Originality and Intellectual Property in the French and English Enlightenment

Routledge Studies in Eighteenth-Century Literature

1. The Epistolary Novel
Representations of Consciousness
Joe Bray

2. Slavery and Augustan Literature
Swift, Pope, Gay
John Richardson

3. The Rise of Literary Journalism in the Eighteenth Century
Anxious Employment
Iona Italia

4. Gender and the Fictions of the Public Sphere, 1690–1755
Anthony Pollock

5. The Female Reader in the English Novel
From Burney to Austen
Joe Bray

6. Originality and Intellectual Property in the French and English Enlightenment
Edited by Reginald McGinnis

Originality and Intellectual Property in the French and English Enlightenment

Edited by Reginald McGinnis

Routledge
Taylor & Francis Group
New York London

First published 2009
by Routledge
711 Third Ave, New York, NY 10017

Simultaneously published in the UK
by Routledge
2 Park Square, Milton Park, Abingdon, Oxon OX14 4RN

Routledge is an imprint of the Taylor & Francis Group, an informa business

First issued in paperback 2012

Typeset in Sabon by IBT Global.

Library of Congress Cataloging in Publication Data

Originality and intellectual property in the French and English Enlightenment / edited by Reginald McGinnis.
p. cm. — (Routledge studies in eighteenth-century literature ; 6)
Includes bibliographical references and index.
ISBN-13: 978-0-415-96288-9
ISBN-10: 0-415-96288-9
1. English literature—18th century—History and criticism. 2. Plagiarism—Great Britain—History—18th century. 3. Plagiarism—France—History—18th century. 4. Originality in literature. 5. Imitation in literature. 6. Intellectual property—Great Britain—History—18th century. 7. Intellectual property—France—History—18th century. 8. Copyright—Great Britain—History—18th century. 9. Copyright—France—History—18th century. I. McGinnis, Reginald, 1959–
PR448.P55O75 2009
700.942'09033--dc22
2008018808

ISBN13: 978-0-415-96288-9 (hbk)
ISBN13: 978-0-415-54298-2 (pbk)

Contents

Illustrations

Preface

The idea for this volume began with a session at the 2006 meeting of the American Society for Eighteenth-Century Studies in Montreal, Canada, entitled "Originality and Intellectual Property in the Eighteenth Century." The papers presented on that occasion have been either extensively or entirely rewritten and are included here, along with three further contributions. While originally conceived as a comparative study of law and literature, the scope of this volume has been expanded to include a chapter on painting. The editor wishes to thank the Barber Institute of Fine Arts, the British Museum, Gainsborough's House Society, the Huntington Library, the J. Paul Getty Museum, the Royal Academy of Arts, and the Tate Gallery for granting permission to use their images.

Introduction

Reginald McGinnis

That discussions of intellectual property and copyright surfaced in eighteenth-century England and France at a time when originality is said to have emerged as a new aesthetic category is a point that appears to have been largely neglected by legal as well as literary scholars. Are legal concepts of intellectual property and copyright related to artistic notions of invention and originality? Do literary and legal scholars have anything to learn from each other or should the legal debate be viewed as separate from questions of aesthetics? Bridging what are usually perceived as two distinct areas of inquiry, this interdisciplinary volume begins with a reflection on the "origins" of literary and legal questions in the Enlightenment to consider their ramifications in the post-Enlightenment and contemporary world.

In the opening chapter, Robert W. McHenry, Jr. considers the question of literary paternity in John Dryden's dramatic adaptations. Writing in the late seventeenth century when, as in the Renaissance, imitation of models was still accepted literary practice, Dryden's usage of "originals" was nonetheless a subject of controversy. From the Duke of Buckingham's parody *The Rehearsal* to Gerard Langbaine's critical catalogues, accusations of plagiary afforded Dryden an opportunity to explain his ideas on imitation and the appropriation of earlier writings. Comparing reflections from Dryden's essays and prefaces with his plays and critical responses, McHenry outlines a debate that helps to formulate definitions of originality and plagiarism at the dawn of the Enlightenment.

Dryden's case is interesting because he combines a strong sense of his own originality—and an aggressively competitive attitude toward other writers—with an easy acceptance of imitation and appropriation as legitimate elements of original composition. Relying on a distinction derived from Petrarch, who said that the borrowing of another man's ideas makes poets whereas the usage of his words makes apes, McHenry shows how, apart from spawning controversy over plagiarism, literary filiations also elucidate Dryden's sense of his place in the emerging history of English drama. Whereas the "resemblance of a son to his father endows the newcomer with an honorable heritage and may confer the benefits of having a nurturing and protecting family, the appellation of 'ape' suggests not only mindless mimicry, but also banishment from the human and literary families."

The question of paternity considered by McHenry with respect to literary filiations appears in a different light in the second chapter exploring authors' parental interests in their fictional characters. Importing a term from present-day internet culture, referring to newly written fiction by fans featuring characters created by another author, Elizabeth F. Judge considers the cultural and legal consequences of "fan fiction" associated with the novel during the eighteenth century, when "reading circles penned annotations in the margins, circulated alternate endings, corresponded with authors to advocate for happier endings, and shared their revisionist interpretations with other fans (as with Lady Bradshaigh and her sister Lady Elizabeth Echlin and their happier endings for Samuel Richardson's *Clarissa*)."

The 1710 Statute of Anne defined rights with respect to the "book" as a whole, leaving individual elements such as fictional characters unprotected. And while eighteenth-century English law did not prohibit people from including famous characters in spurious sequels to novels, in plays, or in satires, such appropriations were often condemned by the original authors and likened to legal wrongs against a person—"ravishing, counterfeiting, and kidnapping." Tracing legal history through the treatment of fictional characters rather than fictional works, Judge offers a new perspective on the relation between authors and their readers (including fan fiction writers) and questions the traditional views of copyright opposing English economic rights with continental European authorship rights (*droit d'auteur*). During a time that saw the emergence of both the novel and copyright law, authors' interests in their characters are shown to have been "custodial" and "moral," rather than solely proprietary.

The contributions to this volume share a common concern with comparing twenty-first-century views of law and literature to those of the Enlightenment. As observed by Simon Stern, "theories of aesthetic originality have been so massively influential since the early nineteenth century that, to modern eyes, any reference to originality seems necessarily to include some element of creativity." Reviewing the eighteenth-century debate over copyright, from the passage of the 1710 *Act for the Encouragement of Learning* to the writings of lawyers such as William Blackstone and Francis Hargrave, Stern challenges the assumption that legal accounts of literary property during this period were based on aesthetic theories of creative genius. Although the eighteenth century is rightly associated with discussions of literary creativity, such as Edward Young's *Conjectures on Original Composition*, the connotation of creativity or novelty was absent from legal discussions of "originality," principally concerned with the reprinting of texts, and where a work was said to be "original" so long as it was not a reproduction of another work. Opposing our modern "high-threshold" definition of originality whereby novelty and ingenuity are considered as the justification for authorial property with an earlier "low-threshold" definition where originality was taken to mean only that a text had not been reproduced, Stern considers the implications of these views for literary culture and for individual writers in their continued reliance on the public domain.

From English discussions of copyright, originality, and the public domain, we turn to the French context in the chapter by Anne Sechin. If the eighteenth century established a legal basis for the notion of intellectual property and witnessed the emergence of originality as an aesthetic category, certainly no other figure reflects this convergence more than Denis Diderot, who, apart from being considered an original author, was accused of plagiarism in his *Encyclopedia* and held what is still perceived to be a controversial position regarding copyright and "privileges" in his *Letter on the Book Trade*. Focusing on *Jacques The Fatalist and His Master*, a novel known for its innovation and originality as well as for its borrowings, Sechin shows how this work of fiction, written after the *Encyclopedia* and the *Letter on the Book Trade*, allows us to make sense of Diderot's seemingly paradoxical and reputedly antimodernist theories. Whereas Stern recalls Henry Fielding's view of the public domain as a "rich common" from which authors should be free to borrow, Diderot's ideas on intellectual property are illustrated in particular by one of his characters, the "landlady," whose worth as a storyteller is undiminished by her habit of telling second-hand stories.

Philosopher, author, and editor of the *Encyclopedia*, Diderot is also remembered for his influential art criticism. Turning to England and painting in Cristina S. Martinez' chapter on Thomas Gainsborough, we are never far from Diderot and France. Not only does Martinez' discussion of Gainsborough include frequent references to the French, but at times closely echoes the preceding chapter. The example of an English master, Joshua Reynolds, for instance, who "admitted that he had been obliged to examine for a longtime a copy by Gainsborough of a Vandyke before he could decide if it were an imitation or an original," recalls a passage on painting from *Jacques the Fatalist* where the master concedes that "[he] could take a bad copy for a sublime original." Although issues of copying among painters could seem distant from the concerns of writers, the world of Gainsborough shows striking parallels between art and literature, as, for instance, when Reynolds, accused of plagiarism "for having borrowed attitudes from ancient masters," was defended on the grounds of "quotation."

Exercising his profession at a time when the issue of copyright was frequently discussed by artists as well writers and jurists, Gainsborough was aware of the abuses associated with copying. With piracy a constant threat and the demand for copies increasing in England and on the European continent, he cultivated a singular style that effectively served to protect his works. As observed by one of his biographers, "[his] manner of penciling was so peculiar to himself, that his works needed no signature." But if Gainsborough's idiosyncratic style is attributed to his "touch" or "handling," it was also related to his unusual choice of painting tools—such as sugar-tongs, bits of sponge or paper dipped in skimmed milk—which he guarded with secrecy. In the context of this volume, the example of Gainsborough as an artist protective of his secrets offers an interesting contrast with the attitude of Diderot, who emphasized the importance of disseminating knowledge and who wrote in *The History and Secret of Painting in Wax* that "nothing is more contrary to the progress of knowledge than mystery."[1]

In the following chapter, Tilar J. Mazzeo takes us from the Enlightenment to issues of plagiarism and copyright associated with the anonymous publication of Lord Byron's *Don Juan*. Beginning with the print culture surrounding Byron's domestic scandals, from his failed marriage and adultery to his illegitimate and legitimate daughters, Mazzeo shows how, during the Romantic period, metaphors of paternity and moral rights became increasingly linked with discussions of intellectual property. Tying in with the opening chapters of this volume where paternity is related by Judge and McHenry to kidnapping and to improvement of one's sources, Mazzeo's discussion of Byron highlights his reputation as a father as related to parental authority and authorship as well as to borrowings and the theft, not of fictional characters, but of authorial identity. What may appear surprising to modern readers is the "essentially aesthetic nature" of plagiarism in the early nineteenth century when "immoral works" were not considered property and only works publicly recognized as "literary" were granted legal protection. In light of the new legal emphasis on the individuality of authors, this chapter reviews the standards required to "prove" a charge of plagiarism in the Romantic period and focuses on the ways in which the conventions of literary appropriation were historically distinct from both earlier eighteenth-century and later modern constructions.

The final chapter by John Vignaux Smyth picks up where Mazzeo leaves off, questioning portrayals of Romanticism in recent scholarship. In contrast with supposedly Wordsworthian notions of poetry and solitary genius, Smyth recalls Friedrich Schlegel's insistence on the novel as the modern literary form *par excellence* and particularly on the "proto-Romantic" and comically plagiaristic works of Diderot and Laurence Sterne. "Sterne's most obvious technique, openly imitated by Diderot in *Jacques The Fatalist,* stages the abstract difficulty of distinguishing between law and arbitrariness very concretely for his readers, since precisely where he and Diderot appear or claim to narrate most arbitrarily we would be well advised to suspect the opposite"—a problem that becomes particularly pointed when it is a matter of deciding whether "what looks superficially like an arbitrary or 'original' maneuver is in fact a conscious plagiarism, or whether the resemblance we see belongs to a more fundamental law, where (like Leibniz and Newton) two authors arrive independently at similar results." "The trouble," as Smyth observes, "is that a theory of originality seems sometimes to amount to a theory of almost everything and sometimes to almost nothing." While not venturing so far as to discuss "everything," Smyth expands reflection on originality beyond the legal and literary spheres to include theories of law and arbitrariness in philosophy, anthropology, science, and mathematics.

NOTES

1. Regarding *The History and Secret of Painting in Wax*, see Arthur M. Wilson, *Diderot* (New York: Oxford University Press, 1972), 225–228.

1 Plagiarism and Paternity in Dryden's Adaptations

Robert W. McHenry, Jr.

John Dryden thought a great deal about literary paternity during his career as a successful playwright especially because he spent a great deal of his time during the 1670s and 1680s writing appropriations and adaptations of Shakespeare and other writers. While he did so, he also wrote extensively about the proper relationship between contemporary writers like himself and the literary ancestors with whom they competed and simultaneously honored as paternal figures. One of the main elements defining this issue was that of plagiarism because Dryden faced accusations that he both stole from his predecessors and showed them no respect. When Gerard Langbaine published his attacks on plagiarism in English drama, concentrating especially on Dryden, he seemed particularly offended that Dryden took elements from the very authors he disparaged. Not that Langbaine was the first to adopt this line of attack, but his criticisms provided a more specific and sweeping set of arguments. Ironically, these allowed Dryden to defend his approach to the appropriation of earlier writings, but they also exposed areas of the discussion that he avoided. The result is a debate that helps to formulate definitions of originality and plagiarism for the Restoration. In addition, the controversy over plagiarism and the idea of literary filiations help to reveal Dryden's sense of his place as an heir of the great earlier figures in the emerging history of English drama.

By Dryden's time, distinguishing the proper imitation of a writer's sources versus slavish copying was already a well-explored topic, as shown by Harold Ogden White, who declared in his groundbreaking 1935 book that "English writers from Sidney to Jonson [argued] that originality of real worth is to be achieved only through creative imitation."[1] These sixteenth- and seventeenth-century poets insisted on their right to appropriate materials from their predecessors. Even earlier, Petrarch, in 1366, sought to make a clear distinction between acceptable imitation and plagiarism when he declared that the "proper imitator should take care that what he writes resembles the original without reproducing it," and he introduced the influential idea of literary paternity into the discussion when he insisted that the resemblance should be like "a son to his father":

> Therein is often a great divergence in particular features, but there is a certain suggestion, what our painters call an "air," most noticeable in the face and eyes, which makes the resemblance. As soon as we see the son, he recalls the father to us, although if we should measure every feature we should find them all different. But there is a mysterious something there that has this power.[2]

His application of this distinction is as simple as it is revealing:

> Thus we may use another man's conceptions and the colour of his style, but not use his words. In the first case the resemblance is hidden deep; in the second it is glaring. The first procedure makes poets, the second makes apes.

Jonathan Bate, who quotes elements of this letter in his brilliant study of Shakespeare's relationship to Ovid, goes on to argue that Shakespeare's imitation of Ovid is of the kind approved by this tradition, an affiliation, as Petrarch described it, "often more easily felt than defined" and "planted so deep that it can only be extricated by quiet meditation."[3] The connection between writers of different eras was important to early criticism, as it remains today, and in many ways the polar alternatives for describing that relationship, from the perspective of the imitating younger writers, is well expressed in Petrarch's "son" and "ape." The resemblance of a son to his father endows the newcomer with an honorable heritage and may confer the benefits of having a nurturing and protecting family. The appellation of "ape" suggests not only mindless mimicry, but also banishment from the human and literary families. Because both terms recur explicitly in Dryden's discussions of plagiarism and imitation, and because in the Restoration the issues addressed by Petrarch and others in the Renaissance received a higher degree of often acrimonious airing in the public press, it seems useful to explore the question of the value of those terms for describing the relationship between Dryden and other writers, particularly Shakespeare. Can Petrarch's quiet meditation yield an understanding of Dryden's imitations of Shakespeare and other great writers that can be considered filial? Or would his injunction against using another writer's words properly condemn Dryden's appropriations, at least for those applying Petrarch's values?

Petrarch's notion of a literary "son" would certainly not be surprising to Dryden, for whom the idea that there were lineal relationships among poets of different eras was important to his sense of himself as an artist. In the retrospective Preface to *The Fables, Ancient and Modern* (1700), he observes that the major English poets of the Renaissance eagerly placed themselves with their literary genealogies. Having praised Spenser and Edward Fairfax, the translator of Tasso, as great Elizabethan "Masters [of] our Language . . . who saw much farther into the Beauties of our Numbers, than those who immediately followed them" (7:25),[4] he records as their true descendents—not those who "immediately followed them," but those who understood their styles and adapted them for their own:

> *Milton* was the Poetical Son of *Spencer*, and Mr. *Waller* of *Fairfax*; for we have our Lineal Descents and Clans, as well as other Families: *Spencer* [sic.] more than once insinuates, that the Soul of *Chaucer* was transfus'd into his Body; and that he was begotten by him Two hundred years after his Decease; *Milton* has acknowledg'd to me, that *Spencer* was his Original; and many besides my self have heard our famous *Waller* own, that he deriv'd the Harmony of his Numbers from the *Godfrey of Bulloign*, which was turn'd into *English* by Mr. *Fairfax*. (7:25)

Clearly, these descendents are proud of their literary progenitors and wished to acknowledge them because they regarded such lineal descents as wholly honorable. As Laura Rosenthal points out, images of descent are even important in satires, when the implications were dishonorable. The most famous example is in Dryden's own *MacFlecknoe* (1682), where Dryden's ironic coronation of Thomas Shadwell as king of dullness includes a hyperbolic account of his descent from the odious poet Richard Flecknoe. "MacFlecknoe" means "son of Flecknoe." There it is an important means of defining his lineal right to reign and be acknowledged throughout the literary world as the absolute monarch of nonsense.[5]

That sense of literary forbears seems always to have been important to Dryden, and he often invoked this traditional image of Shakespeare as a literary father. Yet in his earliest criticism, his attitude is complex because it is not uniformly deferential. Indeed it is sometimes openly rebellious. Being a literary son did not for Dryden always lead to expressions of respect or admiration. In the "Essay of Dramatic Poesy" (1667), for example, his witty image for the Shakespeare and his Elizabethan contemporaries is surprising because his spokesman Neander paints these "honour'd and almost ador'd" ancestors as wastrels:

> We acknowledge them our Fathers in wit, but they have ruin'd their Estates themselves before they came to their childrens hands. There is scarce an Humour, a Character, or any kind of Plot which they have not us'd. All comes sullied or wasted to us: and were they to entertain this age, they could not now make so plenteous treatments out of such decay'd Fortunes. This therefore will be a good Argument to us either not to write at all, or to attempt some other way. There is no bayes to be expected in their Walks. (*Works*, 17:73)

Dryden transforms the plentitude of his predecessors into a liberating fault: since they've used up everything, those of his generation must begin anew. This witty complaint forms the basis for an important argument against imitating the masters of the previous age, yet it also suggests that imitation, if not plagiarism, is almost inevitable because the "fathers" have seemingly already been everywhere or—perhaps more accurately—the lands they have explored now seem to be all that can be conquered. His main concern here is that respect for literary fathers not result in a generation of "apes" who copy too much from such powerful fathers. That fear justifies his emphasis on the rebellious side of the filial relationship.

That the attitudes of actual sons might include a range of emotions beyond love and reverence should come as no surprise in our post-Freudian age, in which the Oedipus complex is a well-known tenet of psychoanalysis. As a common dictionary definition has it, the "libidinal feelings in a child, especially a male child, for the parent of the opposite sex [is] usually accompanied by hostility to the parent of the same sex."[6] Generational conflict, especially between fathers and sons, is surely a frequent pattern in human behavior. Indeed, the great authority exercised by fathers in the seventeenth century could easily result in sons having negative feelings about their fathers. About the period in which Dryden was a child, Lawrence Stone observes that, "from 1540 to 1660 there is a great deal of evidence, especially from Puritans, of a fierce determination to break the will of the child, and to enforce his utter subjection to the authority of his elders and superiors, and most especially of his parents."[7] During this time, it was commonly expected that children would "kneel before their parents to ask their blessing every morning, and even as adults on arrival at or departure from the home."[8] Not surprisingly, some parents' demands or punishments were so excessive that they resulted in abhorrence and fear as well as outward deference. Stone cites the example of Bishop Gilbert Burnet—born in 1630, a year before Dryden—whose childhood memories included "much severe correction; the fear of that brought me under too great an uneasiness, and sometimes even to a hatred of my father."[9] Clearly, what Stone calls "this pattern of extreme deference to parents in the home"[10] could also result in antagonism, however suppressed or regretted. Although we have no evidence that Dryden's puritan upbringing led to fear or hatred of his father, it is important to recall that in a period in which parental authority was enforced with severity, the idea of "paternity" could represent an ambiguous claim on loyalty or affection.

In just the same way, the claims of paternal literary masters result in a coiled nest of conflicting motives that include admiration and distaste, submission, and competitive pride. This combination of emotions can result in considerable complexity when applied to literary relations between generations because the acknowledgment of paternal authority might take the form of imitation and of what some would call plagiarism, whereas rebellion might encompass both a rejection of early models and a inclination to fall short of adequate acknowledgments of the influence of past masters on new works. In fact, Dryden was judged by some to be guilty on both counts, but he steadily denied the charges.

Some insight into Dryden's complex feelings about the paternal figures of the English dramatic tradition may be gained indirectly from examining his comedy, *Sir Martin Mar-all* (1667), written in collaboration with the Duke of Newcastle (1592–1676) during the same period that saw the publication of the *Essay of Dramatic Poesy*. After collaborating with the elderly Newcastle, known for his earlier patronage of Ben Jonson, Dryden may well have imagined the play's final conflict between old Moody, the heroine's father, and the amorous Sir Martin as representative of the clash of old and new theatrical styles. Even the play's two authors may be implicated in this satirical theme. Moody has the blunt, inelegant style of one "bred up in the old *Elizabeth* way of plainness" (3.1.33–34; 9:237) while the heedless Sir Martin enrages him with his modish language usually based on French words. Moody demands that he speak in plain English: "If thou wilt have a foolish word to lard thy lean discourse with, take an *English* one when thou speakest *English*" (3.1.83–85; 9:239). While Moody is otherwise a standard blocking figure whose efforts to marry off his daughter to a man she dislikes are clearly doomed, he is not such a fool as Sir Martin. Moody easily sees through Sir Martin's inept plotting, even having Sir Martin beaten for pretending, ineptly enough, to be Moody's long-lost son. Moody as a father seems close to Dryden's sense of the older writers he admired, once powerful and still upright, but now unfashionably plain, blunt, and inelegant. In the same way, Sir Martin is a parody of the faults of the new style because he is full of French elegance, but senseless and ineffective.

However, Moody does have a true son in this play. He is Warner, who, in the end, marries Moody's daughter Millisent and reveals himself to be a nobleman. Once that fact has been established, Moody quickly accepts Warner as a son-in-law and offers to pay off the mortgage to his estate (5.2.126–127; 9:289). This turn of events is not in the play's sources; there the title character gets the girl. Dryden and Newcastle, however, make Sir Martin into such a dolt that no audience would want him to succeed with an attractive heroine like Millisent. By contrast, Warner, once revealed to be of the proper class, is a perfect match in wit for her and a good alliance for Moody. Though young, he does not use the Frencified cant of Sir Martin. Warner's unexpected success suggests that an alliance between the honest but unsophisticated style of the pre-Civil War days and an intelligent English contemporary manner can happily succeed, much as the collaboration of Newcastle (at age 74) and Dryden (at age 36) did in writing this play.

One last image concerning Moody serves to reinforce this connection. In the play's farcical final scene, Moody is tricked into standing on a high stool while the young people sneak into the next room to get married. When they return to unmask and reveal what they have done, Moody is left high above on his stool, unable to get down. Now his high position suggests not exalted status, but powerlessness. Finally, he asks: "What am I kept here for?" The question is both challenging and pitiable; it is just the sort of question that those who valued the old style of drama might well ask, as new plays began to push the old from the repertory. Warner's reply is generous:

> I might in policy keep you there, till your Daughter and I had been in private, for a little consummation: But for once, Sir. I'le truste your good nature. [*Takes him down too.*] (5.2.114–116; 9:288)

The play's conclusion shows that Warner is right to trust Moody; once assured of his status as a gentleman, Moody does accept him with the same degree of generosity that Warner showed in helping his new father-in-law down from his high and precarious isolation. Is it too much to conclude that this action serves as a symbol of the proper relationship of the old and new styles? Moody returns to the practical ground level and finds a son-in-law he can respect, and Warner helps him to rejoin the party and demonstrates his own worthiness. Amid the farce and the contrived happy marriages decreed by convention—and by the two main sources, Molière and Philippe Quinault—this play contains some notions about generational conflict and reconciliation that have implications about the proper relations between literary fathers and sons.

These issues of paternity and filial imitation were especially on Dryden's mind during this period because he was then establishing his reputation in the theater and as a critic of drama. They appear once again in the Preface to his much rewritten version of Shakespeare's *The Tempest*, published with the title, *The Tempest or the Enchanted Island. A Comedy* (1670). Having worked once again with an older collaborator, Sir William Davenant, Dryden uses this Preface to record his sense of filial piety toward Davenant, who died shortly after the play began its successful run in the theater, some two years before the text saw publication. Since then, Dryden had succeeded to the position of Poet Laureate that Davenant had held (unofficially), so the notion of filial succession seems apt. His attention to Davenant's memory also allows him to address the accusations of plagiarism that followed those like Davenant and himself who took up the popular practice of adapting old plays. Davenant was by then well known for appropriating or adapting Shakespeare's plays. Dryden begins his defense by citing two much earlier precedents for appropriating elements from *The Tempest*: John Fletcher had "*thought fit to make use of the same Design*," specifically the "*Storm, desart Island, and the Woman who had never seen a Man*" (10:3) in his (and Massinger's) *The Sea Voyage* (first performed in 1622).[11] Sir John Suckling's *The Goblins* (first performed in 1638) is also invoked as a play that appropriated the characters of Miranda and Ariel.[12]

Audiences were likely to know of these plays, since the rival theater, the King's Company, revived both of them in the fall of 1667, just before the premiere of Dryden and Davenant's *Tempest*. It is unlikely that Dryden would attempt to mislead his audience about the nature of these other appropriations of *The Tempest*, when many members of it had probably seen one of the recent performances of them. However, it is less clear how many would know of their connection to Shakespeare, which is not mentioned in Suckling's Prologue and Epilogue, and Fletcher's play includes neither prologue nor epilogue. Samuel Pepys saw both when they were revived in 1667, but his diary entries make no connection to Shakespeare.[13]

Modern commentators are apt to think that Dryden exaggerated the indebtedness of these plays to Shakespeare's. Paulina Kewes, who describes them, accurately enough, as "loosely inspired" by *The Tempest*, argues that Dryden provides this "spurious history" of their use of Shakespearean elements to "create the impression that dramatic appropriation is a legitimate and time-honoured practice."[14] Of course appropriation of earlier material was then often considered legitimate and was certainly persistent from the time of Jonson and Shakespeare onward. What was new is the interest in full adaptations of Shakespeare—and Davenant was the first important practitioner to create them—in which the adaptor took over the main elements of the plot and most of the original characters, rewrote his lines and added new scenes, while following some parts of the original play closely.[15] However, the distinction between an adaptation and a play "loosely inspired"‘ by another is not as clear as Kewes seems to assume, despite the adaptors' use of some of Shakespeare's scenes with few changes beyond the wholesale modernization and simplification of the language. Even *The Tempest or The Enchanted Island* could be described as 'loosely inspired' by Shakespeare. Because the new version offered several new characters and changed the plot radically, while omitting much that was distinctive in the original, it seems unlikely that Dryden would expect to be convicted of plagiarism for following the original play too closely.

The emphasis of his argument falls on the role of Shakespeare's *Tempest* as the source of the "design" of the appropriating works—the basic plot elements, such as the magical island, the storm, the woman ignorant of men, and the "monster" Caliban who inhabits the place. Further, he is implicitly relying on Petrarch's distinction between filial imitation and the plagiarism of apes when he argues that others had merely copied Shakespeare—although to be fair, Dryden should have added "in some respects," but that Davenant had the notion of adding wholly original new elements, "*of which neither* Fletcher *nor* Suckling *had ever thought*" (10:4).

Like Petrarch, Dryden assumes that all authors borrow. He and the Duke of Newcastle, after all, had just written *Sir Martin Mar-all*, which Davenant had produced and whose plot was borrowed from Molière and Quinault, who had appropriated elements from Niccolò Barbieri's *L'Inavertito* (1630) (9:365). Like good literary sons, all used the appropriated material differently, added features from other sources, and invented elements of their own. In fact, Dryden sees no irony in using the occasion of a commentary on their adaptation of *The Tempest* to stress Davenant's originality. After all, Davenant invented Hippolyto, the male counterpart of Miranda, and the "*Saylors were also his invention, and for the most part his writing*"

(10:4). Dryden stresses that when he got to know Davenant, he was struck by his lively and original imagination: "*And as his fancy was quick, so likewise were the products of it remote and new. He borrowed not of any other; and his imaginations were such as could not easily enter into any other man*" (10:4). More than his eulogy for a colleague fondly remembered, this declaration is a useful way to address the criticisms of both authors for their appropriations of Shakespeare. In particular, Davenant had been attacked for them by Richard Flecknoe, not as a plagiarist, but for "spoiling and mangling" the Shakespearean originals—an accusation implying a lack of filial piety and of dramatic skill that calls into question the adaptor's literary lineage.[16]

Dryden defiantly began this Preface with a satire on mere copiers, singling out "some Ape of the French Eloquence" (possibly Richard Flecknoe himself) and at the end of the Preface, he returns to the idea of originality to express his disapproval of plagiarism. He cites writers who ungratefully gave no credit to Davenant for "*whole Scenes together*" (10:5) that he contributed to their plays. Dryden strongly condemns such silent appropriations of another's work, declaring "*there [is] nothing so base as to rob the dead of his reputation*" (10:5). Taking such a firm stance condemning plagiarism, Dryden implicitly treats Shakespeare's play as a mere source for the adaptors' "design" and argues—accurately enough—that it is a source from which they immediately, radically, and determinedly depart. In his Preface, he acknowledges Shakespeare as fully as possible. As Kewes notes,

> to "improve" one's source [in the plays of this period] was to demonstrate one's skill, and to enhance the quality both of the current repertory and of the native dramatic tradition. To absorb "respectable" sources was quite different from filching from outlandish romances or from obsolete plays. By contemporary standards, the plays of Shakespeare and Fletcher needed upgrading and modernization, even if their authors were revered in literary circles.[17]

Does Dryden also have the assurance to claim that his use of Shakespeare is good enough to justify the theft? He is, of course, too sophisticated to boast about his own work. He declares that he is writing his Preface "*not to set a value on any thing I have written in this Play, but out of gratitude to the memory of Sir* William D'Avenant, *who did me the honour to joyn me with him in the alteration of it*" (10:3).

Thus, Dryden sidesteps the question of the adaptation's literary worth (as he is well aware, it is the right of the audience to judge it) so that he can stress the argument that a writer who makes original use of borrowed material justifies the appropriation. On that issue, he and Davenant are on firm ground, at least insofar as the design of their new play is concerned: it contains a great deal of new plot, many new characters, revisions of the treatment of several characters, and the radical modification of Prospero in particular.

The most important aspect of the issues surrounding plagiarism that this argument leaves out is that of the language, which in Petrarch's distinction is linked to the imitation of a mere "ape." Sometimes the adaptors do not scruple to use Shakespearean language, but, more frequently, they revise it to achieve a sort of simplified modern paraphrase, not unlike what Davenant employed for his earlier adaptations. Perhaps revising Shakespeare's obsolete Jacobean style into Restoration English seemed little different from translating Molière's French into English because once the necessity of changing the words made copying the original out of the question, then it seemed as pointless to complain about the appropriation of an older work as it would to object that a translation copied the ideas or plot of the foreign work that was translated. Also, the issue may have seemed too difficult to discuss in the context of his attempt to establish his filial respect for both Davenant and Shakespeare because he wished to stress that his using Shakespeare as a source was neither disrespectful nor unethical.

Nevertheless, in the "Defence of the Epilogue" to *The Conquest of Granada* (1672), Dryden returns to the image of literary fathers and sons, in a more aggressively satirical manner, as he treats the statements of respect by contemporary critics for past authors as a backhanded means of denigrating present ones. Of the old, he acknowledges that "we contend with them for the preheminence" (11:203) and invokes the idea of progress to bolster the new writers, expressing the hope that "Poetry may not go backward, when all other Arts and Sciences are advancing" (11:203). At the essay's conclusion, he delivers a savage account of "some few old fellows" who remember the days of Jonson and like to be "call'd his Sons." He denies them any claim to learning and wit (except for "what they could remember") and dismisses their criticisms of new plays as the mere effects of complacent nostalgia: "Not contented to have known little at the age of twenty, they boast of their ignorance at threescore" (11:216). This satire on claims of those representing the literary inheritance is followed by attacks on the fathers:

> let any man who understands *English*, read diligently the works of *Shakespear* and *Fletcher*; and I dare undertake that he will find, in every page either some Solecism of Speech, or some notorious flaw in Sence: and yet these men are reverenc'd when we are not forgiven. (11:205)

In this contrast between the indulgence granted to Shakespeare and Fletcher and the harshness reserved for writers such as himself, Dryden employs the rhetoric of outrage at injustice to rationalize his harsh view of his literary fathers. He then moves to specifics, stressing in addition to faults of language and sense the "lameness of their Plots"—defined as "some ridiculous, incoherent story, which, in one Play many times took up the business of an

Age" (11:206). Here the faults are in both a lack of mimetic naturalness and flaws in coherence, usually the result of multiple plots. For examples of such flaws, Dryden turns first to Shakespeare:

> I suppose I need not name *Pericles Prince of Tyre*, nor the Historical Plays of Shakespeare: Besides many of the rest as the *Winters Tale, Love's labour[s] lost, Measure for Measure,* which were either grounded on impossibilities, or at least, so meanly written, that the Comedy neither caus'd your mirth, nor the serious part your concernment. (11:206)

This critique is surprisingly comprehensive. Although Dryden is willing to mitigate his condemnation a little by noting that some of the plays he censures are early works (he mistakenly puts *Pericles*, a late romance, in that category), these rigid classical standards for plot and language seem to relegate much of Shakespeare's plays to the dustbin. Dryden effectively invokes his audience's own taste to support his argument that they are poorly written. The proof is that these plays are not effective in the theater. "You" in the audience do not laugh at these comedies or feel moved by the serious plays. Here, of course, is the ultimate justification for the Restoration's impulse to revise Shakespeare's plays: they no longer move readers or audiences. An avid playgoer like Samuel Pepys, for example, thought *A Midsummer Night's Dream* "the most insipid ridiculous play that ever I saw" and *Twelfth Night* "one of the weakest plays that ever I saw upon the stage."[18] But this line of attack, however justified, makes Dryden seems like an ungrateful son. Must he, like Zeus, kill his father to secure his own birthright?

Not surprisingly, in the Preface to *All for Love* (1678), he returns to this competitive image when discussing his decision to write a tragedy about Antony and Cleopatra, a subject that seemed to be owned by Shakespeare, despite the fact that his tragedy was no longer a favorite with audiences:[19]

> The death of *Antony* and *Cleopatra*, is a Subject which has been treated by the greatest Wits of our Nation, after *Shakespeare*; and by all so variously, that their example has given me the confidence to try my self in this Bowe of *Ulysses* amongst the Crowd of Sutors; and, withal, to take my own measures, in aiming at the Mark. (13:10)

Commentators have often mistaken this passage to mean that the unyielding bow represents Shakespeare's play, but the grammar is unmistakable in showing that the bow is the hard subject, the story of the death of Antony and Cleopatra; its Ulysses (the owner) is Shakespeare, the only playwright who could master it, and the suitors are the other poets, like himself, who hope to be regarded as proper heirs to Ulysses by revealing their prowess in their own versions.[20] As a classicist like Dryden would have been the first to notice, the only other person who could draw the bow is Ulysses' son,

Telemachus, who, in *The Odyssey*, Book 21, shows that he has the strength, but then leaves off for tactical reasons. Dryden clearly wishes to reassume the role as Shakespeare's true heir, not to be ranked as merely another of the suitors. He must have been aware that the other efforts at this subject that followed Shakespeare's were not successful. This appropriated image from Homer is a masterful, characteristic blend of arrogance and modesty. In attempting to draw the bow, he is claiming his right to be considered the true heir to Shakespeare, but he acknowledges that, until the results are in, he is just another one of the "Crowd of Suitors," who are mere usurpers. The distinction is crucial. Dryden is not like the other would-be heirs seeking to master the subject that has so far yielded only to Shakespeare. He is to be finally revealed as the true son.

However, Dryden's approach is so different from Shakespeare's that there seems little possibility that he could succeed. If he does, his achievement would not show that he could improve on Shakespeare, but that he is Shakespeare's heir, not a mere "ape." The competition is in a real sense filial, and it is to be accomplished exactly by Petrarch's sort of filial imitation, in which the spirit of the original is occasionally invoked, but not slavishly copied. The most famous examples of such efforts are in the speeches in which Dryden "translates" Shakespeare's words into his own idiom. These are the parts of the play that Shakespeareans tend to despise, as they read now like weak and simplified reductions of extraordinary originals. If we read Antony's speech describing his first meeting with Cleopatra, taken closely from Enobarbus's speech in Shakespeare, itself borrowed directly from North's translation of Plutarch, it is difficult not to recognize the great distance between Dryden and Shakespeare. In the beginning of Shakespeare's speech, the lavish details find a unity in the metaphoric language of passion attributed to them, as in this brief example from the beginning of the speech:

> The barge she sat in, like a burnished throne
> Burned on the water. The poop was beaten gold;
> Purple the sails, and so perfumèd that
> The winds were lovesick with them.[21] (2.2.201–204)

Dryden's version of this speech lacks Shakespeare's personifications, concentrating instead on a direct and colorful portrait of the scene:

> Her Gally down the silver *Cydnos* row'd,
> The Tacking Silk, the Streamers wav'd with Gold,
> The gentle Winds were lodg'd in Purple sails. . . . (3.1.163–165; 13:60)

These two passages may be said to define much of Dryden's filial method of imitation because he clearly appropriates the description while changing most of the words and eliminating the distinctive poetic elements of the original. Dryden's passage is simpler, more direct, and, for most readers, less poetical, but it does replace Shakespeare's stylistic devices with his own while providing those who know Shakespeare with the pleasure of recognizing the parallels—comparisons that originally did Dryden no harm, because few in his audience were likely to be well versed in Shakespeare's language and most had not yet elevated him and this play, in particular, to the high position they later enjoyed. In his day, such moments of imitation could be regarded as innocently filial, neither plagiarism nor desecration. Now they are sometimes denounced as both.

Still it could be argued that Dryden's strategy for demonstrating his claim for Shakespearean inheritance resides as directly in the more original contributions to the dramatic treatment of the story as in his explicit evocations of Shakespeare's language. His version of the story remained popular for over a century, eclipsing Shakespeare's play, and is even now considered by many to be his masterpiece. It remains one of the most highly regarded and frequently reprinted of what is now a distinctly minor genre, the Restoration tragedy, because it manages to combine eloquent blank verse with the concentrated, unified, heroic plot so admired by neoclassical dramatic critics. It replaces many of Shakespeare's characters or so remodels them that they are wholly changed. This change is most especially true of Cleopatra. Dryden's character is not an attempt to rival the tempestuous figure in Shakespeare, but to recast the part, radically, as a sympathetic, romantic heroine defined by her loyalty to Antony. As such, she cedes center stage to Antony, who is closer to Shakespeare's and Plutarch's character, but who now becomes the clear focus for the conflicts that lead to the lovers' deaths. That sort of imitation allows Dryden to adopt his own version of the passionate style of Shakespeare's blank verse, without mere copying, whereas his treatment of plot, characters, ideas, and atmosphere is wholly different from his father's. The result is a play that cannot really be considered an adaptation at all, although it is often classified as one, because so few of the older play's components are appropriated—and those historical elements that they share are usually taken from Plutarch. Thus, it may be said that *All for Love* is filial both in its piety toward Shakespeare's achievement and in its competitive determination to approach the challenge in a wholly different manner.[22] For real success, it had to be so; as Dryden declared in the *Essay*, "There is no bayes to be expected in their Walks."

In the autumn of the same year, 1678, when Dryden's version of Sophocles' *Oedipus*, a collaboration with Nathaniel Lee, was first performed at Dorset Garden, Dryden returns to the question of imitation of past masterpieces that he had considered in *Sir Martin Mar-All*, *The Tempest*, and in *All for Love*. In *Oedipus*, he and Lee confront an undoubted masterpiece from the Ancients, but one that, in its original form, they were certain would not appeal to their audiences. Thus, their version is a thoroughgoing transformation of Sophocles' play into an English tragedy of the sort that Restoration audiences would recognize as typical of Shakespeare or another

Jacobean master. Their version has many of the characteristics of tragedies, such as *Macbeth* that had a proven appeal in London. It is written in blank verse, has an extensive subplot, features many characters and special effects involving spirits and a ghost, and ends with plenty of deaths on stage. In the Preface to the printed text, published in March 1679, Dryden supports his heavily altered version by citing the precedents of a number of other versions of *Oedipus*, including those by Seneca and Corneille. Although he borrows from these, here he criticizes the major alterations they had introduced, much to the annoyance of Langbaine, who lambastes Dryden for ingratitude to "two such Great Men, without any provocation, and to whom he has been more than once oblig'd for beautiful Thoughts."[23] Typically, Langbaine has no interest in the question of the accuracy of Dryden's criticism. Still, it is worth noting that Dryden does not abuse these earlier adaptors for altering Sophocles' masterpiece, but only complains about their introducing what he considers unsuccessful or discordant elements. For the story of Oedipus, Corneille and Seneca represent the rival suitors who have failed to string this bow, whereas he and Lee become the true heirs of Sophocles. Thus, Corneille is blamed for making his Oedipus too unappealing to be a tragic hero and for introducing the heroic Theseus into his subplot, thus upstaging his titular hero (13:115–116). These changes are ineffective because they essentially break essential rules for tragedy as Dryden saw them. Heroes had to be basically good, and their struggles had to be at the center of the plot.

In his treatment of *Oedipus*, Dryden might be said to adopt the filial approach to imitation at its closest to rebelliousness. Sophocles is never subjected to criticism, yet his play is transformed; by the standards of Petrarch and his own arguments, no one should be able to accuse Lee and Dryden of apish plagiarism. Dryden is quite willing to praise Sophocles and then part company with him. In this case, he claims that "Sophocles *indeed is admirable every where: And therefore we have follow'd him as close as possibly we cou'd*" (13:116). The reservations that follow, however, show that in many ways they did not think they could follow Sophocles very closely at all. Dryden knows that the conventions of Sophocles' theater, such as the single plot and the large role for the chorus, would not do for his time. The ancient Greek theater "*had a perfection differing from ours*" (13:116). Clearly he was aware that he and Lee would be vulnerable to attack from the ferociously classical critic, Thomas Rymer, for most of the alterations to Sophocles were in the spirit of the Elizabethan and Jacobean plays Rymer had scourged for deviations from the neoclassical rules in his *Tragedies of the Last Age* (1678). Dryden defends the changes, rather tentatively, by appealing to the conventions of his own theater:

> *Custom likewise has obtain'd, that we must form an under-plot of second Persons, which must be depending on the first, and their by-walks must be like those in a Labyrinth, which all of 'em lead into the great*

> *Parterre: or like so many several lodging Chambers, which have their out-lets into the same Gallery.* (13:116–117)

These images from garden design and architecture show that Dryden thinks of the problem as a structural issue. Because a play's structure is designed to produce a unified effect, he argues that, although the ancient way of a single plot is ideal: "*as 'tis the easiest, is also the most Natural, and the best*" (13:117), a play with a subplot can still achieve the same concentration and focus if carefully constructed. Thus, Dryden stretches the classical rules to include elements from the English tradition that are essential to the box office while attempting to maintain their aims. Dryden does not argue for a return to the sort of classical plot that he used in *All for Love*; instead, he contends that a more varied plot can avoid "distraction" if carefully constructed. Although the result is more of a homage to dark Jacobean revenge tragedies than to Sophocles, in the Prologue, Dryden invokes the authority of the Greek drama, virtually daring the audience to dislike the new play: "*For were it known this Poem did not please,/You might set up for perfect Salvages*" (Prologue, 15–16; 13:118). And in the play's Epilogue, Dryden again dares the audience to reject a play whose classical stature has given it "*the Vote of full two Thousand years*" (Epilogue, 23; 13:214), but yet in a less conventionally filial mood, he admits that much struggle was required to "*draw the ponderous Mass from Greece*," joking that the effort defeated Seneca and Corneille and that because of its weight this version required more than a single poet: "*Two lay tugging at the piece*" (Epilogue, 3–4; 13:214). This stress on struggle, as if the play were a huge piece of statuary, suggests how onerous Dryden found the task of adapting the conventions of the ancient Greek theater to his own. Sophocles' play, however admired, was both a heavy and a distant monument. Sophocles' way of handling the story may be the best, and his theater may have been greater than any other, but his achievement would still remain in Greece and for scholars of the distant past without such efforts at adaptation as this version represents. Like old Moody, Sophocles is both an admired father and a relic.

If Dryden's allegiance to Sophocles' dramatic paternity seems doubtful in his *Oedipus*, his claims for a filial link to Shakespeare are explicit in his adaptation of *Troilus and Cressida* (1679) because Dryden has Shakespeare's ghost arise to speak the Prologue. His defining emblem, an evergreen wreath of laurel, suggests both his role as Britain's natural laureate and his ability to inspire "*vulgar Poets,*" who find that if they touch his wreath, "*their wither'd Bays revive*" (Prologue, 5–6; 13:249). Dryden, the current laureate, suggests the inspirational power that Shakespeare's achievements have for him. Not only are both laureates, but this Shakespearean ghost sounds a great deal like Dryden, as he launches into a satire on modern plays—"*Weak, short-lived issues of a feeble Age*" (Prologue, 19; 13:249) and on dull churchmen and politicians in rhymed couplets. He admits that his "*rough-drawn Play*" (Prologue, 13; 13:249) needed work, but boasts that some parts are too good to be altered; there are

> *Some Master-strokes, so manly and so bold*
> *That he who meant to alter, found 'em such,*
> *He shook; and thought it Sacrilege to touch.* (Prologue, 14–16; 13:249)

Here Dryden, as he imagines Shakespeare's ghost paternally observing his own struggles, provides an early expression of Bardolatry. Shakespeare is the ark of the literary covenant, at least for those like Dryden who have the sense to understand his excellence. Dryden's boldness in altering the works of such a genius is justified by his admitting the roughness of the original.

Yet commentators like Gary Taylor and Michael Dobson have interpreted Dryden's treatment of Shakespeare as a full-fledged Freudian instance of filial anxiety justified, not by the fact that Dryden had just adapted *Oedipus*, but by giving Dryden a tormenting Oedipus complex that explains what they see as his oblique antagonism toward Shakespeare. Dobson detects "the adaptor's oedipal relation to this 'awful ghost'" in this Prologue.[24] Taylor also begins his discussion with an attempt to connect Shakespeare's ghost in this prologue to the ghost in *Hamlet*. "Thomas Betterton," he comments, "who spoke this prologue, was most famous for his portrayal of Hamlet; Hamlet was haunted by his father's ghost; Dryden's play is haunted, preceded, simultaneously recommended and condemned, by Shakespeare's."[25] Taylor's comment allows his modern Freudian analysis to overwhelm the perspective established in Dryden's text. Although Dryden knew that fathers, and the ghosts representing them, could be both fearful to and judgmental of their offspring, this ghost is not like that. Dryden's text clearly suggests that the ghost is on stage to protect Dryden from imputations of disrespect for Shakespeare and to encourage the audience to approve the play. This ghost admonishes it to "*Sit silent then, that my pleas'd Soul may see/A Judging Audience once, and worthy me*" (Prologue, 35–36; 13:250). Ironically, the haunting and condemnation read into this prologue come from the bardolatry of later judges, including Taylor himself, who cannot help thinking that Dryden's effort is unworthy of the original and that he is a guilty son, if not a false one. His one strand of evidence—the connection to *Hamlet* via Betterton—is tenuous. As the California editors note, the stage was filled with ghosts at this time, including one of Ben Jonson, which arises in the prologue to Edward Howard's *The Women's Conquest* (1671), also with "Bays till now unwither'd." He returns to life to "a vengeance here denounce/On all the Stages Crimes" (13:549).

Shakespeare's ghost does not haunt Dryden in his Prologue because Hamlet was haunted by his father's fearful demands. This cooperative if paternal ghost recommends Dryden's adaptation by encouraging patriotic feelings for English drama. He greets the audience as "*my lov'd Britons*" and refers to himself as "*your Shakespeare*" (Prologue, 1; 13:249). He also claims that this adaptation will improve the contemporary theatre because "*Bad plays are best decry'd by showing good*" (Prologue, 34; 13:250). Dryden is here announcing that he is trying to combine the best of the past and the present. This play is supposed to show the excellences of Shakespeare, pruned of perceived faults and improved by the classicism of the Restoration, a style that is tempered by an awareness of the distinctive national and contemporary cultural imperatives represented by the ghost. In a sense, this prologue is Dryden's published answer to Thomas Rymer's *The Tragedies of the Last Age Considered* (1678), which had blasted the Elizabethan tragedians. This prologue is not, as Taylor claims, a work that "damns his great predecessor,"[26] but one that attempts to glorify Shakespeare as the necessary foundation of a new English tragedy.

Still, it is equally true that Dryden's representations of his relationship with Shakespeare are misleading. If, as his Prologue suggests, he is calling up Shakespeare's ghost to haunt the Restoration stage, he does so only to challenge him, like a champion wrestler. That is, indeed, his conception of "imitation" defined in the Preface to the printed play; there, quoting Longinus but then adding his own image, he compares a good imitation to a wrestling match:

> We ought not to regard a good imitation as a theft; but as a beautiful Idea of him who undertakes to imitate, by forming himself on the invention and the work of another man; for he enters into the lists like a new wrestler, to dispute the prize with the former Champion. (13:228)

The challenge may seem hopeless if the shade of Shakespeare is, as in Dryden's images, "that Divine Poet" (13:246) or "an Universal mind, which comprehended all Characters and Passions" (13:247). The image of wrestling with the "former Champion" who is also a father may suggest Oedipal struggles more than the appearance of the ghost in the Prologue did, but his unequal contest still can result in distinct benefits for the new contender. Like Jacob, who wrestled all night with the Angel, he is transformed; he produces a play that he could not have written alone. Dryden declares that those great writers who are imitated "serve us as a Torch, which is lifted up before us, to enlighten our passage; and often elevate our thoughts as high, as the conception we have of our Authors Genius" (13:228). For this and other reasons, if the contest with Shakespeare favors the father over the neophyte, the role of collaborator favors the newcomer, who has the inestimable advantages of knowing his audience for this theater—and of being alive during what he considered a more modern, refined, and civilized time.

This dramatic image suggests that, in a sense, Dryden anticipated the recent analysis of literary influence by Harold Bloom, who in *The Anxiety of Influence* returns to this motif in a similar if more oracular manner. Bloom declares: "the strong poet in his daemonic elevation is empowered to turn his energy upon himself, and achieves, at terrible cost, his clearest victory in wrestling with the mighty dead."[27] Dryden may or may not be a "strong poet," in Bloom's terms, and he chooses to show little sign of demonic elevation or the terrible cost of his filial struggles with Shakespeare's ghost, but he does recognize that struggle with the mighty dead is important to his artistic identity.

It remains to ask whether the awareness of Dryden's filial relationship to older writers contributes to a more appropriate and useful definition of "originality" as it relates to Dryden's sense of his place as an inheritor of the great earlier figures in the emerging history of English drama. Does his attitude toward charges of plagiarism emerge from his sense of allegiance and his filial rebellion against many of those from whom he borrowed?

This issue of Dryden's habitual borrowing from literary sources became a source of controversy throughout his long career as a dramatist. In 1672, the Duke of Buckingham and his associates parodied Dryden as imaginatively barren in *The Rehearsal*, where the foolish Bayes declares that he needs no "invention" because he simply takes the thoughts of older writers and then "by leaving out a few words, or putting in others of my own, the business is done."[28] Later, when Gerard Langbaine published his critical catalogues, which denounced plagiarism at every turn, he concentrated on Dryden. In his first pamphlet, which was mysteriously issued with the satirical title *Momus Triumphans: Or The Plagiaries of the English Stage* (1688), Langbaine offers a sweeping denunciation of all appropriations of older writers, which he calls "*Thefts*." He reports that "*I found that our modern Writers had made incursions into the deceas'd Authors Labours, and robb'd them of their Fame.*"[29] He knows that the Ancients borrowed—"Homer himself is not free from it"—and that their practice might seem to give a certain authority to the practice, but he argues that the contemporary writers borrowed in less acceptable ways. The Ancients borrowed only from works they used as models, selected only what they considered the most beautiful parts of them, confessed their takings, and altered what they took to make it more beautiful. Further, Langbaine expresses particular impatience with Dryden because in his critical Prefaces he criticized some of those from whom he took materials and taxed others with plagiarism while being guilty of it himself. This passage makes nothing of the distinction between taking elements of the plot versus taking words from earlier texts. Thus, Langbaine's animus is sweeping, and in the case of Dryden it seems to derive from personal and political differences. While lecturing Dryden on the importance of modesty, he defends "Old Flecknoe, *whom he so much despises*," and Shadwell because "*none of our* modern *Poets has borrowed less*" and because he has admitted to his borrowings (Preface, [8–11]). Because these two are well-known objects of Dryden's political satire, one suspects that Langbaine may be a Whig.[30]

When Langbaine came to publish his lengthy catalogue, *An Account of the English Dramatic Poets* (1691), he refined his critical doctrines in response to Dryden's defense of his practice of using old works for his plots in his Preface to *Don Sebastian* (1690). Rather surprisingly, given his censorious references to "*Thefts*" earlier, Langbaine now declares:

> I have not that I know of, any where accus'd the Poets in general, or Mr. *Dryden* in particular, for borrowing their Plots; knowing that it is allow'd by *Scaliger, M. Hedelin*, and other Writers. . . . But tho' the Poet be allow'd to borrow his Foundation from other Writers, I presume the Language ought to be his own; and when at any time we find a Poet translating whole Scenes from other Writings, I hope we may without offense call him a Plagiary: which if granted, I may accuse Mr. *Dryden* of Theft, notwithstanding this Defense.[31]

Viewing this attempted differentiation of Langbaine's as an important effort to "distinguish legitimate literary borrowing from plagiarism, the borrowers from the thieves," Paulina Kewes concludes, nonetheless, that "in practice, he finds this an impossible task."[32] One difficulty is that, although earlier Langbaine exempted translators from his strictures, now he seems to think that even translated words are thefts.[33] As Brean S. Hammond observes, "what Langbaine upbraids as intellectual dishonesty is not usually what would now be considered plagiarism: the adaptation of plots from plays and novels written by authors no longer living, and/or in languages other than English."[34]

Dryden, by then reaching the end of his career as a dramatist—he wrote only one more play after 1692—never addresses the specific complaints that Langbaine lays out about the use of translated language or the ethics of deriving fame or profit from the plays that contain borrowings from other writers. He always had rejected accusations of theft based on his belief that the practice of borrowing is sanctioned by the ancient tradition of imitation and on the principle that if he makes his own changes and improvements to borrowed material, he may—as he writes of Ben Jonson in *An Essay of Dramatic Poesie*—"[invade] Authours like a Monarch" (17:57). Langbaine does not accept this reasoning, often writing as if all appropriation is theft, even if the borrowing is acknowledged and the result is a superior work. For him, even improvements do not excuse the borrowing. In his discussion of Dryden's *Amphitryon* (1691), for example, he notes that Dryden acknowledged his sources, and he admits that, in his judgment, "what he has borrow'd, he has improv'd throughout."[35] But the praise that he offers Dryden for having "outdone" Molière is lessened in his image of the English poet as a mere polisher of gems:

> The truth is, our Author so polishes and improves other Mens Thoughts, that tho' they are mean in themselves, yet by a *New Turn* which he gives them, they appear Beautiful and Sparkling: Herein resembling Skillful Lapidaries that, by their Art, make a *Bristol* Stone appear with almost the same Lustre, as a Natural Diamond.[36]

Here is the restriction on Dryden's praise at the basic level. No matter how skillful or successful he is, he is still a mere craftsman, and one who perpetuates deceit. He is astonishingly able to make his creations look like real gems, but they are still counterfeits.

Clearly attacks on his artistic integrity were of concern to the poet. Earlier in his career, he made several attempts to answer them in his critical writings, but he never went much beyond his argument that he was justified in his appropriations so long as he made original use of the borrowed material. Langbaine's argument that borrowing was theft even if the new work was an improvement over the original did not elicit from Dryden any refutation. Perhaps Dryden merely felt that Langbaine's arguments did not merit further debate. His extreme views may have seemed obviously faulty, as they frequently do to modern commentators, or he may have thought that these criticisms never took hold in a way that demanded a reply because he was no longer writing for the stage.

My analysis suggests that Dryden's attitude toward his forebears always allowed for both imitation and competition in ways alien to Langbaine's construction of the issue. Langbaine saw those who appropriated earlier writers' ideas as stealing from worthy and undefended authors of earlier times. Dryden seems to regard those earlier writers as both fathers, whose patrimony consisted of precisely those literary elements that should benefit those now writing, and as rivals whose legacies must be addressed. As those whose achievements set standards and offered comparisons that made life difficult for new writers, their work demanded engagement, often in the forms of appropriation, adaptation, or allusion. As fathers, their powerful influence required attention, which sometimes took the form of adaptation. Ironically, their strong examples made innovation difficult, just as the different culture, audience, and degrees of "refinement" made it inevitable. But for Dryden, innovation or invention never was *ex nihilo*; the literary fathers like Shakespeare would always be sources of inspiration and models for both imitation and rebellion.

NOTES

1. Harold Ogden White, *Plagiarism and Imitation During the English Renaissance: A Study in Critical Distinctions* (Cambridge, MA: Harvard University Press, 1935), 202.
2. *Letters from Petrarch*, ed. & trans. Morris Bishop (Bloomington: Indiana University Press, 1966), 198–199.
3. Jonathan Bate, *Shakespeare and Ovid* (Oxford: Clarendon Press, 1993), 87–88.
4. *The Works of John Dryden*, ed. Edward Niles Hooker, H. T. Swedenberg, Jr., Vinton A. Dearing et al., 20 vols. (Los Angeles: University of California Press, 1956–2000); references to these texts are given in parentheses; in the case of plays, references are to act, scene, and line, with volume and page numbers following the semicolon; italics in the original.

5. Laura J. Rosenthal, *Playwrights and Plagiarists in Early Modern England: Gender, Authorship, Literary Property* (Ithaca: Cornell University Press, 1996), 44–57, where she stresses the masculine role in the trope.
6. *The American Heritage Dictionary of the English Language*, ed. William Morris (New York: American Heritage Publishing Co., 1969), s.v. "Oedipus complex."
7. Lawrence Stone, *The Family Sex and Marriage in England 1500–1800*, abridged ed. (New York: Harper & Row, 1979), 116.
8. Ibid., 122.
9. Ibid., 121.
10. Ibid., 123.
11. *The Dramatic Works in the Beaumont and Fletcher Canon*, ed. Fredson Bowers et al., 10 vols. (Cambridge: Cambridge University Press, 1966–), 9:3–89.
12. *The Works of Sir John Suckling*, ed. Thomas Clayton and L. A. Beaurline, 2 vols. (Oxford: Clarendon Press, 1971), 2:121–182.
13. *Pepys on the Restoration Stage*, ed. Helen McAfee (New York: Benjamin Blom, 1964), 99, 128.
14. Pauline Kewes, *Authorship and Appropriation: Writing for the Stage in England, 1660–1710* (Oxford: Clarendon Press, 1998), 58.
15. Jean I. Marsden, *The Re-Imagined Text: Shakespeare, Adaptation, & Eighteenth-Century Literary Theory* (Lexington, Kentucky: University Press of Kentucky, 1995), 17.
16. Quoted by Kewes, *Authorship and Appropriation*, 58; the author is Richard Flecknoe in *Sir William D'avenant's Voyage to the Other World* (1668), 8–9.
17. Kewes, *Authorship and Appropriation*, 94–95.
18. McAfee, *Pepys*, 72, 78.
19. Although the King's Men obtained the right to produce the play in 1669, no evidence of any performances of it during the Restoration exists. See William Shakespeare, *Antony and Cleopatra*, ed. David Bevington (Cambridge: Cambridge University Press, 1990), 46.
20. Compare Marcie Frank, *Gender, Theatre, and the Origins of Criticism: From Dryden to Manley* (Cambridge: Cambridge University Press, 2003), 76–78, who sees the image of competition as displaced into the rivalry between Cleopatra and Octavia in the play. She forgets, however, that Telemachus, the true son, can string his father's bow, and so she concludes that in the analogy, "literary failure must, in any case, result" (77).
21. William Shakespeare, *Anthony and Cleopatra*, 124.
22. Gerard Langbaine, finding a parallel between a passage spoken by Don John in *Much Ado About Nothing* ("Even she, Leonato's Hero, your Hero, every man's Hero") and those of Ventidius in *All for Love* ("Your *Cleopatra;/Dollabella's Cleopatra:/*Every Man's *Cleopatra*") indicts Dryden for plagiarism of language. *An Account of the English Dramatic Poets*, ed. Arthur Freeman (New York: Garland Publishing, 1973), 153; cf. Kewes, *Authorship and Appropriation*, 117.
23. *Account*, 167.
24. Michael Dobson, *The Making of the National Poet: Shakespeare, Adaptation and Authorship, 1660–1769* (Oxford: Clarendon Press, 1992), 75.
25. Gary Taylor, *Reinventing Shakespeare: A Cultural History, From the Restoration to the Present* (New York: Oxford University Press, 1989), 45.
26. Ibid., 44.
27. Harold Bloom, *The Anxiety of Influence: A Theory of Poetry*, 2nd ed. (New York: Oxford University Press, 1997), 116.

28. Quoted by Brean S. Hammond, *Professional Imaginative Writing in England, 1670–1740: "Hackney for Bread"* (Oxford: Clarendon Press, 1997), 84.
29. (London, 1688), *Preface*; Langbaine's text omits page numbers.
30. See Kewes, *Authorship and Appropriation*, passim, for a good account of Langbaine.
31. Langbaine, *Account*, 162.
32. See Kewes, *Authorship and Appropriation*, 117.
33. Compare Petrarch, who condemns the use of words from others' writings, but admits that Virgil and many others are guilty of just that (*Letters*, 199–200).
34. Hammond, *Professional Imaginative Writing*, 103.
35. Langbaine, *Account*, 001 [appendix].
36. Ibid., 001–002 [appendix].

2 Kidnapped and Counterfeit Characters

Eighteenth-Century Fan Fiction, Copyright Law, and the Custody of Fictional Characters

Elizabeth F. Judge

> Those cartoons are my "children" of sorts, and like a parent I'm concerned about where they go at night without telling me. And seeing them at someone's web site is like getting the call at 2:00 a.m. that goes, "Uh, Dad, you're not going to like this much, but guess where I am."
>
> —Gary Larson, syndicated cartoonist of the *Far Side*[1]

Reacting to his *Far Side* cartoon characters' renegade afterlife, Gary Larson issued his plea for people to remove his *Far Side* cartoon characters from their unauthorized websites. The similarities between eighteenth-century writers' reactions to their characters' surprise appearances in unauthorized sequels and the objections raised by authors today are striking, both lamenting the too easy migration of characters from their original medium and work to another and the degenerate lives their characters experience after hours. Both debates arise from transitional views of copyright, and in both cases strong authorial attachments to fictional characters triggered serious debates over what constitutes protected original expression and when this should be untouchable by others, as readers and authors engaged in a discourse that was struggling to adjust to diverging norms and new laws.

Analyses of the intellectual history of eighteenth-century copyright typically focus on unauthorized printed editions (that is, the entire copying of another author's works verbatim) and the associated copyright case law in the literary property debates, such as *Millar v. Taylor* and *Donaldson v. Becket*, which tested the status of authors' common-law rights.[2] I turn here to eighteenth-century fan fiction, to import a term that has become popular recently to refer to newly written fiction by fans featuring fictional characters created and made famous by another author, and especially online publication of fan fiction. Although seemingly an anachronistic pairing to speak of "fan fiction," which has been so strongly associated with the internet, and the eighteenth century, the characteristics that define internet fan fiction appositely describe the eighteenth-century phenomenon, excepting the medium of dissemination. As with fan fiction today, which has been at the locus of cultural and legal debates around the meanings of authorship, originality, interests, and rights, fan fiction in the eighteenth century was a focal point for unresolved and evolving views on those same issues, especially the nature of authorship and originality, the integrity of fiction, and the reader's role. This chapter examines the cultural discourse around fan fiction in the eighteenth century to shed light on eighteenth-century interpretations of originality and imitation and the extent to which copyright law shaped (and was shaped by) cultural perceptions about the ownership and care of fictional characters and how competing interests in fictional characters contributed to the debate on copyright law.

FAN FICTION

The status of being a "fan," as Matt Hills argues in *Fan Cultures*, is "always performative; . . . it is an identity which is (-dis)claimed, and which performs cultural work. . . . Fandom . . . is never a neutral 'expression' or a singular 'referent'; its status and its performance shift across cultural sites. What different 'performances' of fandom share, however, is a sense of contesting cultural norms."[3] "Fan fiction" as a colloquial term is now primarily associated with the internet-centered practices of fans who write short stories or screenplays based on their favorite fictional characters and share them electronically. The stories typically add new characters, change settings, alter character traits of popular characters, and incorporate elements from multiple works. Fans post these revisionist interpretations to unofficial fan websites or to fan fiction archives online, and it is widely rumored, and occasionally confirmed, that fan fiction based on serial works influences future story arcs by the original authors. Everything old is new again, and, like much on the internet, there are strong historical precedents. Cultural and literary critics have located the origins of Web fan fiction in the 1970s photocopied fanzines by Star Trek conventioneers.[4] But the historical origins can be traced much further back, indirectly to prewritten oral storytelling, which thrived on episodic embellishment by individual bards, and more directly to the avid fan circles of the early novel, where fictional characters were "ravished" and "counterfeited" by fans for further adventures.

Although "fan fiction" has strong cyber-connotations, the phenomenon has been associated with the novel from its origins, albeit in different media and through different modes of dissemination than fan fiction on the internet. Reading circles penned annotations in the margins,[5] circulated alternate endings, corresponded with authors to advocate for happier endings, and shared their revisionist interpretations with other fans (as with Lady Bradshaigh and her sister Lady Elizabeth Echlin and their happier endings for Samuel Richardson's *Clarissa*). Rival authors wrote parodies (such as Henry Fielding's *Shamela* reply to Richardson's 1740 novel *Pamela*), while lesser known authors profited by writing unauthorized sequels featuring the continued adventures of popular characters before the original author could satisfy popular demand (as with Daniel Defoe's Robinson Crusoe). In reply, contemporary fans made fascinating interventions in these characters' lives by casting them in sequels, migrating them to different genres, honoring them with namesake racehorses, and spawning character merchandise, such as waxworks, silk fans, and china sets.

Fan fiction, then and now, incorporates audience and reader responses to copyrighted expression through alternate endings, reinterpretations, and sequels, and more transgressively, through reimaginings of the original characters in different places or eras or with modified traits, such as the oddly prolific Harry Potter erotica.[6] Henry Jenkins, in his cultural studies examination of modern fan fiction about television, *Textual Poachers: Television Fans & Participatory Culture*, catalogued ten strategies by which today's fan writers "do not so much reproduce the primary text as they rework and rewrite it, repairing or dismissing unsatisfying aspects, developing interests not sufficiently explored."[7] These strategies of "interpretation, appropriation, and reconstruction" include recontextualization (writing "missing scenes" comprising off-screen actions and discussions that motivate perplexing on-screen behavior), expanding the series timeline (elaborating on hints about the characters' backgrounds to provide back stories or carrying through scenes that ended abruptly, where "writing beyond the ending" constitutes a "refusal to legitimize unpopular endings"), refocalization (shifting attention to secondary characters, especially women and minority characters with limited screen time), moral realignment (inverting or questioning the moral universe in the original text; for example by portraying villains as sympathetic protagonists), genre shifting (often shifting toward relationship-centered narratives), cross-overs with other texts (displacing generic and textual boundaries so characters from different series interact or characters are placed in a different environment), character dislocation (removing characters from the original context and providing them with different names and identities), personalization (erasing the line between the fan's experience and the fictional space by inserting the author as a character in the story, denigrated as "Mary Sue" stories), emotional intensification (emphasizing narrative crises, especially one character's response to another character's crisis, called "hurt-comfort" stories), and eroticization (transforming the merely suggestive to the explicitly sexual, which can include changing characters' sexual identities and "slash" homoerotic fiction).[8]

Many of these practices are equally apt descriptions of the rewriting strategies employed by eighteenth-century fans seeking to improve, eroticize, personalize, or elongate the original beloved, or at least provocative, narrative experience. Peter Sabor and Thomas Keymer's description in "*Pamela*" *in the Marketplace* of the inauthentic sequels to *Pamela* could just as easily stand as a defense for the modern fan fiction writer on the internet, speaking of the "self-sustaining dynamism in which new contributions could appropriate, recycle, or respond to other appropriations as much as to the original novel, in ways that kept the process alive and carried it forward well beyond the furore surrounding first publication."[9] Likewise, the following cultural studies definition of "fandom" in relation to today's popular culture can easily apply to eighteenth-century readers' interactions with the popular, and frequently critically maligned, newly emerging genre of the novel: "Fandom . . . is a peculiar mix of cultural determinations. On the one hand it is an intensification of popular culture which is formed outside and often against official culture; on the other it expropriates and rewords certain values and characteristics of that official culture to which it is opposed."[10]

I import the modern "fan fiction" term back to the eighteenth century to highlight similar instabilities in copyright as are invoked by fan fiction practices today (particularly with respect to internet archives of fan fiction) and, as is the custom today, use the term "fan fiction" to denote the enthusiasts' homages as well as the critics' parodies. I do so intentionally as a way to deflect attention (at least temporarily) away from the economic and juristic aspects and toward the expressive qualities of these eighteenth-century reworkings. Admittedly, the catholic view adopted here of what constitutes "fan fiction" could be challenged as embracing too many mere readerly interpretations or criticisms of novels under the rubric of "fan fiction." However, the distinctions between reader and critic, and indeed author and critic, are always subtle, as Richard Cumberland remarked in his 1795 novel *Henry*:

> We talk of critics as of men set apart on purpose to annoy and censure us, whereas every reader is a critic and publishes his opinion of us where he goes; we ourselves are critics in our turn, and what we complain of in our own persons we do to others; and though few think it worth their while to publish their criticisms, let it be remembered that some men's voices circulate farther than other men's publications.[11]

These already elusive distinctions are naturally exaggerated by a project that seeks to study fan writings about novels, where those fans may be "readers," "professional" writers, or other novelists, and to study the reader and author responses to each others' treatment of the fictional characters. Because there was an active dialogue *in writing* among authors, readers, and critics, all participants assume all these roles as an inevitable by-product of contributing to the exchange. With some novels that were published serially, the "roles of text and reception are peculiarly intertwined," as Keymer observed about *Clarissa*, a particularly pointed example of a novel where the "fan fiction" writer is at once a reader, writer, and critic and the author himself a borrower of fan fiction as he revised his novel. "Whether Richardson is anticipating reader response or reacting to it is not so easily distinguished. By exploring the possibility of alternative endings *inside* the closing volumes, he not only set the terms of the debates that followed publication but also parodied and answered responses of which he was aware well before his extensive final revisions. . . ."[12] Although the terminology of "fan" and "author" suggests stark delineations between the two groups, as is also true of today's nomenclature that oddly calls authoring fans "users" and, in demarcating them, undermines their legitimacy as "authors," the categories in fact are mutually permeable: Eighteenth-century authors of the original works, like Laurence Sterne with *Tristram Shandy*, Cervantes with *Don Quixote*, and Richardson, were not averse to integrating and reworking reader comments back into their subsequent volumes to enrich them, in the same way that some screenwriters of serial programming candidly acknowledge that they read and are influenced by the narrative suggestions on fan sites.

In what follows I examine a few key historical examples of fan fiction and set them in their legal context to examine eighteenth-century notions of cultural properties like fictional characters and the relationship between the multiple claims in those characters and copyright. Well-documented examples of extensive reader response to fictional characters that became cultural phenomena—spawning numerous unauthorized sequels in novels, plays, and short stories; lively correspondences between fans and the author; satires by rival established authors; and character merchandising—illustrate how appealing fictional characters who reach iconic status within a culture, like Pamela and Defoe's Robinson Crusoe, are subject to competing claims of ownership as well as competing affections. The chapter focuses especially on when and why popular, creative, and often affectionate inclusions of these eighteenth-century fictional characters into works by other people were, more often than not, treated by the original authors as akin to legal wrongs against a person—ravishing, counterfeiting, and kidnapping—and treated analogously to the word-for-word copying of entire works that was condemned as "pirating," despite the lack of legal foundation in English copyright law to underlie these assertions.

EIGHTEENTH-CENTURY COPYRIGHT AND AUTHORIAL PERSPECTIVES ON LITERARY PROPERTY

The 1710 Statute of Anne, or *An Act for the Encouragement of Learning by vesting the Copies of Printed Books in the Authors or Purchasers of such Copies, during the Times therein mentioned*, was intended, as its introductory section asserts, to prevent the "very great detriment" of "printing, reprinting, and publishing" of "books and other writings," by "printers, booksellers, and other persons" without the consent of their "authors or proprietors."[13] The Act's objective, as set out it in its long title, is explicitly utilitarian: *for* the encouragement of learning *by* vesting legal rights in the copies, an idea that is recapitulated in the preamble, stating the legislation is "for preventing therefore such practices for the future, and for the encouragement of learned men to compose and write useful books," that is, to prevent what contemporary usage called piracy and to provide incentives for writing.[14] Under this public bargain, in exchange for writing "useful books," authors were granted a limited-term monopoly over the reproduction (printing) right. For books that had already been printed, the Act granted the "sole right and liberty of printing" to authors, if they had not transferred the rights in the "copy" or "shares," or to booksellers or printers or anyone who had purchased or acquired the copy or shares to print or reprint the book, for a term of twenty-one years, "and no longer." For "books already composed, and not printed and published," or books written after the Act's effective date, the Act granted the "sole liberty of printing and reprinting" for a term of fourteen years to the author, counting from the date of first publication. If the author was still alive at the end of that period, the Act provided for a reversion term of another fourteen-year period for the "sole right of printing or disposing of copies" that shall "return to the Authors" only, not to booksellers. The statutory rights, the enforcement of which were conditioned on the proprietor having entered the title of the copy in the Stationer's registry, were infringed if any bookseller, printer, or other person printed, reprinted, or imported a book without the proprietor's written consent, or sold, published, or advertised for sale any books known to be printed or reprinted without the proprietor's consent. The penalties consisted of forfeiting the books and sheets and paying one penny for every sheet in possession, printed, published, or advertised for sale, with half going to the Crown and half to the proprietors.

The legislation thus set out in whom the "copy" right initially vested; in practice, the author as first owner subsequently assigned the right to the booksellers, as had been the norm before the Statute of Anne, usually exchanging the full rights for a lump sum, but more complicated arrangements in which authors retained some control or revenue sharing were possible and increasingly common as the century progressed.[15] For *Pamela*, for example, Richardson "accepted of 20 Guineas for two Thirds of ye Copy-Right; reserving to my self only one Third," but he must have rued that arrangement of only one-third coproprietorship shared with the two booksellers in light of *Pamela*'s phenomenal sales success.[16]

The intended objectives and the actual results of the Statute of Anne continue to be debated. A standard scholarly interpretation of the Act contends that it primarily protected the booksellers, despite the statute's long title reference to vesting copies in the "authors." Thus, Lyman Ray Patterson in *Copyright in Historical Perspective* describes the emphasis on the author as "more a matter of form than of substance," with authors used primarily as a weapon against the Stationers' monopoly.[17] John Feather strangely contends, controverting the clear text of the statute, "The so-called Copyright Act of 1710 mentions neither copyright nor authors," and calls it "little more than a codification, an inadequate and inaccurate codification as it proved, of existing book trade practices." An "author's right to be treated as the creator and owner of literary property," he continues, "is not defined in any English statute before the Copyright Act of 1814."[18] Revisionist interpretations have questioned whether the Act was as deeply centered in the booksellers and on trade regulation as the standard histories assert. According to this view, the facial reading of the preamble accurately reflects Parliament's objectives, but their efforts were thwarted by poor drafting or subsequent judicial glosses that read back into the statute a meaning that it had not been born with. According to this revisionist line of thought, the legislators were indeed concerned with securing the "free market of ideas," as Ronan Deazley has concluded, "not the marketplace of the bookseller," and the societal bargain represented in the legislation was struck not between the two parties of "the bookseller and censorial state," but among three parties, "the author, the bookseller, and the reading public."[19]

Although the Act describes the exclusive right as the "sole liberty of printing and reprinting . . . books," it did not protect the physical artefact of the printed book itself but the intangible expression that was embodied in the book. It is possible to discern this distinction between the tangible and intangible in the Act, as the statute does specifically target piracy, including, notably, *re*printing. The language in which this is articulated in the Act, however, is both opaque and inconsistent because the statute refers to unauthorized "printing and reprinting," which must relate to the intangible expression, but also to "books and other writings," which might be expected to refer to the tangible material in which that expression was embodied. Modern intellectual property scholars would have recourse to the idea of a "work" to describe the subject matter of copyright law and to distinguish it from the book as a material object, which is properly the subject of classical property law (governing real property and chattels). The contemporary connotation of the terms used in the Statute of Anne, "books" and "copies," however, did not observe such nice distinctions and "could and did refer to interests in physical objects or in incorporeal property, or to both simultaneously."[20] Thus, though Parliament "may have fully appreciated the rationale of their actions" and intended the utilitarian objective for the statute, it "does not necessarily mean," as Deazley remarks of the act's conceptual fluidity, "that anyone full understood what was meant by a statutory property in books."[21] Compounding the interpretive difficulties in reading the statute in hindsight, the meaning of an "author" for both cultural and legal purposes was just developing its modern connotations in this period, as Martha Woodmansee, Peter Jaszi, and Oren Bracha have emphasized.[22] "The 'authorship' construct, although still incomplete when introduced into English law in 1710, was a charged receptacle," Jaszi writes, and the "term took on a life of its own as individualistic notions of creativity, originality, and inspiration were poured into it."[23]

However, conceding the lack of consensus on the objectives of the statute, whether Parliament intended to secure or regulate the Stationers' monopoly, to grant rights or to recognize preexisting rights, to benefit authors, or to protect the reading public, and conceding the inchoate definitions of key copyright concepts—including what constituted the exact contours of the protected subject matter and the rights holder—it is clear that the Statute of Anne, in both letter and spirit, defined rights with respect to the "book" as a whole, not its individual parts. More precisely, the Act protected the intangible expression in the book, through "vesting the copies of printed books," and granting the "sole liberty of printing such book," as the legislation put it, or in modern parlance, through granting a negative right to the author to exclude others from reproducing the work without the right's holder's consent. The Statute of Anne, significantly, did not protect individual elements of a fictional work, such as fictional characters, and, as judicially interpreted, did not grant authors the right to prevent others from creating new works derived from the authors' original books, such as adaptations and abridgments. In today's discourse, one might explain that this period took a narrow view of the "expression" that would be legally protected and, perhaps only as a corollary rather than as an ideology, a broad view of what constituted the "ideas" that the law would leave open to the public and from which other writers would be free to seek inspiration and use for their own writings.

Given that this eighteenth-century copyright law formally protected economic interests in print, it left many potential "rewritings" and "reuses" by other authors unaddressed and, evaluated from the cascade of exclusive rights that copyright owners hold today, protected the proprietor against a fairly narrow compass of potential infringements best described as piracy of the verbatim text. Certainly eighteenth-century authors were concerned about the type of rights that the Statute of Anne protected, legal rights in the work as a whole, and in the loss of revenue occasioned by piracy.[24] In the years preceding and following the Statute of Anne, "book" and the "work" figure as ontologically relevant categories for authors to define their interests in their writings. Both terms repeatedly appear in authorial statements on piracy, addressing the financial detriments and the existing ethical claims to the property interest in the book, which, authors argued, underwrote the necessity to recognize the ownership in law. This strain is evident in Defoe's periodical writings on literary property, where he declares, "A Book is the Author's Property," and later, "Every Man who writes *what is no Breach of the Laws of God or Man* to publish; His Work is his Property, and he cannot be divested of that Property at the Will and Pleasure of any Man," on the Lockean grounds that "to suppress his Labour, is to divest him of his Property."[25] In his 1704 *Essay on the Regulation of the Press*, Defoe strenuously advocated for authors' rights in their literary works, as a necessary corollary, he argued, to the liability authors faced: "For every Author being oblig'd to set his Name to the Book he writes, has, by this Law, an undoubted exclusive Right to the Property of it."[26] In a 1705 article in the *Review*, Defoe points to the conjoining of rights and liabilities in authorship as a justification for legal ownership and as a reason to distinguish clearly the "work" with which each author should be credited, whether for liability or praise:

> Books are Printed by no body, and Wrote by every body; one Man Prints another man's Works, and calls them his own; again, another Man Prints his own, and calls them another Man's. *A*. is loaded with *B*.'s crimes, and *B*. Applauded with *A*.'s Virtues . . . continual Robberies, Piracies, and Invasions of Property, range among the Occupation.[27]

He continued to press this theme in the years preceding the Statute of Anne, paralleling property interests in writing with those in real and personal property and stressing the Lockean justifications, as in his 1709 *Review* article where he describes an author whose work is taken as having "his Goods stollen, his Pocket pick'd, his Estate ruin'd, his Prospect of Advantage ravish'd from him, after infinite Labour, Study and Expence."[28]

To move to an example of an author at mid-century treating the "book" and the "work," Samuel Richardson, as both a printer and an author, was more imbricated in the literary property debates than most writers, more savvy about his legal rights under the copyright act, and possessed a great deal of business acumen about the trade.[29] In the wake of an Irish bookseller who had obtained Richardson's advance copies of sheets advertising unauthorized copies of Richardson's final novel, *Sir Charles Grandison*, for sale, he was prompted, by this "wicked Invasion of my Property," to write *The Case of Samuel Richardson, of London, Printer; with regard to the Invasion of His Property in The History of Sir Charles Grandison before Publication, by certain Booksellers in Dublin*, where decrying the piracy, he asserted, "Never was Work more the Property of any Man, than *this* is his. The Copy never was in any other Hand: He borrows not from any Author: The Paper, the Printing, entirely at his own Expence."[30] Intriguingly, where Defoe had cited Lockean labor justifications for the author's property in the book, Richardson points not only to his active participation in the entire publishing process but includes aesthetic originality as a criterion for why this Work "is his": "he borrows not from any Author." Richardson elaborated on this theme that the property rights claim ("property all my own") is predicated on the writings having originated from him ("neither a compilation, nor borrowed from any body") in a letter addressing the Irish piracy, complaining to Anne Dewes in 1756,

> . . . I have owned the laying down of my pen. . . . And have I not written a monstrous quantity; nineteen or twenty close written volumes? And for what? To propagate, instead of virtue, theft, robbery and abuse,

> from the wild Irish, and to be forced to defend a property all my own; that is to say, neither a compilation, nor borrowed from any body.[31]

However, while asserting proprietary interests in the book, the full possessive claims that authors pronounced over their writings were seemingly not strictly reflective of and not defined by the narrow sphere of legal rights in the copyright statute. Authors as vigorously asserted interests in their fictional characters as they did in the printing rights in the book and made wider claims to control the integrity of the writings that ranged far beyond the rights that proprietors would have under the Statute of Anne. It is not that authors misunderstood the scope of their legal rights, but that the Statute of Anne merely reflected a crystallization in law of one interest within a wider set of interests that many authors had been claiming they already held and for which they cited a constellation of reasons, spanning aesthetic, philosophical, and moral grounds. Copyright law, at least initially, was not the definitional touchstone by which eighteenth-century authors measured their thinking as to the types of interests that could be protectively asserted on behalf of their fictional writing, and this was especially true with respect to fictional characters.

These interests over fictional characters, however, bear close resemblance to what today would be protected as a copyright interest, corresponding to author's moral rights under copyright law, as contrasted with economic rights in reproduction, which describe the type of legal right under the Statute of Anne.[32] The coalescing of legal rights in the aesthetic fictional work (leaving aside the issue of whether the 1710 statute primarily benefited the booksellers or was an important step in establishing copyright for authors) and the emerging genre of the long prose fiction of the novel, for which the fictional character was a central defining characteristic, came together to instill in authors a sense that their custodial interests over their fictional characters were legitimate. Over time, these claims would also crystallize into legally cognizable rights in the form of economic and moral rights in copyright law.

ECONOMIC AND MORAL RIGHTS

Copyright theory today, if one generalizes in broad brushes, typically traces two branches for copyright law: England's economic focus, rooted in Lockean labor appropriation, and a civil law European focus on personality rights, rooted in Hegelian personality theory. Under both systems, copyright comprises economic rights and moral rights, but with varying emphases. Collectively, copyright provides the author, as first owner, with the rights to exploit the work economically, to exclude others from doing so, and to be recognized as the creator of the original expression. Economic rights are exclusive limited-term rights, most notably reproduction rights, to facilitate the economic exploitation of a work, which are granted to the author as first copyright owner but can be subsequently assigned to others (such as a publisher). Moral rights, philosophically based on the idea that art is an expression of the author's personality, belong to the author and cannot be assigned (although they can be waived) and include attribution rights (the right to have one's name attached to one's copyrighted work or conversely have it published anonymously) and integrity rights to protect the work against distortion, modification, or mutilation.[33] Economic rights are usually more strongly associated with the English "copyright" common law tradition, and moral rights with the French "droit d'auteur" civil law tradition. As Justice Binnie, for the majority of the Supreme Court of Canada, recently said of these two traditions:

> It is not altogether helpful that in the French and English versions of the [Canadian Copyright] Act the terms "copyright" and "*droit d'auteur*" are treated as equivalent. While the notion of "copyright" has historically been associated with economic rights in common law jurisdictions, the term "*droit d'auteur*" is the venerable French term that embraces a bundle of rights which include elements of both economic rights and moral rights. As Professor Strowel observes:
>
>> [TRANSLATION] The expressions "droit d'auteur" and "copyright" speak volumes in themselves. It has been pointed out that the distinction between the copyright tradition and the "droit d'auteur" tradition is based on a question of terminology: where the followers of the first tradition, the British and their spiritual heirs, talk about "copyright" to refer to a right that derives from the existence of a "copy," an object in itself, the followers of the second tradition talk about "author's right" (droit d'auteur) to refer to a right that stems from intellectual effort or activity brought to bear by an author, a creator. This is the fundamental difference: on the one hand, a right that is conceived of by reference to the author, the creative person, and, on the other, by reference to the copy of the work, the product of the creative activity that is protected against copying.[34]

Modern intellectual property theory and discourse has been colored by these perceptions of conceptual differences between the "*droit d'auteur*" of the continental *civiliste* tradition and the English copyright tradition as rooted in the eighteenth-century legal history. In particular, modern intellectual property philosophy posits a tension between a natural law idea that views copyright as affirming preexisting rights that authors have in their work and emphasizes the work as an intrinsic part of the author's personality, which is said to be inhospitable to historically rooted English views and the English system based on the idea that copyright consists only of statutory rights and emphasizes economic rights. A copyright system based on the English system from the Statute of Anne characterizes

> copyright primarily as a system designed to organize the economic management of intellectual property, and regards copyright primarily as a mechanism for protecting and transmitting the economic values associated with this type of property and with the use of it.[35]

Whereas,

> [m]oral rights, by contrast, descend from the civil law tradition. They adopt a more elevated and less dollars and cents view of the relationship between an artist and his or her work [than the English copyright tradition]. They treat the artist's *oeuvre* as an extension of his or her personality, possessing a dignity which is deserving of protection. They focus on the artist's right . . . to protect . . . both the integrity of the work and his or her authorship of it (or anonymity, as the author wishes).[36]

However, this traditional way of looking at copyright—with economic rights being traced to eighteenth-century England and its protection of the *copy* (the printing rights in the book) and continental Europe's concern with personality-based rights—does not fully capture how eighteenth-century authors and their readers (including the participating fan fiction writers) perceived authorship and their normative rights in writings. Eighteenth-century copyright law did not prohibit imaginative reworkings of famous characters. But the authorial response to these unauthorized sequels nonetheless figured these fictional escapades in criminal law terms as kidnappings of their beloved characters. When the history of copyright law is traced through the treatment of fictional characters rather than fictional works, we start to get a better sense through authors' perceptions, rather than the trade's perceptions, of the laws and norms that governed authorship and originality and begin to see less divergence philosophically between the two copyright traditions. Although the trade in England focused on how to prevent the literal appropriation of print, authors also posed the different question of when original characters could be prevented from being taken and in so doing formulated a more expansive view of which kinds of expressions' integrity mattered. This, in turn, influenced a more expansive view of copyright property. In many eighteenth-century authors' views, aspirational under the law but descriptive under prevailing norms of authorship, authors could (and should) control the afterhours lives of their characters. Inserted into the legal framework, these authorial (and fan) interests in preserving characters' integrity was subsequently propertized, turning these early moral and aesthetic claims that characters were being kidnapped, counterfeited, ravished, and debased into the later legally cognizable assertions that original characters could be "claimed," "owned," and "taken."

KIDNAPPED, COUNTERFEIT, RAVISHED, DEBASED, PIRATED, AND ENGRAFTED CHARACTERS

Anna Laetitia Barbauld, in her *Life of Samuel Richardson with remarks on his writings*, summarily pronounced Richardson's sequel to *Pamela*, "like most second parts, greatly inferior to the first" and "less a continuation than the author's defence of himself." Second parts are "superfluous," she sniffed, because "the plan was already completed, and they are dull, for instead of incident and passion, they are filled with heavy sentiment, in diction far from elegant."[37] Richardson apparently shared this view: Had another author not begun what Richardson thought a rogue second part to his novel, he would not have done his own sequel, as he defensively explained: "for otherwise I believe I shou'd not have prevailed upon myself to continue it; for Second Parts are generally received with Prejudice, and it was treating the Public too much like a Bookseller to pursue a Success till they tired out the buyers."[38] A sequel by the original author was scorned not only because it was perceived as an unnecessary profit-seeking continuation of a story that may have been creatively exhausted, but also because fake "second parts" were proliferating at a prodigious rate, and in the process even "true" second parts by the original author were devalued, just as counterfeit purses flooding the market degrade the value of the authentic luxury item by deflating the exclusive status associated with owning them. Vulnerable and suspected, "second parts" were plagued not only by condemnations that they were inferior, but by the taint of inauthenticity and mass accessibility. The phenomenon of "second parts" being written by "fans" to provide "further adventures" for the novel's fictional characters was a common enough risk over the eighteenth century that Jonathan Swift was provoked to incorporate a meta-textual discussion of the publishing practice in his *A Tale of a Tub* to preemptively disown any "Second Parts," the "pernicious Kind of Writings," passed off as a production of the "paultry *Scribbler*" who "usually passes under the Name of *The Author of the First*."[39]

Despite the censure of 'second parts,' authors often resorted to writing their own second parts to reclaim characters when spurious sequels circulated. Cervantes, Bunyan, Defoe, and Richardson avowedly wrote their sequels to their massively popular fictions, *Don Quixote* (1605–1615), *Robinson Crusoe* (1719), *Pilgrim's Progress* (1678–1684), and *Pamela* (1740), respectively, to recapture their characters from rival authors of inauthentic sequels who, as they painted it, kidnapped and pirated their popular characters through specious namesakes to run rampant in "second parts." As Cervantes explains in his 1615 Dedication to the *Second Part of Don Quixote of La Mancha*, Don Quixote "has put [his spurs] on and he is on his way. . . . [F]rom many parts I am urged to send him off, so as to dispel the loathing and disgust caused by another Don Quixote who, under the name of *The Second Part*, has run masquerading through the whole world."[40] Bunyan introduces his sequel to *Pilgrim's Progress* by bidding his Pilgrim book to go forth, but to be warned that "some have of late, to Counterfeit/ My pilgrim, to their own, my Title set;" so if the readers do not believe they see the true Pilgrim, "I will Testifie that only you/ My Pilgrims are; And that alone will do."[41] Richardson rushed his own sequel to *Pamela* on learning that John Kelly was engaged to produce a sequel, explaining to his brother-in-law James Leake how:

> [h]aving heard that Mr Chandler, a Bookseller, had employed one Mr. Kelly, a Bookseller's Hackney, who never wrote anything that was tolerably receiv'd, and had several of his Performances refused by the Stage, I remonstrated against it, to a Friend of Kelly's. This brought Chandler to me, who when he found I resented the Baseness of the Proceeding; told me that he understood I had said, I had neither Leisure nor Inclination to pursue the Story. I told him it was true I had said so to several of my Friends who had pressed me on the success to continue it; but that was upon a Supposition no one would offer to meddle with it in which case I had resolved to do it myself. . . . I told him that still I would decline continuing it, if he and others did not force me to it in my own Defence; but if they proceeded I must & would; and Advertise against them, as soon as they Published. . . . And insisted that if their Piece was so well written as he pretended, (and much boasted to me, saying, they fell in nothing short of my two Volumes) he should have it publish'd under some other Title, and not infringe upon my Plan or Characters . . . By these [half sheets sent to Richardson by Kelly] I saw all my Characters were likely to be debased, & my whole Purpose inverted.[42]

Cervantes, Bunyan, and Richardson, as early examples of writers protective of their emerging rounded characters in long prose fiction, see these fan sequels as transgressions of rights (in a strong sense, but not necessarily in a *legal* sense), and yet seek linguistic refuge in terminology suggesting crimes against the person, thus anthropomorphizing their fictional characters with concerns about counterfeits, kidnapping, and masquerading. Today, the copyright owner would likely articulate these claims more juristically as copyright infringements, but the impulse to protect fictional characters still resonates with authors. The difference between characterizing these rogue sequels as a debasement, a ravishing, or an engraftment as opposed to copyright infringement is not insignificant; eighteenth-century authors were not framing the problem of their fictional characters' rebirths and reappearances in other people's work as a matter of lost economic interest, but as a more personalized drive to protect their characters' integrity.

The authors' descriptions of the reimagined characters (as imposters, masquerades, engraftments, and counterfeits), the language for the violations that the characters are suffering (depreciation, ravishing, and debasement), and their choice of rebukes of the writers who perpetrated these sequels (as pirates and conceptually equal to kidnappers) are provocative. Pirates and kidnappers suggest that the later writers are appropriating something that is whole and animated and that can and should be returned to its original home. The fictional characters are being imbued with a recognizable "life" that can be kidnapped and placed in a foreign world or, textually speaking, a new framework of exotic writing. Counterfeits and masquerades, in a slightly different vein, suggest clones, look-alikes, and duplications of the fictional characters, but artificial imitations in which the trained eye of a knowing and "attentive reader" could detect the fraud. Engraftments suggest a monstrous textual corruption, a living tumorous growth, which must be excised or which will spread like cancer, where the very multiplicity of the characters is a sign of the duplicity. Depreciation, ravishing, and debasement suggest that the fictional characters are like living entities against whom crimes against the person can be perpetrated. Although a jaundiced view might assume the authors had dressed up their complaints in hyperbole, the similarity of the lexicon in which the authors register their concerns and its repetition in both professional and personal correspondence should retard a too-facile conclusion that they were not sincere. Richardson exhibits relatively similar levels of ire against "hack writers," accomplished writers like Fielding, and readers who presume to articulate alternative endings (notwithstanding they had been invited by Richardson to do so), and whether the story is an actual continuation of the events in *Pamela I*, a satire, an eroticization, or a moral realignment. Thus, he fulminates against Fielding's *Joseph Andrews*, a refocalization fan fiction, with similar rebukes to those he launched against Kelly's sequel, "*Pamela*" *in the High Life*, which expanded the timeline of Richardson's original, complaining to Lady Bradshaigh that Fielding "abused" Pamela in his *Shamela* and that *Joseph Andrews* had "hints and names taken from" *Pamela* "with a lewd and ungenerous engraftment,"[43] recycling language for Fielding that he had used years before against Kelly's *Pamela* continuation.

The eighteenth century can claim character phenomena that rivaled, perhaps even surpassed, the cult hits of today, and that popularity similarly ignited fan devotion to the characters and an ardor for fan fiction. Richardson refers to "no less than 16 Pieces, as Remarks, Imitations, Retailings of the Story, Pyracies, &c." flowing from *Pamela* alone, and the epistolary novel *Clarissa* inspired his own epistolary correspondents to design alternative endings for the beleaguered heroine.[44] In *Clarissa*, where the eponymous heroine, Clarissa Harlowe, is tricked into running away from home with Richard Lovelace, after her parents insist that she marry another man against her wishes, is confined in a brothel, drugged and raped by Lovelace, and, for hundreds of pages over the serially published seven-volume book, dies, the reading circles, like serial drama and soap opera fans today, had ample time to try to persuade the author to save the heroine and plead that she marry Lovelace. "In short, that I thought my principal Characters could not be rewarded by any Happiness short of the Heavenly," Richardson defends the tragic ending in a letter to Aaron Hill on November 7, 1748. "But now have I suffered by this from the Cavils of some, from the Prayers of others, from the Intreaties of many more, to make what is called a Happy Ending!"[45] Abundant lobbying opportunities were presented to readers over the course of the serial publication of the first edition and the three revised editions that followed. The serial publication, as with series narratives today, provided the temporal space for fans to intercede for their characters and gave at least the illusion that the narrative arcs were not predetermined. As Richardson reflected later to Elizabeth Carter about readers who had misperceived opportunities for participation in a design that the author fought to keep aesthetically closed:

> others . . . wrote to me anonymously, and who professed so much love to Clarissa, as to deny her her triumph, and to grudge her her Heaven. What have I not suffered from an *affectation of a delicate concern for virtue*. A great deal of this trouble I have had from publishing a work in Parts which left everyone at liberty to form a catastrophe of their own.[46]

Lady Bradshaigh (under the pen name "Belfour") wrote Richardson after two installments to beg that Clarissa be saved: "let me intreat (may I say, insist upon) a turn, that will make your almost despairing readers half mad with joy."[47] In the alternative ending that Lady Bradshaigh spins in her annotated copy of *Clarissa*, Clarissa is spared the "last outrage," lives, but apart from Lovelace, and is reconciled with her family.[48] In her correspondence with Richardson, Lady Bradshaigh also describes "another scheme," this time of hurt-comfort fan fiction, in which Clarissa is restored to health, "still steady in her refusal of Lovelace," but Lovelace succumbs to a dangerous fever, and "compassionate Clarissa" is prevailed upon by Dr. Lewen to "make him a visit, as a charitable act." "What an interesting scene might you there introduce!" she tempts Richardson. Continuing to spin her tale, she imagines Clarissa would agree to marry Lovelace if he should recover, and, on his disorder taking "an unexpected turn," they do marry, "her resentment over, her stifled love returning with double force." On behalf of this impassioned scenario, she implores Richardson to consider the aesthetic benefits he would gain, "what moving tender scenes could you draw upon such an occasion," and "with what pleasure could I sob, and dedicate a deluge of tears to those scenes, and to the worthy objects."[49] Lady Bradshaigh's fan fiction explores emotional intensification through Clarissa's bedside visit to the fevered Lovelace and moral realignment with Lovelace's deathbed repentance and marriage.

Lady Elizabeth Echlin, Lady Bradshaigh's sister, wrote a more full-blown alternative ending for Clarissa, where, rather than outlining the events as her sister had done, she writes the fictional prose inset.[50] Like many modern fan fiction writers, Lady Echlin reasons that her emotional attachment provided her with a privileged position to know the character better than even the creator did. "I endeavoured to divert my thoughts from horrible scenes by the strength of fancy, and contented myself with supposing that I had discovered some mistakes in Clarissa's story, which were owing to your being misinformed," and while "sensible of the author's laudable intention, . . . shall ever think him mistaken in the method towards accomplishing his several great ends."[51] That is, the author's characters are so familiar and real that they overtake the narrative in which they appear, and it can be possible for devoted fans to see themselves as rescuers for the characters in whom they are so invested. In one sense, Richardson's success is his downfall: Having succeeded at creating fictional characters with whom readers intensively relate, the readers' relationship with the characters subverts the creator's moral universe and aesthetic design. In her alternative ending, Lady Echlin similarly spares Clarissa from the rape and converts Lovelace's familiars, but has Lovelace die a penitent, at least nominally retaining the tragic nature of the book by preserving Clarissa's death. Though she relates the "different turn" of her story, as Richardson gingerly calls it, to the author, she explicitly notes that she wrote it "with no other view than to please myself."[52]

Richardson objected both to Lady Brashaigh's proposed "happy ending" as contrary to his Christian ethic of an afterlife reward for the meritorious (but long suffering) Clarissa and the displaced tragedy of Lady Echlin's ending. He jokingly wrote the latter that Lovelace may as well have been made governor of an American colony, but his rejection of the revisionist ending was firm.[53] In the Postscript to *Clarissa*, where Richardson laboriously answers readers' "most material objections to different parts of this History" with specific evidence from the novel, he firmly insists that the characters' fate could end in no other way:

> The foregoing Work having been published at three different periods of time, the Author, in the course of its publication, was favoured with many anonymous Letters, in which the Writers differently expressed their wishes with regard to the apprehended catastrophe. Most of those directed to him by the gentler Sex, turned in favour of what they called a *Fortunate Ending*. . . . And how was this happy ending to be brought about? Why, by this very easy and trite expedient; to wit, by reforming Lovelace, and marrying him to Clarissa—Not, however, abating her one of her trials, nor any of her sufferings [for the sake of the sport her distresses would give to the *tender-hearted* reader as she went along] the last outrage excepted: That indeed, partly in compliment to Lovelace himself, and partly for delicacy-sake, they were willing

> to spare her. But whatever were the fate of his work, the Author was resolved to take a different method.[54]

While failing to shape the "official" version of what they had hoped was a malleable work in progress, the slighted fans nevertheless succeeded in broadening the characters' universes through writing and disseminating interleaved copies of the novels and letters that secured the heroine her happier-ever-after, or at least more contented, endings for which they had advocated.[55]

Richardson rebuffed these efforts from the loyal readers of his *Clarissa* as conclusively as he did the bawdy unbowdlerized unauthorized sequels of his first epistolary novel's heroine, Pamela Andrews, albeit more temperately phrasing his refusals to the cognoscenti, whose interest in his novels he courted and who sought to save Clarissa, than the professional writers who financially capitalized on *Pamela*'s fame and eroticized and mocked its protagonist. Pamela, the eponymous heroine of his first novel, is a maidservant who marries her deceased employer's son, Mr B, after he attempts to rape her. Pamela, character and novel, is a confusing admixture. *She* can reasonably be interpreted as a scheming, too-knowing, coarse vixen—a "little pert minx" as The "Lover of Virtue" of the anonymously published *Critical Remarks on Sir Charles Grandison, Clarissa and Pamela* labels her, or a virtuous, ingenuous, refined naïf.[56] Terry Eagleton has contended that how "'bold' or 'devious' Pamela is is finally undecidable." Pamela, he remarks, is "neither 'naturally' saucy nor a straitlaced girl driven desperately to impudence; she is neither deliberately scheming nor in the least blind to self-interest, neither initially high-minded nor a hypocrite."[57] *Pamela*, the novel, meanwhile, as Ian Watt memorably remarked in *The Rise of the Novel*, manages to offer the "combined attractions of a sermon and a striptease," a pornography of prudence, or, as Leslie Fiedler calls it, "at once practical, prurient, and edifying."[58] It is not surprising then that *Pamela* the novel attracted such a proliferation of fan fiction, by devotees and more financially motivated sequelizers, for there was a built-in reading public for these continued adventures. Moreover, the very indecipherability of the original character as schemer or innocent provided fertile ground for exploration (and mockery) with some versions "clarifying" Pamela's character with their decided bent toward the lewd and mischievous.

Richardson, however, was exercised by the wild turns that the namesake character experienced in these escapades and by the supposed revelations of her "real" feelings. Irate over the prospect of John Kelly's unauthorized sequel of *Pamela's Conduct in High Life*, Richardson took umbrage that his characters would be ill-used, much like Gary Larson lamenting the after-hours life of the Far Side characters in cyberspace, censoriously objecting that "my Plan should be basely Ravished out of my hands, and, probably, my Characters depreciated and debased, by those who knew nothing of the Story, nor the Delicacy required in the Continuation of the Piece."[59] Richardson later wrote to Lady Bradshaigh that he hoped his Christ-figure hero Grandison from his final novel "may be suffered to end where I have now concluded it," deflatedly but rightly recognizing that this ability to preclude afterhours adventures of his beloved characters was not a legally enforceable right, but a claim that could be asserted as a culturally cognizable one.[60]

Although Richardson sometimes feigned surprise that readers so actively intervened to plead for their characters and deigned to propose or craft alternative endings for his characters, his characters were carefully constructed to provoke this response, and he was well aware of the likely effect with his readers, owning to Lady Bradshaigh, "I have lost a great part of my Aim, if I do not occasion many Debates upon different Parts of my Management."[61] To Lady Echlin, he similarly conceded that his characters were deliberately designed to provoke active participation: "A good Character is a Gauntlet thrown out. . . . Many things are thrown out in the several Characters, on purpose to provoke friendly Debate; and perhaps as Trials of the Readers Judgment, Manners, Taste, Capacity." Richardson relishes the opportunity furnished him by his "Characters drawn from common Life" of "looking into the Hearts" of his readers "through Windows that at other times have been close shut up."[62] He "designedly, play'd the Rogue" with his readers, as he confesses to Lady Bradshaigh, "intending to make them think now one way, now another, of the very same Characters."[63] However, while enjoying throwing out this gauntlet, there was no question for Richardson when the challenge for his readers ended and that the original author's vision of the characters must prevail: "It is impossible that Readers the most attentive, can always enter into the Views of the Writer of a Piece written, as hoped, to Nature and the Moment," with "every one putting him and herself into the Character they read, and judging of it by their own Sensations."[64]

In reference to the proliferating *Pamela* sequels, Richardson complained of the "Baseness as well as Hardship it was, that a Writer could not be permitted to end his own Work, when and how he pleased, without such scandalous Attempts of Ingrafting upon his Plan."[65] By the time *Clarissa* succeeded *Pamela*, he had learned his lesson and (literally) closed the crypt door to a repeat of the *Pamela* craze: One could argue there was some misdirected spite inspiring him to kill off his heroine, rather than having to be forced to disown her after her reputation was sullied in afterhours antics in someone else's story. Interestingly, the author and proprietors of the unauthorized *Pamela* sequel, *Pamela's Conduct in High Life*, ominously subtitled "*to the Time of her Death*," made the same rhetorical move to buttress their characters' authenticity, adopting the rhetoric of the wounded author protecting a cherished character, insisting that they "*have been obliged to* Kill Pamela, that neither Mr. R——n, or his accomplices might be guilty of Murdering Her," and complaining that Richardson's attack on their publication was "in a most flagrant Manner striking at, and endeavouring to Stain, their Characters, which stand *at least in as fa[i]r a light* as that pretended Author's."[66] Richardson was provoked to point out at least one logical lapse in that curious argument, publishing an advertisement in his own sequel, *Pamela in Her Exalted Condition*, proclaiming that the murder of the spurious Pamela would in turn mean "that Persons may not be wanting, who will impose new Continuations upon the Publick."[67]

Interestingly, although Richardson castigates the *Pamela's Conduct* perpetrators as "Imitators," speaking as if their narrative propagated clones of the characters, he also describes them as having "murder'd that excellent Lady" Pamela, speaking as if a single character could not only be described and recognized, but also could find a home in two different works and maintain her essence. The fan fiction character simultaneously is both an imitation, a clone or counterfeit, but also retains enough of the original character that Richardson can complain of her being murdered. These seemingly contradictory notions are characteristic of the flux in this period in the concepts of originality, imitation, and authorship, especially with respect to interests in fictional characters. The apprehension of the first authors, as Richardson voices the concern of the characters' creators, seems to be both that their *same* fictional characters are making unauthorized appearances in other people's writing *and* that *imitations* of their characters are masquerading in other people's writing, superficially similar in appearance but *not* the same in their essence, a lurking doppelganger rather than a unique and unitary character with life experiences that have not yet been recounted.

In prophesying that the same fate would befall the "imitators," Richardson perhaps is alluding to the idea that once the concept that there could be only one authentic character was broken there was nothing to prevent further spurious sequels. Indeed, Kelly's sequel was fan fictionalized when Mary Kingman published *Pamela in High Life.*[68] With *Clarissa,* and the heroine's memorable, tragic, prolonged, and indubitable death, Richardson can be seen to be testing the theory that providing a definitive conclusion of the character's life, regardless of whether those narrative choices satisfied all the readers' longings and hopes for that character, would set up higher obstacles to dampen the ardor of a devoted fan or dedicated satirist contemplating an unauthorized continuation by forcing would-be fans to rewrite an existing ending, rather than merely continue an open-ended plot. Such final endings might be especially likely to have this dampening effect, Richardson might reason, once the novel proceeded from manuscript stage to publication, when the pleas from the inner circle of fans who were privileged to see the manuscript in progress could no longer affect the original author's published decisions, that is, assuming the author followed the conventions and limitations of narrative realism and did not resurrect his characters after having second thoughts about their demise.

FINANCIAL AND AFFECTIVE AUTHORIAL INTERESTS IN FICTIONAL CHARACTERS

Legal and literary analyses of eighteenth-century copyright law and the novel swirl around the economic repercussions of piracy. Yet as the Richardson fan fiction suggests, these accounts discount the vivid personal attachments and claims to the novel's fictional characters. In "*Pamela*" *in the Marketplace*, for example, Keymer and Sabor posit that Richardson was concerned with revenue loss and would not have been upset with stage adaptations, in contrast to prose adaptations, since the theatre performances would increase his sales:

> [I]deological considerations pale before those of commerce, and there is no reason to think that Richardson would have been greatly distressed by the [Irish] play. As a businessman, and indeed as a father, he objected vehemently to Irish reprintings of his work, which would deprive his family of revenues rightfully theirs. Yet stage adaptations, including the Irish dramatizations, were another matter.[69]

Viewed from an economic perspective, with the whole work as the locus, and based on the rights in law, their case is convincingly and logically made that an author would distinguish between stage adaptations and pirated reprintings.

But what of the authors' *moral interests* (to borrow our modern term) in the fictional characters? Would an author like Richardson really have been sanguine about unauthorized reimaginings of their characters if the aesthetic presumptions by subsequent writers did not affect revenues? As the correspondence between Richardson and Lady Bradshaigh and Lady Echlin suggests, authors and fans had vivid custodial and emotional interests in their fictional characters that they vigorously defended. Highlighting these "moral" interests is not to deny that there were marketplace effects at play here in the elevated rhetoric about fictional characters' reputations. Debased characters could—economically—harm the original author's reputation and hurt sales not only of the novel in which those characters appear but of future novels. The same holds true today. Although the modern distinction between "economic" rights and "moral" rights in copyright law implies a dichotomy, the protection of moral rights under copyright law actually has a financial dimension because safeguarding the author's rights to attribution and integrity of the work can have salutary economic repercussions for the sales of the book. Notably, Richardson's objections often invoke decidedly emotional and parental responses in their allusions to ravishings, lewd engraftments, scandals, and debasements. Of course, this could be calculated hyperbole to mask and make more socially palatable a real concern over money. But the repeated mantra and consistency in both private and public correspondence, the harsh invective, and his choice of how to frame the debate suggests that his concerns were closer to aesthetic interests in the integrity of his novels and, specifically, in his characters.

The elusive distinctions in this period's copyright law occasioned by the uncertain statutory terms of "book" and "copy" has its counterpart in the elusive distinctions in the cultural discourse between the novel and the fictional character. The repeated ambiguity in the correspondence between Richardson and others as to whether a name is intended to signify the character (Pamela) or the title of the work (*Pamela*) is certainly made more pronounced because of the eponymously titled novels and the lack of standardized typesetting formats for delineating titles in printed publications, but is not attributable only to those factors and is evocative of the custodial and emotional attachments to the fictional characters. The almost seamless movement between the work and the character, and the ease with which the fictional character is a synechdoche for the whole work, is indicative of how strongly and quickly the fictional characters, although only one aspect of the genre, came to define the novel in the eighteenth century. In Richardson's correspondence, this practice of what seems a deliberate exploitation of the ambiguity between the name of the character and the title of the work may be seen as his intention to assert not only a claim over the fictional character, but an irrevocably higher claim than anyone else who may write of the character because of the unbreakable lineage between the fictional character child and the author. Richardson's concern for his "Plan" (apprehending it "should be basely Ravished out of my hands") seems to be less about the novel per se than for the fictional characters and the arc of their fictional lives. The intense protective interest he exhibits here toward his characters is more than an economic one—it is custodial and affective, more than proprietary, and aptly characterized as a moral rights type interest in the integrity of the work.[70] This type of custodial integrity interest suggests that the historical narrative about English copyright law and the traditional basis for control and rights requires a reinterpretation, whereby the equivalent of moral rights interests in the early English copyright tradition is accorded a more prominent role in the narrative.

Lacking legal enforcements, eighteenth-century authors deployed creative strategies to protect their moral-rights-type interests in the integrity and aesthetic unity of their fictional characters and the novels that told their characters' stories. One strategy was for authors to mark their own work as authentic or official. Sterne autographed thousands of copies of his authentic continuation of *Tristram Shandy* after spurious volumes appeared.[71] Advertising and public notices furnished other credentialing means for the author to mark the true entrance of their sequels or to disinherit rogue sequels as pretenders, as Richardson in his guise as Editor of *Pamela* does in his December 7, 1741 advertisement, giving "publick Assurance, by way of Prevention, That all the Copies of Mrs. B's Observations and Writings, upon every Subject hinted at in the preceding Four Volumes, and in particular those relating to *Devotion*, *Education*, *Plays*, &c. are now in *One Hand Only*."[72] Another strategy was for authors to insist not only on the authenticity of their original writings but to foreclose the possibility that any authentic continuation would be forthcoming, denying readers the thrill of fictional characters' afterhours experiences.[73]

More obviously, authors could reassert control over the integrity of their aesthetic design by writing the sequel themselves. Cervantes, like Sterne, adopting this tactic was both playful and savvy in his fictional retorts to the sequels, incorporating meta- and paratextual references to the spurious sequel in which his original publication is discussed as an artefact in his own sequel, enabling the original and sequel to reinforce each other's authenticity while reappropriating the choice bits of the fan fiction into the true sequel and displacing the pretenders. As Keymer and Sabor describe this phenomenon, "Parasitism could in the end be made to yield a kind of symbiosis; engraftment could nourish the root."[74] Cervantes marshals his own fictional characters to justify their encore appearance:

> "Does the author promise a second part at all?" said Don Quixote. "He does promise one," replies Sansón, "but he says he has not found it, nor does he know who has it, and we cannot say whether it will appear or not. So on that score, as some say that no second part has ever been good, and others that enough has been already written about Don Quixote, it is thought there will be no second part. Yet there are some who are jovial rather than saturnine. 'Let us have more Quixotic adventures, let Don Quixote charge and Sancho chatter,' they declare, 'and no matter how it may turn out, we shall be satisfied with that.'" "And what does the author mean to do?" said Don Quixote. "What?" replied Sansón. "Why, as soon as he has found the history which he is now searching for with extraordinary diligence, he will at once give it to the press, moved more by the profit that may accrue to him from doing so than by any thought of praise." "The author looks for money and profit, does he?" observed Sancho, when he heard that. "It will be a wonder if he succeeds, because it will be only hurry, hurry, with him, like the tailor on Easter Eve, and works done in a hurry are never finished as perfectly as they ought to be."[75]

In Cervantes's metatextual display, the fictional characters make clear to whom their allegiance lies, promising fidelity to the original author with their precommitment to appear in any of his sequels:

> Let master Moor, or whatever he is, pay attention to what he is doing, and I and my master will give him enough material in the way of adventures and actions of all sorts that he can make up not only one second part, but a hundred. The good man fancies, no doubt, that we are fast asleep in the straw here, but let him hold up our feet to be shod and he will see which foot we're lame on. All I say is, that if my master would take my advice, we would be out there now, redressing outrages and righting wrongs as is the use and custom of good knights-errant.[76]

Richardson was less playful than Cervantes in his actions to guard the integrity of his fictional characters and exhibited a vexed relationship to his fans, soliciting their contributions, coyly drawing them out, teasing them into criticizing, rebuffing their suggestions, and rebuking their critiques, all while sharply asserting his presumptive authority and insistently defending his original aesthetic choices. He sought debate and engagement, after all a "good Character is a Gauntlet thrown out," but with varying degrees of politeness snubbed and spurned any overt fan fiction interventions in the characters' lives.

Of course, the most potent weapon the authors wielded against fan fiction was the extreme measure of killing off their fictional characters, especially the protagonist, which authors remarkably and perversely defended as a way to preserve the characters' memories. After the unauthorized sequel to Part I of *Don Quixote* appeared in 1614, Cervantes wrote his own "second part" but gave Don Quixote his final farewell, explaining in the Prologue to the Reader, *Part 2*,

> you should bear in mind that this *Second Part of Don Quixote* which I offer you is cut by the same craftsman and from the same cloth as the *First*. In it I present Don Quixote continued and finally dead and buried, so that no one may dare bring forward any further evidence against him, for that already produced is sufficient. Suffice it, too, that some reputable person should have given an account of all these shrewd lunacies of his without going into the matter again. Abundance, even of good things, prevents them from being valued, and scarcity, even in the case of what is bad, confers a certain value.[77]

Richardson preempts Aaron Hill's suggested changes for *Clarissa* by bluntly announcing the deaths of all the significant personages: "In her Preparation for Death, and in her Death, I had proposed to make this a much nobler and more useful Story than that of Pamela; *As all must die*."[78] Although he did not repeat this feat in *Grandison*, the fact that he *could* and had the fortitude in the past to have done so seemed to have the desired effect on his fans. After *Clarissa*'s tragic ending, Richardson's fans were particularly chary that this tragic death scene for the fictional characters they had come to love might be replayed, and they tread carefully lest they provoke he who held the official fates of the characters in his hands. As Miss Highmore warned Miss Mulso,

> [L]et us remember he can cut their thread of life at pleasure; their destiny is in his hands, and I am not certain that our security may not provoke him to destroy them, for that has set his imagination on the glow; and he can draw instructions equally from every catastrophe, and can wind nature as he pleases; she presents him with events for every purpose, so probable, that we shall think no other than the chosen fortune could have attended them with propriety.[79]

Although she later thought herself foolish, Lady Bradshaigh "burst into Tears" on Richardson's hints of an unhappy ending in *Grandison* too, and lashed out, "You love to make one weep, you *love* to *kill* people. God forgive you. I *never* can."[80]

Although Miss Highmore treats him as a puppet master over his fictional characters, Richardson is apprehensive that his narrative control over his characters was coming unloose with his final novel precisely because by not killing off his entire cast of characters there was too much thread spooled out, which could be picked up by those who wished to write *Grandison* sequels. Disconcerted by the narrative possibilities left open by characters who survived his fictional end and the latent power that accorded to others, Richardson explains to Lady Bradshaigh why he nevertheless gamely proceeded with that risk so as to honor the characters' integrity:

> But, Madam, could not you have observed, that this Story is laid so near the present Time, that it would have been to be guilty of the highest improbability, had I concluded with the Deaths or Marriages of every one of my principal Characters?. . . . Most of the Persons then must be left alive at the Conclusion of the Story, or I must have a murdering Pen indeed. Something also must be left to the Reader to make out. Perhaps some other officious Pen (as in Pamela in High Life, as it was called) will prosecute the Story; But I hope it may be suffered to end where I have now concluded it.[81]

By the time he wrote *Clarissa*, Pamela had been taken on many further adventures by other pens, and perhaps not surprisingly *Clarissa* has an excessively final ending. There could be no dispute as to her fate, no chance of sequels for Clarissa, only fan disappointment and suggestions for *alternative* endings. In *Clarissa*, Richardson's postpublication discussions take the form of defending his aesthetic choices, repeating the mantra that her only just reward was heaven, not marriage. In *Grandison*, the fates of the characters are more open and the possibility of sequels a viable one. In some senses, it is surprising that, after the *Grandison* piracy and the *Pamela* fan fictions, Richardson would return to an open-ended ending, where the fates of characters could be continued by other hands. Richardson's postpublication correspondence for *Grandison* explains why he is not going to write a sequel but also takes the opportunity to clear the paths his characters will travel; although they live, their fates will not be open ended. In his *Copy of a Letter to a Lady, who was solicitous for an additional volume to the History of Sir Charles Grandison; supposing it ended abruptly, and expressing herself desirous to see Sir Charles in the Parental Character; and to know if the Story were intended to be carried further* (1754), Richardson remains stalwart against fan fiction intrusions into his characters' lives; although he chooses aesthetic unity of their storyline over their premature deaths, he spins some predictive futures of his own for his characters:

> I have no intention of pursuing further the History of Sir Charles Grandison: And hope, when you consider the circumstances of the Story, you will be of opinion, that it ends very properly where it does; tho' at the first perusal it may seem, to a Lady who honours the piece with her approbation, to conclude a little abruptly; and the rather, as the necessary delay in publishing the last volume, occasioned by the treatment I met with, from Dublin, made persons imagine that marvellous events, and violent catastrophes, were preparing; and but for which treatment the three last volumes would have been published together. . . .

After surveying and justifying the fate of each character, Richardson concludes,

> Permit me further to observe, that the conclusion of a *single story* is indeed generally some great and decisive event; as a *Death*, or a *Marriage:* But in scenes of life carried down nearly to the present time, and in which a *variety of interesting characters* is introduced, all events cannot be decided, unless, as in the History of *Tom Thumb the Great*, all the actors are killed in the last scene; since persons presumed to be still living, must be supposed liable to the various turns of human affairs. All that can be expected therefore in such a work, if its ending is proposed to afford the most complete scene of felicity of which human life is capable must be to leave the principal characters happy, and the rest with fair prospects of being so.[82]

THE CHARACTER OF FICTIONAL CHARACTERS IN EIGHTEENTH-CENTURY FAN FICTION

The fact that the history of copyright and the history of the novel developed in parallel, both temporally and discursively, is significant. There are deep connections between the origins of the English novel as a distinct genre and the origins of English copyright law, and the literary property debates are not coincidentally tied in to the development of full fictional characters. Eighteenth-century fan fiction highlights the tentative nature of the "novel" as a literary project, its developing and distinctive practices of fictional characterization, the emerging descriptive and normative definitions of "fictional characters," the scope of public and authorial attachment to fictional characters, the development of identity through a shared lexicon of popular (and "rounded") characters, and early copyright law. The cultural discourse around fan fiction in the eighteenth century sheds light on eighteenth-century interpretations of "originality," "imitation," and "authorship," and the extent to which copyright law shaped (and was shaped by) cultural perceptions about the claims to fictional characters and the emerging genre of the novel.

Fan fiction debates were able to flourish in the eighteenth century because full, or rounded, fictional characters were emerging with the growing popularity of the novel. All contributors to this exchange (the authors of the fan fiction, the authors of the original fiction, and both of their readers) identified and reacted to these unauthorized and, in some views, nonauthorial sequels and revisionist explorations of the characters *because* of the perceived continuity of the protagonist or the cast of characters (regardless of whether the characters are similarly named). What makes the fan fiction identifiable as a "sequel" or reworking is the reader response that recognizes the "same" character in the original and successor writings; for literary works, such recognition is no small feat because there is no visual manifestation to compare two versions of characters (except those novels published with graphic illustrations of the characters in frontispieces or plates, and even those represent a refraction of the author's textual character). Richardson, for example, in his introduction to the second edition of *Pamela*, in accounting for the absence of two planned frontispieces, quotes with approbation Aaron Hill's apprehension that any image of the protagonist would diverge and reduce the one inspired by the text:

> the Proprietors [Richardson with booksellers John Osborn and Charles Rivington] were advised to lay them aside. And were the rather induced to do so, from the following Observation of a most ingenious Gentleman [Aaron Hill], in a Letter to the Editor. "I am so jealous, *says he*, in Behalf of our *inward* Idea of PAMELA's *Person*, that I dread *any* figur'd Pretence to Resemblance. For it will be pity to look at an *Air*, and imagine it *Hers*, that does not carry some such elegant Perfection of Amiableness, as will be sure to find place in the *Fancy*."[83]

Interestingly, such a test for whether two fictional characters are the "same," which relies on visual recognition, in intellectual property terms is more akin to trademark than to copyright concepts, although the formal law of trademark in England lies a century further ahead of this period. From a market perspective, those eighteenth-century fan fiction authors who wished to cash in surely intended the sequels to be interpreted as featuring the same character (even under a name change). The authors thus could hardly be blamed as overreacting that "their" characters were being kidnapped and transported to a new fictional vehicle because the characters were in fact identified by the readers and authors as likenesses, whether twins, counterfeits, or kidnapped characters, when they made encore appearances.

Aesthetically, Richardson was claiming that the circulation of these revisionist endings would fundamentally damage the integrity of Clarissa because these depictions misunderstood her fundamental nature, an intriguing and somewhat paradoxical view that can at once perceive the reworked character *as* Clarissa and yet still fret that the new plots are "out of character" for the character. However, for authors, these concerns over the welfare of their characters, for the integrity of the character of the character, so to speak, were essential claims that were intricately intertwined with the interests over the "book" and, although not formally part of copyright law, informed the larger conversation over authorship and originality.

Fan fiction is problematic to categorize, both legally and aesthetically, because a character can be fully realized for authors and readers even though not everything about the character is shared by the first author. Early novel authors like Richardson were asserting that *they* knew the character, but of course not everything about a fictional character can ever be wholly told within the inherent limitations of finite generic bounds (and limited patience and time among readers). This necessarily invites the possibility that any character, no matter how developed, can have stories that have not been told and thus opens up expressive and economic opportunities for others to explore.

As E. M. Forster has cogently described in his famous study of characters in *Aspects of the Novel*, characters are "real not because they are like ourselves (though they may be like us) but because they are convincing":

> A character is real . . . when the novelist knows everything about it. He may not choose to tell us all he knows—many of the facts, even of the kind we call obvious, may be hidden. But he will give us the feeling that though the character has not been explained, it is explicable, and we get from this a reality of a kind we can never get in daily life. . . . [I]n the novel we can know people perfectly, and, apart from the general pleasure of reading, we can find here a compensation for their dimness in life.[84]

Literature, and notably the novel, excels at introspection and psychology, permitting us to "know" a literary character in a different way than the visual recognition of a pictorial fictional character. Literary characters develop incrementally by nuances, mannerisms, telling incidents, and revealing remarks. Fan fiction's affinity then for crossing boundaries and pursuing the unsaid (or unsayable) in the original work makes it difficult to discern when it is the same character who is reappearing in a different literary work and when, by contrast, it is another character inspired by the first or created specifically to show how a different character could react to similar plot devices.

Henry James rhetorically queried, "What is character but the determination of incident? What is incident but the illustration of character?"[85] Under this Jamesian view, where a fan fiction writer gives a character new incidents that the official work would not pursue as part of a serial development then there is indeed a new character. The reactions by eighteenth-century authors and readers, however, seem to suppose an immanent fictional character, separable from the original work and the original plot, whose integrity can be damaged, but where even injured it is still the same character that is suffering. Eighteenth-century readers and Richardson interestingly interpreted the facility with which a "Pamela" could be detached from her original story and reappear in so many other works *not* as a sign that the character was only a fungible allegorical stereotype, a mere template that each author subsequently gave expression. Rather, the fact that she could step out—or be drawn out—to have further adventures and to travel to other works indicated she was a fully realized character on her first outing in Richardson's novel, even if not every moment of her life could have been entirely recounted there. In this complex interaction, a character that is "round" in its first outing is simultaneously able to move (or be moved) to other works and, in that sense, is less fettered to the first narrative, but in maintaining its recognizability as it travels, the character also enhances the significance of the first author's narrative of that full character.[86]

Eighteenth-century novelists frequently trumpeted the "newness" or novelty of novels, representing their work as significant not merely because their novel contributed to this new *genre* but because their particular manifestations within that generic mode were original and not imitative. Edward Young, in his 1759 *Conjectures on Original Composition in a Letter to the Author of Sir Charles Grandison*, speaks of an "Original" as being of a "vegetable nature" that "grows, it is not *made*"; an *original* organically "rises spontaneously from the vital root of genius," whereas "*Imitations* are often a sort of *Manufacture* wrought up by those *Mechanics, Art,* and *Labour*, out of pre-existent materials not their own." An *Imitation* is read "with somewhat of his languor, who listens to a twice-told tale," whereas an "*Original*, by being as excellent, as new, adds admiration to surprise."[87] In her Preface to *Evelina* (1778), Frances Burney asserts a general principle in line with this denigration of "imitation," averring that in books, "imitation cannot be shunned too sedulously; for the very perfection of a model which is frequently seen serves but more forcibly to mark the inferiority of a copy." Richardson more boldly claimed the mantle of originality, describing *Clarissa* to Johannes Stinstra as "a piece from first to last, that owes its Being to Invention" and *Grandison* as "entirely new and unborrowed, even of myself."[88] Although he speaks here of the work as a whole, it is because of his *characters*' originality, in a sense their fullness, newness, recognizability, and individuality, that Richardson is justifying his continuous custodial interests; they must be cared for because they can move out of the books in which they were incarnated and because they are damaged when they are displaced. That these original individual characters are capable of being recognized when they reappear in other works, albeit that they are, in Richardson's perception, only pale or corrupted images of their original selves, undergirds his inclination to denigrate these unauthorized second parts; they are in effect what Young would later call a "twice-told tale" based on "pre-existent materials," specifically, the preexistent materials of Richardson's original fictional characters.

Yet it must have been especially difficult given the uncertain contours of the new genre of the novel for contemporary readers to know whether fan fiction authors had kidnapped the same characters or whether they were conducting the same generic experiments but creating original characters of their own. That is, were the *Pamela* fan fiction authors mixing some of the same generic antecedents of the novel that Richardson explored and repeating devices and scènes à faires about the *idea* of *a* character of a house staff who is seduced, or raped, by someone within the house or were they specifically replaying the original character of Pamela herself? Fielding's *Shamela* is certainly meant to be a play on *Pamela.* But is Shamela an alias unveiling of Pamela's true self in more forthright colors or is Fielding's critique effected through another character? Is it, following James's definition, another character by virtue of being in a work written by another hand with new incidents? Richardson certainly did not wish to make any claims of ownership over *Shamela* or *Pamela's Conduct* as literary *works.* The nature of his objection may be better understood as an objection that they were imitating his fictional *character* and violating the character's integrity.

The difficulty of distinguishing kidnapped characters from generic imitations would have been compounded by the fact that with eponymously titled novels it is often difficult to tell, as previously alluded to, whether contemporary correspondents were discussing the novel or the character, and if the slippages between the work and the character are intentional, as with Sarah Fielding telling Richardson, "no pen but your's can do justice to Clarissa,"[89] or Aaron Hill writing, "Whoever considers your Pamela, with a view to find matter for censure, is in the condition of a passionate lover, who breaks in upon his mistress, without fear or wit, with intent to accuse her and quarrel."[90] Hester Mulso's letter, discussing *Grandison*, similarly breaches boundaries between character and novel: "I think I am jealous too for my favourite Clarissa; for I verily think this work promises (or threatens, which shall I say?) to excel that. I was angry with Clarissa for eclipsing my Pamela; and I believe I shall now have the same quarrel with her new rival."[91] Catherine Talbot, likewise, moves easily between the novel and characters with "Sir Charles" seemingly standing in for both: "I believe Clarissa *is* a work of higher genius than Sir Charles; yet I do love Sir Charles, and I *admire* Harriet too, gentle and reasonable though she be, and prefer her infinitely to Clementina."[92] One of the prefatory letters to *Pamela*'s second edition slips almost unnoticed between *Pamela* the work and Pamela the character, solidifying the intertwined nature of the two:

> [L]et us have *Pamela* as *Pamela* wrote it; in her own Words, without Amputation, or Addition. Produce her to us in her neat Country Apparel, such as she appear'd in, on her intended Departure to her Parents; for such best becomes her Innocence, and beautiful Simplicity. Such a Dress will best edify and entertain. The flowing Robes of Oratory may indeed amuse and amaze, but will never strike the Mind with solid Attention.[93]

These readerly efforts accrue on eighteenth-century authors' own proclivities toward anthropomorphizing fictional characters, speaking of them as children, and their affinity toward the rhetorical device of prosopopoeia. For many eighteenth-century authors and readers, the essential character of the novel was the full fictional characters with which they were peopled.[94] Thus, in his Preface to *The Adventures of Ferdinand, Count Fathom* (1753), Smollett defines the novel in relation to fictional characters and the essential significance of the eponymous hero/anti-hero(-ine):

> A Novel is a large diffused picture, comprehending the characters of life, disposed in different groups, and exhibited in various attitudes, for the purposes of an uniform plan, and general occurrence, to which every individual figure is subservient. But this plan cannot be executed with propriety, probability or success, without a principal personage to attract the attention, unite the incidents, unwind the clue of the labyrinth, and at last close the scene by virtue of his own importance.[95]

Samuel Johnson, in his famous *Rambler* No. 4 on the novel's instructional purposes, identified the "individuals"—the fictional characters—as central to these pedagogical objectives: The "chief advantage which these fictions have over real life is that their authors are at liberty, though not to invent, yet to select objects and to cull from the mass of mankind those individuals upon which the attention ought most to be employed."[96]

During this emerging period of the novel and copyright law, with uncertain rights and proprietary interests and only a murky sense of the difference between what modern scholars would refer to as a public domain "idea" and copyrightable "expression," it is possible that an author like Richardson might have tried to claim rights in the "idea" that Pamela represented, thus over any representation of a "beautiful young damsel" in similar circumstances. But the essence of his claim seems to rest on different grounds and to be motivated by different reasons: that the "original author" has custody over the life of his original character, which is effected through narrative control. Richardson, that is, seeks to protect *this* character in all her particularity and to do so, moreover, for custodial reasons.

CUSTODIAL INTERESTS IN FICTIONAL CHARACTERS

Significantly in these eighteenth-century conversations, authors were defining their relationship to fictional characters, not merely their relationship to the work and not merely to economic interests. As Mark Rose has described, copyright has been guided by two metaphors: the book as real estate and authorship as paternity.[97] The author as the parent of the book goes back to Plato and is a common metaphor through early modern writings and prevalent over the long eighteenth century. Mary Shelley, for instance, famously confessed her "affection" for her "hideous progeny" in her 1831 Introduction to *Frankenstein*. Defoe, in a 1710 *Review* article, refers to the book as the "Child of his Inventions, the Brat of his Brain . . . these Children of our Heads are seiz'd, captivated, spirited away, and carry'd into Captivity, and there is none to redeem them."[98] Similarly, the realty metaphor is common in eighteenth-century discourse and was a predominant fixture of the copyright debates. Justice Yates, the only judge dissenting from the 1769 case of *Millar v. Taylor* (where the King's Bench upheld an author's perpetual common law rights, a result that was reversed by the House of Lords in 1774 in *Donaldson v. Becket*), referred to the act of publication as a forced dedication to the public: "[W]hen an author prints and publishes his work, he lays it entirely open to the public, as much as when an owner of a piece of land lays it open into the highway."[99] As Rose, David Brewer, and Simon Stern, among others, have discussed with respect to the eighteenth-century literary property debates, the prevalent comparison of books with land established an idea of literary works as scarce physical resources.[100] This elided the distinction between intangible expression and the material object.

The land metaphor has had a tenacious stronghold on the discourse of copyright through the current digital copyright debates, with supporters of greater access speaking in land-based terms of the public commons and public domain. From the eighteenth century forward to today, there is frequent analogizing, with respect to reader access to original works, to real property with terms such as "covenants," "easements," "trespass," and "fences," culminating in the advocacy movement for supporters of a wider public domain finding fertile precedential strategies and resources in the earlier environmental law movement.[101] On the other side, the parental metaphor has been much less influential in shaping contemporary intellectual property debates and framing legal reform. This too muted effect stems from a persistent inattention to *author's* interests (rather than the copyright *owner's* interest, namely the publishing trade) and to a corollary tendency to underestimate the symbolic capital of fictional characters and their attraction as both emotional beings and economic vehicles. From the publisher's perspective and in the Statute of Anne, the main concerns revolved around the treatment of the work in its entirety and its printing as a material object: piracy and counterfeiting, the literal copy right. Even the parenting metaphor has been frequently deployed in reference to the birth of the *book*, displacing the parental interest in the characters and deflecting legal attention away from authorial—and readerly—interests in preserving the characters' integrity. But authors and readers assumed guardianship interests in the fictional characters, not only the book, with Richardson calling Clementina and Harriet his "excellent daughters" and readers claiming that they felt "intimately acquainted" as if they knew them "from my Infancy" or, as Catherine Talbot says, that they could scarce be persuaded that the characters are "not real characters, and living people."[102]

Modern copyright law, in part to keep pace with new technologies for reproduction and dissemination, protects not only the literal right to copy an original work (to prevent pirated editions of verbatim text), but also protects less literal copying, such as the "making of a copy in three dimensions of a two-dimensional work," and grants the author the exclusive rights in creating derivative works, including adaptations such as translations or dramatic versions of nondramatic literary works.[103] Even under modern copyright law's expansive author rights, relative to the eighteenth century, there are continuing legal debates as to when fan fiction infringes the copyright of the original work, when it can be the subject of copyright, and the extent to which modern copyright law permits fictional characters to be copyrightable subject matter independently of the work in which they appear.[104] Copyright legislation in the United States and Canada has resisted extending explicit and separate copyright protection to fictional characters as autonomous copyrightable works, although fictional characters can be protected as component parts of an underlying work (and thus reproducing the fictional characters without the copyright owner's consent could constitute infringement of the larger work in which they appear). A 1965 report to Congress from the United States Registrar of Copyright commenting on a copyright revision bill supported this interpretation. The Registrar advised Congress not to add a legislative category making fictional characters a copyrightable work in themselves. The Registrar acknowledged that characters could be "developed in detail and with such breadth and depth" as to have the appropriate quantum of expression to be copyrightable as a separately identifiable part of the copyrighted work in which they appear. However, given that "others, perhaps the large majority," of fictional characters are not "independent creations apart from the literary or pictorial works depicting them," it would be "unnecessary and misleading to specify fictional characters as a separate class of copyrightable work."[105] Likewise, England's Whitford committee in its 1973 review of copyright law also stood fast against urgings to introduce a "character right" because "there would be real difficulty in defining exactly what a "character" is, *i.e.*, in deciding what are the essential features that make the character distinctive and which are therefore worthy of protection."[106] These hesitancies among legal policymakers underscore the continuing elusiveness and subjectivity of a legally administrable definition of a "copyrightable fictional character," especially attempts to define the ineffable nature of fictional characters in literary works. This uncertainty was, not surprisingly, even more pronounced in the eighteenth century, when the novel as a genre was emerging and the role of its fictional characters was still developing.

England's 1710 Statute of Anne made few pretenses of providing rights to prevent the "spurious" sequels against which Bunyan, Cervantes, Defoe, and Richardson complained. It did not stretch to protect against the cloned Quixotes and "counterfeited Pilgrims" that appeared in new imaginative works in "second parts" penned by others and more certainly not the purportedly "same" characters when they appeared under different names than the original work. However, during the eighteenth century, although unauthorized sequels featuring someone else's characters were not strictly governed by copyright law, there was an active cultural exchange about the norms that should govern creativity, imitation, originality, and authorship, which was actively played out in this debate about fictional characters and their appearances in fan fiction. Yet there was no consensus between authors and readers about these practices and no clear relationship between the cultural norms of originality and imitation and the law's provisions on copyright.

ENVISIONING A TRADITION OF ENGLISH COMMON LAW MORAL RIGHTS INTERESTS THROUGH EIGHTEENTH-CENTURY FAN FICTION

Through Bunyan's pilgrims, Defoe's Robinson Crusoe, and Richardson's characters in *Pamela*, *Clarissa*, and *Sir Charles Grandison*, the competing claims to fictional characters who reach iconic status within a culture and the intersecting legal and cultural debates can begin to be traced. Situated in the context of the period's copyright debates, the reception of fan fiction, particularly involving iconic characters like Pamela and Crusoe, influenced the meaning of "original expression" for copyright law. Copyright law would later come to influence how fictional characters were culturally constructed as a legal property that could be owned, appropriated, and reclaimed, but the authorial inclination to protect characters' integrity as independent creations, which was a prevalent strain of the discourse around the newly emerging novel in this period, has had less of an identifiable effect on the development of common law jurisdictions' copyright law. Because there was no established legal precedent for claiming intellectual property in fictional characters per se, these debates between authors and readers and their contending claims to characters help to identify norms that were circulating over the long eighteenth century. These norms were then incorporated into descriptive legal categories of proprietary claims, which reformed the governing legal framework and repositioned the cultural claims from custodial to proprietary interests. Shifting the focus from the pirating of fictional works (by which we view the debate primarily from the booksellers' and printers' lens) to the kidnapping of fictional characters (by which we view the debate from the authors' eyes) highlights how "copying" began to be transformed from a mere literal copy-right to a more expansive protection against fictional character kidnappings and counterfeiting and sets the groundwork for copyright protection for nonliteral reworkings that are "original." However, the authorial interests in preserving characters' integrity, which were so prevalent in the early discourse, have not had as direct an effect back on the legal constructions and current copyright conversation to shape the interest away from proprietary- toward integrity-based protection. When viewed from eighteenth-century authors' and readers' perspectives and when focusing on fictional characters, a more complicated narrative emerges than a sharp dichotomy between an economically oriented eighteenth-century English history versus the authorial personality-rights oriented continental European history of copyright traditions.

This period's authors and readers are typically viewed in hindsight as actively engaged in creating contending constructs of "fictional characters" as private property, on the one hand, and as public commons, on the other hand, and as key players in widening the scope of controlled original expression under copyright law. But their participation in the imaginary welfare of the characters was articulated more often at the time in a discourse of less proprietary terms. Speaking at the end of the century of the "high Dignity, Powers, and Prerogatives of the Novel-Writer," for example, Richard Cumberland remarked on the awesome responsibilities that novelists held toward their fictional characters:

> I know that the privileges of the novelist are more than can well be defined, and his range wider than that portion of created nature which is known to us. . . . I know that I could play my puppets after my own fancy, for the wires are in my hand . . . but I have lived long enough to see wonderful revolutions effected by an intemperate abuse of power and shall be cautious how I risque privileges so precious upon experiments so trivial.[107]

Although the custodial interest for the welfare and integrity of fictional characters was so prevalently and persuasively expressed by both authors and readers over the eighteenth century, it has not been attended to as a part of the copyright history as much as have the property interests of the publishing trade with respect to the book. Reframing the debate in terms of fan fiction foregrounds the ways that both authors and readers participated in the characters' lives and the degree to which both authors and readers treasured these characters for personal and aesthetic, and not merely proprietary reasons.

The focus on the entire work does not adequately capture the felt response of authors and their interests during these eighteenth-century debates, which included demands by authors for attribution and for preserving integrity and calls by readers as fan fiction writers for their own vision of aesthetic integrity. Authors' concerns were often about the welfare of their fictional characters and not merely the handling of the book. Eighteenth-century novel writers applied the parenting metaphor to the fictional characters as distinct beings, and indeed such a domestic noncommercialized metaphor of parenting seems to find a more comfortable home when applied to characters than to books. When these novelists referred to the ownership of their fictional characters, the connotation is ownership not as an assertion of a *proprietary* interest, as would be true for a sovereign control over chattels or land, but a *custodial* interest in a sentient being (a child or, if one prefers, a domestic pet). Authors' responses to fan fiction, where they speak of the fictional characters as if they can be adopted, kidnapped, seduced, escape, and run away, brings into relief the trope of parenting (or its converse of "disowning" a child) and dims the legal metaphor of landownership (or its converse of a dedication of land to the public domain). In other words, when Bunyan laments the counterfeitings of his characters or Richardson decries the debasement of his, they embrace a guardianship interest, rather than a market-oriented status for the characters. That *plagiary* comes from Latin as "one who abducts or steals the child or slave of another, a kidnapper," provides further rhetorical echoes of the injustice these authors perceived.[108]

Notably, the fans, too, invoked custodial interests, and their perception of the conflict was that it was less about a struggle over rival property rights than a disagreement with the author over the best interests of the character. Clarissa, as Lady Bradshaigh and Lady Echlin ardently pleaded, deserved a better ending here on earth than the one her author-parent provided, and they lobbied for her to win both the rewards of the afterlife *and* the here and now (with a comfortable and quiet life in the country or death only after familial reconciliation). Even the writers of the bawdy Pamelas might see themselves as giving her the liberty to live in accord with her "true" character, much as the website creators today who provide the *Far Side* characters with the freedom to roam the internet. For many first authors, however, the tension is better described as the guardian authors against fan fiction corruptors.

Eighteenth-century sequels and rewritings have often been analyzed primarily as marketable commodities within a consumer culture, and the characters, too, are viewed as dislocatable and circulating figures, as marketplace subjects.[109] This theory is consistent with the prevailing narrative of England's economic copyright rights, but an alternative literary history can be constructed and would affect how the legal history is understood; focusing on custodial interests and fictional characters in the literary history in turn indicates a more profound role and more deeply rooted history for moral rights interests under English common law. To be sure, some fan fiction writers who wrote spurious sequels were "cashing in," as the economic view suggests, in a "Grub Street grabfest" as Keymer and Sabor dubbed it.[110] Yet in many other cases, the fiction was written by inspired fans who were prompted by noncommercial, expressive, and aesthetic reasons. That said, these more loving re-uses also tended to receive a chilly response from the original authors.

When fan fiction is repositioned within the literary property debates—as the authors (rather than the trade) viewed the issues that were at stake—the literary significance of fictional characters within the history of the novel and the legal significance of moral interests within the history of copyright is illuminated. Seen as a *relationship* of reader and authors to *fictional characters*, not printed works, and the ongoing *custodial* interests that *both* readers and authors felt toward these characters helps to illustrate another side of this debate which has been lost among the talk of landed metaphors, the marketplace, and the focus on the Stationers' property in the copy, all of which have dominated the legal articulation of the contending interests. As between eighteenth-century authors and their fan reader-writers, the dynamic, despite the lack of legal rights for support, is about authors as their fictional characters' guardians, protecting them against corrupting outside influences. This was true even as to those seemingly benevolent fans who wished for "better" lives for the characters, as can be seen in Richardson's reaction to the campaign to save Clarissa waged by Richardson's devoted fans. These fan fiction exchanges, evidencing textual responses to *fictional characters* and not merely to the novel as a work, suggest fictional characters were key defining aspects of the novel and that authors persistently claimed interests over fictional characters regardless of the lack of foundation for these rights in copyright law. Their interests were parental and custodial, rather than proprietary or legal, seeking to safeguard the integrity of their fictional characters.

This literary history evocatively suggests that the legal history of copyright may be recounting a fictionalized story. In narrating copyright as a binary story of English economic rights and continental European authorship rights (moral and personality rights), we may not be listening to what these emerging English novelists were saying about their characters or giving due regard to the reader reception and fans' zealous engagement with the characters' lives. The suggestion that "author's rights," in the sense of moral rights and the *droit d'auteur* tradition, are not as much a part of the English history—that it is absent in norms, rhetoric, and law—is belied by the custodial interest in which authors expressed their concerns about characters' afterhours lives: the gee, Mom, I'm in someone else's book and I'm behaving badly and I don't feel quite like myself. Can you come get me? Or, to convert this to the eighteenth-century language, the concerns that characters were being "debased," "pirated," kidnapped, and "ravish'd."

ACKNOWLEDGMENTS

Elizabeth F. Judge, JD, PhD, Associate Professor, University of Ottawa, Faculty of Law. I thank the participants at the "Originality and Intellectual Property in the Eighteenth Century" panel at the 2006 American Society for Eighteenth-Century Studies conference in Montreal, Quebec, and the Con/texts of Invention conference, sponsored by The Society for Critical Exchange, at Case Western Reserve University in Cleveland in 2006 for their comments on earlier versions of this chapter, and the organizers of those panels, Reginald McGinnis and Martha Woodmansee, Peter Jaszi, and Mario Biagioli, respectively. I am grateful to Deina Warren for her excellent research assistance. This research has been generously supported by the Social Sciences and Humanities Research Council of Canada.

NOTES

1. Gary Larson's remarks on his *Far Side* cartoon characters' renegade afterhours lives were included in his 1999 plea to website operators asking them to remove *Far Side* cartoons from their sites. In his personal appeal, he describes "the intangible impact, the emotional cost to me, personally, of seeing my work collected, digitized, and offered up in cyberspace beyond my control." Larson's approach is strongly reminiscent of the approach many eighteenth-century authors took in response to their fictional characters' appearances in fans' sequels: directly approaching fans to seek their cooperation, articulating aesthetic rather than legal interests, and emphasizing the emotional connections between authors and their fictional characters. Larson sentimentally concludes his entreaty by reiterating the great personal—indeed parental—attachment he has to his cartoon children: "I hope my explanation helps you to understand the importance this has for me personally, and why I'm making this request. Please send my 'kids' home. I'll be eternally grateful." ("A Note from Gary Larson: RE: Online Use of Far Side Cartoons," <http://www.creators.com/a-note-from-gary-larson.html>).
2. *Millar v.Taylor* (1769), 98 *English Reports* 201; *Donaldson v. Becket* (1774), 4 Burr 2408. On the literary property debates, see Trevor Ross, "Copyright and the Invention of Tradition," *Eighteenth-Century Studies* 26, no. 1 (1992): 1–27; Brad Sherman and Lionel Bently, *The Making of Modern Intellectual Property Law: The British Experience, 1760–1911* (Cambridge: Cambridge University Press, 1999), chap. 1; Ronan Deazley, *On the Origin of the Right to Copy: Charting the Movement of Copyright Law in Eighteenth-Century Britain (1695–1775)* (Oxford: Hart Publishing, 2004); Ronan Deazley, *Rethinking Copyright: History, Theory, Language* (Cheltenham: Edward Elgar, 2006); Mark Rose, *Authors and Origins: The Invention of Copyright* (Cambridge: Harvard University Press, 1993); Lyman Ray Patterson, *Copyright in Historical Perspective* (Nashville: Vanderbilt University Press, 1968); Justin Hughes, "Copyright and Incomplete Historiographies: Of Piracy, Propertization, and Thomas Jefferson," *Southern California Law Review* 79, no. 5 (2006): 993–1084; Martin A. Kayman, "Lawful Writing: Common Law, Statute and the Properties of Literature," *New Literary History* 27, no. 4 (1996): 761–783.
3. Matt Hills, *Fan Cultures* (London: Routledge, 2002), xi–xii.
4. For discussions of Star Trek fanzines in the history of fan fiction, see Francesca Coppa, "A Brief History of Media Fandom," in *Fan Fiction and Fan Communities in the Age of the Internet: New Essays*, ed. Karen Hellekson and Kristina Busse (Jefferson, NC: McFarland, 2006), 41–59; Patricia Frazer Lamb and Dianna L. Veith, "Romantic Myth, Transcendence, and *Star Trek* Zines," in *Erotic Universe: Sexuality and Fantastic Literature*, ed. Donald Palumbo (Westport, CT: Greenwood, 1986), 235–255; Henry Jenkins III, "*Star Trek* Rerun, Reread, Rewritten: Fan Writing as Textual Poaching," *Critical Studies in Mass Communication* 5, no. 2 (1988): 85–107, repr. with revisions in *Close Encounters: Film, Feminism and Science Fiction*, ed. Constance Penley, Elisabeth Lyon, Lynn Spigel, and Janet Bergstrom (Minneapolis: University of Minnesota Press, 1991), 171–204; Rosemary J. Coombe, *The Cultural Life of Intellectual Properties: Authorship, Appropriation, and the Law* (Durham: Duke University Press, 1998), 117–118.
5. On the marginalia phenomenon, see H. J. Jackson, *Marginalia: Readers Writing in Books* (New Haven: Yale University Press, 2001).
6. Henry Jenkins discusses Harry Potter fan fiction and the copyright infringement claims in "Why Heather Can Write: Media Literacy and the *Harry*

Potter Wars," in *Convergence Culture: Where Old and New Media Collide* (New York: New York University Press, 2006), 169–205. An example of a cease-and-desist letter sent in response to Harry Potter "adult fan fiction" is available at the Chilling Effects website, <http://www.chillingeffects.org/fanfic/notice.cgi?NoticeID=522>.

7. Henry Jenkins, *Textual Poachers: Television Fans & Participating Culture* (New York: Routledge, 1992), 162.
8. Jenkins, *Textual Poachers*, 162–177. Sheenagh Pugh discusses sequels, prequels, crossovers, missing scenes, Mary Sue, and slash fanfic in *The Democratic Genre: Fan fiction in a literary context* (Bridgend, Wales: Seren, 2005).
9. Thomas Keymer and Peter Sabor, "*Pamela*" *in the Marketplace: Literary Controversy and Print Culture in Eighteenth-Century Britain and Ireland* (Cambridge: Cambridge University Press, 2005), 15.
10. John Fiske, "The Cultural Economy of Fandom," in *The Adoring Audience: Fan Culture and Popular Media*, ed. Lisa A. Lewis (London: Routledge, 1992), 34.
11. Richard Cumberland, *Henry*, in *Eighteenth-Century British Novelists on the Novel*, ed. George L. Barnett (New York: Appleton-Century-Crofts, 1968), 168, book viii, chap. 1.
12. Tom Keymer, *Richardson's "Clarissa" and the Eighteenth-Century Reader* (Cambridge: Cambridge University Press, 1992), 218.
13. *An Act for the Encouragement of Learning by vesting the Copies of Printed Books in the Authors or Purchasers of such Copies, during the Times therein mentioned* [*Statute of Anne*], 1709 [1710], 8 Anne, c. 19. The statute was enacted in 1709 (new calendar 1710) and entered into force the following year. For historical studies and different perspectives on copyright law and the rights of authors and publishers over the eighteenth century, see generally Rose, *Authors and Owners*; Sherman and Bently, *The Making of Modern Intellectual Property Law*; Deazley, *On the Origin of the Right to Copy*; Joseph Loewenstein, *The Author's Due: Printing and the Prehistory of Copyright* (Chicago: University of Chicago Press, 2002); Rosemary J. Coombe, "Challenging Paternity: Histories of Copyright," *Yale Journal of Law and the Humanities* 6, no. 2 (1994): 397–422; Ross, "Copyright and the Invention of Tradition"; Patterson, *Copyright in Historical Perspective*; Martha Woodmansee, "The Genius and the Copyright: Economic and Legal Conditions of the Emergence of the Author," *Eighteenth-Century Studies* 17, no. 4 (1984): 425–448; Harry Ransom, *The First Copyright Statute: An Essay on An Act for the Encouragement of Learning, 1710* (Austin: University of Texas, 1956).
14. "These Miscreants are a Set of Wretches we Authors call Pirates," Joseph Addison states the year preceding the Statute of Anne, following an unauthorized printing of *The Tatler*, "who print any Book, Poem, or Sermon, as soon as it appears in the World, in a smaller Volume, and sell it (as all other Thieves do stolen Goods) at a cheaper Rate," *Tatler* 101 (1 December 1709), quoted in Adrian Johns, *The Nature of the Book: Print and Knowledge in the Making* (Chicago: University of Chicago Press, 1998), 458. Johns describes the contemporary usage for "pirate" in the early modern period as having a "technical meaning" of "someone who indulged in the unauthorized reprinting of a title recognized to belong to someone else by the formal conventions of the printing and bookselling community." But it also came to encompass "a wide range of perceived transgressions of civility emanating from print's practitioners. As such, almost any book could, in principle, find itself accounted a piracy, whatever its actual circumstances of production and distribution" (*The Nature of the Book*, 32).

15. Oren Bracha, "The Ideology of Authorship Revisited," University of Texas Law, Public Law Research Paper No. 82 (2006): 27, available at Social Science Research Network: <http://ssrn.com/abstract=869446>.
16. On *Pamela*'s sales and marketing, see Keymer and Sabor, "*Pamela*" *in the Marketplace*, chap.1, "The Selling Part."
17. Patterson, *Copyright in Historical Perspective*, 148.
18. See John Feather, "From Rights in Copies to Copyright: The Recognition of Authors' Rights in English Law and Practice in the Sixteenth and Seventeenth Centuries," in *The Construction of Authorship: Textual Appropriation in Law and Literature*, ed. Martha Woodmansee and Peter Jaszi (Durham: Duke University Press, 1994), 191, 208–209.
19. Deazley, *On the Origin of the Right to Copy*, 46.
20. Peter Jaszi, "Toward a Theory of Copyright: The Metamorphoses of 'Authorship,'" *Duke Law Journal* 1991, no. 2 (1991): 455–502, esp. 474.
21. Deazley, *On the Origin of the Right to Copy*, 164.
22. Woodmansee, "The Genius and the Copyright"; Martha Woodmansee, *The Author, Art, and the Market: Rereading the History of Aesthetics* (New York: Columbia University Press, 1994); Jaszi, "Toward a Theory of Copyright"; Peter Jaszi, "On the Author Effect: Contemporary Copyright and Collective Creativity," in *The Construction of Authorship*, 29–56; Bracha, "The Ideology of Authorship Revisited."
23. Jaszi, "Toward a Theory of Copyright," 471.
24. Authors continued to suffer financial losses from piracy, however, even after the passage of the 1710 copyright act because of the statute's limited jurisdictional reach.
25. Defoe, December 3, 1709, and February 2, 1710, *Review*, quoted in Rose, *Authors and Owners*, 37 and 39.
26. Defoe, *Essay on the Regulation of the Press* (1704). On Defoe, authorial liability, and the copyright act, see Jody Greene, *The Trouble with Ownership: Literary Property and Authorial Liability in England, 1660–1730* (Philadelphia: University of Pennsylvania Press, 2005), chap. 3; Loewenstein, *The Author's Due*, 214–217; and Rose, *Authors and Owners*, 34–40.
27. Defoe, November 8, 1705, *Review*, quoted in Greene, *The Trouble with Ownership*, 138.
28. Defoe, December 6, 1709, *Review*, quoted in Rose, *Authors and Owners*, 37.
29. For Richardson's own summary of his printing career, see Richardson to Johannes Stinstra, June 2, 1753, *The Richardson-Stinstra Correspondence and Stinstra's Prefaces to "Clarissa,"* ed. William C. Slattery (Carbondale: Southern Illinois University Press, 1969), 25–26: "I continued Five or Six Years after the Expiration of my Apprenticeship (Part of the Time, as an Overseer of a Printing-House) working as a Compositor, and correcting the Press: As I hinted, in a better Expectation. But *that* failing, I began for my self, married, and pursued Business with an Assiduity that, perhaps, has few Examples; and with the more Alacrity, as I improved a Branch of it, that interfered not with any other Person; and made me more independent of Booksellers (tho' I did much Business for them,) than any other Printer. Some of them, even thought fit to seek me, rather than I them, because of the Readiness I shewed, to oblige them, with writing indexes, Prefaces, and sometimes for their minor Authors, *honest* Dedication[s]; abstracting, abridging, compiling, and giving my Opinion of Pieces offered them." On Richardson's printing career, see William M. Sale, Jr., *Samuel Richardson: Master Printer* (Ithaca: Cornell University Press, 1950); T. C. Duncan Eaves and Ben D. Kimpel, *Samuel Richardson: A Biography* (Oxford: Clarendon Press, 1971), esp. chaps. 1–4. Richardson's two wives were both daughters of

printers. See Eaves and Kimpel, *Samuel Richardson*, 11, 17–18; *The Selected Letters of Samuel Richardson*, ed. John Carroll (Oxford: Clarendon Press, 1964), 109 nn. 97, 98.

30. Richardson to Stinstra, September 11, 1753, *Richardson-Stinstra Correspondence*, 56; *Case of Samuel Richardson* (London, September 1753), 2. In 1754, Richardson followed *The Case* with a second offensive against the Irish printers, *An Address to the Public, on The Treatment which the Editor of the History of Sir Charles Grandison has met with from certain booksellers and Printers in Dublin, including observations on Mr. Faulkner's Defence of Himself, Published in his Irish News-paper of Nov. 3 1753* (London, 1754). Richardson also discusses the Irish piracy in his correspondence in Richardson to Sophia Westcomb, July 20, 1753, and August 15, 1753, Richardson to Lady Bradshaigh, October 5, 1753, November 12, 1753, and February 8, 1754, *Selected Letters*, 240, 242–244, 247–248, 279. On Richardson and the Irish piracy of *Grandison*, see Kathryn Temple, *Scandal Nation: Law and Authorship in Britain, 1750–1832* (Ithaca: Cornell University Press, 2003), chap. 1, "Printing Like a Postcolonialist: The Irish Piracy of *Sir Charles Grandison*."
31. Richardson to Anne Dewes, December 15, 1756, *Selected Letters*, 331.
32. Ronan Deazley recently remarked that there is no single axis on which the movement from the Statute of Anne to *Donaldson v. Becket* can be traced and that the "orthodox tale buckles under the weight of numerous identifiable but disparate threads of influence." Deazley, *On the Origin of the Right to Copy*, 222. My intention here is not to propose a single teleology for copyright, but rather to foreground eighteenth-century authors' and fans' responses to fan fiction and fictional characters. By doing so, I hope to highlight another aspect of the literary history, suggest some complications and turns in the narrative of the legal history, and, without adopting a presentist perspective, contribute to the discussion of legal and cultural issues that internet fan fiction raises.
33. In the *Berne Convention for the Protection of Literary and Artistic Works* (1886, as amended), available at the World Intellectual Property Organization, <http://www.wipo.int/treaties/en/ip/berne/>, moral rights are defined in Article *6bis*: "Independently of the author's economic rights, and even after the transfer of the said rights, the author shall have the right to claim authorship of the work and to object to any distortion, mutilation or other modification of, or other derogatory action in relation to, the said work, which would be prejudicial to his honor or reputation."
34. *Théberge v. Galerie d'Art du Petit Champlain Inc.*, (2002) 2 *Supreme Court Reports* 336, 337. A. Strowel, *Droit d'auteur et copyright: Divergences et convergences: Étude de droit comparé* (Bruxelles: E. Bruylant, 1993), 19–20.
35. *Éditions Chouette (1987) Inc. v. Despeuteaux* (2003), 1 *Supreme Court Reports* 178, 215; and see *Théberge*, 347–348.
36. *Théberge*, 348.
37. In *The Correspondence of Samuel Richardson*, ed. Anna Laetitia Barbauld, 6 vols. (London: R. Phillips, 1804; New York: AMS Press, 1966), 1:lxxvii.
38. Richardson to James Leake, August 1741, in Thomas Keymer, introduction to volumes 4 & 5 of *The Pamela Controversy: Criticisms and Adaptations of Samuel Richardson's* Pamela *1740–1750*, 6 vols. (London: Pickering & Chatto, 2001), 4:xii; Keymer and Sabor, "*Pamela*" *in the Marketplace*, 57.
39. Jonathan Swift, *A Tale of a Tub*, ed. Robert A. Greenberg and William Bowman Piper, *The Writings of Jonathan Swift* (New York: Norton, 1973), 357.
40. Miguel de Cervantes, *The Ingenious Gentleman Don Quixote of La Mancha*, ed. Joseph R. Jones and Kenneth Douglas, trans. John Ormsby, rev. ed. (New York: Norton, 1981), 418.

41. John Bunyan, *The Pilgrim's Progress*, ed. N. H. Keeble (Oxford: Oxford University Press, 1984), 136.
42. Richardson to James Leake, August 1741, in *The Pamela Controversy*, 4:xi–xii; Keymer and Sabor, "*Pamela*" *in the Marketplace*, 56–57. A more temperate revised letter is reprinted in *Selected Letters*, 42–45; Alan Dugald McKillop, *Samuel Richardson: Printer and Novelist* (Chapel Hill: University of North Carolina Press, 1936), 51–54. On the spurious sequel by John Kelly, *Pamela's Conduct in High Life,* and Richardson's reaction, see Eaves and Kimpel, *Samuel Richardson*, 135–139. For extensive biographical information on John Kelly, see Keymer and Sabor, "*Pamela*" *in the Marketplace*, 66–82.
43. Richardson to Lady Bradshaigh ["Mrs. Belfour"], [1749], *Correspondence*, ed. Barbauld, 4:286.
44. Richardson to James Leake, August 1741, Forster MSS, xvi, I, f. 56, quoted in Keymer and Sabor, "*Pamela*" *in the Marketplace*, 2. These include Henry Fielding's *Shamela* and *Joseph Andrews*, Eliza Haywood's *Anti-Pamela*, as well as *The True Anti-Pamela, Pamela's Conduct in High Life, Pamela in High Life, The Life of Pamela, Pamela Censured, Pamela Versified, The Virgin in Eden, Memoirs of the Life of Lady H—, The Celebrated Pamela*; the stage plays *Pamela. A Comedy* and *Pamela: or, Virtue Triumphant*; the opera *Pamela: or, Virtue Rewarded, An Opera*; the long verse *Pamela: or, The Fair Impostor, A Poem, in Five Cantos*; as well as *Pamela* poetry, engravings, fans, racehorses, and waxworks. For chronologies of *Pamela*'s sequels and adaptations, see William B. Warner, *Licensing Entertainment: The Elevation of Novel Reading in Britain, 1684–1750* (Berkeley: University of California Press, 1998), 295–296, Appendix 1; Keymer and Sabor, "Chronology, 1740–1750," in *The Pamela Controversy*, 1:xxi–xxix; Keymer and Sabor, "*Pamela*" *in the Marketplace*, 216–224, Appendix. For facsimile texts of most sequels, see Keymer and Sabor, *The Pamela Controversy*, 6 vols. For further discussion of the *Pamela* vogue in addition to these sources, see Eaves and Kimpel, *Samuel Richardson*, chap. 7; McKillop, *Printer and Novelist*, chap. 1; Bernard Kreissman, *Pamela-Shamela: A Study of the criticisms, burlesques, parodies, and adaptations of Richardson's "Pamela"* (Lincoln: University of Nebraska Press, 1960); David A. Brewer, *The Afterlife of Character, 1726–1825* (Philadelphia: University of Pennsylvania Press, 2005), chap. 4; James Grantham Turner, "Novel Panic: Picture and Performance in the Reception of Richardson's *Pamela*," *Representations*, no. 48 (1994): 70–96.
45. Richardson to Aaron Hill, November 7, 1748, *Selected Letters*, 99.
46. Richardson to Elizabeth Carter, December 17, 1748, Ibid., 117.
47. Belfour to Richardson, October 10, 1748, *Correspondence*, ed. Barbauld, 4:179.
48. *The Annotations in Lady Bradshaigh's Copy of Clarissa*, ed. J. Barchas and G. Fulton, ELS Monograph Series no. 76 (Victoria, BC, Canada: University of Victoria, 1998), 140. Lady Bradshaigh suggested two "improved" comic endings. See also Janice Broder, "Lady Bradshaigh Reads and Writes *Clarissa*: The Marginal Notes in Her First Edition," in *Clarissa and Her Readers: New Essays for The* Clarissa *Project*, ed. Carol Houlihan Flynn and Edward Copeland (New York: AMS Press, 1999), 97–118.
49. Lady Bradshaigh [Belfour] to Richardson, November 20, 1748, *Correspondence*, ed. Barbauld, 4:202–206.
50. Lady Elizabeth Echlin, *An Alternative Ending to Richardson's "Clarissa,"* ed. Dimiter Daphinoff, Swiss Studies in English no. 107 (Bern: Francke Verlag, 1982). For a discussion of Lady Echlin's vision of justice in her ending, see Tom Keymer, *Richardson's "Clarissa" and the Eighteenth-Century Reader* (Cambridge: Cambridge University Press, 1992), 214–218.

51. Lady Elizabeth Echlin to Richardson, August 12, 1754, *Correspondence*, ed. Barbauld, 5:19–20.
52. Richardson to Lady Echlin, September 12, 1754, *Correspondence*, ed. Barbauld, 5:24; Lady Elizabeth Echlin to Richardson, August 12, 1754, ibid., 20.
53. See Keymer, *Richardson's "Clarissa,"* 214.
54. Richardson, *Postscript* to *Clarissa*, 348–340, repr. in Samuel Richardson, *"Clarissa": Preface, Hints of Prefaces, and Postscript*, introduction by R. F. Brissenden (Los Angeles: William Andrews Clark Memorial Library, University of California, 1964), 15.
55. Richardson's biographers discussed his friends' attempts to influence the ending for his novel during the manuscript phase. Eaves and Kimpel, *Samuel Richardson*, chap. 10.
56. Anonymous, *Critical Remarks on Sir Charles Grandison, Clarissa and Pamela, enquiring Whether they have a Tendency to corrupt or improve the Public Taste and Morals. In a Letter to the Author* (London, 1754), 58, facsimile repr. in *Three Criticisms of Richardson's Fiction, 1749–1754*, Richardsoniana XIII (New York: Garland, 1974).
57. Terry Eagleton, *The Rape of Clarissa: Writing, Sexuality and Class Struggle in Samuel Richardson* (Oxford: Basil Blackwell, 1982), 34–35.
58. Ian Watt, *The Rise of the Novel: Studies in Defoe, Richardson and Fielding* (Berkeley: University of California Press, 1957), 173; Leslie A. Fiedler, *Love and Death in the American Novel*, with a new afterword by the author (New York: Anchor Books, 1992), 63.
59. John Kelly's *Pamela's Conduct in High Life* was published in two volumes in May and September 1741. Richardson to James Leake, August 1741, in Keymer and Sabor, *The Pamela Controversy*, 4:xi; Keymer and Sabor, *"Pamela" in the Marketplace*, 56. Richardson is here recounting to Leake his earlier reaction when he discovered the plans for Kelly's sequel.
60. Richardson to Lady Bradshaigh, February 25, 1754, *Selected Letters*, 296.
61. Richardson to Lady Bradshaigh, December 8, 1753, ibid., 257.
62. Richardson to Lady Echlin, October 10, 1754, ibid., 315–316.
63. Richardson to Lady Bradshaigh, November 12, 1753, ibid., 248.
64. Richardson to Lady Echlin, October 10, 1754, ibid., 316.
65. Richardson to James Leake, August 1741, in Keymer and Sabor, *The Pamela Controversy*, 4:xi; Keymer and Sabor, *"Pamela" in the Marketplace*, 56.
66. Quoted in Eaves and Kimpel, *Samuel Richardson*, 138 from issues of *Common Sense* published in 1741.
67. Richardson, "Advertisement," in *Pamela in Her Exalted Condition*, December 7, 1741, repr. in Keymer and Sabor, *Pamela Controversy*, 1:130. Richardson's advertisement is discussed in Keymer and Sabor, *Marketplace*, 64; Keymer, introduction to volumes 4 and 5, *Pamela Controversy*, 4:xxii; and Eaves and Kimpel, *Samuel Richardson*, 137–138.
68. *Pamela in High Life: or, Virtue Rewarded* (London, 1741; facsimile repr. New York: Garland, 1975).
69. Keymer and Sabor, *"Pamela" in the Marketplace*, 204.
70. David Brewer discusses Sir Walter Scott's "parental interest" in his afterword to *The Afterlife of Character*; however, he connects parental interests with authorial property claims, pointing to Scott's insistence on his "absolute proprietorship" over his characters and valorization of the "monarchic author." Chronologically, Brewer associates this "newfound assent to proprietary authorship" with the Romantic period, arguing it displaced the "textual commons" of the 1720–1760 period.
71. Keymer and Sabor, *"Pamela" in the Marketplace*, 52.

72. Richardson, "Advertisement" in *Pamela in Her Exalted Condition*, December 7, 1741, repr. in Keymer and Sabor, *Pamela Controversy*, 1:130.
73. Swift's *A Tale of a Tub* provides a pointed example of such preemptive forestalling within the text: "I do here give this publick Notice, that my Resolutions are, to circumscribe within this Discourse the whole Stock of Matter I have been so many Years providing. Since my *Vein* is once opened, I am content to exhaust it all at a Running for the peculiar Advantage of my dear Country, and for the universal Benefit of Mankind" (*Writings*, 357).
74. *"Pamela" in the Marketplace*, 82.
75. Cervantes ["Author of the First Part"], *Second Part of the Ingenious Gentleman Don Quixote of La Mancha*, 1615, ed. Joseph R. Jones and Kenneth Douglas, trans. John Ormsby, rev. ed. (New York: Norton, 1981), 445.
76. Ibid.
77. Ibid., 417.
78. Richardson to Aaron Hill, January 26, 1746[7], *Selected Letters*, 83.
79. Miss Highmore to Miss Mulso [n.d.], *Correspondence*, ed. Barbauld, 2:317.
80. Lady Bradshaigh to Richardson, February 22, 1754, *Selected Letters*, 295 n. 27.
81. Richardson to Lady Bradshaigh, February 25, 1754, ibid., 296.
82. *A Copy of a Letter . . .* in *A Collection of the Moral and Instructive Sentiments, Maxims, Cautions, and Reflections, Contained in the Histories of "Pamela," "Clarissa," and "Sir Charles Grandison"* (London, 1755), 403–406, facsimile repr. in *Samuel Richardson's Published Commentary on Clarissa, 1747–1767*, intro. by John A. Dussinger and afterword by Ann Jessie Van Sant, 3 vols. (London: Pickering & Chatto, 1998), 3:403–407.
83. Introduction to the second edition of *Pamela* (London, 1741), xxxvi–xxxvii, facsimile repr. in Keymer and Sabor, *Pamela Controversy*, 1:38–39. Janet Aikins, "Richardson's 'Speaking Pictures,'" in *Samuel Richardson: Tercentenary Essays*, ed. Margaret Anne Doody and Peter Sabor (Cambridge University Press, 1989), 146–166, notes the illustrations "do not diminish but dramatically expand the startling discrepancy between the reader's mental pictures and those on the page" (152). On the engravings in Richardson's deluxe octavo edition of *Pamela*, see Keymer and Sabor, *Pamela Controversy*, 2: xxxiv–xli, introduction to volume 2.
84. E. M. Forster, *Aspects of the Novel* (San Diego: Harcourt Brace Jovanovich, 1985), 63. Predictable and unsurprising characters are vulnerable to being labeled as stereotypes and excluded from copyright protection on the grounds that they are not original expression but only ideas to which no single author can lay claim. On stock characters, see Northrop Frye, Sheridan Baker, and George Perkins, "Characters," in *The Harper Handbook to Literature* (New York: Harper, 1985), 97.
85. Henry James, "The Art of Fiction," in *The Critical Muse: Selected Literary Criticism* (London: Penguin, 1987), 196–197.
86. David Brewer in *The Afterlife of Character* adopts a different perspective, in which the "fact of multiple and competing reproductions could make the texts in question (and the characters which they contained) seem less tied to any particular manifestation they might take" (97). For him, "the more a text was disseminated (both in terms of number and variety of formats), the more potentially detachable its characters could seem" (95). I argue here that it is not the multiple circulations of the text that give rise to the detachability of the characters; rather, it is the first author's full realization of the character on its initial outing that makes it possible for the character to be moved into

new adventures and for readers to recognize at least essential aspects of the first narrative's fictional character in the new narrative's character.

87. Young, *Conjectures on Original Composition* (London, 1759), 12–13. Martha Woodmansee concludes that Young's essay "attracted relatively little attention in England" but had a "profound impact" in Germany. "The Genius and the Copyright," 430.
88. Richardson to Stinstra, June 2, 1753, *Richardson-Stinstra Correspondence*, 29, 31.
89. Sarah Fielding to Richardson, January 8, 1748[9], *Correspondence*, ed. Barbauld, 2:61.
90. Aaron Hill to Richardson, December 29, 1740, *Correspondence*, ed. Barbauld, 1:55–56.
91. Hester Mulso to Miss Highmore, July 20, 1751, *Correspondence*, ed. Barbauld, 2:269.
92. Talbot to Carter, April 4, 1754, in *A Series of Letters between Mrs. Elizabeth Carter and Miss Catherine Talbot, from the year 1741 to 1770; to which are added, letters from Mrs. Elizabeth Carter to Mrs. Vesey between the years 1763 and 1787*, 2 vols. (London: F.C. and J. Rivington, 1808), 1:358.
93. "To my worthy Friend, the Editor of Pamela," in Richardson, *Pamela: or Virtue Rewarded*, 2nd ed. (London: XXX, 1741), x–xiv, esp. xiii, facsimile repr. in Keymer and Sabor, *Pamela Controversy*, 1:15.
94. E. M. Forster says of "flat characters," "sometimes called types, and sometimes caricatures," that they are "constructed round a single idea or quality" in their "purest form," and are "easily recognized . . . by the reader's emotional eye" and "easily remembered" because they are simple and do not change (*Aspects of the Novel*, 67–73). On round characters and the history of the novel, see Watt, *Rise of the Novel*, and Deidre Shauna Lynch, *The Economy of Character: Novels, Market Culture, and the Business of Inner Meaning* (Chicago: University of Chicago Press, 1998).
95. Tobias George Smollett, *Adventures of Ferdinand, Count Fathom*, repr. in George L. Barnett, ed., *Eighteenth-Century British Novelists on the Novel* (New York: Appleton-Century-Crofts, 1968), 65.
96. Samuel Johnson, *Rambler*, no. 4, March 31, 1750, repr. in Donald Greene, ed., *Samuel Johnson* (New York: Oxford University Press, 1984), 177.
97. See Rose, *Authors and Origins* and "Copyright and Its Metaphors," *UCLA Law Review* 50, no. 1 (2002): 1–15.
98. Defoe, February 2, 1710, *Review*, quoted in Rose, "Copyright and Its Metaphors," 5 n. 23.
99. 98 *English Reports* at 234.
100. David Brewer, *The Afterlife of Character*; Simon Stern, "*Tom Jones* and the Economies of Copyright," *Eighteenth-Century Fiction* 9, no. 4 (1997): 429–444.
101. See "The Public Domain," ed. James Boyle, Special Issue, *Law and Contemporary Problems* 66, nos. 1–2 (2003), esp. contributions by James Boyle, "The Second Enclosure Movement and the Construction of the Public Domain" (33–74), Mark Rose, "Nine-Tenths of the Law: The English Copyright Debates and the Rhetoric of the Public Domain" (75–87), Pamela Samuelson, "Mapping the Digital Public Domain: Threats and Opportunities" (147–171), David Lange, "Reimagining the Public Domain" (463–483). See also Lawrence Lessig, *Free Culture: How Big Media Uses Technology and the Law to Lock Down Culture and Control Creativity* (New York: Penguin, 2004); Lawrence Lessig, *The Future of Ideas: The Fate of the Commons in a Connected World* (New York: Random House, 2001); Yochai Benkler, "Free as the Air to Common Use: First Amendment Constraints on

Enclosure of the Public Domain," *New York University Law Review* 74, no. 2 (1999): 354–446; David Lange, "Recognizing the Public Domain," *Law and Contemporary Problems* 44, no. 4 (1981): 147–178; Jessica Litman, "The Public Domain," *Emory Law Journal* 39, no. 4 (1990): 965–1023.

102. Richardson to Lady Bradshaigh, January 4, 1754, *Selected Letters*, 266; Sarah Fielding, *Remarks on Clarissa* (London, 1749), 8 (in the guise of the "Lady of the House"); Catherine Talbot to Elizabeth Carter, December 28, 1747, in *A Series of Letters*, 1:161.

103. See, for example, the UK's *Copyright, Designs and Patent Act* 1988, c. 48, ss. 16, 17, 21. In Canada, as another example of economic rights under modern copyright statutes, the exclusive rights consist of the following separate rights: "Section 3 (1) For the purposes of this Act, 'copyright,' in relation to a work, means the sole right to produce or reproduce the work or any substantial part thereof in any material form whatever, to perform the work or any substantial part thereof in public or, if the work is unpublished, to publish the work or any substantial part thereof, and includes the sole right (a) to produce, reproduce, perform or publish any translation of the work, (b) in the case of a dramatic work, to convert it into a novel or other non-dramatic work, (c) in the case of a novel or other non-dramatic work, or of an artistic work, to convert it into a dramatic work, by way of performance in public or otherwise, (d) in the case of a literary, dramatic or musical work, to make any sound recording, cinematograph film or other contrivance by means of which the work may be mechanically reproduced or performed, (e) in the case of any literary, dramatic, musical or artistic work, to reproduce, adapt and publicly present the work as a cinematographic work, (f) in the case of any literary, dramatic, musical or artistic work, to communicate the work to the public by telecommunication, (g) to present at a public exhibition, for a purpose other than sale or hire, an artistic work created after June 7, 1988, other than a map, chart or plan, (h) in the case of a computer program that can be reproduced in the ordinary course of its use, other than by a reproduction during its execution in conjunction with a machine, device or computer, to rent out the computer program, and (i) in the case of a musical work, to rent out a sound recording in which the work is embodied, and to authorize any such acts."

104. Discussions of fictional character copyright can be found in Leslie Kurtz, "The Independent Legal Lives of Fictional Characters," *Wisconsin Law Review* 1986, no. 3 (1986): 429–525; Michael Marks, "The Legal Rights of Fictional Characters," *Copyright Law Symposium (ASCAP)* 25 (1980): 35–92; Dorothy Howell, *Intellectual Properties and the Protection of Fictional Characters: Copyright, Trademark, or Unfair Competition?* (New York: Quorum Books, 1990); Kenneth E. Spahn, "The Legal Protection of Fictional Characters," *University of Miami Entertainment and Sports Law Review* 9 (1992): 331–348. On fan fiction and copyright, see Rebecca Tushnet, "Legal Fictions: Copyright, Fan Fiction, and a New Common Law," *Loyola of Los Angeles Entertainment Law Journal* 17, no. 3 (1997): 651–686; Christina Z. Ranon, "Honor Among Thieves: Copyright Infringement in Internet Fandom," *Vanderbilt Journal of Entertainment and Technology Law* 8, no. 2 (2006): 421–452.

105. Supplemental Report of the Registrar of Copyrights on the General Revision of U.S. Copyright Law: 1965 Revision Bill, 89 Congress, 1st Sess. (1965), 6; see Melville B. Nimmer and David Nimmer, *Nimmer on Copyright*, 10 vols. [looseleaf] (New York: Matthew Bender, 1997–), 1, sec. 2.12 n. 2; Kurtz, "Independent Legal Lives of Fictional Characters," n. 67.

106. *Copyright and Designs Law: Report of the Committee to Consider the Law on Copyright and Designs* [*Whitford Report*] (London: H.M.S.O., 1977),

Command Paper 6732 (1977), para. 909, quoted by Steven L. Nemetz, "Copyright Protection of Fictional Characters," *Intellectual Property Journal* 14, no. 1 (1999): 69–70.

107. Cumberland, *Henry*, book 1, chap. 1, in Barnett, *Eighteenth-Century British Novelists on the Novel*, 156.
108. *Oxford English Dictionary*, 2nd ed., s.v. "plagiary." Samuel Johnson's 1759 *Dictionary of the English Language* defines *plagiary* as a "thief in literature; one who steals the thoughts or writings of another."
109. Keymer and Sabor refer to the *Pamela* controversy as a "market phenomenon: as the product, agent, and uniquely visible trace of the new consumer culture that was taking hold, in which the genre was becoming an increasingly important commercial and literary mode and object of fashionable attention" ("*Pamela*" *in the Marketplace*, 15). Other discussions of eighteenth-century marketing of fictional characters include Lynch, *The Economy of Character*; Warner, *Licensing Entertainment*.
110. Keymer and Sabor, General Introduction to *The Pamela Controversy*, 1:xiii.

3 Copyright, Originality, and the Public Domain in Eighteenth-Century England

Simon Stern

Recent efforts to explain the role of originality in the history of copyright law have argued that legal accounts of literary property in eighteenth-century England were based, at least tacitly, on aesthetic theories of creative genius. Although some commentators on aesthetics treated literary creativity and ownership as intertwined concepts, that linkage finds no corollary in contemporaneous legal doctrine. The 1710 Act of Anne prohibited piracy, but did not regulate imitations, condensations, adaptations, anthologies, indexes, and similar partial copies.[1] The profusion of imitative texts testifies to a flourishing public domain that depended on the *absence* of a copyright theory grounded in literary creativity. Neither the law nor its exponents treated aesthetic originality as an ideal condition to which all writings should aspire, in theory, to justify their status as property, nor did any of the legal commentators suggest that works tinged with creativity merited more protection than their most pedestrian counterparts. Copyright applied equally to all publications and provided a limited exception to the general rule that the various ingredients of any work belonged in the public domain. When the House of Lords ruled in 1774 that the Act of Anne limited the term of copyright to twenty-eight years, the public domain gained a new and important dimension, but that development expanded what was already a vital factor in the literary marketplace, rather than bringing it into being for the first time.[2]

As advocates of stronger copyright support have repeatedly invoked the figure of the solitary, self-made authorial genius over the last two centuries to justify longer term limits and an ever-expanding scope for copyright protection, the public domain has diminished accordingly. The idea–expression dichotomy, central to modern copyright jurisprudence, reflects the fencing off of various textual elements that were freely available in the eighteenth century. When piracy is the only prohibited form of copying, it is pointless to ask whether a rewriting of a novel is a recapitulation of its ideas or an appropriation of its expression, because neither one constitutes infringement. Since around the middle of the nineteenth century, the fulcrum has shifted so that features like plot, character, and even style have become potentially eligible for copyright protection—and the drift of aesthetic theories into the legal realm helps to explain that development.[3] But there is little reason to conclude that in the eighteenth century originality (understood as novelty or creativity) played even a tacit role in the definition of literary property.

To question the significance of aesthetic originality in eighteenth-century copyright law is not to deny its importance in contemporaneous literary criticism. Whereas Renaissance English literary culture displayed comparatively little interest in attribution, plagiarism, and textual accuracy,[4] these became matters of much greater concern to readers and writers during the century and a half beginning around the 1670s.[5] By the second half of the eighteenth century, this discussion had led to the publication of numerous efforts to define and illustrate literary genius and originality, including Edward Young's *Conjectures on Original Composition* (1759), probably the best-known contribution to the discussion.[6] Although Young could treat an author's originality as the basis of his property in his work, contemporaneous legal thinkers did not gravitate so readily toward this explanation.[7] Various novelists, poets, and critics may have shared Young's view, but among the commentators who argued about the legal basis and contours of copyright, the only ones to embrace any version of Young's argument were not advocates of literary property, but rather its opponents.

The wide variance between the literary and legal meanings of "originality" has not been sufficiently acknowledged in scholarship on the history of copyright. The Act of Anne says nothing about originality, which helps to explain why many of the statute's legal exponents had nothing to say about the topic. Although the literary concept was being elaborated in terms of exuberant creativity by writers like Young,[8] the few legal commentators who invoked the term were concerned with the statute's bar on mimetic duplication. When William Blackstone, for example, speaks of copyright protection for "original work[s]," he indicates that a written production should be counted as original so long as it is not a reprint of another text.[9] This usage comports with one of the word's earlier senses—"[c]reated, composed, or done by a person directly; produced firsthand; not imitated or copied from another"—which the *Oxford English Dictionary* (*OED*) dates to the mid-seventeenth century. By contrast, the *OED* dates the usage of "original" as "novel or fresh in character or style" to the 1750s.[10] An analysis that conflates these two senses of originality risks misunderstanding the meaning of copyright during its early development.

Such conflations fail to account for the contemporaneous case law, and they also misrepresent its significance for the literary culture of eighteenth-century England, whose legacy includes several highly imitative forms, such as parodic verse and the novel, that continue to flourish and that have figured crucially in defining the scope of copyright protection and fair use. A view of novelty and ingenuity as the justification for authorial property maps onto a high-threshold definition of originality, which looks suspiciously on imitation as theft not only from the perspective of moral rights, but also from an economic perspective, in which imitations threaten to displace the source. Under the low-threshold definition, originality means only that the text has not been reproduced.[11] According to the literary philosophy that aligns itself with this definition, production inevitably depends on revision, and adapting a plot or scene is simply a way to bring it to new readers or satisfy old readers in a new way.

In every era since the Restoration, examples of writers at any place on the spectrum are plentiful. At one end are jealously proprietary figures who insist that their genius is native and that their works reflect no influences. Ignoring the detail that genres, conventions, and stylistic techniques are all born of preexisting models, these writers claim to owe no literary debts, but often police others' writings with an eagle eye for instances of misappropriation. Samuel Richardson, complaining about the piracy of *Sir Charles Grandison* in 1753, wrote that "[n]ever was Work more the Property of any Man, than *this* is [mine] . . . [I have] borrow[ed] not from any Author: The Paper, the Printing, [were] entirely at [my] own Expence . . . [The work is] *New* in every Sense of the Word."[12] Richardson claimed to own the book's ideational aspects as absolutely as its physical aspects. His declaration refuses any awareness of the "gift[] that all artists receive, namely, a tradition and world they have not made."[13] Richardson's case is particularly striking because, although his novels were fresh and innovative in many ways, a careful review of the quotations in his fiction has shown that he relied on the eighteenth-century version of *Bartlett's* for most of his literary references.[14] Although that fact can hardly be thought to reduce Richardson's ownership of the novels he published, it points up his dual role as author and user and highlights his participation in a literary culture that produced such reference aids precisely because this dual role was commonplace.

At the other end of the spectrum are writers who treat adaptation and revision as essential for literary production, who recognize that their work is "embedded in a culture that nourishes and influences them, yet from which they derive their own voice."[15] In *Tom Jones*, for example, Henry Fielding could style himself as the "founder of a new province of writing," while later declaring that the writings of the ancients "may be considered as a rich common, where every [modern writer] hath a free right to fatten his muse."[16] That both assertions carry an ironic charge does not remove the implication that novelty and imitation may coexist, that the public domain—the "rich common"—may support a thriving literary culture, sustaining "new province[s]," which, in turn, provide more fodder for future writers. Alexander Pope, similarly, defended "the liberty of *Borrowing*" by observing that "it seems not so much the Perfection of Sense, to say things that have *never* been said before, as to express those *best* that have been said *oftenest*." He added that "by being grafted upon others, [a writer's work] may yield variety. A mutual commerce makes Poetry flourish."[17] Users' rights, although not styled as such, are clearly central to this "mutual commerce." The term "originality," then, may be decomposed into these two antithetical perspectives on the meaning of indebtedness in the literary universe. Although some writers hold themselves above the disreputable business of borrowing and lending, others view originality as a quality that is perfectly capable of thriving amid such traffic. Rather than one word, we have a pair of homonyms that represent different understandings of how writing takes place and how it circulates.

In what follows, I start by showing that arguments in favor of a public domain were implicit in the efforts by Locke and others at the end of the seventeenth century to eliminate the Licensing Act. Next, I look at the debate over copyright law in the eighteenth century, emphasizing the limited scope of legal protection and the correspondingly wide reach of the public domain. Finally, I discuss the kinds of imitations that were allowed to flourish under this legal regime, and I end with some brief remarks about how writers come to embrace the high-threshold view of originality and the belief in solitary and unaided genius that goes with it.

THE LICENSING ACT AND THE ACT OF ANNE

The Act of Anne is often described as England's first copyright statute. Although it would ultimately provoke an unprecedented public debate over authorial rights as property rights, the statute did not mark the origin of a national copyright policy in English law, nor can it be credited with introducing a view of literary production as property. The statute's primary concern—the right of exclusive publication—had figured as an internal guild policy of the Stationers' Company since the sixteenth century.[18] Crucial to the guild's operation was the convention of the publishers' "copy," the right to forbid others from printing any title already appropriated by a guild member. The first member to enter his copy in the Stationers' Register secured the sole right of publication and was understood to hold the right in perpetuity. As John Feather has observed, this policy introduced, "in all but name, the concept of copyright," and shortly after its introduction, "we have every indication that 'copies' were being treated as property."[19]

The convention moved from guild rule to legal requirement in 1637, when a Star Chamber decree on printing specified that all publications had to be "entred into the Register Booke of the Company of Stationers."[20] The decree prohibited the reprinting of any "Copy, book or books, or part of any book or bookes" already registered by another.[21] The copy system now had the force of law. The Star Chamber decree remained in effect no longer than the Star Chamber, which was abolished in 1641, but the decree's monopolistic powers were revived in various Parliamentary ordinances adopted during the Interregnum.[22]

These ordinances, in turn, gave way to the 1662 Licensing Act. That act differed from the earlier policies, however, in the scope of its application.

The Star Chamber decree, and the acts that followed it, had covered not only entire books, but also any constituent "part"—a term that would seem, at a minimum, to cover extracts. The 1662 statute, by contrast, applied only to "any Booke or Pamphlet,"[23] implicitly leaving others free to reprint excerpts. To eliminate the bar on partial appropriations is to tolerate or even encourage the forms of limited redaction undertaken by abridgements and anthologies. The 1662 statute thus relies on much the same view of literary property that would reappear nearly fifty years later in the Act of Anne, and that was generally accepted throughout the eighteenth century. Under the terms of both statutes, the book is the unit of property, and its components (excerpts, scenes, characters, and style) are free for the copying.

In focusing its attention on piracy, the Licensing Act reflected the norms of Restoration literary commerce. Despite the language of the earlier prohibitions, there is no evidence that any seventeenth-century century writers or publishers who excerpted or revised others' writings were ever sued or proceeded against by other guild members, although anthologies and literary imitations were commonplace.[24] Accusations of plagiarism became increasingly common during the Restoration, but they seem to have served primarily as a means of asserting one's literary status, particularly among members of literary factions, who used this charge to signal their affiliation by attacking outsiders.[25] The decision to provide more limited coverage in the Licensing Act than in the Star Chamber decree and its interregnum successors, then, seems to reflect not so much a change in legal and social norms as simply the abandonment of an excessively broad provision that no one had bothered to enforce (and that perhaps no one had even noticed) in the first place. The basic assumption that others' writings were available for adaptation and revision remained unchanged throughout the seventeenth century. The literary culture of the day took it for granted that writers could make what use they liked of others' ideas, and also of what today would be deemed protected expression.

The Licensing Act was renewed periodically during the later seventeenth century, but met with heated opposition when it came up for renewal in Parliament during the 1692–1693 session. Although critics of press regulation had long argued against licensing as a form of censorship, the debate in 1692–1693 also referred specifically to authors' rights. An anonymous pamphlet, probably submitted in late December, a few days after the Commons resolved to continue the act, declared that "[m]any learned Authors have been defrauded of their Rights . . . who, after many years Pains and Study . . . have been barred by surreptitious Entries made in the [Stationers'] Register."[26] This allegation of fraud was later confirmed by a member of the guild. On March 7, 1693, an affidavit was presented in the House of Lords from a stationer who testified that when he came to search the Register for his own entries in 1691, he "found several leaves rout out of the Register-book about the date or time of the entry of most of the said copies" and "saw several of his copies entered again to other persons."[27] The following day, eleven members of the Lords opposed the renewal of the Licensing Act, translating this violation of stationers' property rights into the language of authors' rights. The policy, it was affirmed, "subjects all Learning, and true Information to the arbitrary Will and Pleasure of a mercenary, and perhaps ignorant Licenser, destroys the Properties of Authors in their Copies; and sets up many Monopolies."[28] The opponents ultimately failed to block the act, but their criticisms may have been instrumental in limiting the renewal period to the unusually brief term of one year plus one session of Parliament.[29] When the act came up for renewal again in 1695, the opposition was much better organized, and they had the help of John Locke.

Locke had already shown some interest in the question of licensing during the 1692–1693 debate. He owned several of the antilicensing pamphlets, including the anonymous pamphlet that decried the stationers' frauds against "learned Authors."[30] While the proposal to renew the Licensing Act was pending, the issue figured prominently in his correspondence with his friends Edward Clarke and John Freke, two members of "the College," a club that Locke had founded several years earlier as a forum for political debate. Freke was a lawyer and Whig activist. Clarke, a Whig who represented Taunton in the Commons, would play a crucial role in the rejection of the Licensing Act in 1695. Through both men, Locke also maintained contact with the club's patron, John Lord Somers, the Lord Keeper under King William.

Locke's criticisms of the Licensing Act during the 1692–1693 debate refer obliquely to authors' rights and the public interest in having access to accurate and scholarly texts. On January 2, 1693, more than a week after the vote in Commons to renew the act, Locke wrote to Clarke:

> I wish you would have some care of Book buyers as well as all of Book sellers and the Company of Stationers who haveing got a Patent for all or most of the Ancient Latin Authors (by what right or pretence I know not) claime the text to be theirs and soe will not suffer fairer and more correct Editions than any thing they print here or with new Comments to be imported without compounding to them whereby these most usefull books are excessively dear to schollers and a monopoly is put into the hands of the company of ignorant and lazy stationers. . . . By this monopoly also of these ancient authors noe body here, that would publish any of them a new with comments or any other advantage can doe it without the leave of the learned judicious stationers, for if they will not print it themselves nor let any other be your labour about it never soe usefull . . . it is to noe purpose.[31]

Locke focuses here primarily on the rights of readers, forced to pay for "excessively dear" editions when "fairer and more correct" ones might be sold for less. What should be cheaply available to the public has been monopolized by the booksellers. Locke also hints at the injustice to scholarly editors, whose "useful" "labour" in annotating classical writers goes for naught. These objections were prompted in part by the guild's opposition to one of his own editorial projects—an edition of Aesop that Locke had planned in the early 1690s, but did not publish until 1703.[32] If these objections sound like the complaints of a curmudgeonly professor, lamenting the stationers' low editorial standards, Locke was to reframe his argument significantly within a few years.

Clarke and his associates were unable to block the renewal of the Licensing Act in 1693, but when it came up for consideration again, in early 1695, they prevailed. A committee in the Commons brought in a resolution to renew the act on January 9, 1695.[33] In a memorandum probably sent off later that month to Clarke and Freke, Locke provided a point-by-point critique that dealt with preprint censorship and the stationers' monopolistic practices, and that also attacked the exclusionary system of copy registration, "[w]hereby it comes to passe that sometimes when a book is brought to be entred in the register of the Company of Stationers, if they thinke it may turne to account, they entre it as theirs."[34] Advocating an end to the stationers' convention of perpetual copyright, Locke proposed a limited term, arguing that "noebody should have any peculiar right in any book which has been in print fifty years."[35] Fixing the duration of copyright would mean that all books would eventually become available for users to edit and would be affordable for the public.

When the renewal bill, which Locke had criticized, was brought to a vote on February 11, 1695, it was rejected.[36] A new committee was appointed "to prepare and bring in a Bill for better Regulating of Printing and Printing Presses,"[37] and this bill incorporated many of the objections Locke had sent to Freke and Clarke in January. After receiving a draft of the proposed bill, on March 14, Locke sent Freke and Clarke his own model, which included a clause "[t]o secure the Authors property in his copy." Leaving a blank space where the agreed-on period would be inserted, this clause specified that "noe book . . . shall within years after its first edition be reprinted . . . without Authority given in writeing by the Author."[38]

This suggestion found no place in the legislation presented in the Commons; in fact, the new bill included no provision at all for the protection of copies. If adopted, the bill would have eliminated the registration requirements that had served to protect the stationers' copies for more than a century. Not surprisingly, the stationers objected, and the Lords, seeking to pacify them, appended to another bill, in the form of a rider, a clause that would simply have renewed the old Licensing Act.[39] The Commons removed the rider,[40] and, in justifying that action, Clarke echoed Locke's complaint about stationers who happen on a promising manuscript and "entre it as theirs." However, Clarke couched this objection in stronger and more suggestive terms: "They [the publishers] enter a Title to themselves, and their Friends, for what belongs to, and is the Labour and

Right of, others."[41] Without articulating a full-fledged theory of literary property, Clarke's protest joins labor and rights in a fashion that unambiguously recalls the principles underlying Locke's theory of acquisition. Locke must at least have known about the contents of Clarke's protest, and some forty years later, the *Craftsman* would assert that the whole memorandum was "drawn up by the great Mr. *Locke*."[42] The immediate effect of this confrontation, in any case, was to ensure the elimination of the system of preprint licensing and the copy-registration arrangements that accompanied it.

The stationers, however, refused to allow their copyright system to disappear so easily. A new bill for the regulation of printing, prepared by Edward Clarke and Robert Harley, was introduced on November 30, 1695.[43] This bill, which would have created an optional licensing system, also marks the first legislative effort in England to impose a limited term for copyright protection.[44] The extant drafts of the bill do not specify the proposed term of copyright protection; instead, like Locke's memorandum of January 1695, they include blank spaces where the terms were to be inserted.[45] The bill initially seemed likely to pass, and on December 2, Locke thanked Clarke for his help, remarking that "[t]he Printing Act has been taken care of to its utmost and I thank you it is lodgd, and that's well."[46] Ultimately, however, the bill failed. Numerous attempts followed over the next fifteen years,[47] but not until 1710 did Parliament adopt a statute replacing some of the functions of the Licensing Act.

Seen against this backdrop, two aspects of the Act of Anne take on a different appearance. First, although the publishers may have meant for the author to serve as a convenient repository for their own interests, the idea of authorial control over the manuscript dovetailed nicely with one of the reasons for dismantling the stationers' monopoly in the 1690s. Members of the bookselling industry may have used the call for authors' rights as a self-serving feint, but its appeal to those who heard the argument may also be traced to a fledgling Lockean theory that had already been aired during the previous decade. Second, the limitation of protection to no more than twenty-eight years, although perhaps inspired by hostility to legal monopolies, mirrored a kind of literary antimonopolism. The editorial work that Locke had described in his correspondence promotes a form of public access that is not possible through abridgment or literary imitation. Moreover, the statute provided for a full twenty-eight-year term of protection only if the author was still living at the end of the first fourteen-year term. In practice, the bookselling industry successfully ignored the term limits up until the 1770s. The statute's provisions, however, established a scheme that complemented the extant view of users' rights so that when the term limits came into force in 1774, the public domain gained a temporal aspect that had previously been lacking. Whereas users' access had formerly been limited to various aspects of works, now users would ultimately be able to use the entire work.

ORIGINALITY IN EIGHTEENTH-CENTURY COPYRIGHT LAW

As we have seen, the Act of Anne regulated piracy, not imitations or excerpts. Partisans in literary feuds might accuse each other of illegal borrowing of plots, characters, and language, but those of a more doctrinal bent observed that the law did not touch such offenses. A commentator in 1767, for example, noted that most writers "never stole any thing except lines and sentences, which by the bye is not made penal as yet by any statute."[48] Samuel Richardson could declare in 1742 that the authors of a sequel to *Pamela* had "invaded the author's literary property," but the publication of such sequels was a routine part of the book trade.[49] Booksellers and magazine publishers took it for granted that the statute prevented verbatim reprints of entire books and permitted more partial uses, including the wholesale reprinting of newspaper and magazine articles, which did not qualify for copyright protection in the first place.[50] The mid-eighteenth century witnessed various suits over piracy, but the publication of imitations, anthologies, revisions, and the like proceeded with little fear of threat. Only in the case of abridgments was there any uncertainty, and even then only in the case of an abridgment that reprinted virtually all of the original book.

In *Gyles v. Wilcox* (1741), for example, Lord Hardwicke explained that "abridgments may with great propriety be termed a new book," and that a rule "restrain[ing] all abridgments . . . would be of mischievous consequence."[51] In declaring that an abridgement is permissible only if it is a "real and fair" one, involving more than merely cosmetic changes, Hardwicke signaled his impatience with "mere evasion[s] of the statute," but in practice his standard was easily satisfied. In the case at bar, the plaintiff objected to a legal treatise that, he claimed, "borrowed verbatim from Sir Matthew Hale's *Pleas of the Crown*," reproducing "the greatest part thereof in the very words thereof."[52] Hardwicke referred the case to a Master of the Court, who compared the two texts and found no infringement. Recalling the details eleven years later, Hardwicke said that the abridgment was deemed permissible because it was one-eighth the length of Hale's book.[53] It is doubtful that Hardwicke remembered the case accurately, given that the defendant's counsel had made the similar, but feebler, argument that Wilcox had left out "severall intire chapters" from Hale's 128-chapter treatise and had added "several chapters of [new] Material."[54] Even on Hardwicke's own reckoning, however, it was the book's condensed form, and not any creativity on the part of the abridger, that made it a "real and fair" abridgment.

In 1761, in *Dodsley v. Kinnersley*, Samuel Johnson's publisher unsuccessfully sued the owners of the *Grand Magazine of Magazines* for reprinting *Rasselas* with the moral reflections excised.[55] Again, the court explained that only a "fair abridgment" was permissible and then concluded that the defendants had not reprinted enough of the book to be liable for infringement.[56] In *Strahan v. Newbery* (1774), an abridgment of Hawkesworth's *Voyages* was similarly held to be noninfringing, in an opinion that endorsed the practice of abridgment as "an act of understanding" that saves the reader's time.[57]

There appear to be four or five eighteenth-century cases in which a defendant did not successfully defend his publication by characterizing it as an abridgment, but only the last case (whose outcome remains unclear) actually features an abridged text. In two cases decided in 1739, Lord Hardwicke granted injunctions barring any further publication after he concluded that, in both instances, the defendant was attempting to use his magazine to publish an entire book serially in installments.[58] In *Tonson v. Walker* (1752), the defendant printed Milton's *Paradise Lost*, having added twenty-eight notes to the fifteen hundred in Tonson's edition.[59] Walker's counsel initially took the position that *Paradise Lost* had fallen out of copyright, but after gaining no traction with that argument, he turned rather lamely to the theory that Walker's edition was a revision or abridgment ("Dissatisfied with the text and notes, Walker planned a new edition from various sources"[60]). Lord Hardwicke enjoined the publication until there could be a further hearing on the question of "whether the alterations make it a new work"—a hearing that Tonson's counsel did not trouble himself to arrange. *Macklin v. Richardson* (1770) recalls the magazine cases of 1739: This time the defendant published the first act of *Love-à-la-Mode* and planned to publish the second (and final) act.[61] The defense relied primarily on the claim that because Macklin had arranged for the play to be performed publicly, and had not published it himself, he "gave a right to any of the audience to carry away what they could, and make any use of it."[62] As in Walker's case, it was only after this argument failed that the defendant implausibly called his publication an abridgment.

Finally, in *Bell v. Walker and Debrett* (1785), the plaintiff objected to a one-volume abridgment of a five-volume autobiography by the actress George Anne Bellamy. After being presented with identical passages from the two books, Lord Thurlow stated that he was not ready to decide whether the defendant's edition was a permissible abridgment or a piracy, but he had seen enough to merit a temporary injunction until the question could be resolved. The following month, the defendants' counsel moved to dissolve the injunction, but there seems to be no record of the court's final ruling. If the injunction remained in place, then *Bell* would mark the first instance in which a condensed version of a book was deemed to be equivalent to a piracy. The early nineteenth century offers clearer instances of this view. What is significant, however, is that in *Gyles*, *Dodsley*, and *Strahan*—all of which featured direct and extensive copying—the courts declined to find infringement.[63] Not until well after the turn of the century did courts begin to recognize anything resembling a right against the more attenuated kinds of imitation.[64]

Although some novelists, like Richardson, were outraged that the law did not reach this kind of conduct, many commentators on literary commerce found this state of affairs quite acceptable. In *A Vindication of the Exclusive Rights of Authors to Their Own Works* (1762), an anonymous pamphlet arguing for strong copyright protection, the author endorsed the practice of revision by rearrangement, objecting only to revisers who content themselves with "an *inconsiderable* addition or improvement," such as "the supplying literal or verbal omissions."[65] To qualify a text for copyright protection, the author explained, "it is not necessary that the ideas be original. It is sufficient, that by a new combination of known ideas, the author has produced a different composition."[66] Here is a defense of copyright that shows no interest in novelty and genius.

That view was consistent with the understanding of copyright articulated by the leading legal commentators of the day.[67] In the quest to weld literary property and aesthetics, scholars frequently turn to Blackstone, but the *Commentaries* cannot easily support a high-threshold view of originality. Those who treat Blackstone as an exponent of creativity have relied primarily—and often exclusively—on Mark Rose's influential study of eighteenth-century copyright law and literary culture, and so I focus here on Rose's discussion. Central to this line of argument is Blackstone's assertion that

> [w]hen a man by the exertion of his rational powers has produced an original work, he has clearly a power to dispose of that identical work as he pleases, and any attempt to take it from him, or to vary the disposition he has made of it, is an invasion of his right of property.[68]

Explaining the significance of this passage, Rose concludes that "the production of the discourse of original genius coincided with that of authorial property. The logical point of connection was the idea of value: both were concerned with the worth of texts."[69] It is not difficult to see why some have taken Rose to mean that Blackstone invokes "the discourse of original genius."[70] For Blackstone, however, a work is "original" so long as it is not a reproduction of another work. Nothing suggests that Blackstone, any more than the anonymous author of the *Vindication*, took the view that imitations and anthologies were lacking in value or worth.

Consider the passage from which this line is drawn. First, Blackstone says that an author has a right "in his own original literary compositions" and that "no other person without his leave may publish or make profit of the copies." Unauthorized publication is the focus. Then we are told, in the line quoted earlier, that the author who produces an original work has the power to dispose of it as he likes. Finally, to clarify the nature of this "original work," Blackstone explains that "the identity of a literary composition consists intirely in the *sentiment* and the *language*; the same conceptions, cloathed in the same words, must necessarily be the same composition."

If a second writer repeats those words, "it is always the identical work of the [first] author which is so conveyed, and no other man can have a right to convey or transfer it."[71] Someone who expresses the same conceptions in different words, then, has created an 'original' work according to this definition and is entitled to copyright protection. Lord Ellenborough uses the word in the same sense when he explains, in *Cary v. Kearsley* (1802), that a writer may "use a work [by another writer] to make extracts from it into any original work of his own."[72] On this view, a writer may convey another's ideas in the cognitive sense without being liable for conveyance in the legal sense.

When Blackstone speaks of a prohibition against any effort to "vary the disposition" of the work, he might seem to contemplate a right against adaptation or imitation. But when a work is revised in this manner, it is no longer "cloathed in the same words." Rather, the author's right of disposition is the right to arrange for the book's publication, which no one else may "vary" by printing copies without authorization (or, Blackstone adds, by "recital, [or] by writing"). Some thirty years later, John Trusler took up the question of adaptation, asking whether "compilations and abridgments [are] to be considered [original works]" and immediately answering in the affirmative:

> They are all works of labour and invention. . . . [Even if some texts] may introduce the same matter, the arrangement may be different . . . [and even if] various writers and compilers . . . draw their materials from the same source, [they] not only vary in their arrangement of facts, . . . *but have cloathed their conceptions in different language*. . . . [E]ach man's work stands distinct by itself, new and original in its kind.[73]

Trusler's gloss on Blackstone is consistent with the account in the *Commentaries*: In both cases, the term 'original' is used in its low-threshold sense and does not rely on any notion of novelty or creativity to rationalize the author's property right.[74]

In limiting his concern to imitations that repeat "the same conceptions, cloathed in the same words," Blackstone may find little kinship with the more expansive aesthetic theorists of his day, but he comes close to the views of Samuel Johnson and Richard Hurd, who had both written on imitation from a forensic perspective some fifteen years earlier. Johnson, in a *Rambler* paper from 1751, observes that charges of plagiarism, "even when . . . false, . . . may somctimes be urged with probability" because writers use "a common stock of images, a settled mode of arrangement, and a beaten path of transition, . . . which produce the resemblance generally observable among contemporaries."[75] After enumerating examples, Johnson concludes that a writer may not be

> fully convicted of imitation, except where there is a concurrence of more resemblance than can be imagined to have happened by chance;

as where the same ideas are conjoined without any natural series or necessary coherence, or where not only the thought but the words are copied.[76]

Richard Hurd pursues the same theme, at greater length, in *A Discourse Concerning Poetical Imitation* (1751). Hurd explains that different writers of "genius" may produce similar phrases, allusions, and comparisons, but these resemblances are not evidence of copying unless the texts include "*the same arrangement of the same words*."[77] The standard of proof is so high because "the same ideas and aspects of things constantly admonish the poet of the same *resemblances* and *relations*." Writers acting "under the influence of the same *national character*" and "liv[ing] together in the *same period of time*" may use "some considerable *similarity* of expression." Hurd allows that similar texts may possibly be copies even when such starkly incriminating evidence is absent—but without verbatim repetition, it is impossible to be sure.[78]

Elsewhere in the essay, Hurd discusses "genius" in terms that resonate with those of his most energetic contemporaries, saying, for example, that a "true genius" has been "touched with a ray of celestial fire"—which does not prevent him, however, from treating genius and imitation together. Even deliberate imitations may outshine their sources, according to Hurd, because the imitator "may possess a stronger, and more plastic genius, and therefore be enabled to touch, with more force of expression, even those particulars, which he professedly imitates."[79] As with Pope's approval of the "mutual commerce [that] makes Poetry flourish," Hurd treats imitation not as a vice, but as something to be encouraged. Hurd, like Young, is concerned with "the idea of value" and "the worth of texts," but for Hurd those considerations are not premised on novelty. If Blackstone's account of copyright in "original works" converges with an aesthetic theory, it is a theory that gives imitation a vital role in literary production.

That perspective is also evident in a letter to George Steevens in 1779, in which Blackstone explained that a modern rewriting of a classical text "may safely [be] pronounce[d] an imitation, for it is not I presume the same train of ideas that follow in the same description of an Ancient and a modern." The same description yields a different meaning when the modern writer borrows from an ancient source. If one kind of copy may express the same conceptions in different words, another kind might use the same words, in a new context, to express different conceptions. In both cases, the text is an 'original work' according to the *Commentaries*. In the remainder of the letter, Blackstone filled two pages with parallel passages from Addison's *Cato* and its Shakespearean and Latin sources, remarking that he took "pleasure [in] setting down some imitations [he] observed in [Addison's play]."[80] Again, like Hurd, Blackstone emphasizes the productive potential of literary imitation.

Besides Blackstone, the other principal source usually cited to connect eighteenth-century copyright law with aesthetic originality is *An Argument in Defense of Literary Property*, published in 1774 by Francis Hargrave, a barrister and legal historian. Again, the scholarship that draws on Hargrave is based on Rose's analysis.[81] Rose quotes Hargrave at length, in a passage that is worth reproducing in full, not least because of its echoes of Blackstone:

> The subject of literary property is a *written composition*; and that one written composition may be distinguished from another, is a truth too evident to be much argued upon. Every man has a mode of combining and expressing his ideas peculiar to himself. The same doctrines, the same opinions, never come from two persons, or even from the same person at different times, cloathed wholly in the same language. A strong resemblance of stile, of sentiment, of plan and disposition, will be frequently found; but there is such an infinite variety in the modes of thinking and writing, as well in the extent and connection of ideas, as in the use and arrangement of words, that a literary work *really* original, like the human face, will always have some singularities, some lines, some features, to characterize it, and to fix and establish its identity; and to assert the contrary with respect to either, would be justly deemed equally opposite to reason and universal experience. Besides, though it should be allowable to suppose, that there *may* be cases, in which, on a comparison of two literary productions, no such distinction could be made between them, as in a competition for originality to decide whether both were really original, or which was the original and which the copy; still the observation of the possibility of distinguishing would hold in *all other* instances, and the Argument in its application to them would still have the same force.[82]

Here are Blackstone's "sentiments" and "language" again, presented in terms that closely track the account in the *Commentaries*. Rose suggests that, in referring to "a literary work *really* original, like the human face," Hargrave's usage is ambiguous: "Does Hargrave merely mean a composition that has not been copied? Or does he mean one that is novel, that exhibits a certain freshness of character?"[83] This ambiguity, however, seems to depend on the high-threshold sense of "originality." Throughout the passage, Hargrave treats originality in its low-threshold sense, insisting that human expression is so various, so "peculiar" to each individual, that some minimal degree of variation is inevitable. His analogy between the human face and an original work makes exactly this point: If two nearly identical faces can be differentiated by "some singularities, some lines, some features," then human identity, like literary originality, depends on minor differences, rather than on the more demanding criteria of "novel[ty]" and "freshness of character." The confusion evidently stems from the phrase "a literary work *really* original," by which Hargrave does not mean a remarkably or outstandingly original work, but one that is actually original (in the sense of being independently created), as opposed to a reproduction holding itself out as an original.

The last line of the passage is also ambiguous, Rose explains, because Hargrave may be taken to mean either that some writings are "unindividuated" or that some texts resemble each other so closely as to make it "impossible to determine which is the original."[84] But Hargrave has not set up a category of banal and nondescript writing to be contrasted against meritorious works with singular attributes. Rather, he has made a practical observation about limit cases. Hargrave's "competition for originality" involves an effort to determine whether two texts were independently produced ("whether both were really original") or whether one was based on the other. Such a "competition" may be difficult with nearly identical texts, but the problem is an uncommon one: "the possibility of distinguishing would hold in *all other* instances."

Rose is right to note the contradiction: Having begun by claiming that no two texts are alike, Hargrave now admits that some may be indistinguishable. But that contradiction need not be taken to mean that a "*really* original" work requires creativity, nor that Hargrave is concerned to differentiate "hack writer[s]" who are not capable of "produc[ing] distinct literary works" from those "with at least moderate powers of original genius."[85] Far from seeking to raise some talented group to the literary firmament, Hargrave merely acknowledges that sometimes we may be incapable of *telling* whether a text was created independently—just as Hurd argues that our suspicions about copying are often incorrect because some writings are in fact independent creations, although they look like duplicates of another text. The trivial variations that constitute originality in Hargrave's view ("some lines, some features") do not bespeak a requirement of creativity. Novelty figures nowhere in his argument, and indeed the conceptual problem that novelty would solve—the need to provide a basis for separating duplicates from non-duplicates—is handled just as well by the notion of minor variation, which Hargrave explicitly adduces.

Once one looks for evidence of a link between aesthetic theories of creativity and legal theories of literary property, it is striking how rarely anyone invoked the concept of aesthetic originality during the eighteenth-century copyright debates. References to authorial labor abound in this literature, but there is little discussion of novelty—even by figures such as William Warburton, who, as a lawyer, literary critic, and copyright advocate, would seem an obvious candidate.[86] Among the contributions to the legal debate over copyright, the only extended discussion of aesthetic originality appears in *An Enquiry Into the Nature and Origin of Literary Property* (1762), an anonymous pamphlet that attacks the concept of literary property as quixotic and incoherent.[87] Even if the law recognized this form of incorporeal property, the writer explains, few would be able to recover in court because among "the Productions of modern Authors, [there are] very few . . . whose Sentiments are new or original. Authors who seek Redress for Invasion of their Property, must prove the Originality of their Sentiments."[88] Even where recovery is possible, damages must be based on the singular features "wherein the excellency of the Book consists." The value of a book of poetry, for example, depends on "the Elegance of Diction, and Propriety of Metaphors, . . . in the Richness of Invention, and turn of Thought," whereas in fiction and drama, the value lies in "the Truth of Character, the Vein of Humour, the Sentiment and Conduct of the Story." But these features, the author concludes, cannot be assigned any market value: "Juries would be puzzled, what Damage to give for the pilfering of an Anecdote, or purloining the Fable of a Play."[89]

Here at last we see aesthetic considerations emphatically adduced as the proper basis for literary property—but only because the commentator means to ridicule the whole enterprise. In the *Enquiry*, literary property is made to seem a bad deal for modern writers because, on the one hand, they own only the original aspects of their own productions, which leaves much of their work available for appropriation by others, whereas, on the other hand, those original aspects are so hard to identify, and the value is so hard to quantify, that any suit looks like a futile proposition. In short, aesthetic originality appears only as an imaginary and impossible prerequisite, advanced by a skeptic who means to question the basis for any claim whatsoever to authorial property. That attitude makes sense, because even a requirement for "modest powers of original genius" would have entailed a radical expansion of copyright's scope beyond the terms specified in the Act of Anne and a corresponding diminution of the public domain.

Ironically, the catalogue of absurd conflicts evoked in the *Enquiry* as a threat has turned out to offer a prescient gloss on the development of copyright law during the nineteenth and twentieth centuries. Courts and legislatures have developed increasingly intricate distinctions and exceptions as they have looked beyond wholesale piracy to isolate smaller elements that qualify for protection while continuing to insist they are not in the business of making aesthetic judgments. Thus, the unthinkable task of having to evaluate an anecdote or a fable has found doctrinal footing in the protection now afforded to plots and plot devices. The problem of originality has become even more difficult in light of the U.S. Supreme Court's 1991 opinion specifying that an original work must have "at least some minimal degree of creativity," "some creative spark, no matter how crude, humble or obvious it might be."[90] The *Enquiry*'s warning may have amused its first readers, but probably did not alarm them, because the pamphlet invented a precondition that had no legal role. In the interim, however, the conflicts rehearsed in the *Enquiry* have gained force—as vindications of authorial merit by those who embrace a high-threshold view of originality, and as evidence of doctrinal confusion by those who take the low-threshold view.

IMITATION AND EIGHTEENTH-CENTURY LITERATURE

In addition to a copyright doctrine that showed no interest in aesthetic originality, the eighteenth-century literary marketplace testifies to an ongoing enthusiasm for many kinds of imitation and revision—forms of copying that publishers would have been reluctant to gamble on if there were a likelihood that the books would be damasked and made into waste paper.[91] These practices were not new; for the most part, they had been an essential part of literary commerce for centuries. Parodic poets, like their Elizabethan counterparts, showed no hesitation in recycling numerous verses from the poems they targeted, often changing only a few words here and there to make the heroic seem comic, bathetic, or simply idiotic.[92] Novelists copied plots, scenes, characters, and jokes with the same rapidity and enthusiasm as dramatists during the previous century. The imitations that writers produced in both of these contexts may not have been innovative, but the fact that they continued to thrive for many decades after the passage of the Act of Anne has considerable significance for the modern forms of both genres.

Considering the omnipresence of parody in modern culture, the history of parody has received surprisingly little attention. However, in a study of parody in early modern England, Robert Mack carefully distinguishes the dominant forms of parody up to the end of the sixteenth century from the new forms that emerged during the decades before the English Civil War. Mack notes that, although "the fundamental, referential 'idea' and impulses of parody" were not new to English authors in the Jacobean period, in previous centuries, parody tended not to target individual writers or texts, but traditions, genres, schools, and "literary style[s] somehow divorced from any particular author."[93] In Ben Jonson's plays around the turn of the sixteenth century, Mack argues, we see the emergence of "wholesale and text-specific parodic appropriation."[94] These plays, in which Jonson pillories his competitors by mimicking their words and throwing them back at the author, feature a "tense staccato quality of . . . rapid-fire exchange that . . . is almost nowhere to be found in the more established traditions of medieval verse satire."[95]

In the wake of Jonson's efforts, imitative parody became one of the characteristic features of English literary culture—a feature whose growth increased rapidly after the Restoration in response to the popularity of such landmark contributions as Buckingham's verbally precise mockery of Dryden in *The Rehearsal* (1672) and John Philips's bathetic revision of *Paradise Lost* in *The Splendid Shilling* (1701). As Richmond Bond notes, this change is also apparent from the evolving vocabulary used for poetic mockery:

> Blount's *Glossographia* . . . in 1656 gave *burlesque* as "drolish, merry, pleasant," . . . [whereas] the *Glossographia Anglicana Nova*, 1707, added "or a mock Poetry" . . . Edward Phillips's *New World of English Words*, 1658, defined *burlesque* as "merry, drolish," *travested* as "shifted in apparel, disguised"; the sixth edition, by John Kersey in

> 1706, expanded both terms like the 1707 book cited above and introduced *parody* as "a Poetick Sport, which consists in putting some serious Pieces into Burlesk, and affecting as much as is possible, the same Words, Rhimes and Cadences."[96]

Finding oneself the object of this "Poetic Sport" was the price of literary fame, as Dryden discovered, for example, in the early 1680s when "Absalom and Achitophel" generated numerous mocking attacks such as Samuel Pordage's "Azariah and Hushai."[97] Pope encountered much the same treatment in "Aesop at the Bear-Garden: A Vision . . . In Imitation of the Temple of Fame," by "Mr. Preston" (1715) and Giles Jacob's "The Rape of the Smock" (1717). Ambrose Philips was an especially popular target in the mid-1720s, as were Colley Cibber's odes to King George in the early 1730s.[98] By the mid-century, Gray's reluctance to publish his "Elegy in a Country Churchyard" (1751) proved fully justified, given that it provoked dozens of mocking lampoons replete with insulting lines like: "For Science frowned not on his humble Birth/And smooth-tongued Flattery marked him for her own."[99]

The growing cultural emphasis on aesthetic originality over the last two hundred years, however, has produced an increasing hostility to imitative writing in some quarters. In 1994, the U.S. Supreme Court suggested that verbal similarity might, by itself, support a finding of infringement:

> Once [the parodist has used] enough . . . to assure identification [of the source], how much more is reasonable will depend, say, on the extent to which the . . . overriding purpose and character is to parody the original or, in contrast, the likelihood that the parody may serve as a market substitute for the original.

This formulation might be thought to set out a two-part test (first, ask whether the work is essentially parodic and, if not, then assess the risk of market substitution), but on the previous page, the opinion treats the amount taken as itself a determinant of market substitution: "the amount and substantiality of the portion used will . . . tend to reveal[] the degree to which the parody may serve as a market substitute for the original or potentially licensed derivatives."[100] Thus, rather than allowing the parodic purpose to excuse a greater amount of borrowing, the test suggests that (at some threshold, at least) the quantity used may simply be regarded as too great, and that finding then points to the conclusion that the work, regardless of any parodic elements, is not essentially a parody, but instead is a market substitute. Under this analysis, many parodists of the eighteenth century would have fared poorly. In justifying its reasoning, the Court purports to rely on eighteenth-century literary culture, invoking Johnson's maxim that "[n]o man but a blockhead ever wrote, except for money."[101] But it hardly follows that parodies—even wholesale parodies—usurp the source's place in the market. As Johnson observed elsewhere, two books on the same subject might "do good to one another" because "[s]ome will buy the one, some the other, and compare them: and so a talk is made about a thing, and the books are sold."[102]

A concern with market substitution would also have constrained the production of eighteenth-century fiction. It had long been conventional among writers to exploit others' successes by recycling their plots. This practice was to prove especially popular among eighteenth-century novelists as they discovered the market niche. Because the novels' bid for readers often depended on the affiliation with an earlier work, it was common to advertise the genetic relationship. *Yorick's Sentimental Journey Continued*; *Pamela in High Life*; *Gulliveriana: Or, a Fourth Volume of Miscellanies, Being a Sequel to the Three Volumes Published by Pope and Swift*; *Charlotte, or, a Sequel to the Sorrows of Werter*; *Delineations of the Heart: or, the History of Henry Bennett, a Tragic-comi-satiric Essay, Attempted in the Manner of Fielding*—all of these appealed to potential readers by capitalizing on a popular title or author. Today, these might be treated as infringements of the original author's plot or characters. The same could be said for the imitations that J. M. S. Tompkins finds in later eighteenth-century recyclings of Richardson: "The abduction of Miss Byron from the masquerade, Mr. B.'s disguised attempt on Pamela, Clarissa's home-coming to the stony-hearted Harlowe family, these are the patterns from which are drawn the chief incidents of scores of books, with remarkably little variation, and sometimes with a literal closeness."[103] Another form of novelistic imitation may be seen in the proliferation of works following the model of a newly popular subgenre, such as the novel of sentiment, the gothic, the "it" narrative, and the Jacobin novel. Even when these books do not wear their literary lineage on the title page, their plots and characters readily indicate the source of inspiration.[104] The penchant for treading over familiar ground led to a vast quantity of fiction that today goes unread even by the most diligent historian of the novel, but that is hardly surprising, because the conditions that make for a flourishing public domain are conditions that foster literary production in general.

Nowhere is the importance of the public domain clearer, perhaps, than in the Fielding–Richardson rivalry. *Shamela*'s title and many of its sentences represent only slight variations from *Pamela*, while *Joseph Andrews* names itself as *Pamela*'s sibling. If the *Pamela-Shamela* controversy were to arise today in the United States, Fielding's contribution would likely be treated as an infringement under the ruling cited earlier. Although certainly not seeking to provide the same kind of satisfaction as Richardson, Fielding would have been delighted if *Shamela* had put an end to *Pamela*'s sales. To a court trying to predict the future, the extent of Fielding's copying would be more than sufficient to demonstrate the risk of market substitution. Similarly, *Joseph Andrews*, with its various references to the correspondence between Joseph and his sister, might run afoul of the doctrine that treats characters as a form of protected expression.[105] The broader understanding of the public domain in the eighteenth century provided the crucible for the debate over the novel's moral aims and means of representation—a debate that had formative consequences for the development of the genre.

In addition to parodic and imitative writing, some writers built their careers on collecting and condensing others' works. John Trusler, author of one of the treatises cited earlier,[106] is a particularly instructive example. Trusler published numerous abridgements and compilations, including *Principles of Politeness, Being a Compilation From Lord Chesterfield's Letters* (1775); *A Descriptive Account of the Islands Lately Discovered in the South Seas* (1778; an abridgment of Captain Cook's *Voyages*); *A Concise View of the Common and Statute Laws of England* (1784; an abridgment of Blackstone's *Commentaries*); *A Compendium of Useful Knowledge* (1784); *A Compendium of Sacred History* (1797; an abridgement of Stackhouse's *History of the Bible*); and *Detached Philosophic Thoughts of the Best Writers, Ancient and Modern* (1810). Along the way—as if to underscore his interest in the principle of minimal differentiation that separates the abridgment from the piracy—he was also one of the first English writers to produce a thesaurus (*The Difference, Between Words, Esteemed Synonymous, in the English Language*, 1766) and a rhyming dictionary (*Poetic Endings, or a Dictionary of Rhymes*, 1783). That Trusler worked so energetically to mine others' works helps to explain why he would have cared to insist that compilations and abridgments should be regarded as original for purposes of copyright protection. Although he may have had a more significant stake in the answer than the other legal commentators who addressed this issue, his view was consistent with theirs.

This description of eighteenth-century literary culture returns us to the question of why modern scholars might find a greater emphasis on aesthetic originality than the contemporaneous legal discussion seems to support. There is no doubt that writers like Richardson and Young were eager to associate creativity and property (although it is hardly clear that they were prepared to discuss the issue with any kind of legal precision or that they could have responded to the remarks in *An Enquiry Into the Nature and Origin of Literary Property* about the prerequisites for the property right and its limits). To anyone who comes to the legal debate after being immersed in eighteenth-century literature, the views of novelists and poets are likely to color the whole question and provide the backdrop for any legal references to originality. Moreover, theories of aesthetic originality have been so massively influential since the early nineteenth century that, to modern eyes, any reference to originality seems necessarily to include some element of creativity. This is why ambiguities can appear to arise in the writings of commentators like Blackstone and Hargrave even when their arguments are perfectly consistent with the low-threshold notion of originality that they invoke throughout.

Not only do we have difficulty separating originality and creativity, but, as it turns out, we also delude ourselves into believing that a high-threshold originality requirement would be a painless one for writers to live by. A recent study by a team of cognitive scientists shows that we find it harder to recognize our creative debts to others than to believe in our own creative power.[107] Participants in the study were asked to propose new uses for familiar items, and then all of the ideas were gathered and divided into several groups. Next, the participants were asked to rate one set of ideas (Group 1) according to their practicality and to suggest improvements for another set of ideas (Group 2). One week later, the participants were given lists with items from both groups and were asked which ones they had proposed. When reviewing an idea from Group 2 in its unimproved state, the participants were three times more likely to claim it as theirs than when reviewing an idea from Group 1. Once they had performed the imaginative work of revision—the Lockean "mixing" of labor—people were more likely to take credit for the idea in its original form.[108] This study suggests that, even when authorial claims about novelty sound exaggerated, they may represent the author's sincere belief. But the author's sincerity does not diminish her reliance on the public domain. Rather, it explains why writers who argue for a high-threshold copyright regime may fail to understand that reducing the rights of users would have devastating effects on their own productivity.

If our eagerness to exaggerate our own role in any creative endeavor accounts in part for this tendency, another explanation, paradoxically, involves the low-threshold view of originality that these writers disdain. Even *Feist*, with its demand for "some minimal degree of creativity," hardly threatens to deny protection to any work intended as a creative effort by its author. The publication that flunked *Feist*'s "originality" standard was a phone book, and no court has suggested that the standard does anything to disqualify certain novels, restaurant reviews, or blog postings from copyright protection. As long as the aim to be creative is sufficient and questions of aesthetic merit do not enter into the analysis, writers remain free to take from the public domain without needing to ask themselves whether a more demanding criterion for originality would have limited their opportunities.

A significantly heightened originality requirement, if imposed tomorrow, would serve to deny copyright protection to new works that fail to display sufficient creativity while leaving intact the protection already afforded to existing works. Over the last century and a half, a similar effect has been achieved—not through any significant revision of the threshold originality requirement, but instead by recharacterizing the elements of the work that qualify for protection or, what amounts to the same thing, by recharacterizing what counts as copying. The anonymous author of *An Enquiry Into the Nature and Origin of Literary Property* could imagine a work that had no original aspect except for "the Conduct of the Story," so that only that slender reed could sustain a claim for damages against a verbatim reproduction of the work, and there could be no compensation for any of the other copied elements. In modern copyright law, conversely, once a work has been deemed "derivative" because it copies a single protected element of another work, the derivative work may be regarded as thoroughly indebted to the source. Together, an increasingly fine-grained specification of what constitutes protected expression and an ever-longer term of protection have produced the same kind of effect, although not on the same order of magnitude, as a redefinition of "originality." Precisely because this change was not effected through the latter route, it is still possible for writers to regard themselves as thoroughly innovative even as they work with borrowed tools. When these writers continue to object that their highly original works are being unfairly appropriated, the response cannot involve a more demanding originality requirement, because that solution will always be regarded as doctrinally unworkable. So long as these complaints are heeded, then, the only possible solutions involve an ever-more atomized view of the work's elements and an ever-growing copyright term.

ACKNOWLEDGMENTS

Thanks to Ronan Deazley, Trevor Cook, Holger Schott Syme, and Reginald McGinnis for their helpful suggestions.

NOTES

1. *An Act for the Encouragement of Learning*, 8 Anne c. 19 (1710).
2. The same point is implicit in Tilar J. Mazzeo's observation that "[t]he primary obstacle to the development of copyright law during the first part of the [eighteenth] century . . . was the widespread cultural belief that knowledge should be held in common by all members of society, in order to ensure the development of civilization." Mazzeo, "Plagiarism, Composition Pedagogy, and the History of the Book," *Pacific Coast Philology* 40, no. 2 (2005): 92. For a useful analysis of the public domain's role in copyright law generally, see Jessica Litman, "The Public Domain," *Emory Law Journal* 39 (1990): 965–1023. As Litman explains, "the public domain is the law's primary safeguard of the raw material that makes authorship possible" (967).
3. See, e.g., Susan Eilenberg, "Mortal Pages: Wordsworth and the Reform of Copyright," in *Strange Power of Speech: Wordsworth, Coleridge, and Literary Posession* (New York: Oxford University Press, 1992), 193–212; Bradley Deane, *The Making of the Victorian Novelist: Anxieties of Authorship in the Mass Market* (New York: Routledge, 2003), 39–43; Clare Pettitt, *Patent Inventions: Intellectual Property and the Victorian Novel* (Oxford: Oxford University Press, 2004), 60–80.
4. G. W. Pigman III, "Versions of Imitation in the Renaissance," *Renaissance Quarterly* 33, no. 1 (1980): 1–32; Stephen Orgel, "The Renaissance Artist as Plagiarist," *ELH* 48, no. 3 (1981): 476–495; Harold Ogden White, *Plagiarism*

and Imitation During the English Renaissance (Cambridge, MA: Harvard University Press, 1935).

5. Laura Rosenthal, *Playwrights and Plagiarists in Early Modern England: Gender, Authorship, Literary Property* (Ithaca, NY: Cornell University Press, 1996); Paulina Kewes, *Authorship and Appropriation: Writing for the Stage in England, 1660–1710* (Oxford: Clarendon Press, 1998); Brean S. Hammond, *Professional Imaginative Writing in England, 1670–1740: "Hackney for Bread"* (Oxford: Clarendon Press, 1997); Paulina Kewes, ed., *Plagiarism in Early Modern England* (New York: Palgrave Macmillan, 2003).
6. Whether Young's essay had much influence on his contemporaries is another question. According to Martin William Steinke, Young's *Conjectures* "did not attain . . . much significance in their own country" and the book "was appreciated far more in Germany." Steinke, *Edward Young's "Conjectures on Original Composition" in England and Germany* (New York: Stechert, 1917), 14–15. James Sambrook similarly notes that "Young's treatise became well-known in Germany" and "enjoyed renewed influence in England when its ideas were reimported by Coleridge"; Sambrook, "The Psychology of Literary Creation and Literary Response," in *The Cambridge History of Literary Criticism*, ed. Hugh Barr Nisbet, 9 vols. (Cambridge: Cambridge University Press, 1989), 4:630. For other discussions of genius in eighteenth-century aesthetics, see Gilberta Golinelli, "The Concept of Genius and Its Metamorphoses in Eighteenth-Century English Criticism," *Textus* 18, no. 1 (2005): 189–204; John Hope Mason, "Thinking about Genius in the Eighteenth Century," in *Eighteenth-Century Aesthetics and the Reconstruction of Art*, ed. Paul Mattick, Jr. (Cambridge: Cambridge University Press, 1993), 210–239; George J. Buelow, "Originality, Genius, Plagiarism in English Criticism of the Eighteenth Century," *International Review of the Aesthetics and Sociology of Music* 21, no. 2 (1990): 117–128; Paul Kaufman, "Heralds of Original Genius," in *Essays in Memory of Barrett Wendell by His Assistants* (Cambridge, MA: Harvard University Press, 1926), 191–217, esp. 200–207.
7. Edward Young, *Conjectures on Original Composition in a Letter to the Author of Sir Charles Grandison* (London: Millar, 1759), 53–54. Young advises his reader to "prefer the native growth of thy own mind to the richest import from abroad"; the writer who relies on his native talents will find that "[h]is works . . . stand distinguished; his the sole Property of them; which Property alone can confer the noble title of an *Author*." See also Mark Rose, *Authors and Owners: The Invention of Copyright* (Cambridge, MA: Harvard University Press, 1993), 117.
8. For example, Young writes that "[t]he mind of a man of Genius is a fertile and pleasant field, pleasant as *Elysium*, and fertile as *Tempe*; it enjoys a perpetual Spring. Of that Spring, *Originals* are the fairest Flowers: *Imitations* are of quicker growth, but fainter bloom" (Young, *Conjectures*, 9). For similar treatments of originality, see William Duff, *An Essay on Original Genius; and Its Various Modes of Exertion in Philosophy and the Fine Arts, Particularly in Poetry* (London: Dilly, 1767); William Duff, *Critical Observations on the Writings of the Most Celebrated Original Geniuses in Poetry* (London: Becket, 1770); Alexander Gerard, *An Essay on Genius* (London: Becket, 1771); and the sources cited in note 77.
9. William Blackstone, *Commentaries on the Laws of England*, 4 vols. (Oxford: Clarendon Press, 1765–1769), 2:405–406.
10. The two definitions appear respectively under uses 5.a. (which the OED traces to 1650) and 6.a (traced to 1756).

11. A classic articulation appears in *University of London Press v. University Tutorial Press*, [1916] 2 Ch. D. 601, 608–609: "The word 'original' does not in this connection mean that the work must be the expression of an original or inventive thought. Copyright Acts are not concerned with the originality of ideas, but with the expression of thought. . . . [T]he Act does not require that the expression must be in an original or novel form, but that the work must not be copied from another work—that it should originate from the author." As discussed below, the U.S. Supreme Court raised the threshold for originality in the ruling in *Feist Publications, Inc. v. Rural Telephone Service Co.*, 499 U.S. 340 (1991), which held that an original work must have "some minimal degree of creativity."
12. *The Case of Samuel Richardson, of London, Printer, with Regard to the Invasion of His Property in The History of Sir Charles Grandison* (London, 1753), 2–3.
13. Wendy J. Gordon, "Render Copyright unto Caesar: On Taking Incentives Seriously," *University of Chicago Law Review* 71, no. 1 (2004): 77.
14. Michael E. Connaughton, "Richardson's Familiar Quotations: *Clarissa* and Bysshe's *Art of English Poetry*," *Philological Quarterly* 60, no. 2 (1981): 183–195. Bysshe's compilation included famous poetic extracts (often of twenty lines or more), arranged topically, along with a rhyming dictionary and a treatise on versification. The book, which went through nine editions between 1702 and 1762, attests to the importance of anthologies in eighteenth-century literary culture.
15. Abraham Drassinower, "Taking User Rights Seriously," in *In the Public Interest: The Future of Canadian Copyright Law*, ed. Michael Geist (Toronto: Irwin Law, 2005), 466.
16. Henry Fielding, *The History of Tom Jones*, ed. John Bender and Simon Stern (1749; Oxford: Oxford University Press, 1996), 68 (Book II, chap. 1), 540 (Book XII, chap. 1).
17. Pope to William Walsh, 2 July 1706, in *Alexander Pope: Selected Letters*, ed. Howard Erskine-Hill (Oxford: Oxford University Press, 2000), 13. Pope's remarks in this letter offer a new light on his famous couplet, "True wit is nature to advantage dressed /What oft was thought but ne'er so well expressed."
18. See John Feather, "From Rights in Copies to Copyright: The Recognition of Authors' Rights in English Law and Practice in the Sixteenth and Seventeenth Centuries," *Cardozo Arts & Entertainment Law Journal* 10, no. 2 (1992): 455–473; reprinted in *The Construction of Authorship: Textual Appropriation in Law and Literature*, ed. Martha Woodmansee and Peter Jaszi (Durham, NC: Duke University Press, 1994), 191–209.
19. Feather, "From Rights in Copies to Copyright," in *The Construction of Authorship*, ed. Woodmansee and Jaszi, 197. As evidence for this view, Feather mentions "transfers [of 'copies'] by purchase, inheritance and gift, subdivision into shares, and similar commercial activities" and notes that "[a]s early as 1579, a copy was used as security for a debt" (197–198). For another version of this argument, see John Feather, *Publishing, Piracy and Politics: An Historical Study of Copyright in Britain* (London: Mansell, 1994), 18.
20. *A Decree of Starre-Chamber, Concerning Printing* (London: Barker, 1637), signatures B2r–B2v.
21. *A Decree of Starre-Chamber*, signatures C2r–C2v.
22. Frederick Seaton Siebert, *Freedom of the Press in England, 1476–1776: The Rise and Decline of Government Controls* (Urbana: University of Illinois Press, 1952), 165–233.

23. 13 & 14 Car. 2, c. 33 § 6 (1662).
24. On excerpting and anthologizing during this period, see John H. Astington, "Dramatic Extracts in the Interregnum," *Review of English Studies* 54, no. 217 (2003): 601–614; Leah Price, *The Anthology and the Rise of the Novel: From Richardson to George Eliot* (Cambridge: Cambridge University Press, 2000), 15–16; Barbara M. Benedict, *Making the Modern Reader: Cultural Mediation in Early Modern Literary Anthologies* (Princeton: Princeton University Press, 1996); Adam Smyth, *"Profit and Delight": Printed Miscellanies in England, 1640–1682* (Detroit: Wayne State University Press, 2004); Arthur Ellicott Case, *A Bibliography of English Poetical Miscellanies, 1521–1750* (Oxford: Bibliographical Society, 1935). On literary imitations during the seventeenth century, see the sources cited in notes 4 and 5. Focusing mainly on poetry and ballads, William St Clair has shown that there were fewer anthologies than one might expect, and he concludes that some members of the bookselling industry may have agreed not to abridge or anthologize each other's publications. St Clair, *The Reading Nation in the Romantic Period* (Cambridge: Cambridge University Press, 2004), 66–74, 490–498.
25. Neither Rosenthal nor Kewes (cited in note 5) frames the politics of Restoration plagiarism in these terms, but their examples—particularly those involving Dryden, Shadwell, and Settle—bear out the point. See Rosenthal, *Playwrights and Plagiarists*, 44–49, Kewes, *Authorship and Appropriation*, 52–54. Marilyn Randall, *Pragmatic Plagiarism: Authorship, Profit, and Power* (Toronto: University of Toronto Press, 2001), 134–135, discusses *tu-quoque-ism*, a particular form of literary feuding in which one partisan uses the accusation of plagiarism against a rival, who responds by detecting the accuser's thievery.
26. *Reasons Humbly Offered to Be Considered Before the Act for Printing, Be Renewed* (1692). Raymond Astbury, "The Renewal of the Licensing Act in 1693 and Its Lapse in 1695," *Library* 33, no. 4 (1978), 300 n. 19, assigns the leaflet to "late December" 1692.
27. *Manuscripts of the House of Lords, 1692–93* (Historical Manuscripts Commission, Fourteenth Report, Appendix, Part VI, 1894), 381 (affidavit of Peter Parker).
28. *Journal of the House of Lords*, 15:280 (March 8, 1693). The argument appears in the course of an effort to amend the Licensing Act by stipulating that entry in the Stationers' Register should not be required so long as the book's printer and author included their names on the title page. For further discussion of this proposal, see Siebert (note 22), 260.
29. *Journal of the House of Commons*, 10:847; *Journal of the House of Lords*, 15:280 (March 8, 1693). In its two most recent versions, the act had remained in effect for fourteen and eight years, respectively.
30. See John Harrison and Peter Laslett, *The Library of John Locke*, 2nd ed. (Oxford: Clarendon Press, 1971), 214 (item 2390).
31. Locke to Edward Clarke, January 2, 1693, in *The Correspondence of John Locke*, ed. E. S. De Beer, 8 vols. (Oxford: Clarendon Press, 1976–1989), 4:614–615.
32. For Locke's discussions of the project in his letters, see Locke to Edward Clarke, February 18, 1687, *Correspondence*, 3:128–132; Locke to Edward Clarke, November 23, 1691, ibid., 4: 331–332; Awnsham Churchill to Locke, November 17, 1703, ibid., 8:121. See also Robert B. Horwitz and Judith B. Finn, "Locke's Aesop's Fables," *Locke Newsletter* 6 (1975): 71–88; James L. Axtell, *The Educational Writings of John Locke* (Cambridge: Cambridge University Press, 1968), 271 n. 2.

33. *Journal of the House of Commons*, 11:200 (January 9, 1695).
34. *Correspondence*, 5:786. See also 5:785 (noting that, because the Commons made the recommendation for renewal on January 9 and rejected it on February 11, the memorandum "probably belongs about January").
35. Ibid., 5:787. Later in the memorandum, Locke offers a variation on this proposal, suggesting that for "Authors that now live and write it may be reasonable to limit their property to a certein number of years after the death of the author or the first printing of the book as suppose 50 or 70 years." Ibid., 5:791.
36. *Journal of the House of Commons*, 11:228 (February 11, 1695).
37. Ibid.
38. See John Freke and Edward Clarke to Locke, March 14, 1695, *Correspondence*, 5:291, 5:795; see also ibid., 5:796 (including clause vesting "a priviledg in the Author of the said book his executors administrators and assignes of solely reprinting and publishing the said book for years from the first edition thereof").
39. *Manuscripts of the House of Lords, 1693–95* (Historical Manuscripts Commission, 1900), 540 (April 3, 1695); *Journal of the House of Lords*, 15:532 (April 8, 1695) ("An Act for continuing and making perpetual several Laws therein mentioned").
40. *Journal of the House of Commons*, 11:301 (April 12, 1695).
41. *Journal of the House of Commons*, 11:306 (April 17, 1695); see also *Journal of the House of Lords*, 15:545 (April 18, 1695). For another discussion of this protest in terms of Lockean approaches to copyright, see Alfred C. Yen, "Restoring the Natural Law: Copyright as Labor and Possession," *Ohio State Law Journal* 51, no. 2 (1990): 523.
42. *Craftsman* 281 (November 20, 1731). Some historians have also ascribed Clarke's protest directly to Locke. See, e.g., Laurence Hanson, *Government and the Press, 1695–1763* (London: Oxford University Press, 1936), 1.
43. *Journal of the House of Commons*, 11:343 (November 30, 1695).
44. The stationers, presumably anxious about the limited-term copyright provision, petitioned Parliament on December 5, declaring themselves "very much concerned in the consequences of the . . . bill." *Journal of the House of Commons*, 11:354.
45. *See* Cambridge University Library Manuscripts, shelfmark Oo.vi.93, folios 45r–46v ("no person or persons hath or shall have any sole property or sole Right of printing any Book pamphlet portrait or paper for any further or longer tyme than years to be accounted from an ensueing the first printing of the same"). A later draft of the bill is included among the papers of Archbishop Tenison at Lambeth Palace Library (shelfmark Codices Tenisoniana, 640:17).
46. Locke to John Freke and Edward Clarke, December 2, 1695, *Correspondence*, 5:471.
47. See Ronan Deazley, *On the Origin of the Right to Copy: Charting the Movement of Copyright Law in Eighteenth-Century Britain (1695–1775)* (Oxford: Hart, 2004), 10–29; Feather, *Publishing, Piracy, and Politics* (cited in note 19), 51–63; John Feather, "The Book Trade in Politics: The Making of the Copyright Act of 1710," *Publishing History* 8 (1980): 19.
48. Archibald Campbell, *The Sale of Authors: A Dialogue, in Imitation of Lucian's Sale of Philosophers* (London: [s.n.], 1767), 5. Similarly, an anonymous essayist observed in 1751 that "there is no statute law enacted against this kind of theft." *The Student: Or, The Oxford and Cambridge Monthly Miscellany* (Oxford: Newbury, 1751), 2:211. Arthur Murphy, a playwright and barrister, found himself unable to decide about the permissibility of the "Kind of Imitation . . . which consists in adopting the Sentiments and Phrases

of others," concluding that its "Legality is yet a Question." *The Gray's-Inn Journal*, no. 16 (February 3, 1752/1753, reprinted in *The Gray's-Inn Journal*, 2 vols. (London: Vaillant, 1756), 1:107. For more on Murphy and copyright law, see Richard W. Schoch, " 'A Supplement to the Public Laws': Arthur Murphy, David Garrick, and *Hamlet, with Alterations*," *Theatre Journal* 57, no. 1 (2005): 21–32; Don Nichol, "Arthur Murphy's Law: The Man Who Won the First Decisive Battle in the Literary Property Wars," *Times Literary Supplement* 4855 (April 19, 1996): 15–16; Judith Milhous and Robert D. Hume, "Profits from Play Publication: The Evidence of *Murphy v. Vaillant*," *Studies in Bibliography* 51 (1998): 213–229.

49. David A. Brewer, *The Afterlife of Character, 1726–1825* (Philadelphia: University of Pennsylvania Press, 2005), documents numerous examples of such sequels; see also Thomas Keymer and Peter Sabor, "Literary Property and the Trade in Continuations," in *"Pamela" in the Marketplace: Literary Controversy and Print Culture in Eighteenth-Century Britain and Ireland* (Cambridge: Cambridge University Press, 2005), 50–82; Betty A. Schellenberg, "'The Measured Lines of the Copyist': Sequels, Reviews, and the Discourse of Authorship in England, 1749–1800," in *On Second Thought: Updating the Eighteenth-Century Text*, ed. Debra Taylor Bourdeau (Newark: University of Delaware Press, 2007), 25–42, esp. 26, 29–30.
50. Iona Italia notes that the Act of Anne "only applied to publication in volume form and did not affect periodicals" and that many magazines "were scissors-and-paste operations, offering little or no original material. . . . Many of the same tales, letters, poems, and essays were reprinted on numerous occasions in many different publications." Italia, *The Rise of Literary Journalism in the Eighteenth Century: Anxious Employment* (New York: Routledge, 2005), 20, 21. (See Italia, 110–114, for further elaboration of this point.) As Christine Y. Ferdinand observes, "Even more than other periodicals, the magazines capitalized on this practice [of reprinting articles], taking the name—*magazine*—from this characteristic." Ferdinand, *Benjamin Collins and the Provincial Newspaper Trade in the Eighteenth Century* (Oxford: Clarendon Press, 1997), 146.
51. *Gyles v. Wilcox*, 26 Eng. Rep. 489, 490 (Ch. 1740). Jane C. Ginsburg suggests that by establishing a "fair abridgment doctrine," *Gyles* shows that copyright protected more than the antipiracy provisions of the Act of Anne, so that authors' rights were greater (and the public domain correspondingly smaller) than the statute's terms would imply. Ginsburg, " 'Une Chose Publique'?: The Author's Domain and the Public Domain in Early British, French, and US Copyright Law," *Cambridge Law Journal* 65, no. 3 (2006): 647–648. The language of *Gyles* might appear to carry that implication, but in practice, the "fair abridgment doctrine" created only the most miniscule limitation on the public domain. The abridgment cases generally display a presumption that the work is available for other writers to use.
52. These arguments from the counsels' pleadings (now housed at the Public Records Office in Kew) are quoted by Deazley in *On the Origin of the Right to Copy*, 82.
53. "In *Gyles v. Wilcox*, the abridgment contained 35 sheets, the original 275; it was referred to an award and held a fair abridgment." *Tonson v. Walker*, 36 Eng. Rep. 1017, 1020 (Ch. 1752).
54. Deazley, *On the Origin of the Right to Copy*, 82. No copies of Wilcox's publication seem to have survived.
55. "[Dodsley's] argument rested on the fact that the best parts, the moral reflections, had been edited from the abridgment and only the plot remained. This was his only course of action because in 1761 the one [potentially] successful

argument against the abridgment [was] that the abridgment devalued rather than enhanced Johnson's novel." William J. Howard, "Literature in the Law Courts, 1770–1800," in *Editing Eighteenth-Century Texts*, ed. D. I. B. Smith (Toronto: University of Toronto Press, 1968), 87. See also William F. Patry, *The Fair Use Privilege in Copyright Law* (Washington, DC: BNA, 1985), 8 n.11.

56. 27 Eng. Rep. 270, 271 (Ch. 1761).
57. *Strahan v. Newbery*, 98 Eng. Rep. 913 (Ch. 1774). For a discussion of the facts and the background to the litigation, see Mark Leeming, "Hawkesworth's *Voyages*: The First 'Australian' Copyright Litigation," *Australian Journal of Legal History* 9, no. 2 (2005), 159–173. The action is styled merely as "Curia Cancellaria" (i.e., "Court of Chancery") in Lofft's report and has been designated by others variously as "Newbery's Case" and "*Hawkesworth v. Newbery*." Strahan, who was the publisher or Lofft's report, evidently preferred not to mention his role in the litigation. See Leeming, 172.
58. The two cases—*Austen v. Cave* and *Hitch v. Langley*—are discussed in Deazley, *On the Origin of the Right to Copy*, 79–80. In the first case, Hardwicke observed that piracies are impermissible "whether you print all at once or not." Ibid., 80.
59. *Tonson v. Walker*, 36 Eng. Rep. 1017, 1020 (Ch. 1752).
60. Ibid. Deazley explains the parties' litigating positions and the previous twenty years worth of Chancery case law that Tonson's counsel invoked (and recharacterized) to sabotage his opponent's argument based on the term limits in the Act of Anne. Deazley, *On the Origin of the Right to Copy*, 133–136.
61. *Macklin v. Richardson*, 27 Eng. Rep. 451, 452 (1770). Richardson's main argument was that, because Macklin had arranged for the play to be performed publicly and had not published it himself, he "gave a right to any of the audience to carry away what they could, and make any use of it." Ibid. It was only after this argument failed that Richardson called his publication an abridgment. For further discussion of the background to this case, see W. Matthews, "The Piracies of Macklin's *Love-à-la-Mode*," *Review of English Studies* 10, no. 39 (1934): 311–318.
62. Ibid.
63. It should also be noted that in *Read v. Hodges* (Ch. 1740), the court ultimately refused to enjoin the publication of a one-volume abridgment of the plaintiff's three-volume biography of Peter the Great. The court granted a temporary injunction against the publisher of the abridgment, but then compared the two publications and lifted the injunction. The case was not published in a reporter, but is discussed in Deazley, *On the Origin of the Right to Copy*, 81–82.
64. *Millar v. Taylor*, 98 Eng. Rep. 205 (K. B. 1769) (per Willes, J.) (explaining that the category of "new works" protected by the statute includes "bona fide imitations, translations and abridgments"). For a fuller discussion of the eighteenth-century case law on abridgements and the like, see Deazley, *On the Origin of the Right to Copy*, 79–85; Melissa de Zwart, "A Historical Analysis of the Birth of Fair Dealing and Fair Use: Lessons for the Digital Age," *Intellectual Property Quarterly*, no. 1 (2007): 74–79; Robert Burrell and Allison Coleman, *Copyright Exceptions: The Digital Impact* (Cambridge: Cambridge University Press, 2005), 254–256. On the origins of derivative rights, see L. Ray Patterson, "*Folsom v. Marsh* and Its Legacy," *Journal of Intellectual Property Law* 5 (1998): 431–452.
65. *A Vindication of the Exclusive Rights of Authors to Their Own Works* (London: Griffiths, 1762), 14. This explanation finds a striking parallel in

the delineation of "originality" in *CCH Canadian Ltd. v. Law Society of Upper Canada* [2004] 1 SCR 339 (para. 35), in which the Court held that the reporter's headnotes in judicial decisions were protected by copyright because they exhibited "skill and judgment," but that the reporter's rendition of the decisions themselves were not protected, because "the publishers add[ed] only basic factual information . . . [and] correct[ed] minor grammatical errors and spelling mistakes. Any skill and judgment . . . involved in making these minor changes and additions . . . are too trivial to warrant copyright protection." On the treatment of originality in *CCH* by contrast with *University of London Press* and *Feist*, see Drassinower, note 15, and Drassinower, "Sweat of the Brow, Creativity, and Authorship: On Originality in Canadian Copyright Law," *University of Ottowa Law & Technology Journal* 1, no. 2 (2004): 105–133.

66. *A Vindication of the Exclusive Rights of Authors*, 9. In a book review, William Kenrick approved this view, observing that "he who obtaineth the copy of a book, may appropriate the stock of ideas contained therein, and, by opposing such sentiments, may give birth to a new doctrine." *Monthly Review* 27 (1762): 183. Writing twelve years later, in the wake of the *Donaldson* opinion, Kenrick observed that under the statute, "it does by no means appear that *abstracts, abridgments and compilations* (of which the greater number of new books now published consist) are at all contrary to law." William Kenrick, *An Address to the Artists and Manufacturers of Great Britain* (London: Domville, 1774), 65 (italics in original). For more on Kenrick and his views on literary recycling, see Brewer, *The Afterlife of Character*, 12, 87–95.
67. Oren Bracha similarly observes that "[t]he image of the romantic original author was not even uniformly accepted in theory [in eighteenth-century England]. In copyright doctrine it was hardly present." Bracha, *Owning Ideas: A History of Anglo-American Intellectual Property* (S. J. D., dissertation, Harvard Law School, 2005), 234.
68. Blackstone, *Commentaries*, 2:405–406. Quoted in Rose, *Authors and Owners*, 115.
69. Rose, *Authors and Owners*, 115.
70. For example, in the course of a cogent discussion of the process by which "literature became a form of commerce [so that] writers had a new reason to display their uniqueness," John Hope Mason draws on Rose's discussion of Blackstone and Hargrave. Mason, *The Value of Creativity: The Origins and Emergence of a Modern Belief* (London: Ashgate, 2003), 109–110 and 265 nn.33–34. Similarly, Catherine Fisk cites Rose's discussion for the view that, in this discussion of the "original work," Blackstone was "stat[ing] the classic mixed-labor and genius-based justification for copyright." Fisk, "Authors at Work: The Origins of the Work-for-Hire Doctrine," *Yale Journal of Law & the Humanities* 15, no. 1 (2003): 12. Others have concluded that Blackstone would protect not only the language of the text, but also the author's style. See, e.g., Hannibal Travis, "Pirates of the Information Infrastructure: Blackstonian Copyright and the First Amendment," *Berkeley Technology Law Journal* 15, no. 2 (2000): 782; Richard R. Yeo, *Encyclopaedic Visions: Scientific Dictionaries and Enlightenment Culture* (Cambridge: Cambridge University Press, 2001), 203. Finally, some have concluded more generally, on the basis of Rose's discussion, that novelty was regarded as a prerequisite for legal ownership of the work. See, e.g., David Higgins, *Romantic Genius and the Literary Magazine* (London: Routledge, 2005), 5, 152 n.16; Martin A. Kayman, "Lawful Writing: Common Law, Statute and the Properties of Literature," *New Literary History* 27, no. 4 (1996): 774, 783 n.46; Ellen Gardiner, *Regulating Readers: Gender and*

Literary Criticism in the Eighteenth-Century Novel (Cranbury, NJ: University of Delaware Press, 1999), 39.

71. Blackstone, *Commentaries*, 2:405–406.
72. *Cary v. Kearsley*, 170 Eng. Rep. 679, 679 (K. B. 1802).
73. John Trusler, *An Essay on Literary Property* (London: Printed for the author, 1798), 15 (italics added).
74. Blackstone even went so far as to endorse the practice of abridgment, helping Lord Chancellor Apsley to conclude, in the case of Hawkesworth's *Voyages*, that Newbery's version was "allowable and meritorious." According to Lofft's report of the case, Apsley sought Blackstone's aid, and after "spen[ding] some hours together," they concluded that, despite the verbatim repetition of material from the source, Newbery's abridgment eliminated various "unnecessary and uninteresting circumstances" and was "not an act of plagiarism upon the original work, nor against any property of the author in it." *Strahan v. Newbery*, 98 Eng. Rep. 913 (Ch. 1774).
75. *Rambler* 143 (July 30, 1751). Hurd's essay, published two months earlier (see note 77), may have inspired Johnson's.
76. Ibid. Johnson returned to theme, and the legal rhetoric, in *Adventurer* 95 (October 2, 1753), reprinted in *The Adventurer* (London: Payne, 1753), 2:145–150. Similarly, Boswell, in an essay published a quarter century later in the *London Magazine*, wrote that "the sameness or similarity which we frequently find between passages in different authors cannot be with absolute certainty ascribed to its proper origin unless where there is a passage of considerable length in one author, which we can discover in the very same words in another author." James Boswell, *The Hypochondriack*, ed. Margery Bailey, 2 vols. (Stanford: Stanford University Press, 1928) 1:276 (essay originally published in July 1779).
77. Richard Hurd, *Q. Horatii Flacci Epistola ad Augustum. With an English Commentary and Notes. To Which Is Added, A Discourse Concerning Poetical Imitation* (Cambridge: Thurlbourn, 1751), 186 (italics in original). Hurd's book was published on May 21, 1751; see Sarah Brewer, ed., *The Early Letters of Bishop Richard Hurd, 1739–1762* (Woodbridge, Suffolk: Boydell Press, 1995), 223 n. 2. Hurd would return to these issues in *A Letter to Mr. Mason; on the Marks of Imitation* (London: Dodsley, 1757), which in turn provoked Edward Capell's *Reflections on Originality in Authors, Being Remarks on A Letter to Mr. Mason on the Marks of Imitation: In Which the Absurd Defects of That Performance Are Pointed out, and the Absolute Uncertainty of Imitation in General Is Demonstrated in Various Instances* (London: Horsfield, 1766). For more on Hurd, see Richard Terry, " 'In Pleasing Memory of All He Stole': Plagiarism and Literary Detraction, 1747–1785," in *Plagiarism in Early Modern England*, ed. Paulina Kewes (New York: Palgrave, 2003): 181–200; Bertrand Goldgar, "Imitation and Plagiarism: The Lauder Affair and Its Aftermath," *Studies in the Literary Imagination* 34 (2001): 1–16. John W. Draper provides a useful summation of changing attitudes toward literary imitation in "Aristotelian 'Mimesis' in Eighteenth Century England," *PMLA* 36, no. 3 (1921): 372–400, esp. 386–387.
78. Hurd, *Discourse Concerning Poetical Imitation*, 177, 183. For more examples of the same argument, see Arthur Murphy's *Gray's-Inn Journal* essay, cited in note 48; Joseph Warton, *Adventurer* 63 (June 12, 1753), reprinted in *The Adventurer* (London: Payne, 1753), 1:373–378.
79. Hurd, *Discourse Concerning Poetical Imitation*, 114, 112.
80. Blackstone to George Steevens, 1 April 1779, in *The Letters of Sir William Blackstone, 1744–1780*, ed. W. R. Prest (London: Selden Society, 2006),

178. Thanks to Wilf Prest for bringing this letter to my attention. In identifying these parallel passages, without adducing them as evidence of plagiarism or lack of wit by the later author, Blackstone was engaging in a popular literary pastime that is also illustrated in Hurd's and Johnson's examples. Its popularity suggests, again, that originality as novelty was not the only measure of poetic excellence.

81. In addition to the sources cited in note 70, see, e.g., Jane M. Gaines, *Contested Culture: The Image, the Voice, and the Law* (Chapel Hill: University of North Carolina Press, 1991), 62–63; Rebecca Elisabeth Connor, *Women, Accounting, and Narrative: Keeping Books in Eighteenth-Century England* (New York: Routledge, 2004), 144–145.
82. Francis Hargrave, *An Argument in Defence of Literary Property*, 2nd ed. (London, 1774), 6–7. Quoted in Rose, *Authors and Owners*, 125.
83. Rose, *Authors and Owners*, 126.
84. Ibid., 126.
85. Ibid., 127.
86. See Warburton's anonymous *A Letter From an Author to a Member of Parliament Concerning Literary Property* (London: Knapton, 1747). As noted above, another procopyright pamphlet, *A Vindication of the Exclusive Right of Authors to Their Own Works*, expressly rejects the idea that originality is a prerequisite for copyright.
87. *An Enquiry Into the Nature and Origin of Literary Property* (London: Flexney, 1762). For more on this pamphlet, see Don Nichol, "Warburton (Not!) on Copyright: Clearing up the Misattribution of *An Enquiry into the Nature and Origin of Literary Property* (1762)," *British Journal for Eighteenth-Century Studies* 19, no. 2 (1996): 171–182. The pamphlet has occasionally been misattributed to Warburton; Nichol speculates that Arthur Murphy may have been the author. See also Chris Mounsey, *Christopher Smart: Clown of God* (Lewisburg, PA: Bucknell University Press, 2001), 262–264, which considers the possibility that Christopher Smart was the author and discusses Smart's relations with William Flexney, the pamphlet's publisher.
88. *Enquiry*, 12.
89. Ibid., 13–14. Similarly, Lord Kames, declining to find a common-law copyright in *Hinton v. Donaldson*, pronounced Hogarth to be "the only truly original author which this age has produced in England" and concluded that a doctrine protecting original works would entail a prohibition against taking the author's "ideas, his sense and meaning, which is really his literary property, from him." Kames sarcastically added, citing the example of Bays, the plagiarist in Buckingham's *The Rehearsal*, that this view of literary property could amount to a prohibition against "stealing wit from conversation." James Boswell, *The Decision of the Court of Session, upon the Question of Literary Property; in the Cause [of] John Hinton of London, Bookseller, Pursuer; against Alexander Donaldson* (Edinburgh: Donaldson, 1774), 24, 25.
90. *Feist Publications, Inc. v. Rural Telephone Service Co.*, 499 U.S. 340, 345 (1991) (internal quotation marks and citation omitted). *Feist*'s treatment of originality has provoked extensive discussion; some of the most useful contributions include Diane Leenheer Zimmerman, "It's an Original! (?): In Pursuit of Copyright's Elusive Essence," *Columbia Journal of Law & the Arts* 28, no. 2 (2005): 187–212; Daniel J. Gervais, "*Feist* Goes Global: A Comparative Analysis of the Notion of Originality in Copyright Law," *Journal of the Copyright Society of the USA* 49 (2002): 949–981; Russ VerSteeg, "Rethinking Originality," *William & Mary Law Review* 34, no. 3 (1993): 801–883.

91. Under 8 Anne c. 19, subsec. II, infringing publications were to be turned over to the "proprietor or proprietors thereof, who shall forthwith damask, and make waste paper of them."
92. According to Richard Terry, "The Augustan Age was first great age of parody, the period in which it became both prolific and mainstream." Terry, "The Circumstances of Eighteenth-Century Parody," *Eighteenth-Century Life* 15, no. 3 (1991): 76.
93. Robert L. Mack, *The Genius of Parody: Imitation and Originality in Seventeenth- and Eighteenth Century English Literature* (New York: Palgrave Macmillan, 2007), 72, 73.
94. Ibid., 72.
95. Ibid., 74.
96. Richmond P. Bond, *English Burlesque Poetry, 1700–1750* (Cambridge, MA: Harvard University Press, 1932), 19.
97. Mack, *The Genius of Parody*, 147, 153–156.
98. Bond, *English Burlesque Poetry*, 276–277, 290–291 (Pope); 325–329 (Philips); 357–358, 363–364, 369–370 (Cibber). Moyra Haslett remarks that, "[i]n the disputatious print culture of the eighteenth century, parodies, burlesques, and absurd imitations were deployed more frequently than any other kind of attack." Haslett, *Pope to Burney, 1714–1779: Scriblerians to Bluestockings* (New York: Palgrave Macmillan, 2003), 228.
99. Marcus, "Epitaph," *London Chronicle*, July 27–29, 1769, 103. For more examples (such as "An Elegy Wrote under a Gallows," 1770; "Hackfall: An Elegy," 1772), see Clark Sutherland Northup, *A Bibliography of Thomas Gray* (New Haven: Yale University Press, 1917), 123–144.
100. *Campbell v. Acuff-Rose Music, Inc.*, 510 U.S. 569 (1994).
101. Ibid., 584, citing James Boswell, *The Life of Johnson*, ed. G. B. Hill, 6 vols. (Oxford: Clarendon Press, 1934), 3:19.
102. James Boswell, *Journal of a Tour of the Hebrides* [with Samuel Johnson, *A Journey to the Western Islands of Scotland*], ed. Allan Wendt (Boston: Houghton Mifflin, 1965), 162 (entry for March 20). As a poet, critic, journalist, and editor who knew a good deal about the economics of publishing, Johnson expressed shifting views on literary property and the public domain that are not easily summarized in a pair of quotations. For further discussion, see Edward A. Bloom, "Samuel Johnson on Copyright," *Journal of English and Germanic Philology* 47, no. 2 (1948): 165–172; Alvin Kernan, *Samuel Johnson and the Impact of Print* (Princeton: Princeton University Press, 1987), 101–102; and Kevin Hart, *Samuel Johnson and the Culture of Property* (Cambridge: Cambridge University Press, 1999), 71.
103. J. M. S. Tompkins, *The Popular Novel in England, 1770–1800* (London: Constable, 1932), 34. To show how readily the examples come to hand, Tompkins documents her point with six novels published in the space of six years—1771 to 1776 (34 n. 1).
104. For example, reviewers of gothic novels in the 1790s complained widely about the "vapid and servile imitations" of Ann Radcliffe's fiction, as Lauren Fitzgerald notes in "The Gothic Villain and the Vilification of the Plagiarist: The Case of *The Castle Spectre*," *Gothic Studies* 7, no. 1 (2005): 5.
105. For a discussion of the doctrine, see Francis M. Nevins, Jr. "Copyright + Character = Catastrophe," *Journal of the Copyright Society of the U.S.A.* 39 (1992): 303–344.
106. See note 73.
107. Louisa-Jayne Stark, Timothy J. Perfect, and Stephen E. Newstead, "When Elaboration Leads to Appropriation: Unconscious Plagiarism in a Creative

Task," *Memory* 13, no. 6 (2005): 561–573; see also Louisa-Jayne Stark and Timothy J. Perfect, "Elaboration Inflation: How Your Ideas Become Mine," *Applied Cognitive Science* 20, no. 5 (2006): 641–648.

108. As the authors put it, "real-life plagiarists inevitably think about appropriated ideas and accordingly invest considerable time and efforts in these ideas." Stark et al., "When Elaboration Leads to Appropriation," 562.

4 On Plagiarism, Originality, Textual Ownership, and Textual Responsibility

The Case of *Jacques le fataliste*

Anne Sechin

While some scholars question the relevance of comparing fields of knowledge as far apart as literary aesthetics and legal philosophy,[1] others wonder why so little research has been done at the crossroads of two closely related areas.[2] The emergence of originality as an aesthetic category appears to coincide with the legal birth of intellectual property. As Linda Zionkowski has observed, not only is the former connected to the latter, but both concepts depend on the rise of individuality: "Northrop Frye and R.G. Collingwood both relate the modern stress on individualism in art to copyright—the legal enforcement of originality. But while it encourages originality by law, copyright itself is not responsible for 'aesthetic individualism.'"[3] Prior to the eighteenth century, individuality was seen in a negative light. If we have learned to consider intellectual ownership and the afferent legal concepts as "natural," they did not always appear as such.[4] Reviewing the emergence of "originality" as an aesthetic category in relation to copyright laws will help us look more critically at individuality and originality during a period when they were not taken for granted.

Diderot's *Jacques le fataliste* is relevant to this debate not only because it appears, chronologically, before French copyright laws and after classicism,[5] but also because it exemplifies the paradox of originality as an aesthetic value. It also provides a literary illustration of Diderot's views on aesthetic and legal matters, which he had considered in his *Salons* and *Letter on the Book Trade*. Studying *Jacques le fataliste* in this perspective allows us to show the legal side of what appears to be only an aesthetic question while underlining the aesthetic assumptions pertaining to originality in legal texts.

Let us start from an aesthetic point of view in an attempt to shed some light on the philosophical grounds that sustain the legal notion of intellectual property. Diderot, more than any other eighteenth-century figure, catalyzes the convergence of intellectual property, originality, and plagiarism. Concerning intellectual property, he wrote his *Letter on the Book Trade*, a text largely misinterpreted today because of the lens of "copyright righteousness" through which it is read. With respect to originality, Diderot was perceived as an "original," and he created the two most famous literary "originals" of his times: Rameau's Nephew and Jacques. As to plagiarism, the accusations that the authors of the *Encyclopedia* had to defend themselves against are well known, and, though it remains largely unsaid, most Diderot scholars *know* that Diderot plagiarized.[6] As regards *Jacques le fataliste* specifically, it is worth noting that Diderot worked on this novel between 1765 and 1783, that is to say after six of his *Salons*, after his *Letter on the Book Trade* (1763 or 1764[7]), and after *Rameau's Nephew* (begun in 1761–1762)—in other words, at a time when his thoughts on what constitutes originality and intellectual ownership had come to maturity.

Surprisingly few scholars have given careful consideration to eighteenth-century notions of originality, either in aesthetic terms or as related to copyright. Roland Mortier wrote an essay on the transition from the concepts of ideal beauty and mimesis to "the aesthetics of surprise and shock" and, more specifically, an article summarizing Diderot's views on originality. Although Mortier mentions the ambivalence this notion acquires during the Enlightenment period, he depicts a quite clear transition between the seventeenth century, where an "original" is to be understood as a model to be imitated, and the eighteenth century, where an original is a "prospector of new forms" who rejects models, who "may be of bad taste, but never leaves us indifferent,"[8] thereby emphasizing the peculiar, unique, and exceptional character of the individual.

We can easily understand now that the matter is more complex than it first appears. If in the seventeenth century mimesis was an imitation of models, it must have undergone some shift in a world that no longer believed in such imitation. A further change would have had to occur from the dominant aesthetic principle of "good taste" to an aesthetics of effect, aimed at producing surprise. By abandoning a world in which there was an ideal beauty to be imitated and an aesthetic standard to be trusted, one would arrive at an unprecedented aesthetic responsibility.

As illustrated by recent cases of plagiarism, the heightened importance of originality in aesthetics that influenced the eighteenth-century legal debate on intellectual property is still fundamental in present-day legislation. It would seem crucial, then, to consider contemporary perspectives on copyright and to define the modern notion of textual ownership. According to Martha Woodmansee, an author is "an individual . . . solely responsible—and therefore exclusively deserving of credit—for the production of a unique work." Authorship, as such, is based not only on originality, but entails the notions of "individuality," "responsibility," and "unique work." Individuality is associated with the ability to distinguish oneself from the group, and "unique work," renouncing imitation of models, implies the denial of a stable aesthetic reference, placing authority and responsibility in the hands of the individual producing the work. *Originality, then, asserts the individual against the group or the group's interest.*

According to Woodmansee, the emergence of the idea of the "original author" also entails "a minimization of the element of craftsmanship in favour of the element of inspiration." Whereas the author was previously considered a mere vehicle for the truth and the difference from one author to the next was a difference in craftsmanship, Woodmansee describes a gradual secularization of the notion of inspiration, formerly equated with God's intervention and now perceived as "emanating from within the writer himself."[9] The author, as such, is no longer an ordinary person learning a trade, receiving inspiration from God, and acting as a vehicle for the truth. Rather, he is a magical being, possessing inner qualities that enable him to create truth or beauty out of thin air. The fact that "inspiration" had a "sacred" meaning and did not yet apply to writers is illustrated by the article on "Inspiration" in the *Encyclopedia*.[10]

The modern notion of authorship coincides, moreover, according to Woodmansee, with a shift away from the notion that "writing was considered a mere vehicle of received ideas which were already in the public domain."[11] What we see here, then, is a subtle transition from classical aesthetics, where truth belongs to everyone and where the individual strives for self-denial, to romantic aesthetics, where emphasis is on "the individual rather than the collective." In a preoriginality world, the "public domain" was the eternal truth that belonged to everyone and that served the collectivity. The individual was expected to disappear behind the text.

A further ideological shift was necessary before the notion of intellectual property could take hold. As Woodmansee and Jazsi have observed, "to merit copyright, an 'expression' must be 'fixed.'"[12] Although we may now take this for granted, for many centuries, literary production was far from being fixed. Diderot considers this question in his *Letter on the Book Trade*, complaining, for instance, about the printing permissions that were to be renewed only if the work was proven to be augmented at least by a quarter of its volume:

> I confess to feeling highly indignant at these successive reprints that have shrunk my library to a quarter of its worth in ten years. But beyond that, should an author be kept from continuously correcting the errors he finds, deleting what is superfluous and adding what is missing in his work? Could the bookseller not be required to distribute the additions, corrections, deletions and changes separately, with each reprint?[13]

This objection to fixed form is even better illustrated in Diderot's literary works. *Jacques le fataliste*, for instance, was written over a period of nearly two decades and was transformed by several addenda.[14] As Mark Rose points out, "copyright depends on drawing lines between works, on saying where one text ends and another begins,"[15] which in turn raises the question not only of intertextuality, but also of borrowings, plagiarism, and quotations.

In the evolution from classicism to premodernism, on the one hand, and the development of the contemporary notion of authorship, on the other hand, where does *Jacques le fataliste* fit in? What do Diderot's texts, and particularly *Jacques le fataliste*, tell us about this pivotal period when aesthetic values were shifting? On the one hand, Diderot is seen as a precursor of the modern (possibly even the postmodern) novel, whereas, on the other hand, he is solemnly condemned by posterity for his views on copyright because he is usually thought to have sided in his *Letter on the Book Trade* with the rich and powerful against economic compensation for writers. We may wonder whether there is a way to reconcile these two contradictory assessments and whether *Jacques le fataliste* conforms to the modern notion of authorship considered as the result of inspiration, where the author is "solely responsible for the production of a unique work" and the text is set within a "fixed expression."

If we are to search for indicators of a modern notion of authorship as it may appear in *Jacques le fataliste*, we must begin by acknowledging that Diderot never favored inspiration over craftsmanship. On the contrary, he often asserted that the writer is a worker. Indeed, in his *Letter on the Book Trade*, he refers to a writer's property as "the fruit of his education, of his studies, of his wakes, of his time, of his research and observations,"[16] thus describing the author as a worker and basing intellectual property on the Lockean notion of property, based itself on labor. The fact that "inspiration" according to the *Encyclopedia* does not pertain to secular writing confirms the notion that secular writing is the result of work, rather than outside intervention. If in *Jacques* the author is often mirrored by a narrator who is describing his own writing in a postmodern way, this is done with great pride. The narrator repeatedly praises his own craftsmanship and justifies his status as an "author" by asserting regularly that it is easy to write novels. He nevertheless cultivates his reputation by reminding us of his skills—namely, how much he knows about writing techniques, as well as about other works: he is skillful and knowledgeable. The chosen medium, however (i.e. the novel and the impression of improvisation it is associated with) implies a minimization of craftsmanship when compared, for instance, with a full-fledged tragedy adhering to classical rules. This does not, however, prevent the narrator-author from showcasing his craftsmanship, effort, and skill, as, for instance, when he talks about the degree of hardship involved in giving us the letter written by Mme de la Pommeraye: "Although writing that one would have been difficult in a different way from Agathe's letter, and even though I don't presume too much on my talent, I think I could have pulled it off."[17]

A writer, then, is above all depicted as a craftsman. Does this leave any room for inspiration? Although the best stories in the novel are admittedly reworked versions of other previously told ones, inspiration has particular importance for Jacques, whose ability to speak is largely dependent on wine:

> When destiny became mute in his head, he took counsel by the gourd; it was a sort of portable Pythia, which was silenced the instant it was empty. At Delphi, the Pythia, with skirts pulled up, and seated barebottomed on her tripod, received her inspiration from the bottom up; Jacques, on his horse, his head turned up toward heaven, his gourd uncorked and the mouth of the vessel near his own, received inspiration from the top down. When the Pythia and Jacques pronounced their oracles, both were drunk. (207)

The notion of inspiration is obviously mocked here as the "barebottomed" Pythia invites us to laugh at a sacred notion of inspiration nobody believes in (unlike the Christian notion of inspiration we found in the *Encylcopedia*). So in what can seem to be a somewhat confusing passage, inspiration is equated with intoxication, fantasy, and disrespect for rigid rules. Inscribed in a tradition of (pagan) disrespect, folly, and disorder, and by no means taken seriously, inspiration in this novel is largely equated with passivity, lack of will, and lack of talent. Accordingly, it becomes the Master's prerogative: "If . . . you . . . choose to keep the master company, you will be polite but very bored. You don't know that type of fellow. He has very few ideas in his head; if he happens to say something that makes sense, it's either from memory or momentary *inspiration*" (24, my emphasis). Indeed, the only thing the Master says that impresses us or Jacques is taken from Dante. When Jacques compliments his Master, congratulating him on the fact that his "imagery is charming," the latter replies: "It's not mine. I read it, I believe, in some Italian poet named Dante, who wrote a work entitled: *The Comedy of Hell, Purgatory and Paradise*" (182). Other than this rather exceptional moment of both "memory" and "inspiration," the master is the epitome of flatness, stiffness, and predictability. From his "Nothing multiplies like the rabble" (20) to his "Just one of those strange whims of women, impossible to understand" (187), the master takes material from the "public domain," as do Jacques and the Landlady, but with different results. Taking from the public domain is no more a determining factor in establishing a text's aesthetic quality than originality is reliant on rejecting or adopting imitation.

The Master, we are told, is interesting only occasionally in moments of "memory" (that is to say, when he has memorized Dante) or "inspiration." It is noteworthy that both terms are associated in *Jacques le fataliste* with haphazard appearances of talent: that is to say, when the text is a success only by accident (the Master quotes Dante and commonsense maxims without necessarily making the difference, so he does not do it knowingly or intentionally) or when by chance and not through any effort whatsoever he produces something, that is, inspiration. Inspiration and memory, then, are opposed to skill, work, and knowledge. According to our current notions of aesthetics, memory and inspiration are on opposite ends of the spectrum: inspiration is not equated to passivity and lack of will and in no way stands comparison with works produced by memory only. So if in *Jacques*'s world it is not in rejecting or adopting imitation that aesthetic value is to be found, it is not "inspiration" either that distinguishes a good textual production from a bad one because inspiration is mocked as being passive, external, and foolish.

The second element we noted as being constitutive of the emergence of the modern notion of authorship was the shift away from the idea that writing belonged to the public domain because it was thought of as a vehicle for truth. This implies, of course, the novel's relationship to other works.

Diderot scholars will immediately think of his ability to make someone else's thoughts his own (a quality used by Diderot's enemies to discredit him) and will associate *Les Bijoux Indiscrets* with Crébillon's *Le Sopha*. They will recall what *La Religieuse* owes to Richardson and what *Jacques le fataliste* owes to *Tristram Shandy*. When Jean Starobinski underlines these borrowings, he quotes what Diderot said about Shaftesbury: "I read him over and over again. I was imbued with his spirit and shut my book, so to speak, when I picked up my pen. Never has anyone so freely partaken of another's work."[18]

We commonly read that *Jacques le fataliste* is a modern novel. Although valid to some degree, this line of interpretation has unfortunately distracted us from the fact that, in many respects, Diderot's novel bears closer resemblance to Scarron's *Roman comique*, Lesage's *Gil Blas*, or Cervantes's *Don Quixote* than to the novels of Butor or Robbe-Grillet. It is also closer philosophically to the previous centuries than it is to the *Nouveau Roman*, with which it is often associated. Echoes from sixteenth- and seventeenth-century texts resonate throughout *Jacques*, which makes use of literary practices reminiscent of the Renaissance. In keeping with the melting pot of the almost universal public domain, Diderot composed his novel as a patchwork of collated texts and second-hand discourses. Jacques, for instance, has no pretense of having created his own philosophy. He tells us that it was imparted to him by his Captain, who found it in Spinoza: "[Jacques]'s captain had filled Jacques's head with all these ideas drained out of Spinoza, which he knew by heart" (166–167). Similarly, the narrator who calls himself the author retells the story of Aesop (45), and most of the embedded stories are not said to have been produced either by pure genius or divine intervention, but rather to be borrowed from a common bank, as is the case even with those of one of the book's most masterful storytellers, the Landlady: "It makes an interesting story . . . I should tell it you exactly as their servant told it to my servant, who happened by chance to be from her part of the country. She told it to my husband and he told it to me" (84). What seems to matter is not so much the uniqueness of the story or the narrator's exclusive capacity to produce a discourse. Narrators, even the one calling himself the author, willingly help themselves to the large melting pot of freely circulating textual matter.

So, whether the story is borrowed, repeated, or modified has essentially no bearing on its aesthetic quality. This, however, does not prevent Diderot from experimenting with copying and repeating. On the contrary, plagiarism is taken to its extreme limits, whereby texts are copied and creatively displaced from their original contexts. The clearest example of this practice is in a passage where the Master, "like a parrot" (47), repeats word for word a funeral oration so as to console Jacques from the pain he feels in thinking of his Captain's death: although the text is formally plagiarized, modifying its context causes a shift in meaning. From an aesthetic point of view, it is worth noting that what matters here is neither form nor originality, but rather the effect produced: the Master achieves his desired result as Jacques is so surprised that he stops crying. The attitude pervasive of this novel promotes borrowing from what is perceived as an almost universal public domain and where texts, discourses, and stories are intended to be circulated, transformed, and retold. The constantly shifting meaning of a text is brought to the fore along with the various changes it must undergo through its successive interpretations. The nature of a text is to be in perpetual flux. Aesthetic criteria do not derive from the consideration given to a particular work as opposed to others (the "distinguishing" originality by which one work can clearly be differentiated from all others), but from a shift from formal aesthetics to what Mortier calls the "aesthetics of effect."[19] What is noteworthy, however, is that those strategies and explorations (including where the text is aimed less at producing meaning than an immediate emotional effect, as in the funeral oration) introduce a mechanism whereby the truth appears relative and where immutability is questioned.

As regards the association between fixed expression and copyright, we may note that *Jacques le fataliste* is the result of successive reworkings. The patchwork-like character of the novel reminds us that it evolved over a period of nearly twenty years, beginning in 1765. If there is any unity or fixed form to be assigned to this novel, as is the case today probably as a result of copyright laws, we owe this perhaps less to the author than to his editors.

Although its genesis is relevant to the denial of fixed expression, the structure of this novel seems even more opposed to the notion of textual stability. Several episodes in *Jacques le fataliste*, as in the following passage, question the work's unity: "There are two versions as to what happened after he blew out the lights. . . . Of these two versions, tomorrow, or the next day, having rested your weary head, you may take your choice of the one you like better" (150–151). Dividing the narrative into two equally valid outcomes, this passage is one of several examples illustrating a strategy aimed at *not* imposing definite limits on the text or, in other words, at resisting the idea that a novel could ever be a "fixed expression."

If there was any uncertainty as to whether this deliberate refusal of a fixed expression is linked to literary aesthetics and copyright laws, this would seem to be addressed in the following passage, where duplication of the text into two different outcomes is specifically related to plagiarism: "But what follows leaves absolutely no doubt about the plagiarism. The plagiarist adds: If you are not satisfied with what I reveal to you about Jacques's loves, reader, do better yourself; it's quite all right with me. However you go about it, I'm rather sure you will finish up just where I did" (268). If the narrator happily gives up ownership of his narration so as to shift responsibility onto someone else, he also says unambiguously that this novel, and words in general, actually belong to everyone.

In this respect, we undoubtedly find ourselves closer to the Renaissance than to the twentieth century. In premodern aesthetics, imitation and respect for rules were of the utmost importance. As Mortier observes, "the eighteenth century, especially in France, is firmly anchored in a rational ideal of beauty, implying an inalterable nature and a need to learn, that is, a need to imitate."[20] The eighteenth-century's affinity with what may appear to us as traditional views is supported by the article *Imitation* in the *Encyclopedia*, where Diderot writes: "He who invents a type of *imitation* is a genius. He who perfects a form of *imitation* or who excels in it may also be called a genius."[21]

The Master is an occasional advocate for the older rules and imitation. In his critique of the Landlady's story, he mentions the lack of stability and consistency he noticed in her characters.[22] We could interpret this as an affirmation of belief in stability and consistency, but two things call this into question: (1) the master's lack of talent as a storyteller, and (2) the fact that the Landlady's story was captivating and effective, which leads us to believe that the rules she broke are no indicator of aesthetic worth.

Stability and fixed expression do not appear as determining factors, and the narrator challenges the notion that imitation and respect for tradition should guarantee aesthetic value: "I felt that you were hurt by the word Bogger. I should like to know why. For it's the real name of my wheelwright's family. When their children, who are pretty, go through the streets, people say: 'Look at those cute little Boggers' . . . Can a family name be in good or bad taste? The streets are full of alley cats called "Pompey'" (195–196).[23] In a subtle reversal, bad taste is said to ensure proper imitation (which reminds us of what Diderot says about portraits and the wart in *Les Deux Amis de Bourbonne*).[24] But contrary to what is often observed in our postromantic world of originality, nonadherence to fixed forms does not appear as an end in itself, but as a means toward perfect mimesis. In perfect conformity with classical aesthetics, the narrator claims to disappear behind the reality he describes, erasing his role as intermediary, while putting himself in plain view on the narrative stage. In this way, he is not responsible for the text he produces. In perfect mimesis, there is no visible mediator between reality and representation. Mimesis (and classical aesthetics) is dissolved, nonetheless, when we reveal the paradox on which it relies, namely the assertion of one's own absence.

To depict an *authentic* image—and we see how close we come here to the notion of originality—we need to assert our vision of the particular and reject the general.

The narrator further challenges tradition insofar as it proves to be an insufficient standard of aesthetic quality: "How can a sensible man," he affects to question, "a man of morals, who pretends to know philosophy, amuse himself at spinning out tales of such obscenity?—First of all, reader," he replies, "these are not tales, this is history. And I feel no more guilty, perhaps less, when I write of these tricks of Jacques, than did Suetonius when he transmitted to us the debauchery of Tiberius. And yet you read Suetonius and find no reproach for him. Why don't you lift your eyebrows at Catullus, Martial, Horace, Juvenal, Petronius, La Fontaine, and a host of others?" (205). We are not far from the wart on the temple, but we are moving to moral considerations: Is the artist to depict an idealised world, pure of all obscenity, as suggested by tradition? Or, is he supposed to depict the world adequately and follow models by imitating them? Working through his narrator, Diderot introduces one of the numerous paradoxes of imitation and tradition. Imitation and tradition appear as inadequate tools for measuring a work's quality and are at best arbitrary. Before we questioned tradition insofar as it imitates models, here we question imitation as to how it is perceived by the reader because the novel *does* belong to a tradition and should be read as such. There is no special merit in being different or distanced from the models.

If we consider the idea that copies and originals are simply reversible categories—which, of course, dissolves the notion of imitation—we may note that if, in *Jacques*, the novel is meant to be an adequate reflection of life, life is a copy of what is written on the "Great Scroll." So a text is not a mimetic representation of the world. On the contrary, the world is a mimetic representation of a text, and the entire notion of mimetic value in art is consequently bracketed. The classical notion of self-denial, although still asserted and even confirmed in *Jacques*, when taken to the extreme, paradoxically results in the notion of asserting one's absence, from which we can conclude, again paradoxically, that the more we try to deny ourselves, the more likely we are to establish a vision that is uniquely our own.

After examining the essential components of premodern authorship, we can conclude that, rather than anticipating *our* aesthetics of originality, this novel illustrates the "ambivalence" of the aesthetics of its time. It illustrates the paradoxes classical aesthetics rely on and brings to light the full complexity of questions relating to imitation and originality. We need not be surprised or reminded that Diderot did not write tragedies, but novels, and that he attempted to renew dramatic conventions. His notion of authorship as it appears in *Jacques* is not visionary, at least not in any sense that would anticipate our own. Maybe that is the mistake we make when we read *The Letter on the Book Trade*: We are expecting Diderot to come up with the answers we have come to take for granted regarding intellectual property.

Based on Diderot's belief in freely borrowing from the public domain and his denial of fixed forms, we may expect that his notion of "originality" would have little to do with "distinguishing itself from the rest." If Diderot's conclusions on authorship and aesthetics are complex and if, in fact, they elucidate certain questions, they do not necessarily anticipate our own conclusions or even the way we have come to frame our aesthetic questions. But what, then, are Diderot's conclusions?

We have observed that the status of *originality* in contemporary aesthetics results from the gradual secularization of the notion of inspiration is to be linked with one individual and applied to a fixed expression. Copyright is closely linked to originality, to the point that it could not exist without it.

The word "original" appears regularly in the French text and can be categorized into three types of contexts, all consistent with the definitions given in the *Encyclopedia*. The first describes people, the second paintings, and the third refers more closely to literary aesthetics. In the first case, Gousse and Jacques are two of the most notable originals in the novel. One could consider Mme de la Pommeraye or Hudson to be "originals," but the word is never used to describe them. Gousse, quite appropriately, does not teach his children anything and claims he did not learn anything either: "What! Neither reading nor writing nor their catechism?—neither reading nor writing nor their catechism. And why, pray tell?—Well, they taught me nothing and I am not the more ignorant for it. If they have a mind, they'll do as I did. If they're stupid, what I should teach them would make them only more stupid" (60). Gousse, then, cannot be a product of tradition nor hold a place within a tradition that he would imitate or reject. He is *outside* of mimesis, just as he is outside of morals, not *im*moral but *a*moral. Being "original," then, would amount to being external to all influences. Originality is to be equated with detachment from tradition, culture, and usual forms of knowledge. In the *Encyclopedia*, "original" has both positive and negative connotations. Although Diderot may have praised this kind of "originality" as "natural" elsewhere, in Gousse's case, *Jacques*' narrator gives a mitigated portrait and is obviously bothered by the fact that an "original" would be amoral:

> I suppose you think Gousse an exceptionally good, moral man. Well, disillusion yourselves; he had no more sense of morality than a fish head.—That's impossible.—It's true. I employed him once. I gave him a check for eighty francs on my constituents. The sum was written in figures, and what does he do? He adds a zero and gets paid eight hundred francs—Ah! How horrible!—And he's no more dishonest when he robs me than he is honest when he gives up all for a friend. He's a character completely without principles. (61–62)

In the French text, the word "original" applies to Jacques, who is described as such by Richard, who finds him "a likeable character" ("*qui le trouvait un franc original*"). The text continues: "This would happen more often among men if, first of all, education and, secondly, the experience of society did not wear them down like coins that, as a result of circulation, lose their stamp" (179). This passage illustrates as clearly as possible the meaning of "unadulterated" or "staying true to nature." It is the Master, however, who first calls Jacques "*un original*"; the same meaning is present—unpolished, natural—but something is added: "It was written up yonder that I should never be rid of that character (*original*) and that as long as I live he would be my master and I, his servant" (160). Jacques is therefore said to be the "original" at the moment the master yields his title or position as master to Jacques, and originality is linked to the reversal of the master–servant dichotomy. Originality can therefore be perceived as a serious threat to the established order.

The one and only time we encounter "original" as "being the first chronologically" is when the master talks about paintings, conceding: "I could take a bad copy for a sublime original" (179). While confirming that the Master should not be taken for an expert in aesthetics or good taste, this passage also suggests a potential reciprocity between copies and originals. In its third type of use, when the word is applied to literature, it refers to various versions of a manuscript and subsequent copies corrupting it: "I have read the memoirs in question. Of the three paragraphs that I find not an integral part of the manuscript in my possession, the first and the last seem original, but the middle one is, to my way of thinking, obviously interpolated" (266).[25] The meaning common to all three types of occurrences is that of "unspoiled" or "unadulterated." The secondary meanings deal with a search for origins, made difficult or impossible by copies (in paintings) or by insertions, corrections, and modifications (in texts).

"Originality" also can be applied to literary aesthetics:

> I could have pulled [the letter Mme de La Pommeraye dictated to her two religious friends] off, but it wouldn't have been original. It would have been like those sublime haranguings of Titus Livius in his *History of Rome*, or of Cardinal Bentivoglio in his *Flemish Wars*. One reads them with pleasure but they destroy all illusion. For a historian who imagines conversations his characters did not have, can also conjure up actions which they did not perform. (229)

We find here a paradox similar to the one we noted on mimesis. "Originality" is to be sought aesthetically, and a writer has to aspire to it; it gives the appearance of unspoiled and unadulterated reality and therefore cannot be overworked (an excessively skillful writer who masters his craftsmanship cannot be original). It follows that the key function of originality in literary aesthetics, then, is not mimesis or closeness to reality because we are seeking the *appearance* of reality. Or, to put it differently, *originality* cannot be equated with faithfulness to the *original* it strives to represent. Not in the least: originality serves the *illusion* of reality. To give the illusion of mimesis is to master aesthetics.

Aesthetically then, "originality" is something a writer has to aspire to, and that has two functions. The first is to maintain the illusion. In that sense, it is not so much how it differentiates itself from other works or from tradition. Occurrences of the word "original" in *Jacques* suggest that the meaning we, as twenty-first-century readers, associate it with, namely "unique and distinguishing itself from others," is not of great importance to Diderot. The chronological meaning (i.e., "the one coming first") and the meaning of "uniqueness" appear as secondary to the notions we have just considered: "close to the truth." "unadulterated," and "unmodified."

Let us return now to another prerequisite for modern authorship: the notion of "fixed expression" and its corollary, plagiarism. Plagiarism can only exist where works are clearly separated. Plagiarism, then, rests on the integrity of a given expression with clear borders and defined limits. To threaten those borders is to threaten the integrity of a given expression, which explains why plagiarism is often associated with theft.

The article *Plagiarisme* from the *Encyclopedia*—probably written by Diderot—distinguishes borrowing (consciously and quoting the reference) from stealing, thus reflecting rather closely our conception of what constitutes plagiarism. However, when discussing the commonality of sources and themes, the author of this article goes on to suggest a possible "commonality of goods" in literature. Of course, we can clearly establish a link between, on the one hand, the notions of "commonality of goods" or "commonality of sources and themes," and, on the other hand, the fabric of *Jacques le fataliste*. One of the most striking illustrations of the "commonality of goods" in literature is to be found in the "distributive justice" practiced by Gousse. The narrator recounts the incident:

> I needed a rare book; he [Gousse] brings it to me. Sometime later I need another; again he brings it to me. When I try to pay him, he refuses the just price. Then I need a third rare book. "As for this one," he says, "you won't get it for you have spoken too late. My Sorbonne doctor friend is dead." "And what has your Sorbonne doctor to do with the book I want? Did you take the two others from his library?" "Why, certainly." "Without his permission?" "What need of permission is there in making a fair redistribution? I only changed those books about for the best by transferring them from a spot where they were useless to another spot where someone could make use of them." (62)

This exchange is quite tellingly followed by a passage highlighting the notion of Gousse's "amorality," which we have already discussed. It is worth noticing that this "amorality" roughly amounts to a disregard for economic and material property. In giving consideration only to intellectual rights, however, Gousse is quite consistent. A work's best place is where it is best used.

In literature, then, "commonality of goods" would obviate plagiarism *if what the writer creates is always (at least) as good as what he borrows.* In his article "Diderot, Creator and Compiler," Laurence L. Bongie quotes from the anonymous article *Compilateur* in the *Encyclopedia* in characterizing a plagiarist "as someone without genius or talent who copies not only phrases, but entire pages and sections from other authors and who has the bad faith not to acknowledge his source."[26] As Bongie clearly shows, the notion of "compiling" provides the Encyclopedists with a conveniently blurred notion somewhere between plagiarism and compilation. Having to defend themselves against the claims that they were plagiarists, the makers of the *Encyclopedia* insisted that "plagiarism is a sin," but justify their practices in the article *Compilateur* from which Bongie quotes the following passage:

> The characteristics of a good dictionary such as we would like ours to be, require in large part that we make use of the best discoveries of others. But our borrowings are open and public and we cite our sources. Our role as compilers allows us to take advantage of everything that can add to the perfection of our work, wherever it may be found. Our pilfering is like that of the bee; it steals nectar for the public good. It cannot be said that we pillage authors but rather that we draw from them contributions for the benefit of literature in general. . . . [27]

Borrowing knowledge becomes justified insofar as it is aimed at the public and serves the general interest. If Mortier has shown the ambivalence of aesthetic values surrounding originality in the eighteenth century, we certainly see here the same ambivalence in the legal, moral, and ethical issues surrounding the justification of 'borrowing' knowledge from other texts. This theory clearly contrasts with the modern notion that literary borrowings of any kind are to be avoided.

Diderot was a compiler and even, as Bongie puts it, a "brazen-faced plagiarizer."[28] Bongie mentions that "many of Diderot's philosophical articles were lifted, usually without acknowledgement, from Brucker's Latin history of philosophy," and goes on to quote similar examples including his art criticism.[29] The same is true, ironically, of his *Letter on the Book Trade*, largely inspired by the *Mémoire d'Héricourt* with which it not only shares the premise of intellectual property being similar to all other types of property, acquired and transmitted in a fashion no different from other goods, but also shows structural and stylistic resemblance.[30]

While showing that Diderot is a "brazen-faced plagiarizer," Bongie nonetheless appears to justify Diderot's plagiarism by saying that he used other people's writings only for his least artistic work, such as the *Encyclopedia* or the travel literature. Emphasizing, on the one hand, the haziness of the Encyclopedists' notions of "borrowing" and "plagiarism," Bongie suggests, on the other hand, that their definition "seems clear enough unless, of course, we are perverse enough to interpret the exclusion of genius and talent as meaning that the gifted, who have *no need* to plagiarize, *may be allowed to do so. . . .*"[31]

Although the notion that plagiarism is not plagiarism so long as it is a good writer taking from a bad one may seem dishonest and questionable from our perspective, it has clear applications in the aesthetics of *Jacques le fataliste*, which offers numerous examples to illustrate this point. If it is true that Diderot had followed the same practice in his literary works as he did in his travel literature, in the *Encyclopedia*, in his *Salons*, and in his *Letter on the Book Trade*—namely, the habit of working with other books open in front of him and lifting full passages from them—this only reinforces Bongie's theory, which appears then in a different light: it is not so much that Diderot was an occasional plagiarizer, that is to say that he did it when he had to, but rather this was his general way of working, thinking, and functioning, and from which we can conclude that he did *not* consider plagiarism a 'sin,' but could not see it or think of it in terms similar to ours. Such would seem to be the case because, in *Jacques le fataliste*, it matters not so much, for instance, who told the story of Mme de la Pommeraye *first* as who told it *best*. Similarly, as a writer, Diderot quotes his sources when they are Spinoza, Sterne, or Rabelais, but not when it is someone obscure. As Émile Lizé has shown, the story of M. Le Pelletier d'Orléans in *Jacques le fataliste* is a story taken, quite literally, from a book written by Mlle d'Alès du Corbet, god-daughter of M. Le Pelletier: *Abrégé de la vie de M. le Pelletier, mort à Orléans en odeur de sainteté (le 29 août 1756) par Mademoiselle d'Alès du Corbet.*[32]

In his literary as in his less literary works, Diderot did, in fact, borrow freely. As suggested in the *Encyclopedia*, Diderot's practice seems to confirm a distinction between plagiarism and borrowing, as well as the notion that "pilfering" is perfectly acceptable.

Can we, then, conclude that *Jacques le fataliste* illustrates a distinction between plagiarism and borrowing? We may recall Jacques's habit of filling a big goblet with herb tea, pouring in a little white wine, and swallowing it: "It was a recipe he had gotten from his captain and one which M. Tissot, who got it from Jacques, recommends in his treatise on common illnesses. The white wine, said both Jacques and M. Tissot, causes pissing, is diuretic" (153). The content of this sentence is shown to be common knowledge that deserved to be known by all. It is no surprise that when such a statement is true and useful, it will be shared, which will inevitably lead to repetition and duplication. The same is true of other texts, and the principle at work here, as shown by Zionkowski, is reminiscent of the argument used by adversaries of originality in literary aesthetics: "For Johnson . . . writing is shared labour which involves collective ownership. Complaints of plagiarism, Johnson observes, are often mistaken because the uniformity of human nature creates in writers 'unexpected coincidences of sentiment.'"[33] There is no such thing as a "unique" text; there is no possible "textual integrity." We are left to wonder who, between Jacques and Tissot (and the captain?), is the plagiarist. The *Letter on the Book Trade* tells us the same thing, revealing a surprising consistency rarely noted by scholars.[34] Using Locke's argument on ownership being legitimate so long as it does not overstep someone else's capacity to have enough, Diderot argues that knowledge is infinite: "This manuscript . . . is personal property but that does not prevent writing and publishing on the same subject *ad infinitum*."[35] The logic at work here stems from a philosophy based on the commonality of intellectual goods: knowledge belongs to everyone. The whole letter has to be understood under this prism. Diderot's aim is, above all, to ensure the circulation of *knowledge*, clearly separating the intellectual value of a book from its economic value. Intellectual property has to be based first on "general interest,"[36] which has to take priority over economic interest. Economic interest must be taken into account insofar as it serves to expand the common intellectual wealth.

If texts are a vehicle for knowledge, if they do seek a universal truth, in which case they should seek the most widespread audience possible, they cannot be individualized as self-contained units. Texts will "repeat" aspects of the truth, they will borrow from each other, and are essentially intended to be shared, and hence they belong to everyone. "Plagiarism," then, becomes a blurry notion because sharing and borrowing are authorized and encouraged. The source or the origin of the "truth" is not to be found or even sought: it does not matter who said something first; it matters that what is said is right or useful, as we see in the famous passage on plagiarism in *Jacques le fataliste*: "Here is the second paragraph, copied from *The life of Tristram Shandy*, unless, of course, the discourses of *Jacques the Fatalist and his master* are not anterior to that work, and Mr. Sterne be not himself the plagiarist" (267). Plagiarism cancels itself in its reversibility, giving precedence to the free circulation of knowledge over clear delimitation between works or even over chronology. Reversibility would not occur had we had a clear notion of the "origins" of a text, but this appears to be an impossible, obsessive quest that never arrives at clear answers.

Perhaps we should pause momentarily to consider the unsolvable question of origins. We have seen this illustrated in literary aesthetics as the impossibility to access an original manuscript prone to corruption or the inability to distinguish it from copies. But the matter of origins is thoughtfully illustrated by the Master's son, who is not his son and whose origins have been "duplicated" in the same pattern as the text was duplicated. Just as the text occasionally bifurcates into two acceptable endings, the paternity of the Master's son isn't established, and the son's quest for "origins" would be a useless one. This is not the only occurrence in the text where genealogical matters echo textual matters: "There is at this point a truly lamentable lacuna in the conversation of Jacques and his master. Some fine day a descendant of Nodot, or the Président de Brosses, or Freinshémus, or Father Brottier will fill it up perhaps, and the descendants of Jacques or his masters, owners of the manuscript, will have a good laugh" (210). In light of our subject, this passage is extremely rich: genealogically, we are going toward descendants, so the point of origin should be more reliable. Yet we notice that it undergoes the same kind of textually destabilizing permutation as we have seen elsewhere: the point of origin is multiple, and fictional characters are put at the same level as real, historical people, thus creating confusion between the textual and the metatextual levels. There is also, of course, the matter of imitation because Nodot, the Président de Brosses, Freinshémus, and Father Brottier were all scholars working on classical manuscripts As such, they reiterate the problematic nature of origin, through the classical writings they are working on, such as Tacitus, meant to be used as models, but needing some work, some translation, some interpretation, and, hence, some shifting. In this passage specifically concerned with intellectual property, ownership of the manuscript is assigned, but to posterity—not surprisingly, as Diderot always asserted that writers should write for posterity. Comically enough, ownership of the manuscript is assigned to its characters, and the integrity of the manuscript cannot be protected (nor is it the owners' responsibility to preserve it). The "original" manuscript, its ownership, and the will to create or restore its integrity are all *fictional*. They are the result of a desire for stable, reassuring answers for shifting and fragmentary realities: the question of the ownership of a manuscript is as cryptic, fragmentary, and elusive as its final and definite meaning.

The problem of origins leads us to the same conclusions we arrived at concerning plagiarism and identity: there is a strong denial of stability, of any fixed form in literary aesthetics. Texts belong to everyone, and the endless quest for a final version is as futile and illusory as a quest for origins. A text is and should be constantly modified, scrutinized, perpetually imperfect, and in need of completion, wrongly most of the time. Its origins are multiple, and its essence is in its movement.

In contrast with our own views on intellectual property, and specifically with Woodmansee's idea of "an individual solely responsible . . . for the production of a unique work," we now come to another matter that confirms the notion of perpetual movement and common ownership. In *Jacques le fataliste*, individuality is, at the least, strongly questioned, starting with the following passage where the master has hurt his knee: Although he had failed to believe Jacques's claims as to the intensity of a knee wound, he now agrees that "it is one of the worst. *Jacques*: That is to say, if it's *your* knee? *The Master*: No, no, no. Yours, mine, all the knees in the world" (17). This passage portrays commonality of experience as a necessary point for communication, suggesting that individuality carries the risk of incommunicability. The danger of individuality, in this respect, is to fail to reach into "otherness." Whenever Diderot has to choose, philosophically, between individuality and "otherness," he opts for "otherness."[37]

As Diderot scholars have noted, one cannot claim any kind of individuality when the sign of individuality (i.e., names) is interchangeable:

"Language becomes a very fragile tool for identification or even expression when even proper nouns can be exchanged, when Suzon becomes Marguerite, Fourgeot de Mathieu becomes Mathieu de Fourgeot, and when signs happily interchange, taken into the spiralling movement of variation."[38] Some critics interpret this denial of individuality as a sign of "literary collectivism," where every individual can only be seen as a part of the whole and where the subject can never claim any certainty.[39] This seems, however, to be only part of the equation and only hints at the paradox we noted earlier. The concept of individuality in Diderot's *Jacques le fataliste* must be linked to the ownership of texts and to originality: The more one asserts one's individuality, the more it disappears; and the more one asserts one's function in the group, the more one's individuality emerges.

In this novel as in others by Diderot, the narrator, whoever he may be at a given moment, is never single, consistent, unique, and individual. The narrator constantly defers power, knowledge, and responsibility to a further entity, be it the Great Scroll, the translator, the plagiarizer, the editor, and so on. . . . The text cannot, therefore, claim any kind of authority or integrity. The following passage is one of numerous examples of the text multiplying into different possibilities, contesting "fixed expression," deferring authority, and, therefore, losing any hope for stability: "And in a week I shall give you a judgment (about the different versions of the rest of the story) which will be definitive, except that I reserve the right to retract should someone more intelligent than myself prove to me that I was wrong" (266). Philosophically, assertions such as this separate Diderot from the commonly held opinion placing the individual at the forefront of autobiographical writings in the nineteenth and twentieth centuries[40] and from the premises leading to our copyright laws. For we have to remember that intellectual property laws posit the existence of an *individual.* Copyright is at odds with the idea of multiple authors, but also with the schizophrenic fragmentation of identity. Diderot's notion of the individual could not be further from the one that modern intellectual ownership presupposes. For Diderot, philosophically and literarily, "an individual can only be a discontinuous series of influences and tendencies,"[41] and "self-judgement has less to do with someone's qualities as an individual than with the merit of his actions in the eyes of posterity."[42] This notion is confirmed again in *The Letter on the Book Trade*, where it is quite striking to see that, although it is an author writing the *Letter*, he is consistently defined by his right to self-denial and constantly asserting his right to *give away* the product of his work.[43] The individual is to be defined in terms of self-spending; it can exist only if the limits between self and others are blurred and only if the self belongs to the common group: everything, ideologically, philosophically, morally, and economically, stands in stark contrast to the romantic idea of a solitary genius becoming original by distancing himself from everything that came before him, an ideology we may wrongly associate with the ideals of the Enlightenment. James Creech, who wrote extensively on Diderot, brought attention to this point in underlining what he referred to as Diderot's "focus on dispossession."[44] Certainly this is relevant to the depiction of intellectual property from an author's point of view in the *Letter on the Book Trade*, where, in the words of Starobinski, Diderot "asserts himself by agreeing to self-alienation, by being helpful, and by reinforcing eloquently a *common cause*."[45]

The ideological distance that we easily perceive between Diderot and ourselves in *The Letter on the Book Trade* becomes all the more apparent when we examine the aesthetic principles at work in *Jacques le fataliste*. We have seen that "originality" in this novel has more to do with truth and universality than with exceptions and coming first. The discrepancy that is evident in *The Letter on the Book Trade* between our own ideas on intellectual property and those of Diderot is strikingly consistent with what we can draw from *Jacques le fataliste*. The *Letter on the Book Trade* relies on a notion of intellectual ownership entirely based on truth, universality, general interest, self-denial, and dispossession. If we are not at ease when we read this text, this is most likely due to the point of view from which we read it, according to which the Enlightenment appears as a time of triumph for the individual. As stated by Jaszi, "Foucault . . . located the emergence of the 'author' in the cultural context of the eighteenth-century," arguing that "the coming into being of the notion of the 'author' constitutes a privileged moment of *individualization* in the history of ideas."[46] Diderot's notion of the individual, especially in his relation to the group or to the general interest, seems to be quite different, then, from what we commonly qualify as coming from the Enlightenment.

In Diderot's view, there is no fixed expression, there is no reliable author, and the notion of an individual, consistent, delimited, one, and unique, is strongly questioned. Because the "originality" we know is so closely linked to individuality, we have to conclude that, although originality clearly appears in *Jacques* and it does bring about a new sense of aesthetics, it cannot be considered as fundamental to the notion of authorship as we seem to think.

Intellectual property and aesthetic matters are closely intertwined in Diderot's works. Although we commonly read extraordinary praise for *Jacques le fataliste* and its *avant-garde* aesthetics, careful examination shows its aesthetics to be similar to the ideas expressed in his *Letter on the Book Trade*, one of the few texts that still attract harsh criticism for Diderot.

The emerging individual is clearly a relevant issue in both texts, however, just as it is in contemporary aesthetics and intellectual property. However, Diderot consistently opposes the individual with the collective and upholds the classical dogma (aesthetically, legally, and morally) according to which the individual has to serve the group and the general interest, and texts and knowledge are meant to circulate freely. The individual is to be an effective and, if possible, happy instrument of that mechanism, but the end is never the individual, especially not the writer. The philosopher's prerogative is to ensure widespread circulation of the truth, be it at his own expense.

Similarly, the aesthetics at work in *Jacques le fataliste* function in openness, rather than within a strictly defined framework. As with the *Letter on the Book Trade*, this novel cannot be said to advocate "aesthetic individualism," and Diderot's "originality" is therefore not to be understood in the way originality is usually understood today. In light of these conclusions, we should reread Diderot's writings on intellectual property, knowing that it is the work of a man who does not conceive of the writer as an individual and who does not, therefore, reach the same conclusions we have come to.

Moreover, the functioning of a text as illustrated in *Jacques le fataliste* is incompatible with the notion of "fixed expression." Texts, like the truth, belong to everyone. Individuality endangers textual mechanisms: from the commonality of experience necessary for communication (to say nothing of the commonality of language, which is addressed, for instance, in *Les Bijoux Indiscrets*) to the commonality of sources, but also the necessarily changing nature of a text owing to interpretation and its inherent incompleteness, as well as the necessary participation of at least two agents, the narrator and the reader, everything goes against the idea that the text is the product of an individual.

What we learn from *Jacques le fataliste* is that a text functions only in a perpetual shifting of meaning and that searching for stability is as fruitless as it is undesirable. The novel gives us clear indications that what is most desirable for an author is to reflect the truth and that the best compliment that can be given is the one that Diderot gave to Shaftesbury: to make another's thoughts your own. Intellectually, then, the purpose of a text is to be shared and, ultimately, to belong to someone else, hopefully to everyone else. An author you admire becomes you, and, essentially, thoughts are by nature meant to be understood—in other words, to be shared and fully appropriated. Thought, truth, and texts that support them belong to everyone and are, by nature, meant to be given.

This is not to say that we should give up intellectual property altogether. Diderot did, on this matter as often elsewhere, manage to bring to light its full complexity, but falls short of offering a new system: hence, I believe, his opting for the easiest solution, and the *status quo*. For us, now, as observed by Mark Rose, "copyright is deeply rooted in our conception of ourselves as individuals with at least a modest grade of singularity, some degree of personality." If, as Rose concludes, "we are not ready . . . to give up the sense of who we are,"[47] this should not prevent us from examining closely the components of that identity.

NOTES

1. "Some critics of the 'law and literature' movement have followed the lead of Richard Posner in questioning whether literary and legal studies can illuminate one another, stressing instead the 'profound differences' between the two fields." Martha Woodmansee and Peter Jaszi, eds., *The Construction of*

Authorship: Textual Appropriation in Law and Literature (Durham, NC: Duke University Press, 1994), 13. See Richard Posner, *Law and Literature: A Misunderstood Relation* (Cambridge, MA: Harvard University Press, 1988), 13–14.

2. "Over the past twenty five years, Kaplan's critique of basic copyright concepts has been influential in practical discussion of legal policy, while followers of Foucault have investigated the 'construction of authorship' in the domain of literary culture. In retrospect, however, it is surprising how recently scholars have begun to attend the ways in which the cultural figuration of the 'author,' as the inspired creator of unique works of art, has interacted with the legal notion of the 'author' as the bearer of the portable rights in literary and artistic property." Peter Jaszi, "On the Author Effect: Contemporary Copyright and Collective Creativity," in *The Construction of Authorship*, 30.
3. Linda Zionkowski, "Aesthetics, Copyright, and 'The Goods of the Mind,'" *British Journal for Eighteenth-Century Studies* 15, no. 2 (1992): 171. Copyright and its accompanying aesthetics are seen by Zionkowski as resulting from economic realities: "Initially, the emphasis on original invention was a response to the competitive market in texts—to the never-ending realms of print which provided writers and booksellers with a living" (Ibid., 172).
4. James Boyle underlines "the role of the state in making controversial, policy-laden decisions to define property rights in ways that subsequently become both natural and neutral." James Boyle, "Fencing off Ideas: Enclosure and the Disappearance of the Public Domain," *Daedalus* 131, no. 2 (2002): 14. Other authors argue that copyright laws are far from being universal; see, in particular, Ronald V. Bettig, "Critical Perspectives on the History and Philosophy of Copyright," *Critical Studies in Mass Communication* 9, no. 2 (1992): 131–155.
5. Decrees of January 13, 1791, concerning rights of representation and July 19–24, 1793, on rights of reproduction.
6. In his article "Diderot Creator and Compiler," *Transactions of the Samuel Johnson Society of the Northwest* 15 (1984): 35–44, Laurence L. Bongie documents a few cases of Diderot's plagiarism. Despite making his point on the widespread practice of plagiarism, Bongie *defends* Diderot and finds him excuses for having committed the "sin" of plagiarism. (The word "sin" is actually not Bongie's because it appears in the article *Plagiarisme* from the *Encyclopedia*.) In that sense, Bongie stays true to our values regarding copyright.
7. The date has been the subject of considerable controversy, much of which has been settled by Jacques Proust. See "Pour servir à une édition critique de la *Lettre sur le commerce de librairie*," *Diderot Studies* 3 (1961): 321–345.
8. Roland Mortier, "L'original selon Diderot," *Saggi e ricerche di letteratura francese* 4 (1963): 143.
9. Martha Woodmansee, "The Genius and the Copyright: Economic and Legal Conditions of the Emergence of the 'Author,'" *Eighteenth-Century Studies* 17, no. 4 (1984): 426.
10. "Inspiration se dit particulièrement au sujet des livres de l'Ecriture-sainte: on la définit un mouvement intérieur du Saint-Esprit, qui détermine un homme à écrire, & qui lui suggère le choix des choses qu'il doit écrire. L'idée d'inspiration suppose donc dans celui qui écrit un mouvement du Saint-Esprit qui le porte à écrire ce que la révélation lui a appris, ou ce qu'il sait par lui-même, & qui lui suggère le choix des choses qu'il doit écrire."
11. Woodmansee, "The Genius and the Copyright," 433.
12. Woodmansee and Jaszi, *The Construction of Authorship*, 11.

13. "J'avoue que je suis bien indigné de ces réimpressions successives qui réduisent en dix ans ma bibliothèque au quart de sa valeur; mais faut-il qu'on empêche par cette considération un auteur de corriger incessamment les fautes qui lui sont échappées, de retrancher le superflu, et de suppléer ce qui manque à son ouvrage? Ne pourrait-on pas ordonner au libraire, à chaque réimpression nouvelle, de distribuer les additions, corrections, retranchements et changements à part?" *Lettre sur le commerce de la librairie*, in *Œuvres*, ed. Laurent Versini, 5 vols. (Paris: Robert Laffont, 1994–1997), 3:73 (trans. Don Ullyot).
14. See the chronology established by Paul Vernière in *Jacques le fataliste et son maître* (Paris: Garnier-Flammarion, 1970). Diderot is said to have started working on this novel in 1765. First published in Grimms's *Correspondance littéraire* between 1778 and 1780, the manuscript underwent further additions in July 1780, and then in 1783 for the version prepared by Gribal for Catherine II.
15. Mark Rose, *Authors and Owners: The Invention of Copyright* (Cambridge MA: Harvard University Press, 1993), 3.
16. "En effet, quel est le bien qui puisse appartenir à un homme, si un ouvrage d'esprit, le fruit unique de son éducation, de ses études, de ses veilles, de son temps, de ses recherches, de ses observations." *Lettre sur le commerce de la librairie*, 78 (my translation).
17. *Jacques the Fatalist and His Master*, Translated and with Introduction and Notes by J. Robert Loy (New York: New York University Press, 1959), 229. Subsequent page references are placed in the text.
18. Jean Starobinski, "Diderot et la parole des autres," *Critique* 28, no. 296 (1972): 4. "Je l'ai lu et relu. Je me suis rempli de son esprit, et j'ai, pour ainsi dire, fermé mon livre lorsque j'ai pris la plume. On n'a jamais usé du bien d'autrui avec autant de liberté" (trans. Don Ullyot).
19. Roland Mortier, *L'originalité: une nouvelle catégorie esthétique au siècle des lumières* (Paris: Droz, 1982), 90. "From now on [literature] will be judged on its power to shock, on the emotion it arouses in us, on its capacity to surprise us . . . The freedom of the art disappears behind a highly emphatic dual relationship: a relationship with the author . . . and with the spectator or the reader (shock, emotion, reaction)" (trans. Don Ullyot).
20. Ibid., 27. "Le XVIIIème siècle, en France tout particulièrement, reste fidèle à une *rationalité* du beau, ce qui implique son caractère immuable et la nécessité d'un apprentissage, c'est-à-dire d'une imitation" (trans. Don Ullyot).
21. "Celui qui invente un genre d'*imitation* est un homme de génie. Celui qui perfectionne un genre d'*imitation* inventé, ou qui y excelle, est aussi un homme de génie" (my translation).
22. "My landlady, you tell a story well, but you are not yet perfected in the art of dramatics . . . When you create a stage character, his role must be consistent . . . You have sinned against the rules of Aristotle, Horace, Vida and Le Bossu" (146–147).
23. It is actually not "street cats," but "dogs," as there is an error in translation.
24. "How then will the storyteller go about misleading you? This is how: He will scatter little circumstances here and there throughout his story that are so closely related to the thing, with such simple and natural strokes of his pen, and yet are so difficult to imagine, that you will be forced to admit to yourself, 'Well, nobody could invent such things, so they must be true' . . . A painter draws a head on a canvas. The shape is big, bold and uniform; taken as a whole, it is perfect and unique. My impression as I contemplate it is one of respect, admiration, awe. I search for its like in Nature but to no avail. Everything on the canvas is implausible, shallow and offensive by

comparison. I feel and think that what I see is a head in the ideal form . . . If only the artist had drawn my eye to a faint scar on the forehead, a wart at one of the temples, a barely perceptible fold in the lower lip, then his head, as ideal in form as he intended it to be, would have instantly become a portrait. A pox mark beside her eye or nose would have been all that was needed to transform the face of Venus into the likeness of one of the ladies next door." *Les deux amis de Bourbonne*, in *Quatre Contes*, ed. J. Proust (Genève: Droz, 1964), 66–67 (trans. Don Ullyot).

25. See also: "However the truth is that *engastrimyth* is mine, and that in the original text, the reading is *ventriloquist*" (208).
26. "Diderot Creator and Compiler," 36.
27. Quoted by Bongie, Ibid., 35–36.
28. Ibid., 35.
29. He "copied out substantial sections of Hagedorn's work, imitating sequences and structures as well as adopting Hagedorn's words and ideas, all without any acknowledgement except for a misleadingly casual reference to Hagedorn as the source of one unimportant anecdote" (Ibid., 37).
30. Diderot mentions d'Héricourt as if it was purely by chance that he came across the document: "While I was writing to you, I discovered another text written on the same topic, written by one of our best legal experts, M. d'Héricourt. I read it, and I am pleased to say that we are sharing the same views, and that we both drew the same consequences." Some parallels between Diderot's *Letter on the Book Trade* and the *Mémoire* d'Héricourt have been mentioned by Jacques Proust in "Pour servir à une édition critique de la *Lettre sur le commerce de la librairie*" (331)—for instance d'Héricourt's stating as well as Diderot that a manuscript belongs to the author as it is the fruit of his labour (23), and is then legitimately transmitted legally to the booksellers (29). Proust seems to believe, nonetheless, that Diderot's piece shows some *originality* compared to the *Mémoire d'Héricourt.* Citations from d'Héricourt's *Mémoire* refer to *La Propriété littéraire au XVIIIe siècle: recueil de pièces et de documents*, ed. Edouard Laboulaye and Georges Guiffrey (Paris: Hachette, 1859).
31. Bongie, "Diderot Creator and Compiler," 36.
32. Émile Lizé, "Une source de Diderot dans *Jacques le fataliste*: Qui était Monsieur Le Pelletier d'Orléans?" *Revue d'histoire littéraire de la France* 82, no. 3 (1982): 438–440.
33. Zionkowski, "Aesthetics, Copyright, and 'The Goods of the Mind,'" 169.
34. With the notable exception of Martial Poirson, "Portrait de l'artiste en propriétaire: le dramaturge fortuné ou les avatars du statut de la propriété intellectuelle au XVIIIe siècle," *Littératures classiques* 40 (2000): 119–140.
35. "Il s'agit d'un manuscrit . . . dont la propriété individuelle n'empêche point d'en composer et d'en publier à l'infini sur le même objet." *Lettre sur le commerce des livres*, 80 (trans. Don Ullyot).
36. The notion of "bien général" appears in modified forms no less than fourteen times in La *Lettre sur le commerce de la librairie.*
37. The point has been made by several critics: Starobinski, "Diderot et la parole des autres," 3–22; Poirson, "Portrait de l'artiste en propriétaire," 119–138; James Creech, "Diderot and the Pleasure of the Other: Friends, Readers, and Posterity," *Eighteenth-Century Studies* 11, no. 4 (1978): 439–456.
38. Caroline Jacot-Grappa, "Redites et identité: *Jacques le fataliste* et la pédagogie des Lumières," in *Le Travail des Lumières*, ed. Caroline Jacot Grappa, Nicole Jacques-Lefèvre, Yannick Séité, and Carine Trévisan (Paris: Champion, 2002), 418. "Le langage se révèle un fragile instrument d'identification, ou d'*expression*, quand les noms propres mêmes s'échangent, Suzon pour

Marguerite, Fourgeot de Mathieu pour Mathieu de Fourgeot, quand les signes permutent allègrement, pris dans la spirale de la *variation*" (trans. Don Ullyot).

39. Ibid., 426.
40. "The need to reproduce one's life in words, to preserve some written trace of a personality, is contemporary with the political declaration of the rights of the individual who breaks free from his family and the legal definition of copyright." Michel Delon, "Confessions et Contre-Confessions," *Le Magazine Littéraire*, Hors-Série (2007): 37–41.
41. "L'individu n'y est qu'un faisceau momentané de tendances et d'influences." Ibid., 40 (trans. Don Ullyot).
42. "Le jugement porte moins sur la valeur d'un individu que sur le mérite de son action du point de vue de la postérité." Ibid. (trans. Don Ullyot).
43. "If my condition is not enviable, are you making it better by preventing me from the right to alienate and by cancelling my assignment to my buyer?" and "I have, neither in this matter nor in any other in my life, put my own interest above the general good; I have therefore the reputation of being a good man, and I am not very rich." *Lettre sur le commerce de la librairie*, 94, 101 (trans. Don Ullyot).
44. "There is nothing that can be read as an index of 'le propre' or of self-*possession*. Diderot's characterization of 'âmes fortes' at least initially and in its specificity, focuses rather on *dis-possession*." James Creech, "Diderot and the Pleasure of the Other," 447.
45. Starobinski, "Diderot et la parole des autres," 11. "Diderot . . . s'affirme *lui-même* par l'aliénation consentie, le service rendu, le renfort d'éloquence qu'il apporte à une *cause commune*" (trans. Don Ullyot).
46. Jaszi, "On the Author Effect: Contemporary Copyright and Collective Creativity," in *The Construction of Authorship*, 29.
47. Rose, *Authors and Owners*, 142.

5 "Odd Scratches and Marks"
Thomas Gainsborough and the Idiosyncrasy of the Brush

Cristina S. Martinez

> He detested reading; but was so like Sterne in his Letters, that, if it were not for an originality that could be copied from no one, it might be supposed that he had formed his style upon a close imitation of that author.
>
> —William Jackson of Exeter, *The Four Ages*[1]

What Jackson so expressively remarked here of Gainsborough's letters was equally true of his paintings. If there is one word that characterizes Gainsborough's painterly style it is "originality." His handling and fluent brushwork, what William Jackson called his "hatching style of penciling,"[2] was unlike any other. Philip Thicknesse, Gainsborough's close friend and early biographer, wrote at the beginning of his account of the life of the artist: "To do Mr. Gainsborough justice, it requires a pen, equal to his own inimitable pencil, to hold forth the powers it possessed."[3] It is within the context of such claims that I wish to explore the nature of Gainsborough's work, focusing particularly on the period's growing debate around copyright law, and further considering the extent to which this debate and the problem of the proliferation of copies accounted in part for Gainsborough's idiosyncratic style. Indeed, originality was a prevailing concern of English writers in the eighteenth century. It would become the single most distinguishing feature of British art and remain so a full generation later. Nowhere was this made clearer than in 1855, when English works were sent to the International Exhibition in Paris and the French affirmed that there were only two schools of painting, "ours and yours." "Other schools," they said, "are founded on ours; yours is an original school."[4]

It would be a long while before a British school would rise to prominence. Works produced by early eighteenth-century artists were mostly decorative and far from original, as Edward Edwards, author of *Anecdotes of Painters*, noted:

> Not that the arts were at this period unemployed, for the painting of ceilings and staircases was much in vogue: sometimes the pannels of the room, but more frequently the compartments over the chimney and doors, were filled with some kind of picture, which was seldom the original work of any master, but commonly the production of some practical copyst,

> who subsisted by manufacturing such decorative pieces, and was glad to furnish a landscape on a half length canvas for forty or fifty shillings.[5]

The rank and conditions of artists in Britain were far removed from the well-established traditions of Italy and France. The British art world, by contrast to the Italian and French, was largely dominated by foreign artists and lacked an institutional basis. There was no Academy under royal patronage founded on hierarchical values as in France, hardly any bodies of formal instruction, and no places to exhibit art. By mid-century, however, painting in Britain had assumed greater prominence and gained prestige. With the foundation in 1768 of the Royal Academy of Arts, of which Reynolds was first president and Gainsborough a founding member, the English art scene underwent a crucial transformation. An exhibition culture and a widespread interest in art collecting emerged, along with Gainsborough as one of the foremost painters of the British school. Gainsborough's peculiar and original style drew great attention and did much to enhance the reputation of English art. It also reveals Gainsborough's familiarity with eighteenth-century concerns and reflects an awareness of discussions regarding originality and imitation.

Thomas Gainsborough was born in Sudbury, Suffolk, in 1727. From an early age, he demonstrated an exceptional artistic ability, focusing primarily on drawing and painting from nature.[6] At the age of thirteen, he was sent to London, where he made the acquaintance of the French illustrator Hubert François Gravelot (1699–1773), who kept a thriving studio of draughtsmen and engravers. Gainsborough studied along with the engraver Charles Grignion (1721–1810), and it is believed that he attended St. Martin's Lane Academy. It was at the Academy that Gravelot taught alongside the painter Francis Hayman (1708–1776), the French sculptor Louis-François Roubillac (c. 1705–1762), and the engraver and painter William Hogarth (1697–1764), the latter of whom had attained an extraordinary and international success through his conversation pieces and popular prints.

This stimulating environment provided the young Gainsborough with opportunities not only to develop his art, but also to exhibit his work. In 1748, he was invited to contribute to the project led by Hogarth to hang pictures in the recently established Foundling Hospital. Hogarth contributed a full-length portrait of *Captain Coram* and other prominent painters followed suit, including Thomas Hudson (1701–1779) and Allan Ramsay (1713–1784), each of whom presented an example of their work. Gainsborough's painting, a view of *The Charterhouse*, was part of a series of round pictures representing public institutions in London. The work subscribed to Hogarth's ideals and gained high praise from the engraver and chronicler George Vertue (1684–1756).[7] The composition, constructed around careful perspective lines, is described by John Hayes in his comprehensive study of Gainsborough's landscape paintings as "one of the most original topographical pictures ever painted in eighteenth-century England."[8]

Gainsborough, it should be noted, hardly ever painted topographical views. He expressed no interest in a field in which the landscape painter Paul Sandby so excelled, and he refused to include historical subjects in his landscapes. In a letter to his friend William Jackson, he declared self-assuredly:

> But are you sure you don't mean instead of the flight into Egypt, my flight out of Bath! do you consider my dear Maggotty Sir, what a deal of work history Pictures require to what little dirty subjects of Coal horses & Jack asses and such figures as I fill up with.[9]

Gainsborough had a predilection for local scenery and English subjects and was drawn to Hogarth's naturalistic style. Sir Joshua Reynolds (1723–1792), Gainsborough's contemporary and greatest rival, affirmed: "his grace was not academical or antique, but selected by himself from the great school of nature."[10] The *Morning Herald* similarly noted that

> he appears to have found a preferable school in sequestered nooks,—woody uplands,—retired cottages,—the avenues of a forest,—sheep, cattle, villagers and woodmen.—These were the true sources for the cultivation of a mind so strongly impregnated with the seeds of fine fancy, attached to the wild beauties of nature;—and whose inclination for *landscape*, was drawn forth by these *rustic objects*,—rather than by the example of the laboured *pictures* of any master whatever.[11]

Indeed, Gainsborough did not work in the classical manner or receive academic training, although he did make copies of earlier artists' works as a means of learning. His approach, however, diverged from that of his contemporaries, in that he followed the work of seventeenth-century Dutch painters, rather than the classicism of Italian and French Masters. Gainsborough had an opportunity to see Dutch landscape paintings and prints in private collections and London salesrooms and studied and made copies after Jan Wijnants (c. 1625–1684) and Jacob van Ruisdael (1628–1682). He found inspiration in characteristic Dutch motifs, such as tree trunks, clumps of foliage, woodland lanes, and grey skies. In later years, he would recall with "fondness" these "first imitations of little Dutch landskips."[12]

Gainsborough was also influenced by the French Rococo style and, in particular, the painter Jean-Antoine Watteau (1684–1721), known for his exquisite drawings and poignant courtship scenes. Like Watteau, Gainsborough drew with a naturalness and an easiness envied by his contemporaries and developed a most personal and intimate style. Gainsborough's numerous drawings display the forceful originality and audacity of his markings. His rhythmic and rapid strokes are evident in his *Self-Portrait* (c. 1750), notable for its natural simplicity and casual elegance and clearly indicative of his love of sketching directly from nature (see Figure 5.1). Interestingly,

Figure 5.1 Thomas Gainsborough, *Self-Portrait*, c. 1750. Pencil on paper, 35.9 x 25.8 cm. Trustees of the British Museum, London.

the artist has cut out the figure of himself, which has been drawn separately, and pasted it against a landscape background.

Gainsborough "never did attempt that style of historical painting, for which his previous studies had made no preparation" (254), but turned to the Old Masters to "learn the language of the art" (253).[13] He was mostly influenced by two of the greatest Flemish painters, namely Anthony Van Dyck (1599–1641), who had "a peculiar genius for portraits," and Peter Paul Rubens (1577–1640), whose "pictures were equally adapted to please the ignorant and connoisseurs" and his art "never greater than in landscape."[14] Gainsborough studied their works and on some occasions even copied them, learning about color, the effects of light and shadow, and general composition.

Copying and imitating were seen as essential aspects of academic practice.[15] Since the Renaissance, artists were expected to learn by copying works of past masters and by observing and assimilating their methods and techniques. The Italian painter Cennino Cennini, for example, advised in *Il libro dell'arte* (c. 1390): "Always take pains in drawing the best subjects which you can find, done by the hand of the great masters . . . and it will happen that if nature has bestowed on you any invention, you will acquire a manner of your own, which cannot be other than good."[16] Later in the eighteenth century, Reynolds advocated the same method of study. In his *Discourses*, delivered to the Royal Academy, he maintained that, "by imitation only, variety, and even originality of invention, is produced" (96). He praised the artist "who borrows an idea from an antient, or even a modern artist not his contemporary, and so accommodates it to his own work, that it makes it a part of it, with no seam or join appearing" as one who "can hardly be charged with plagiarism" and further explained that an artist should "enter into a competition with his original, and endeavour to improve what he is appropriating to his own work" (107).[17] Already in the 1760s, Gainsborough was doing just that. He made a copy of the central panel of Rubens's *Descent from the Cross* (1611–1614), most likely from an engraving (see Figure 5.2), and used it as the basis for the main group of figures in *The Harvest Wagon* (1767), a work noted for its natural grace and admirable illustration of English rural life (see Figure 5.3). The painting is noteworthy for its unique and original adaptation of the past. Gainsborough copied, as Reynolds later remarked, "not in the manner of those masters, but in his own" (253).

Gainsborough's adaptation of old motifs was manifested not only in his landscapes, but also in his portrait paintings. He had a preference for landscape painting, but was well aware, as he told his friend Jackson, that in his profession, "a Man may do great things, and starve in a Garret, if he does not conquer his Passions and conform to the *common Eye* in chusing [*sic*] that branch which *they* will encourage, & pay for."[18] Gainsborough frequently borrowed and assimilated Van Dyck's poses and dress and made several copies of his works, among them the portrait of *The Pembroke Family* (c. 1760–1770), which is said to have been painted from memory. Reynolds, in the fourteenth *Discourse*, which he devoted entirely to Gainsborough, stated:

> to satisfy himself as well as others, how well he knew the mechanism and artifice which they employed to bring out that tone of colour which we so much admire in their works, he occasionally made copies from Rubens, Teniers, and Vandyck, which it would be no disgrace to the most accurate connoisseur to mistake, at the first site, for the works of those masters. (253)

Figure 5.2 Thomas Gainsborough, *The Descent from the Cross* (after Rubens), 1760s. Oil on canvas, 125.5 x 101.5 cm. Gainsborough's House, Sudbury, Suffolk.

Gainsborough possessed an extraordinary ability for making exact copies. It is reported that "Sir Joshua himself admitted that he had been obliged to examine for a longtime a copy by Gainsborough of a Vandyke before he could decide if it were an imitation or an original."[19] Borrowing from the ancients was an accepted, and indeed required, practice in art, but Reynolds cautioned that the great aims of art could not be attained by slavish copying, in which the "powers of invention and composition . . . lie

Figure 5.3 Thomas Gainsborough, *The Harvest Wagon*, 1767. Oil on canvas, 120.5 x 144.7 cm. Trustees of the Barber Institute of Fine Arts, The University of Birmingham.

torpid" (29). He warned against "the dangerous habit of imitating without selecting" (29) and also advised: "Instead of copying the touches of those great masters, copy only their conceptions" (30). Reynolds saw a selective approach to imitation as a superior skill and one that revealed the artist's true proficiency. Praising Gainsborough's ability at copying, whether it was the exact copying of a face or the copying of a work of art, was Reynolds's backhanded way of relegating his rival's preeminent skill to the lower mechanical side of art.

Gainsborough certainly did not want to be a servile copier or mere mechanic and, as will be demonstrated, was deeply troubled by the general status of copies and became increasingly aware of the individuality of his style. He was well acquainted with the economic demands of the contemporary art market, which was saturated with imitations, fraudulent copies, and counterfeits. The painter James Barry, in his *Inquiry Into the Real and Imaginary Obstructions to the Acquisition of the Arts in England* (1775), commented: "Artful men, both at home and abroad, have not failed to avail themselves of this passion for ancient art, . . . for vending, in the name of those great masters, the old copies, imitations, and studies, of all the obscure artists that have been working in Italy, Flanders, and other places, for two hundred years past."[20] Reynolds, speaking of Watteau, an artist he greatly admired and whose works were particularly in demand, lamented:

> His works being extremely dear on the Continent the brokers and dealers bring us over copies of his pictures, or those of his imitators, Lancret and Pater, which they impose upon as originals.[21]

Problems of authenticity and attribution became increasingly common in mid eighteenth-century England, resulting in passionate disputes and lengthy debates. This was clearly evident in the celebrated trial of 1787, which pitted the picture dealers Noel Joseph Desenfans (1744–1807) and Benjamin Vandergucht (1753–1794) against each other in a dispute over the authenticity of a picture, which Vandergucht professed to be a work of the seventeenth-century French classical painter Nicolas Poussin (1594–1665). Gainsborough was called as a witness at the trial and reportedly testified that "having had no opportunity for the study, he was no judge of the hands of the masters," but that "he had seen and studied most of the celebrated works of Poussin" and that the picture "produced no emotions."[22] It was "so deficient in harmony, taste, ease, and elegance," he added, "that if he had seen it in a broker's shop, and could have bought it for five shillings, he should not have done it."[23]

As previously mentioned, the Academy endorsed copying only as an exercise necessary to the training of artists. According to its usual announcement for submission, copies were prohibited in its annual exhibitions:

> No Copies whatever, nor any Imitations of Painting in Needle-work, artificial Flowers, Shell-work or any thing of that Kind will be admitted, nor any Pictures, &c. without Frames.[24]

When Gainsborough did make copies, he was clearly preoccupied with keeping track of them and sought to maintain a certain control over them. In a letter to his physician, Dr. Rice Charlton, he writes: "My dear Doctor I forgot entirely that you had a Copy of the little dutch Spire of my Hand, tis not worth a Farthing, so do what you please with it, hang it in your Study at [Wood]house, where it may not be compared with the Original, and I shall be easy."[25] Gainsborough much preferred to keep the copies for his benefit and also out of sight of the public. He refused, for example, to sell a copy he had made of *The Conspirators*, a work by Diego Velázquez, to the Spanish Ambassador in England.[26]

Nor did Gainsborough like for anyone to copy his own works. This is most clearly evidenced in his reply to a request from the painter Ozias Humphrey (1742–1810), who followed and admired Gainsborough's work:

> I should be glad to lend you any of my Landskips to copy, did it not affect the sale of new Pictures, to have any copies taken of them. for which reason I have often been obliged to refuse, when it would have given me pleasure to Oblige my friend.[27]

Gainsborough's position contrasted with that of such contemporaries as Reynolds, Benjamin West (1738–1820) and Joseph Farington (1747–1821), all of whom allowed their work to be copied by students.[28] It is also significant that, although it was common practice at the time among portrait painters to employ assistants to paint the drapery and landscape backgrounds, Gainsborough did not do so.[29] With the exception of his nephew, Gainsborough Dupont (1754–1797), it would appear that he did not employ anyone else in the studio and would do all of this work himself, including painting the additional copies of a work he had been commissioned to produce. When his friend, the celebrated actor David Garrick, expressed an interest in purchasing a copy of his own portrait as a gift for his business advisor James Clutterbuck, Gainsborough flatly refused:

> I never will consent that any body makes a present of your Face to Clutterbuck but myself, because I always intended a Copy (*by my own hand*) for Him, that he may one day tell me what to do with my Money, the only thing he understands except jeering at folks[.] I shall look upon it that you break in upon my Line of happiness in this World if you mention it; and for the Original, it was to be my present to Mrs. Garrick, and so it shall be in spight of your blood.[30]

Gainsborough's concern with copies was so pervasive that he seemed to demand full control over the execution of his paintings. Didactic and economic considerations, however important, were never as great as his concern for the originality and individuality that he valued above all in his art. As is seen, this focus on a highly individual and inimitable style not only served to elevate Gainsborough's professional standing, but also ensured the uniqueness and exclusivity of his art.

HOGARTH'S ACT

Gainsborough began his career in contact with prominent artists and the finest draughtsmen and engravers of the day. The inspiring example of Hogarth and the French engraver Gravelot at St. Martin's Lane Academy, combined with his interest in experimenting in a variety of media, directed his attention to engraving, an art he practiced at times throughout his career and that, in mid-eighteenth-century England, developed considerably. The tremendous popularity of Hogarth's prints and the passing of the *Engravers' Copyright Act* of 1735, often referred to as "Hogarth's

Act," did much to stimulate and advance the English print trade. The French enamel painter André Rouquet, who lived in England for thirty years, wrote that the Act

> had quickly a very considerable influence on the art of engraving. Before that time there were only two print shops in London; but since this act, they suddenly increased to some hundreds: and if we consider the number and abilities of the engravers who are now in that metropolis, we must allow that of all arts relative to design, that of engraving has made the greatest progress in England.[31]

Gainsborough's early training as a professional artist coincided with an extraordinary proliferation of printed imagery and the emergence of a highly competitive market in England. Hogarth offers up a serious account on the state of affairs in his *Battle of the Pictures* (1745), in which he represents his contempt for the Old Masters and, more precisely, the wicked copies of their pictures, in great demand by the wealthy classes (see Figure 5.4). In an undoubtedly novel approach to advertising his work, the engraving was the subscription ticket to the sale of his works at an auction.[32] Notably, on the left of the image, exact replicas of foreign paintings, including *St Andrew on the Cross*, *The Flaying of Marsyas*, and *The Rape of Europa*, each inscribed with *Ditto*, are lined up en masse like an infantry in perfect formation, posing a serious threat to the works of Hogarth and his contemporaries.

Hogarth openly challenged not only the prevailing taste for old pictures, but the treacherous dissemination of copies, which extended to the piracy of his own works and rapidly prompted him to act against the brisk traffic in copies of his series of the *Masquerades and Operas* (1724) and *A Harlot's Progress* (1733–1734). Hogarth's initiative to defend the rights and property of artists was introduced in an open letter, *The Case of Designers, Engravers, Etchers &c. Stated in a Letter to a Member of Parliament*, and followed by a petition presented to the House of Commons, claiming:

> That the Petitioners, and others, have with great Industry and Expence, severally invented, designed, or engraved, divers Sets of new Pictures and Prints, in Hopes to have reaped the Benefit of such their own Labour, and the Credit thereof; but that divers Printsellers, Printers, and other Persons, both here and abroad, have, of late, too frequently taken the Liberty of copying, printing, and publishing, great Quantities of base, imperfect, and mean, Copies and Imitations thereof; to the great Detriment of the Petitioners, and such other Artists, and to the Discouragement of Arts and Sciences in this Kingdom: And therefore praying, That Leave may be given for a Bill to be brought into the House, for preventing such Frauds and Abuses for the future, and securing the

Figure 5.4 William Hogarth, *The Battle of the Pictures*, 1745. Etching, 20.1 x 21.3 cm. Trustees of the British Museum, London.

> Properties of the Petitioners, as the Laws now in being have preserved the Properties of the Authors of Books; or in such other manner as by the House shall be thought fit.[33]

The *Engravers' Copyright Act* (8 George II, c. 13) received Royal Assent on May 10, 1735, and was substantially based on the Statute of Anne of 1710 (8 Anne c. 19/5), which was limited to books and granted the exclusive right of publication to the bookseller or the author. The prestige and esteem enjoyed by authors was envied by engravers, who had hardly overcome the lowly status of craftsmen. Hogarth insisted that he was a "dramatic writer"[34] and described himself as "the Author" of the series in the advertisement for *A Harlot's Progress*, the "most remarkable Subject of painting that captivated the Minds of most People persons of all ranks & conditions."[35]

There is no doubt that the issue of copyright was a frequent topic of discussion at St. Martin's Lane Academy and one that certainly interested Gainsborough. It would be surprising if Gainsborough were not familiar with the rights of engravers over their designs. Although no editions of Gainsborough's works appear to have been published in his lifetime, as early as 1744, John Boydell published prints after his drawings.[36] Interestingly, the Act only provided protection to artists who had both designed and published their own prints, and this for a period of fourteen years from the date of first publication.[37] As Timothy Clayton has pointed out in his comprehensive study of *The English Print*, "the Act was framed in such a way as to be peculiarly useful to [Hogarth], the only artist in the country who designed, engraved and published prints on any scale."[38]

Gainsborough may have been acquainted with Hogarth. The two may have been introduced by Joshua Kirby (1716–1774), a well-known figure in the artistic world and a close friend of Gainsborough and Hogarth, both of whom contributed illustrations to his book *Dr Brook Taylor's Method of Perspective Made Easy* (1754). Clearly, Hogarth and the St. Martin's Lane circle provided young Gainsborough with a contemporary outlook as opposed to a historic and intellectual one. There he found himself in a milieu of engravers, illustrators, and booksellers far removed from the intellectual approach and academic tradition advocated by Reynolds.

The status of the engraver in England was a matter of some controversy. Although Reynolds, as the painter and biographer Joseph Farington reports:

> held the ingenuity of able engravers in high consideration . . . he would not admit that works purely imitative should be classed with original productions, or that the professors of the former were entitled to the distinction granted to the latter, which requires more profound study and greater powers of mind.[39]

Nevertheless, most painters, Reynolds included, relied on engravers to disseminate their works. Robert Strange, in his *Inquiry Into the Rise and Establishment of the Royal Academy of Arts* (1775), observed:

> No body knew better, or has more experienced, than Sir Joshua Reynolds the importance of engraving. . . . Since the memorable aera [*sic*] of the revival of the arts, in the fifteenth century, I know no painter, the remembrance of whose works will depend more on the art of engraving than that of Sir Joshua Reynolds.[40]

Reynolds did not experiment with printing, but a great number of prints were produced after his works. A note in the *Morning Chronicle, and*

London Advertiser in 1787 stated: "The Nobility, Gentry, and the Amateurs of the Arts, is most respectfully informed, that there is two thousand proofs and fine impressions" of various "capital portraits, engraved after the original pictures of Sir Joshua Reynolds, &c. complete for sale."[41]

Unlike Reynolds, who used engraving as a means of becoming known and raising public interest in his work, Gainsborough was interested in exploiting the medium and its artistic capabilities. The English painter and writer Jonathan Richardson, who produced a few etchings, was among those who pioneered the thinking that there should be a distinction made between prints "such as are done by the masters themselves whose invention the work is; and such as are done by men not pretending to invent, but only to copy (in their several ways) other mens [*sic*] works."[42] Gainsborough, whose work would clearly have fallen into the former category, used a variety of printing techniques and produced increasingly personal and original works. One example is the *Wooded Landscape With Peasant Reading Tombstone, Rustic Lovers and Ruined Church* (1779–1780), remarkable for its versatile style and rapid strokes, and possibly also a work he may have intended to publish as it bears an inscription that would have been in keeping with the Act, "Publish'd as the Act directs, Feby 1st 1780" (see Figure 5.5). It is probable that Gainsborough, never fond of copying, was disinclined to do so and felt uneasy with the idea of his work being widely disseminated and therefore even more vulnerable to copying. Reynolds, as previously noted, advocated imitation as the best means of academic training, a practice that brought about great controversy and important concerns about plagiarism. As Richard Shiff points out in his article on *Originality*, Reynolds "appears to condone eclecticism and repetition, perhaps even plagiarism, at the expense of authenticity and innovation."[43] He had been "accused of plagiarism for having borrowed attitudes from ancient masters," but was defended on the grounds of "quotation."[44] The English writer and connoisseur Horace Walpole argued that

> when a single posture is imitated from an historic picture and applied to a portrait in a different dress and with new attributes, this is not plagiarism, but quotation: and a quotation from a great author, with a novel application of the sense, has always been allowed to be an instance of parts and taste; and may have more merit than the original.[45]

Borrowing, for Gainsborough, did not play so dominant a role as it did with Reynolds. In this way, he was much like Hogarth, who "never accustomd himself to coppy [*sic*]"[46] and became a well-known advocate of the *Engravers' Copyright Act*. Gainsborough became fascinated with soft ground etching as a means of reproducing his drawings, but,

Figure 5.5 Thomas Gainsborough, *Wooded Landscape With Peasant Reading Tombstone, Rustic Lovers and Ruined Church*, c. 1779–1780. Soft ground etching, 29.7 x 39.4 cm. The Huntington Library, Art Collections, and Botanical Gardens, San Marino, California.

remarkably, abstained from publishing his prints. The threat of being copied became a constant preoccupation in his approach regardless of the medium and throughout his career. The influence of Hogarth and his circle in Gainsborough's formative years can hardly be overstated. These were artists who clearly alerted him to the economic harm and detrimental effects of piracy.

A GENTLEMAN OF THE BRUSH

If Hogarth's social circle played a key part in Gainsborough's career, so, too, did his group of close friends and prominent figures who flocked to his studio. Although, as his friend William Jackson remarked, he "avoided the company of literary men, who were his aversion"[47] and preferred not to comment upon literary or political matters, Gainsborough was far from indifferent to the intellectual and literary culture of his time. Among his closest friends were the actors David Garrick and James Quin, as well as Richard Brinsley Sheridan, who was also an author and a political orator,

Figure 5.6 Thomas Gainsborough, *Self-Portrait*, c. 1787. Oil on canvas, 77.3 x 64.5 cm. Royal Academy of Arts, London.

the Italian violinist Felice de Giardini, and the celebrated German composer Carl Friedrich Abel, "whose great musical ability was an honor to the age in which he lived" and held Gainsborough in "all his confidence and esteem!"[48]

Gainsborough was lively in conversation and, as his self-portrait of 1787 reveals, elegant in his bearing (see Figure 5.6). "His favourite subjects were music and painting; which he treated in a manner peculiarly his own."[49] Reynolds noted approvingly that Gainsborough "neglected nothing which could keep his faculties in exercise" and acknowledged that he also developed painting practices through "his own natural sagacity," which were "worthy of imitation" (250–251). He would go on to note that Gainsborough "saw [nature] with the eye of a painter; and gave a faithful, if not a poetical, representation of what he had before him" (253).

Portraiture drew Gainsborough to the fashionable city of Bath and later to London, where he gained a reputation as one of the leading portrait painters of his age and became the King's and Royal family's preferred painter. Gainsborough's success was founded on his ability to capture a 'likeness,' which he considered "the principal beauty & intention of a Portrait,"[50] and he attracted the attention of the poet laureate William Whitehead, who wrote to a friend in 1758:

> We have a painter here, who takes the most exact likeness I ever saw. His painting is coarse and slight, but has ease and spirit. Lord Villiers sat to him before he left Bath, and I hope we shall be able to bring his picture to town with us, as it is he himself, and is preferable in my opinion to the finest unlike picture in the universe, though it might serve for a sign; he sate [sic] only twice. The painter's name is Gainsborough.[51]

Gainsborough's exceptional ability in catching a likeness was praised not only by friends and patrons, but by critics as well. Speaking of the portrait of the auctioneer *James Christie* (1778), for example, one reviewer in the *Morning Chronicle, and London Advertiser* noted that it was "so striking a resemblance, that the name need not have been printed in the catalogue"[52] (see Figure 5.7). Gainsborough's technique became increasingly thin and sketch-like, as can be seen in the sitter's stylish brown jacket, rendered in rapid fluid brushstrokes, and in his own self-portrait, where fast vigorous strokes also give life to the graceful cravat and bow. He was probably "the only painter of this country" who painted in "the thin brilliant style of pencilling of Vandyke,"[53] asserted the writer of the obituary notice of Gainsborough in the *Morning Chronicle, and London Advertiser.*

Gainsborough's talents attracted the attention of fashionable people, writers, politicians, lawyers, and clerics. Among his numerous sitters were the author Laurence Sterne, the Prime Minister William Pitt, and the celebrated jurist Sir William Blackstone, who, interestingly, referring to a print of his portrait, wrote to a friend:

> I have rec[eive]d a Proof of Mr. Hall's Print, & think it extremely well executed. I am no Judge of my own Likeness: But Lady Blackstone thinks the Contraction of the Brows, & consequent Sternness of Look, a little too strongly marked. I hope Mr. Gainsborough has seen a Proof of it; & if he approves the Engraving, I am sure I can make no Objection.[54]

Figure 5.7 Thomas Gainsborough, *James Christie*, c. 1778. Oil on canvas, 126 x 101.9 cm. J. Paul Getty Museum, Los Angeles.

Lady Blackstone was probably quite astute in her thinking, and there would have been good reason to blame the engraver for the "sternness of look" of her husband. Gainsborough's fluent handling and spontaneity achieved effects that no engraver could adequately reproduce (see Figure 5.8). Not surprisingly, the number of prints made after Gainsborough's paintings is significantly smaller compared with those after Reynolds. As Antony

Figure 5.8 Thomas Gainsborough, *Sir William Blackstone*, 1774. Oil on canvas, 76.2 x 63.5 cm. Tate Gallery, London.

Griffiths observed in his study of Reynolds and Gainsborough's prints, "Gainsborough's style of painting was an engraver's nightmare."[55]

In Gainsborough's painted portrait of Blackstone, his subject, renowned for his *Commentaries on the Laws of England* (1765–1769), is shown in the robes and wig of a judge. However, Gainsborough concentrates his efforts on the face, suggesting the fleeting nature of expression, by the slightly discernible movement of the lips and vivid luminous eyes, which engage the viewer directly, but serenely. The portrait was painted in 1774, the year the seminal case of *Donaldson v. Becket* concerning literary property was decided by the House of Lords, with Blackstone among the eleven judges to give an opinion.[56] "No private cause has so much engrossed the attention of the public," the *Edinburgh Advertiser* reported, "and none has been tried before the House of Lords, in the decision of which so many individuals were interested. During the whole time of its duration in the House of Lords, (three weeks including adjournments, and eight days debate) a great number of peers were present, and paid the greatest attention."[57] The *Morning Chronicle* informed that "Mr. Edmund Burke, Dr. Goldsmith, David Garrick, Esq; and other literary characters, were among the hearers."[58]

Blackstone, a supporter of the author's right to perpetual copyright in the case, stood out as a particularly important advocate in the discussion of property rights. "There is nothing which so generally strikes the imagination, and engages the affections of mankind, as the right of property,"[59] wrote Blackstone in the *Commentaries.* As to literary property, he appealed to the concept of originality and observed that "when a man by the exertion of his rational powers has produced an original work, he has clearly a right to dispose of that identical work as he pleases, and any attempt to take it from him, or vary the disposition he has made of it, is an invasion of his right of property."[60] Earlier in the century, the poet and statesman Joseph Addison had already advocated the superiority of original over imitative works: "An Imitation of the best Authors, is not to compare with a good Original." Addison further wrote, "and I believe we may observe that very few Writers make an extraordinary Figure in the World, who have not something in their Way of thinking or expressing themselves that is peculiar to them and entirely their own."[61] Gainsborough was the epitome of natural genius, a truly original painter, with a peculiar manner of his own. "His cranium is so crammed with genius of every kind that it is in danger of bursting upon you, like a steam-engine overcharged,"[62] wrote his friend the actor David Garrick.

Clearly, this moment was important in the development of copyright, a time when the debate over the value of creativity and the notions of property and originality occupied many of the leading writers and jurists of the day. Not surprisingly, as disputes over copyright augmented and as piracy and plagiarism became increasingly sensitive issues, lawyers, too, found themselves increasingly more occupied, a circumstance they obligingly exploited. Gainsborough's opinion of the legal profession is most clearly expressed in his letter to a lawyer, in which he alludes to a prior conversation with a friend:

> I little thought you were a lawyer when I said one in ten were not worth hanging. I told Clubb of that, and he seemed to think I was lucky that I did not say one in a hundred. It's too late to ask your pardon now, but really, Sir, I never saw one of your profession look

> so honest in my life, and that's the reason why I concluded you were in the wool trade.[63]

Although his opinion of lawyers was not the most favorable, Gainsborough, as most of the fashionable people of London did, went to the courts to enjoy the superb spectacle of the law. For example, he attended the trial of Warren Hastings, a memorable event that "gathered together, from all parts of a great, free, enlightened, and prosperous empire, grace and female loveliness, wit and learning, the representatives of every science and of every art,"[64] and where Burke and his friend Sheridan delivered eloquent speeches that won them the reputation of orators of the highest stature. More important, as has already been noted, Gainsborough was a primary witness at the celebrated trial between two renowned picture dealers, which certainly made him aware of the abuses associated with copying. Interestingly, he was questioned on the relevance of a painter's "touch," as the English artist Benjamin Robert Haydon reported in his account of Gainsborough's cross-examination:

> What do you mean by a "touch"? what has a "touch" to do with character or thinking? said a counsel to Gainsborough on a trial. What! as much as the stroke of a pen has to do with either, inasmuch as the separate strokes of the pen make the word "mountain" and fill the mind with grand associations, so do separate "touches" of the brush express feature, form, colour, action, and expression, and convey associations of character.[65]

Gainsborough's "observations" and "remarks," as Henry Angelo noted in his *Reminiscences*, "were no less original than the style of his art"[66] and hardly those of an illiterate person. His explanation of the painter's "touch" and his putting it on a level with the "strokes" of the pen, a clear reminder of Leonardo's *Paragone*, laid emphasis on the most important quality of Gainsborough's own work, namely the distinctive character of his brushwork.

"NOVELTY AND PECULIARITY"

Gainsborough's methods and choice of materials were highly intuitive and noted for their idiosyncrasies. Among them was "a process rather capricious, truly deserving the epithet bestowed upon them by a witty lady, who called them moppings," and which consisted, as Edwards explained, of "a small bit of sponge tied to a bit of stick, [that] served as a pencil for the shadows, and a small lump of whiting, held by a pair of tea-tongs was the instrument by which the high lights were applied."[67] Angelo similarly notes that, "instead of using crayons, brushes, or chalks, he adopted for his painting tools his fingers and bits of sponge . . . one evening . . . he seized the sugar-tongs, and found them so obviously designed by the *genii* of art, for the express purpose, that sugar-tongs at Bath were soon raised two hundred per cent."[68]

In a letter to his friend Jackson, in 1773, Gainsborough explained the meticulous drawing technique he had developed, which included the use of a special paper that had to be cut, glued, let to dry, stretched, dipped in skimmed milk, let dry again, and varnished three times to intensify the effects. Significantly, Gainsborough ends his letter entreating his friend to "swear now never to impart my secret to any one living,"[69] a clear indication of his intention to protect his laborious method.

Luckily, details of Gainsborough's unusual studio practices are well documented. Humphrey, who followed Gainsborough's work with great interest, notes that Gainsborough's pictures "were frequently wrought by candlelight" and that "even by Day" his painting room "had scarcely any light."[70] Another contemporary, who saw Gainsborough at work, says that he painted "with pencils on sticks full six feet in length" and explains that "he placed himself and his canvas at a right angle with the sitter, so that he stood still and touched the features of his picture exactly at the same distance at which he viewed his sitter."[71] Not surprisingly, Gainsborough would become deeply concerned with the hanging and viewing conditions of his pictures.[72] This is evident in the much quoted letter to one of his sitters, a lawyer at Colchester, where he also speaks of the advantages of his peculiar style:

> You please me much by saying that no other fault is found in your picture than the roughness of the surface, for that part being of use in giving force to the effect at a proper distance, and what a judge of painting knows an original from a copy by; in short being the touch of the pencil, which is harder to preserve than smoothness. [. . .] I don't think it would be more ridiculous for a person to put his nose close to the canvas and say the colours smell offensive, than to say how rough the paint lies; for one is just as material as the other with regard to hurting the effect and drawing of a picture. Sir Godfrey Kneller used to tell them that pictures were not made to smell of; and what made his pictures more valuable than others with the connoisseurs was his pencil or touch.[73]

Gainsborough was both proud of and pleased with the unusual "touch" of his pencil, which not only served to protect his works, but was also crucial in giving a surprising appearance to the picture when viewed at "a proper distance." Reynolds acknowledged the "novelty and peculiarity" of Gainsborough's manner and described how "all those odd scratches and marks," which he referred to as "chaos," magically assumed "form" at a certain distance so that "all the parts [seemed] to drop into their proper places" (257–258).[74] He also admired the way in which "this hatching manner of Gainsborough did very much contribute to the lightness of effect which is so eminent a beauty in his pictures; as on the contrary, much smoothness, and uniting the colours, is apt to produce heaviness" (258–259). The reviewer of the *St. James Chronicle*, on seeing one of Gainsborough's landscape paintings exhibited at the Royal Academy in 1777, was rendered practically speechless in his attempt to describe this never-before-seen style:

> But what shall I say of the Pencilling [brushwork]? I really do not know; it is so new, so very original, that I cannot find Words to convey an idea of it. I do not know that any Artists, living or dead, have managed their Pencil in that Manner, and I am afraid that any Attempt to imitate it will be attended with Ill-success.[75]

The difficulty in reproducing what Reynolds called his "hatching manner" made Gainsborough's work inimitable. As the French engraver and author Abraham Bosse asserted, highly finished styles were easier to copy than those displaying bold and spontaneous handling, "where a single stroke of the brush creates what is hard to replicate in a hundred."[76] Edwards similarly opined that "Mr. Gainsborough's manner of penciling was so peculiar to himself, that his works needed no signature." "Nor is it known," Edwards continues, "that he ever made use of any to his pictures" and only exceptionally in some drawings used "a mark in gold letter, which he himself had applied by the same process that is used by the bookbinders, in the decorations of their book covers."[77]

It is important to emphasize in the present context that the provisions of the *Engravers' Copyright Act*, the first legislation to give protection to artists, were limited to works that were both designed and engraved by the same artist. Paintings and drawings were not protected as such. Surprisingly, only in 1862, with the *Fine Arts Copyright Act* (25 and 26 Victoria, c. 68), were paintings and drawings granted protection by statute. This fact is of the utmost significance because, as I have tried to show, Gainsborough's response to what he saw as the dangers of copies was to develop a peculiar and idiosyncratic style. Recognizing the defects and precarious standing of artistic copyright in eighteenth-century England, he responded cleverly. One commentator in more recent times summed it up as follows:

> That inimitable painter unwittingly set the fashionable world agog after style; but he did not enter the lists as a teacher, nor would he have allowed youth who had advised with him upon art to waste their time in attempting to learn what no one could teach. The copyists, or rather dabblers in his new style, were full grown amateurs, polite idlers at Bath, who vainly fancied, forsooth, because this rare genius could, by a sort of graphic magic, dash off romantic scraps of landscape, rural

> hovels, wild heaths; and picturesque groups of rustics, that they had but to procure his brown or blue paper, and his brushes and pigments, and do the like . . . The Gainsborough mania was long the rage; and there are yet some antique beaux and belles of *haut ton*, who recollect their many friends who, with themselves, were stricken with this sketching phrenzy [*sic*].[78]

Among those imitators were the English landscape painter Julius Caesar Ibbetson; the amateur painter George Frost, who copied Gainsborough's drawings extensively; and the artist Thomas Baker, a skillful copyist.[79] For the most part, however, Gainsborough's works were readily distinguished from copies, and, if newspapers reports are any indication, the quality of the imitations of his drawings was poor. One report in the *Morning Herald* alerted the public to "attempts having been made by the *Fabricators* in the polite arts, to pass off some very *miserable imitations* of Mr. GAINSBOROUGH's Beautiful stile of drawing."[80]

Gainsborough's quick and spontaneous manner was not easy to copy, and it is significant that he never took a didactic approach, caring little about educating and training students. Unlike Reynolds, Gainsborough consistently objected to the copying of his pictures and never felt comfortable publicizing his works. This approach served his purposes well, as the end result was that his portraits and landscape paintings were less copied or imitated than those of his contemporaries.[81] This is not to say that artists did not follow Gainsborough's style or that it had no impact on the development of English art. On the contrary, many were directly influenced, including the prominent landscape painter John Constable and skillful draughtsman Thomas Rowlandson. Interestingly, as Mary Woodall observes in her insightful study, *Gainsborough's Landscape Drawings*, Constable was someone "profoundly influenced by the spirit of Gainsborough's work, but who never really copied it," whereas Rowlandson, "on occasion, imitated Gainsborough's methods and characteristic penciling, without really exploring his attitude to nature."[82] Renowned foreign painters also became interested in Gainsborough's distinctive style, including the leading French neoclassical painter Jacques-Louis David (1784–1825), who copied a mezzotint of his portrait of the *Prince of Wales.*

Gainsborough was not a history painter, betraying the Academy's hierarchy of genres and Reynolds's aspirations. Within his own genre, however, whether it was landscape or portrait painting, he was unique. Although Reynolds lamented that Gainsborough preferred "the lesser excellencies to the greater" (260), he could not help but confer praise on him: "If ever this nation should produce genius sufficient to acquire to us the honourable distinction of an English School, the name of Gainsborough will be transmitted to posterity, in the history of the Art, among the very first of that rising name" (248).

Gainsborough's art was undeniably admired in the eighteenth century and greatly in demand by collectors and connoisseurs in England and abroad. One newspaper felt it necessary to claim that it was "hoped" that his "magical performances" would not "for the honor of *England* and the *Arts*, be ever in a situation of being sent out of this country."[83] No other English artist in his time possessed a more distinctive or more highly personal style than Gainsborough. His inimitable handling, whether it was in his prints, drawings, landscape paintings, or portraits, effectively functioned as his signature and, as he was well aware, secured his work from copying. The "odd scratches and marks," as Reynolds called them, that Gainsborough used in his work were deliberately meant to make his paintings unique and became an essential means of protecting them. The real threat of piracy and the extensive demand for copies in England and in continental Europe were powerful incentives to Gainsborough's originality.

ACKNOWLEDGMENTS

The author wishes to thank William Vaughan and Nadia Marshy.

NOTES

1. William Jackson of Exeter, *The Four Ages* (London, 1798), 160.
2. Ibid., 155.
3. Philip Thicknesse, *A Sketch of the Life and Paintings of Thomas Gainsborough, Esq.* (London, 1788), 32.
4. For this remark, see Richard and Samuel Redgrave, *A Century of British Painters* (London: Phaidon Press, 1947), 1.
5. Edward Edwards, *Anecdotes of Painters Who Have Resided or Been Born in England, With Critical Remarks on Their Productions* (London: Leigh and Sotheby, 1808), viii.
6. Gainsborough's friend Henry Bate-Dudley recalls that he had painted "several landscapes from the age of ten to twelve." *Morning Herald*, August 4, 1788. Allan Cunningham says that "at ten years old he had made some progress in sketching, and at twelve he was a confirmed painter." Allan Cunningham, *The Lives of the Most Eminent British Painters, Sculptors, and Architects*, 6 vols. (London: John Murray, 1830), 320.
7. See John Hayes, *The Landscape Paintings of Thomas Gainsborough*, 2 vols. (London: Sotheby Publications, 1982), 1:54.
8. Ibid., 53.
9. Gainsborough to William Jackson, August 23 [1767], as cited in *The Letters of Thomas Gainsborough*, ed. John Hayes (New Haven, CT: Yale University Press, 2001), 39.
10. Sir Joshua Reynolds, *Discourses on Art*, ed. Robert R. Wark (New Haven, CT: Yale University Press, 1975), 254. Hereafter page references to this edition are given in the text.
11. *Morning Herald*, March 12, 1788 (original emphasis and punctuation).
12. Gainsborough to Thomas Harvey, May 22, 1788, *Letters*, 174.

13. For an account on Gainsborough's collection, see "Gainsborough's Collection of Pictures," *The Burlington Magazine for Connoisseurs* 84, no. 494 (1944): 107–110.
14. Horace Walpole, *Anecdotes of Painting in England With Some Account of the Principal Artists*, ed. Ralph N. Wornum, 3 vols. (London: Chatto and Windus, 1876), 302, 305, 316.
15. Today, the words "copying" and "imitating" are mostly used interchangeably. In the past, however, and specifically, in the eighteenth century and earlier, the two activities were distinguished from each other, with "copying" being defined as a mere mechanical process and "imitation" being a less constrained method involving the interpretation and adaptation of old motifs. A copy, therefore, is essentially a reproduction, whether it was made by the artist wishing to learn the technique of a master or by a print maker seeking to disseminate an image. For a discussion of the role of copying in a nineteenth-century context, see Albert Boime, *The Academy and French Painting in the Nineteenth Century* (London: Phaidon, 1971), 42–43, 122–132.
16. Cennino Cennini, *Il libro dell'arte* (c. 1390), cited in Carl Goldstein, *Teaching Art: Academies and Schools From Vasari to Albers* (Cambridge: Cambridge University Press, 1996), 115.
17. Reynolds was an exemplar borrower. See Edgar Wind, "'Borrowed Attitudes' in Reynolds and Hogarth," *Journal of the Warburg Institute* 2, no. 2 (1938): 182–185; E. H. Gombrich, "Reynolds's Theory and Practice of Imitation," *Burlington Magazine* 80, no. 467 (1942): 40–45.
18. Gainsborough to William Jackson, [date unknown], as cited in *Letters*, 74. Hogarth in his *Apology for Painters*, written toward the end of his life, lamented bitterly that in England only portrait painters had any chance of "a tolerable lively hood," adding also that portrait painting is the only brand of the art by which "a money lover (can) get a fortune." William Hogarth and Michael Kitson, "Hogarth's 'Apology for Painters,'" *Walpole Society* 41 (1966–1968): 100.
19. William T. Whitley, *Thomas Gainsborough* (London: Smith, Elder & Co., 1915), 249.
20. As cited in John Pye, *Patronage of British Art* (1845; repr., London: Cornmarket Press, 1970), 29 n. 16.
21. As cited in William T. Whitley, *Artists and their Friends in England 1700–1799*, 2 vols. (London: The Medici Society, 1928), 1:110.
22. *General Evening Post*, June 7, 1787, and June 9, 1787.
23. Ibid. For a detailed discussion of the case, see Cristina S. Martinez, "The Painter's Eye and the Lawyer's Tongue: The Artist as Witness," in *Trials of Art*, ed. Daniel McClean (London: Ridinghouse, 2007), 105–133.
24. For example, the ad appeared on the first page of the *Public Advertiser*, April 1, 3, 5, 1771.
25. Gainsborough to Dr. Rice Charlton, June 24, 1779, *Letters*, 139.
26. See Whitley, *Thomas Gainsborough*, 249.
27. Gainsborough to Ozias Humphrey, [Date Unknown], *Letters*, 32.
28. The painter James Northcote, in conversation with James Ward, went as far as to say it was their responsibility: "Artists of eminence should not withhold their experience from the rising generation of painters. They should even lend them pictures to copy; it's their duty, whenever they can do it, to point out the students' faults, and to lead their minds to excellence." James Northcote, *Conversations of James Northcote R. A. With James Ward on Art and Artists*, ed. Ernest Fletcher (London: Methuen, 1901), 33–34.
29. James Northcote, assistant of Reynolds, comments: "I continued with Sir Joshua near five years, most of which time I spent in making copies from

my master's pictures for him or painting his draperies; and whenever I could gain a little time from those employments I painted heads from the life for my improvement as a portrait painter, but the hours I could gain were few." Stephen Gwynn, *Memorials of an Eighteenth Century Painter (James Northcote)* (London: T. Fisher Unwin, 1898), 110.

30. Gainsborough to David Garrick, [1771], *Letters*, 85 (original emphasis and punctuation).
31. Jean André Rouquet, *The Present State of the Arts in England* (London, 1755), 28.
32. See Frederick D. Leach, *William Hogarth's Subscription-Tickets: A Vehicle for Eighteenth Century Satire on Contemporary Taste* (PhD thesis, State University of Iowa, 1955).
33. *Journals of the House of Commons*, as cited in Ronald Paulson, *Hogarth: His Life, Art, and Times*, 2 vols. (New Haven, CT: Yale University Press, 1971), 1:361. The petition was signed by Hogarth, George Vertue, John Pine, George Lambert, Joseph Goupy, Gerard Vandergucht, and Isaac Ware.
34. "I have endeavoured to treat my subjects as a dramatic writer; my picture is my stage, my men and women my players, who, by means of certain action and gestures, are to exhibit a dumb show," Hogarth declared. As cited in Cunningham, *The Lives of the Most Eminent British Painters*, 1:87.
35. "Vertue Note Books, Volume III," *Walpole Society* 22 (1933–1934): 58.
36. See Hayes, *Landscape Paintings*, 1:37.
37. The Act provided "every Person who shall invent and design, engrave, etch, or work in *Mezzotinto* or, *Chiaro Oscuro*," with the "sole Right and Liberty of Printing and Reprinting" their work "for the Term of Fourteenth Years, to commence from the Day of the first Publising thereof, which shall be truly engraved with the Name of the Proprietor on each Plate, and printed on every such Print or Prints." The Act is reprinted in Paulson, *Hogarth*, 2: 489.
38. Timothy Clayton, *The English Print 1688–1802* (New Haven, CT: Yale University Press, 1997), 87–88. The Act proved less beneficial than Hogarth intended. His new series of prints, *The Rake's Progress* (1735), was pirated by someone who had seen the original works in Hogarth's studio and copied them from memory. To Hogarth's great disappointment, the pirated copies were on sale before his own prints appeared. See David Kunzle, "Plagiaries-by-Memory of the *Rake's Progress* and the Genesis of Hogarth's Second Picture Story," *Journal of the Warburg and Courtauld Institutes*, 29 (1966): 311–348.
39. Joseph Farington, *Memoirs of the Life of Sir Joshua Reynolds; With Some Observations on His Talents and Character* (London: T. Cadell & W. Davies, 1819), 62.
40. Robert Strange, *An Inquiry Into the Rise and Establishment of the Royal Academy of Arts* (London, 1775), 120–121.
41. *Morning Chronicle, and London Advertiser*, April 28, 1786.
42. Jonathan Richardson, *An Essay on the Whole Art of Criticism as It Relates to Painting* (1719), in *The Works* (1773) (Hildesheim: Georg Olms Verlag, 1969), 233.
43. Richard Shiff, "Originality," in *Critical Terms for Art History*, ed. Robert S. Nelson and Richard Shiff (Chicago: University of Chicago Press, 1996), 107.
44. Walpole, *Anecdotes*, 1:xvii n. 2.
45. Ibid.
46. William Hogarth, "The Autobiographical Notes," in *The Analysis of Beauty with the Rejected Passages from the Manuscript Draft and Autobiographical Notes*, ed. Joseph Burke (Oxford: Clarendon Press, 1955), 202.
47. Jackson, *The Four Ages*, 179.
48. *Morning Herald*, June 21, 1787.

49. Jackson, *The Four Ages*, 160.
50. Gainsborough to Lord Dartmouth, April 13, 1771, *Letters*, 90.
51. Whitehead to Lord Harcourt, December 5, 1758. Cited in Whitley, *Thomas Gainsborough*, 28.
52. *Morning Chronicle, and London Advertiser*, April 25, 1778.
53. *Morning Chronicle, and London Advertiser*, August 8, 1788.
54. Sir William Blackstone to William Strahan, January 11, 1778, as cited in Howell J. Heaney and William Blackstone, "The Letters of Sir William Blackstone (1723–1780) in the Hampton L. Carson Collection of the Free Library of Philadelphia," *American Journal of Legal History* 1, no. 4 (1957): 376.
55. Timothy Clifford, Antony Griffiths, and Martin Royalton-Kisch, *Gainsborough and Reynolds in the British Museum* (London: British Museum, 1978), 40–41. Michael Rosenthal, in his thorough study of Gainsborough's art, pointed out that the "four" prints "that James McArdell made after Gainsborough portraits in the 1750s and early 1760s hardly compare with the 'nearly forty' plates that he worked on for Reynolds before his death in 1765." Michael Rosenthal, *The Art of Thomas Gainsborough: "a little business for the eye"* (New Haven, CT: Yale University Press, 1999), 12.
56. In this decision, as Mark Rose explains, the "principle in question was whether literary property was a statutory right, a limited creation of the state, or a common-law right and therefore absolute and perpetual." Mark Rose, "The Author as Proprietor: *Donaldson v. Becket* and the Genealogy of Modern Authorship," *Representations*, no. 23 (1988): 51. See also Ronan Deazley, *On the Origin of the Right to Copy: Charting the Movement of Copyright Law in Eighteenth-Century Britain (1695–1775)* (Oxford: Hart Publishing, 2004), 142–147.
57. *Edinburgh Advertiser*, March 1, 1774.
58. *Morning Chronicle*, February 5, 1774.
59. William Blackstone, *Commentaries on the Laws of England*, 4 vols. (Oxford: Clarendon Press, 1765–1769), 2:2.
60. Ibid., 405–406.
61. Joseph Addison, *Spectator* (September 3, 1711), ed. Donald F. Bond, 5 vols. (Oxford: Clarendon Press, 1965), 2: 129–130.
62. As cited in John Hayes and Lindsay Stainton, *Gainsborough Drawings* (Washington, DC: International Exhibitions Foundation, 1983), 15.
63. Quoted in Lord Ronald Sutherland Gower, *Thomas Gainsborough* (London: George Bell and Sons, 1903), 30.
64. For this remark, see George Williams Fulcher, *Life of Thomas Gainsborough* (London: Longman, Brown, Green, and Longmans, 1856), 144.
65. Benjamin Robert Haydon and Frederick Wordsworth Haydon, *Benjamin Robert Haydon Correspondence and Table-Talk*, 2 vols. (New York: R. Worthington, 1878), 2:291.
66. *The Reminiscences of Henry Angelo*, intro. Lord Howard de Walden, 2 vols. (London: K. Paul, Trench, Trübner & Co., 1904), 1:276.
67. Edwards, *Anecdotes*, 139.
68. Angelo, *Reminiscences*, 1:168–169.
69. Gainsborough to William Jackson [January 29, 1773], *Letters*, 111.
70. Ozias Humphrey, *Memoir* (London: Royal Academy, Humphrey Papers HU I/20–40 fol. 36).
71. For this reference, see Whitley, *Thomas Gainsborough*, 247.
72. Gainsborough's concern for correct viewing conditions was to cause the withdrawal of his paintings from the Royal Academy exhibition in 1784. See *Morning Herald and Daily Advertiser*, April 22, 1784; *Gazetteer and New Daily Advertiser*, April 24, 1784; and *Public Advertiser*, May 26, 1785.

73. Thomas Gainsborough to William Mayhew, March 13, 1758, *Letters*, 10–11.
74. On Gainsborough and the issue of magic in pictorial representation, see William Vaughan, "Magic in the Studio," in *Sensation & Sensibility: Viewing Gainsborough's Cottage Door*, ed. Ann Bermingham (New Haven, CT: Yale Center for British Art, 2005), 165–179.
75. As quoted in *Thomas Gainsborough 1727–1788*, ed. Michael Rosenthal and Martin Myrone (New York: Abrams, 2002), 124.
76. As quoted in Donald Posner, "Concerning the 'Mechanical' Parts of Painting and the Artistic Culture of Seventeenth-Century France," *Art Bulletin* 75, no. 4 (1993): 591.
77. Edwards, *Anecdotes*, 142.
78. W. H. Pyne, *Somerset House Gazette*, as cited in John Lewis Roget, *A History of the "Old Water-Colour" Society*, 2 vols. (London: Longmans, Green and Co., 1891), 58 (original emphasis and punctuation).
79. For a detailed analysis of Gainsborough's copyists and imitators, see Hayes, *Landscape Paintings*, 1:237–298; John Hayes, *The Drawings of Thomas Gainsborough*, 2 vols. (New Haven, CT: Yale University Press, 1971), 1:64–91.
80. As cited in John Hayes, *Gainsborough Drawings* (London: The Arts Council, 1960), 7 (original emphasis).
81. For example, as Hayes points out, the work of Gainsborough's rival, the English landscape painter Richard Wilson, "was widely copied." Hayes, *Landscape Paintings*, 1: 238–239.
82. Mary Woodall, *Gainsborough's Landscape Drawings* (London: Faber and Faber, 1939), 79.
83. *Morning Herald*, February 29, 1788; and *Morning Herald*, August 18, 1788.

6 Byron and the Scandal of Paternity

Anonymity, Plagiarism, and the Natural Rights of Authors

Tilar J. Mazzeo

Matthew Lewis' gothic novel *The Monk* was published anonymously in 1798, with a preface in which the young author acknowledged his literary debts, both conscious and unconscious.[1] Lewis soon discovered, however, that anonymous publication provided little protection from the periodical reviewers. The novel was quickly pronounced obscene, involving Lewis in a series of potential legal difficulties. Perhaps more surprisingly, despite his public avowal of source materials, he was also soon accused of plagiarism.

In the 1820s, with the anonymous publication of *Don Juan*, Lewis' friend and fellow author Lord Byron found himself in much the same predicament: the work was likewise published anonymously and charged with both plagiarism and indecency. My argument here proposes that the legal and rhetorical entanglements of anonymity, plagiarism, and immorality—three different but often associated forms of culturally suspect speech in the Romantic period—reflect an important evolution in public attitudes toward literary property in Britain during the first decades of the nineteenth century.

More specifically, focusing on how these forms of speech converged in the critical conversation surrounding Byron's poetry after 1816, I argue that the poet's literary reception in the period helped to popularize a nascent legal discourse linking property rights (and plagiarism, in particular) to metaphors of paternity and moral rights.

The contemporary parallel between the perceived immorality of Byron's work and his celebrity status as a father is the most straightforward part of an otherwise complex rhetorical knot. In fact, after 1816, it is difficult to underestimate the importance of paternity in the popular representation of Byron. Most obviously, of course, he was known as the son of a famously immoral father, the "mad" Lord Byron. But he was also, and rather more importantly, known as a parent of some dubious report. His failed marriage was the subject of common gossip, and, as Samuel C. Chew revealed in a bibliographic essay published in 1919, public interest in the separation scandal spurred the publication and sale of numerous pamphlets and spurious poems that interrogated Byron as a father.

The print culture surrounding Byron's domestic complications was extensive, and it gives an idea of how intense the public scrutiny of his status as a father became. It also reveals how consistently that scrutiny became tied to issues of language and immoral poetics. In fact, for many commentators, imitating Byron's life and shocking moral conduct was nearly the same thing as imitating him in verse. As one anonymous author (likely the publisher, John Stacey) boasted: "I know of nothing easier than to compose a poem à la Byron: take a (not) human being . . . with every vice . . . borrow as much pride, malignity, and blasphemy as Satan can afford . . . let him have a mistress . . . [and] let her be *insinuated* to be his *sister*."[2] In fact, there were numerous poems along these lines, supplemented by pamphlets that offered detailed accounts of the poet's domestic difficulties and moral irregularities. Lady Byron's legal arguments for separation on the grounds of her husband's "brutally indecent language" were popularized in polemical accounts of the separation, and there were any number of works with titles such as *A Narrative of the Circumstances Which Attended the Separation of Lord and Lady Byron* (London: Richard Edwards, 1816).[3]

Verse accounts of the Byron marriage were particularly popular in 1816, when the lawyers were slowly hammering out the terms for a private separation agreement and when gossip about the separation was circulating broadly in London society. His wife's family and her friends seem to have initiated a further smear campaign when Byron announced his intention to retain custody of his infant daughter, considered a father's right by law. His half-sister Augusta (herself at the heart of some of the most disturbing rumors, focusing on incest and paternity) warned Lady Byron early in the proceedings that "There is one thing . . . you should be prepared for (if worse don't occur) which is about the Child. He seems determined to have it, & I understand that *the Law* wd allow it to him when a year old."[4] By mid-April, the entire affair—from the custody battle to the charges of marital abuse, infidelity, homosexuality, and incest—was more public than any of the principals would have wished. Byron responded to the rumors by publishing his riposte poems "Fare Thee Well!" and "Sketch From Private Life," and Lady Byron was left to lament "The circumstances of my present Situation having, to my great regret, become the subject of the *most* public discussion."[5]

The publication of Byron's verses on his marriage only heightened the public interest in his personal life and placed greater public scrutiny on his character as a father in particular. "Fare Thee Well!" and "Sketch From Private Life" were widely reprinted and by various publishers usually under the title *Poems on His Domestic Circumstances*.

The edition published by Richard Hone in 1816 went to fifteen editions in the course of the first year alone, and "Fare Thee Well!" was a poem very much about paternity and the issues of contested custody that continued to dominate his legal conflict with his wife's family. In the poem,

Byron pointedly asks his wife: "When our child's first accents flow / Wilt thou teach her to say 'Father!' / Though his care she must forego?" (ll. 34–36).[6] The emphasis is on the same linguistic construction (or violation) of fatherhood that dominated in print culture responses to the poem, and his paternal concern in "Fare Thee Well!" is explicitly a fear that his child will not learn to say his name.

But if publishers and printers were doing a brisk trade selling Byron's poems on the separation, they soon discovered that the public was even more eager to read hoaxes, satires, and polemics capitalizing on the scandal. There were popular poetic responses to the separation that provided sharp commentary, works such as *A Reply to Fare Thee Well!! Lines Addressed to Lord Byron* (London: R. S. Kirby, 1816), "To a Sleeping Infant" (London R. S. Kirby, 1816), or *Reply to Lord Byron's "Fare Thee Well"* (Newcastle: S. Hodgson, 1817). There also were hoaxes. Apocryphal works such as Lord Byron's "Pilgrimage to the Holy Land," "The Tempest," "Farewell to England," and "To My Daughter on the Morning of Her Birth" were all published as if they were the new and authentic work of Byron. There were even poems said to have been written by Annabella on the subject of their marriage, most notably *Lady Byron's Responsive "Fare Thee Well"* (London: Richard Edwards, 1816). What all these works shared was an emphasis on Byron's publicly (and legally) contested role as a father. Although the fashion for such imaginative responses to his marital difficulties was at its height during the legal machinations of 1816, publications on the topic continued to be printed until at least as late as 1825.

But if Byron's celebrity persona in 1816 was already firmly linked in the public mind to his new role as an absent and, increasingly, unfit father, his paternity was soon to be even more firmly linked to outrage concerning his morals and his verse. From 1816 to 1819, gossip increasingly associated Byron with the most shocking sorts of family romance and violation. The periodic dark hints of his incestuous relationship with Augusta and the true paternity of her daughter Medora, dating from 1814, were reinvigorated with the publication of *Manfred* in 1817. During the infamous summer of 1816, there had already been scandalous rumors that Byron had formed with Shelley and the Godwin sisters a literary "league of incest" on the shores of Lake Geneva. Before long, there were accounts of the birth of his illegitimate daughter Allegra, the product of his unhappy liaison with Claire Clairmont. Lady Caroline Lamb's revenge novel *Glenarvon* (1816) appeared that same year, casting Byron as a vampire and revolutionary in a novel centered on questions of legitimacy and child murder. In 1818, the publication of the openly licentious *Beppo* confirmed the public opinion of Byron as a libertine and raised legal fears of prosecution for indecency, and in 1819 came the publication of the first two cantos of *Don Juan*—with their exceedingly sharp caricatures of Lady Byron. Once again, his domestic affairs were the topic of fevered public interest, and this time his fitness as a father found even fewer defenders.

The first two cantos of *Don Juan* were published anonymously in July 1819 in an expensive quarto edition, without either the name of the author or the name of the publisher, and it should have been a poem with a modest and almost exclusively aristocratic audience. However, as William St. Clair recently has demonstrated in his study *The Reading Nation in the Romantic Period* (2004), Byron's "*Don Juan* was read by more people in its first twenty years than any previous work of English literature" (333), and this was due, in large part, to the fact that the poem was widely reprinted in pirate copies almost immediately after its publication.[7] This unparalleled circulation was the direct result of the highly public controversy that connected the poem's immorality with the suspension of property rights in the work. Under nineteenth-century British law, immorality was a criminal offense, and those found guilty of it were not allowed to profit from their crimes, especially when those crimes were literary. As a result, there could be no property in works judged libelous, scandalous, seditious, blasphemous, obscene, or morally "mischievous."[8]

However, under nineteenth-century law, it was not only authors who could be denied the rights to their productions on the basis of immorality. Parents could also be deprived of the custody of their children on the same grounds. According to statute, a father's otherwise unquestioned right to authority over his minor children could be dissolved on the "grounds of some moral . . . injury . . . likely to accrue to the child."[9] Ironically, speech was more likely to be viewed as morally harmful than action. Fathers did not lose parental rights for adultery, but they might lose them for blasphemy. Anonymity offered a measure of protection for authors and parents concerned about the legal implications of a risqué poem.

Although there was no way to protect the literary property in an offensive work, anonymous publication could prevent the author from facing the additional personal and legal consequences of this "injurious" speech. Shelley had learned this lesson the hard way in 1817, when the court decided that his *Queen Mab* (1813), published with his name, contained blasphemous libel. From a copyright perspective, such a finding would imply that the poem—having no legal existence as property—could not be protected from reproduction or piracy. Shelley would undoubtedly have welcomed this broader circulation regardless of how it came about. From a personal standpoint, however, the implications were rather more unsettling. The penalties for blasphemy were serious. A second conviction carried a prison sentence of three years.[10] But even a first finding of blasphemy was sufficient to strip him of the parental authority over his minor children.

Shelley's legal difficulties with his poem and his children were well known in Regency society, and his status as an unfit father was the subject of common report. Byron's close association with Shelley only confirmed the suspicions about Byron that had been circulating at least since the celebrated 1816 "Fare Thee Well!" rebuttals. It was Byron's commitment to safeguarding his parental control over his daughter, whose custody had been legally retained by him as the father in the separation agreement, that emerged as the motivation for keeping *Don Juan* anonymous. Although his authorship was always intended to be an open secret, the lack of a name on the title page meant that his wife's family would not be able to take the case to court. As Byron explained to Murray in October 1820: "Recollect, that if you put my name to *Don Juan* in these canting days, any lawyer might oppose my Guardian rights to my daughter in Chancery, on the plea of its containing the *parody* . . . [and] I prefer my child to a poem at any time."[11]

Parental concerns aside, the anonymous publication of *Don Juan* also protected Byron and Murray from personal prosecution for other injurious forms of speech and, notably, from the charges of scandalous libel that Murray feared would result from the open caricatures of so many public figures. Yet the legal benefits of anonymity were a doubled-edged sword. While protecting Byron from individual complaints of libel, it seems actually to have fueled the charges of immorality and indecency in *Don Juan* as a whole. According to contemporary statute, anonymous publication was perfectly permissible under late eighteenth- and early nineteenth-century British law and had no bearing on issues of copyright. In fact, one recent study suggests that more than fifty percent of the novels published during the Romantic period appeared without the legal name of the author, and the absence of an author's name on the title page had little effect on the property rights of the work.[12] In the words of one nineteenth-century legal commentator: "it is not necessary that the author's name should appear to secure any right given by the statutes passed for the protection of literary property."[13] As a matter of convention, however, anonymous publication signaled a work of questionable judgment.

Anonymous publications were aesthetically and morally suspect. Even the legal decisions governing it were contentious. Faced with the question of the author's rights to his or her work in the case of *Tonson v. Collins* (1761), which found that anonymous publication could not be considered the abandonment of property, there were still jurists who argued that a work could be understood as "a gift to the public, like land thrown into a highway . . . [in cases] where the author conceals himself and gives no indicia to distinguish his property."[14] More ominously, the notorious Black Acts—"occasioned by some devastations committed . . . by persons in disguise"—made certain forms of anonymity a criminal offense; according to the statute, a person could be sentenced for "sending anonymous letters, or letters signed with a fictitious name."[15] Following this same cultural logic, pseudonymous publications, often compared to a species of fraud (a capital crime), were considered particularly problematic. In the case of *Hogg v. Kirby* (1803), "in which it was endeavoured to be shewn that a new magazine was a fraudulent continuation of a similar work, the Lord Chancellor expressed a doubt whether he ought to interfere, because the latter book bore *a fictitious name*."[16]

In addition to these opposing cross-currents in the legal discourse surrounding anonymity, there also were pervasive negative cultural associations with anonymous works. To publish a book without a name signaled one of two things, and neither was likely to encourage gentle treatment in the periodical reviews. An anonymous book was either a work of questionable merit—typically a novel written by an appropriately modest gentleman or gentlewoman and published without his or her name to emphasize the essentially private and amateurish (and, therefore, genteel) nature of the effort—or it was a work too inappropriate for the author (or publisher) to dare to claim it.

As John Feather has demonstrated in *Publishing, Piracy, and Politics*, one reason that books were published anonymously was because they were illegal pirate editions. The most determinedly "modest anonymity is an almost infallible indicator of an irregular edition," Feather writes.[17] Where books were published without the name of either the author or the publisher and printer, they are, as Feather suggests, invariably pirate copies. The law positively required the name of the printer, and publishers who held legitimate copyrights to a work had every reason to be sure their property was claimed publicly—and, thereby, protected. There could only be nefarious reasons for omitting such information, including the possible illegality of the imprint.

In other cases, however, a literary work might be published without the name of the author (or even, as in the case of *Don Juan*, without the name of the publisher) because the content was thought to be actionable. As I already suggested, there were several forms of criminal speech in the Romantic period. Generally understood as different types of libel, blasphemy, sedition, and obscenity were all immoral and punishable offenses. Because the courts were disinclined to allow authors or publishers to benefit from these crimes, it also was understood that immoral works could not be treated as literary property. A publisher would not be given an injunction to prevent the illegal reproduction of the work because the copyright was essentially invalidated. In his *Practical Treatise on the Laws of Patents for Inventions and Copyright*, published in 1823, Richard Godson summarized the contemporary conditions succinctly: "There cannot be a copyright in any work, the tendency of which is *obscene* or *immoral*. . . . And if a work be of such a libellous or mischievous nature as to affect the *public morals* . . . a court of equity will not interfere with an injunction, to protect that which by the policy of the law cannot be called property."[18]

Generally, the idea that there were certain forms of publication that could not be considered literary property is an important one, not only for the study of copyright history, but also for the study of plagiarism in the Romantic period. Immoral works were not property, but neither were particular genres. Love letters, no matter how eloquently written, had no legal protection. Only works publicly recognized as literary enjoyed the protections—legal or cultural—that we now apply to a much broader range of writing. As Godson explains, letters of any sort "*cannot be considered as literary* composition, and entitled to protection on the ground of copyright existing in them."[19] Other genres often seem to have been likewise excluded, notably travel writing and histories. They were subject to extensive reemployment in other texts without generating either the lawsuits or charges of plagiarism that we might expect.

For works written in clearly literary genres such as poetry, however, there seems to have been a significant degree of suspicion when they were published anonymously, especially during politically tense national moments, and this was in large part because anonymity was often associated with the radical press or active cultural dissent. As Lisa M. Wilson argues in her reading of the controversy provoked by the publication of *The Monk* at the end of the eighteenth century, the reviews connected "the faceless troop of [gothic] authors with other kinds of anonymous social threats like Jacobins or groups of working-class radicals . . . repeating fears about the lack of social control over anonymous authors."[20] The Seditious Societies Act of 1799 was intended to prevent the circulation of radical books and pamphlets that might foment civil unrest, and it was precisely to prevent the anonymous circulation of "dangerous" works that printers and publishers were required to put their names to all books they produced. Thus, although anonymous publication was legal, it often resulted either in the intense scrutiny of a work for radical elements or in its critical dismissal as subliterary.

Byron surely understood, even from the distance of his self-imposed exile in Italy, the complications that the anonymous publication of a poem as irreverent and politically engaged as *Don Juan* might create. He was in close contact with Shelley during the months given over to Shelley's unsuccessful custody suit, and Byron must have followed with interest and some glee the legal difficulties of his arch-rival Robert Southey, whose efforts to secure an injunction against pirate copies of his early radical poem *Wat Tyler* were refused in 1817 on the grounds that the work demonstrated a "libellous tendency" and could not be protected as literary property.[21] Matthew Lewis visited Byron in Venice that same year, and it is difficult to imagine that Lewis' experience with a similar scandal surrounding blasphemy and obscenity in *The Monk* did not come to mind for both authors. Above all, Byron's letters indicate that he understood the risks as well as the protections of anonymity. Writing to Murray in the summer of 1819, as the first cantos of *Don Juan* were coming to press, he insisted that his publisher should "keep the *anonymous* in every case: it helps what fun there may be; but if the matter grows serious about *Don Juan*, and you feel *yourself* in a scrape or *me* either, *own that I am the author. I* will never *shrink*, even if *you* do."[22]

What Byron had not anticipated, however, was the extent to which Murray's concerns for his own anonymity would exacerbate the situation. As Byron knew, authors published works anonymously on a regular basis;

although it might attract additional attention to the poem, that was part of the amusement. Byron must have expected that *Don Juan*, with its veiled portraits of society figures, would create a scandal among the chattering classes. However, Byron does not seem to have seriously believed that there was anything demonstrably indecent about the poem. Throughout all his long correspondence on the subject in the years after the public abuse and legal entanglements began, he remains insistent on this point. "The reading or non-reading of a book," he wrote with characteristic disdain for the innocence of his female readers, "will never keep down a single petticoat."[23] "Smollet . . . [is] ten times worse; and Fielding no better," he insisted.[24] Murray, however, was far less confident; as a result, when it came time to print the first two cantos of the poem, he refused to put his name on the book either. *Don Juan* was published only with the name of the printer, as minimally required under the law. Murray's evasiveness, however, was a strong cultural message that he considered the poem morally suspect and potentially scandalous. When the publisher signaled his concern that the work was indecent, both the readers and the pirate publishers took note.

The result of Murray's hesitation was a publication that smacked of the illegitimate and untoward. The pirate publishers understood immediately that the poem was fair game. Byron understood the problem quite clearly as well. Recounting *Don Juan*'s entrance into society, he told Thomas Medwin:

> Murray offered me, of his own accord, 1000 l. a Canto for "Don Juan," and afterwards reduced it to 500 l. on the plea of piracy. . . . It is true enough that "Don Juan" has been pirated; but whom has he to thank but himself?. . . . If he had put John Murray on the title-page like a man, instead of smuggling the brat into the world, and getting Davison, who is a printer and not a publisher, to father it, who would have ventured to question his paternal rights? Or who would have attempted to deprive him of them? The thing was plainly this: he disowned and refused to acknowledge the bantling; the natural consequence was, that others should come forward to adopt it.[25]

Byron suggests in this recounting that the rights to a literary work belong essentially to the publisher. Although the matter may seem curious, the representation is historically accurate. Murray owned the copyrights to these first cantos of *Don Juan*, and it was generally understood in the Romantic period that the commercial agents who produced a book were those most responsible for its success—and those who would enjoy any profits from it.

In fact, the idea that the author played a personal role in the creation of literary property had no legal reality until the latter part of the eighteenth century. Although the metaphor of author as progenitor had existed for centuries, it was only with the decision in *Tonson v. Collins* (1761) that the identity of the author was formally recognized as having an inherent connection to the property rights invested in his or her writing. "How," the court had asked, "is an author to be distinguished?"[26] The answer was that the best writers were recognizable by their literary style and individual sentiments, suggesting the importance of identity in the creation—although not yet regulation—of literary property. It was only in the period between 1760 and 1842, with the passage of the revised Literary Copyright Act—in other words, in the period roughly coinciding with the emergence of literary Romanticism—that the personality or persona of the author became legally, culturally, and aesthetically important in publishing history.

The rise of the professional author and its relationship to changes in copyright law, however, has been ably addressed by legal historians and other scholars.[27] What interests me most in Byron's account of *Don Juan*'s publication is not the inherent conflict with Murray that he was negotiating, but the metaphors that he used to describe the origins of the controversy surrounding the poem. What his language suggests is the extent to which paternity was a legal and representational subtext in the scandal of *Don Juan* from the outset. Mary Shelley had spoken of *Frankenstein* (1818) as "my hideous progeny."[28] Byron speaks of *Don Juan* as a bastard child. His recollections cast the poem as a "brat" and a "bantling" that John Murray had smuggled shamefacedly into the world. Elsewhere he emphasizes to his correspondents his own intentions of living up to his responsibilities. "*I* will never *shrink*," he writes.[29] "I am . . . willing to be *both ostensible* and *responsible* for the poem—and to come home and face the consequences on the *Author*," he says in another instance.[30] Where Murray refuses to act "like a man" and acknowledge this literary production as legitimate, Byron insists he is prepared to do so without hesitation, and this macho language also is the language of fatherhood.

These issues of paternity circulating around the poem were publicly intensified when Murray eventually attempted to enforce his copyright in the poem by taking the piracies to trial in 1823. A well-known publisher of pornographic materials by the name of Dugdale argued in court that the work was obscene and won. Even the language of the trial emphasized paternal rights. *Don Juan*, the defendant proclaimed, was "so licentious, that no father of a family would permit the book to be seen in his house."[31] Part of the public scandal of the poem became the injury it might inflict on innocent maidens and the illicit knowledge that it might impart, and this was part of the rhetoric surrounding the poem even before the legal proceedings and the press coverage that followed highlighted the risks to daughters. British fathers did, in fact, take seriously their charge to keep the poem away from women readers, and this cultural exercise of parental authority was an inherent part of the poem's reception history. Byron's dismissive remark about keeping petticoats down is mirrored in his later comment that "No Girl will ever be seduced by reading *D.J.*:—no, no; she will go to . . . Rousseau's romans for that," and well into the Victorian period, fathers even of literary girls like Elizabeth Barrett Browning were known to "keep a canto . . . locked up from wandering eyes."[32]

Perhaps most formative in connecting the moral dangers of *Don Juan* with issues of Byronic paternity, however, was the scandal surrounding the funeral of his illegitimate daughter, Allegra, which coincided with the outraged critical attacks on *Don Juan* and its author in the autumn of 1822. Once again, the parallels between Byron as a father and Byron as a poet were intensified. He had hoped to have Allegra buried in the churchyard of his old school at Harrow, but then word went about that Lady Byron considered this a favorite spot of her own and a personal insult. Public outrage ensued, and the pitch of controversy surrounding indecency in *Don Juan* became fused with the controversy surrounding his illegitimate paternity and other forms of moral degeneracy.

His letters suggest that Byron also saw the emerging parallels. Metaphors of birth, paternity, and death dominate his responses to the charges brought against the poem after Allegra's death in late April 1822. Within weeks, Byron described his literary projects in a letter to Walter Scott as "obstetrical" labors.[33] By autumn, when news of this fresh scandal had broken, he protested to Murray about "the calumnies you have allowed to circulate in the papers on the subject of the funeral of Allegra," and only days later he wrote again defending *Don Juan* as "a *Satire* on *abuses* of the present state of Society, and not an eulogy of vice."[34] The immoral substance of *Don Juan* and the funeral of his illegitimate daughter, both misperceived as eulogies to vice, became linked in the public mind, both concrete evidence of the poet's libertinism.

Don Juan, however, was already associated in the public arena with another form of illegitimacy as well. Byron had been charged with plagiarism in the poem by 1821, when an anonymous reviewer (identified only as C.E.S.) published a series of articles in the *Monthly Magazine* documenting Byron's obligations in the second and third cantos of *Don Juan*. In the essays, Byron was accused of having plagiarized from a broad range of contemporary and historical texts, including a series of narratives describing shipwrecks at sea, and his obligations were outlined in parallel passages. In defending himself against the charge of plagiarism, he suggests that the anonymous publication of the *Don Juan* should have obviated the necessity of any citations. In a letter written to Murray in the summer of 1821, Byron writes:

> With regard to the charges about the Shipwreck,—I think that I told both you and Mr. Hobhouse, years ago, that [there] was not a *single circumstance* of it *not* taken from *fact*; not, indeed, from any *single* Shipwreck, but all from *actual* facts of different wrecks. Almost all *Don Juan* is *real* life, either my own, or from people I knew. By the way, much of the description of the *furniture*, in Canto 3d, is taken

> from *Tully's Tripoli* (pray *note this*), and the rest from my own observation. Remember, I never meant to conceal this at all, and have only not stated it, because *Don Juan* had no preface nor name to it.—If you think it worthwhile to make this statement—do so—in your own way.—*I* laugh at such charges—convinced that no writer ever borrowed less—or made his materials more his own.[35]

The suggestion is that the anonymous publication of the poem would have made the avowal of sources essentially irrelevant. Plagiarism was one author taking credit for the thoughts, ideas, sentiments, and literary style of another writer. But if he did not take the credit—if his name were not attached to the work in question—how had the original author been harmed? Of course, a preface to the poem still might have been included with a catalogue of his debts. But when Matthew Lewis had anonymously published *The Monk* with precisely such a note, it had done nothing to forestall charges of plagiarism. Byron might easily be forgiven for wondering whether there could be any point in announcements of this sort. The truth of the matter, I suspect, is that there was also a complicated cultural relationship between anonymity and charges of plagiarism in the Romantic period, one not simply resolved with a set of notes and citations.

As I already suggested, anonymous publications had about them something of the illicit to begin with. In Byron's case with *Don Juan*, that hint of scandal found its catalyst and central metaphors in a broader controversy surrounding the illegitimate assertion and appropriation of paternity. Anonymous works, however, also were readily assimilated into another cultural narrative that concerned illegitimate appropriation: plagiarism. With the publication of his risqué comic poem *Beppo* in 1818, Byron had anticipated some of the problems that anonymous authorship posed for an author doubly anxious about charges of plagiarism and immorality. The poem also was published without his name, at Byron's insistence, and his primary concern seems to have been that the personal attacks on his morality would be renewed in the periodical press and society gossip. Murray, meanwhile, was concerned that *Beppo*'s vilification of the poet William Sotheby, whom Byron suspected of sending him anonymous poison pen letters, would result in legal proceedings for libel. Byron also seems to have perceived clearly, however, that the poem was liable to charges of plagiarism. He repeatedly wrote to Murray, warning him that the poem was written "in or after the excellent manner of Mr. Whistlecraft," an allusion to the pseudonymous works of John Hookham Frere, and, as one of Byron's most recent biographers observes, "he was still worried enough by the plagiarism issue to repeat his instance that *Beppo* was . . . a pastiche."[36] The evidence is admittedly circumstantial: *Beppo*, *Don Juan*, and *The Monk*. But one begins to suspect that racy anonymous works were particularly liable to additional charges of plagiarism as these three forms of textual license became increasingly entangled.

Certainly Byron's response to the charges of plagiarism in *Don Juan* also highlights the evolving legal notion that authorship was a function of individual character. Not only does he suggest that the anonymous publication of the poem complicates his relationship to the literary property of other writers and makes the acknowledgment of source material both unnecessary and, likely, futile, but he also ends by suggesting that, even in the absence of named authorship, he has nevertheless made the "materials" recognizably his own. The implication is that authorial identity relies less on the public marker of name and more on a private and linguistically textured expression of sensibility.

In fact, Byron's attitude reflects the legal reality during the Romantic period. It was not the name of the author that created literary property. Copyrights were still typically (although not exclusively) owned and controlled by publishers and printers, and it was *their* names that guaranteed certain rights to a work and that were required to be present. But what copyright decisions in the late eighteenth century had decided and what was becoming during the period an increasingly prevalent cultural attitude was the notion that the personal identity of the author, whether named or unnamed, infused the work with unique and recognizable qualities that made a production new and "original." What anonymous publication complicated was not textual authority, but instead the nature of a work's controlling sensibility and, therefore, its identity. Publishers owned their copyrights regardless of whether an author's legal name was present. But to the extent that a uniquely identifiable "style" or voice had become increasingly associated with textual productions of the best sort—in other words, with their identification as "literary"—anonymous texts became rhetorically complex. Put another way, anonymous authors were shady characters in two senses. Their character could not be readily attributed to a precise social identity and required additional interpretive and aesthetic judgments. Because of the tensions created by the absence of the familiar social markers, their character, along with the legitimacy of its origins and intents, were inevitably suspect.

The anxiety that the anonymous publication of *Don Juan* created in the 1820s and its connection to the problems of reading for character in a cultural context is particularly transparent in the controversy surrounding Byron's alleged authorship of the picaresque travel novel *Anastasius* (1820). The novel also was published without the name of an author, and it was first proposed in an essay entitled "On *Anastasius*—by Lord Byron," published in *Blackwood's* September 1821 issue, that Byron was its originator.[37] It is a curious review in that it not only captures the importance of authorial character in the creation of literary property, but also reveals something important about how plagiarism charges operated in the Romantic period: they depended on the same precise aesthetic judgments that were used to construct proper authorship and literary status.

In the *Blackwood's* review, the argument for Byron's authorship of the novel is based on tracing the identifiable characteristics of his style and sensibility in the work. There is no other evidence of his authorship, and the suggestion is that no other evidence is required. This is a critical point. Where the character of the writing is identifiably Byronic, the reviewer contends, it is inevitable that the author is Byron. To this end, the reviewer proposes that "The character . . . of *Anastasius*, is exactly of a piece with Lord Byron's; that is, with the one which pervades all his works, and so charitably considered as his own. The spirit of *Anastasius* is that of *Don Juan*. Would Lord Byron have made so obvious a copy from the work of any other artist?" (201). It is an argument based on persona and, especially, on the public commodity that Byron's authorial identity had become. The "character" of *Anastasius* mirrors that sensibility which is culturally recognizable as Byronic even in the absence of named authorship. In fact, the implication is that even had the name of another author been inscribed on the title page—the name of, say, the actual author of the novel, Thomas Hope—the critic would have exposed the work only as a more complicated form of textual deception. Either Byron would have been charged with perpetrating a fraud on his readers by using a pseudonym or Thomas Hope would have been charged with plagiarism from Byron.

The possibility of Hope being charged with plagiarism from Byron—even in a work that he had, in fact, genuinely "authored"—was a real one in the Romantic period. I have argued elsewhere that plagiarism in the first decades of the nineteenth century did not depend on verbatim parallels, but rested precisely on these sorts of perceived similarities in voice, tone, style, and sensibility.[38] Plagiarism was, above all, a violation of the boundaries of public authorial character, not a simple matter of verbal echoes or missing footnotes. William Wordsworth, for example, accused Byron of plagiarisms from "Tintern Abbey" (1798) in the third canto of *Childe Harold's Pilgrimage* (1816) using much the same language. As Thomas Moore recalled it, Wordsworth had lamented "Byron's plagiarisms from him [alleging that] the whole third canto [was] founded on his style and sentiments."[39] In imitating (in the mind of the reviewer, at least) a "style and sentiment" that was recognizably "Byronic," it was quite possible that Hope could be reasonably accused of having plagiarized from his more famous contemporary.

It is undeniably a curious matter, at least from the vantage point of the twenty-first century. But our modern ideas of plagiarism have their legal and cultural precedents in the late nineteenth century and have little in common with the attitudes toward plagiarism shared by Byron and his Romantic contemporaries. An author might be persuasively charged with plagiarism for similarities that were limited to correspondences in subsemiotic elements such as tone or style. Likewise, extended and unacknowledged verbatim borrowings might be perfectly legitimate appropriations if, for example, the text were dominated and "improved" by a unifying narrative voice.[40] The main point is that plagiarism during the Romantic period was primarily an aesthetic charge—one essential to determining the important question of whether a work was sufficiently "literary" to merit protection as literary property and one that reflected the increasing importance, both legally and culturally, of the personal identity of the author in the creation of literary property.

For a modern reader, the essentially aesthetic, rather than legal, nature of Romantic plagiarism is perhaps one of its more striking features. This distinction is important because plagiarism and copyright are often understood in tandem, in ways that can be misleading and are certainly inaccurate. Many different kinds of speech were criminalized in the Romantic period to be sure, and, as Byron was discovering, even a morally "mischievous" poem like *Don Juan* could create complicated legal entanglements for the author and his publisher. There was a long list of speech acts considered immoral by the courts in the Romantic period, but plagiarism was not on it. In fact, in that important case of *Tonson v. Collins*, even the advocate for the plaintiff was at pains to distinguish clearly between the violations of an author's personal rights and the violation of literary property: "When I speak of the right of property," Wedderburn emphasized, "I mean in the profits of his book, not in the sentiments, style, &c."[41] The unlucky Thomas Hope found himself on the horns of precisely this dilemma. Hope and his publishers were clearly entitled to the profits of the "new" literary work that his intellectual labor had created, but he was potentially not the author of it.

What we see here is the cultural disentanglement of two concepts that often seem logically and even inevitably connected. The legal statutes governing literary property became increasingly distinct from the emerging cultural discourses that defined authorship and the author's personal right to control his or her own identity. The first was a matter of copyright. The second was often a matter of plagiarism. It is important to remember, after all, that plagiarism per se was not illegal. Under early nineteenth-century copyright law, plagiarism was only actionable in the most extreme circumstances. If the verbal parallels were extensive and verbatim and if there were means to prove conclusively that the borrowed passages had not been improved or appropriated, but merely recopied, then the law might offer a remedy. The remedy was a complicated one, however. The obligations needed to represent what was, essentially, a new printing of the work to be actionable under copyright law, and the bar was remarkably high even for verbatim reproductions.

Part of the dilemma was that abridgements of a work protected under copyright were considered new literary productions and were often perfectly legal. Likewise, an author could plausibly "appropriate" the text first created by another writer into his or her own work by adding new notes or commentary to the text. This was how many of the periodical reviews walked the fine line between reporting and reproduction. As Richard

Godson summarized in his contemporary treatise on copyright laws on the period,

> A copyright right exists in *abridgement* or *translations* of works. Also in the *notes and additions*. . . . For one man may compose a work . . . another abridge it, a third translate it, and a fourth write annotations upon it; and every one of them will acquire a copyright in the product of his own ingenuity and labour. (Godson 238)

Even for works that were not abridgements or new editions, in cases where the author had not endeavored to "appropriate" the text with labor and ingenuity, the law was still remarkably generous.

Copyright law only applied to works in which a few pages or more of text had been reproduced verbatim—a standard far different from the kind of borrowings that produced charges of plagiarism. As Godson again reports "To copy a part of a work . . . by taking a few pages *verbatim*, where the sentiments are not new . . . [is] considered to be illegal."[42]

The phrasing of Godson's comment here, however, is of critical importance for understanding the relationship between plagiarism and copyright law in the period. By offering the caveat that extensive verbatim borrowings are illegal only "where the sentiments are not new," Godson distinctly leaves open the possibility of verbatim passages where the sentiments *might* be new and the appropriations, therefore, permissible. Writers in the Romantic period talked about this as a matter of "improvement," and it was the essential component in charges of plagiarism. Where a writer had improved on the textual materials he or she employed—either by making changes to the wording *or* by making changes to subsemiotic elements of a text, such as voice, tone, sentiment, or style—it was not plagiarism. What Godson suggests is that, where it was not plagiarism, a finding dependent on the implicit aesthetic judgment that a work was "original," it also was not a copyright violation. The new work, whatever its antecedents and however extensive its verbal parallels might be, represented original literary property as long as it was controlled and unified by an original authorial identity. But the converse also was true: works that appropriated the public "character" of another author—even when the text represented a distinct intellectual production—were plagiarisms. These are troubling implications for poor Thomas Hope in that anonymous review of *Anastasius*. It was a book that many found excellent. Byron always regretted, or so he said, *not* having written it himself.[43] But in writing *Anastasius* in the voice culturally recognized as Byron's, Thomas Hope had effectively plagiarized another writer in his own work. Put more simply, he had failed to write with the unique expression of "style and sentiment" required to merit the aesthetic judgment of "original."

What we are confronted with, then, is a disjunction between how literary property was treated in the Romantic period and how it was created or evaluated. Clearly, however, one depended on the other. It was a moment in British legal history when only literary works were protected as literary property. Charges of plagiarism, although having no legal standing, were essential to the cultural process of making these important aesthetic judgments. Reflecting on the repercussions of *Tonson v. Walker* (1752), John Feather locates the mid-eighteenth century as the point of origin for what he calls a "split [in] the property of books between a 'natural' property, constituted within the private 'manuscript culture' of the author and a statutory property, constituted by statute within the public sphere of 'book culture'" (236). By the beginning of the nineteenth century, the rhetoric of the author's "natural" property was experiencing, with the rise of literary and cultural Romanticism, a renaissance, and it was coming to dominate the regulation of "public" book culture perhaps for the first time in British history.

Appropriately enough, the increased importance of the natural rights of authorship coincided with the rise of a legal discourse concerning moral rights in early nineteenth-century jurisprudence. Currently under British copyright law, there are implied legal protections against plagiarism. Those protections are protections based on metaphors of paternity and morality. Under the *Copyright, Designs, and Patents Act* of 1988, an author not only has the statutory right to control the sale of intellectual property, but he or she also retains the natural and moral rights of "paternity."[44] This is an explicitly "moral right" based on tort law, and the doctrine of moral rights also has its precedent in nineteenth-century law. Although the identification of the author's right of paternity as one of these explicit moral rights was only formalized in Britain during the early years of the twentieth century, when copyright law was standardized internationally in the Berne Convention of 1928, the rhetorical construction of plagiarism as a violation of an author's moral and natural rights was mirrored in cultural attitudes broadly shared by the end of the Romantic period.

The question is how this evolution in public perceptions of plagiarism—both as a violation of an author's natural moral rights and as related to metaphors of paternity—developed. The answer is only partly a legal one. What changed in British copyright law over the course of the century, in the copyright acts of 1814 and 1842, was the increased prominence given to the personal identity and lifespan of the author in the creation and ownership of literary property. At stake was not the manner in which literary property came into existence, but who had the right to benefit from it and for how long, and the effect was to limit the commercial power of the publishers in favor of the professional writer, who would come to control both the "public" and "private" aspects of authorship that John Feather identifies. Clearly, one of the effects of this shifting legal paradigm was the emerging critical interest in "character" or sensibility of the author as a guarantee of both aesthetic value and literary property rights. This movement toward an assessment of literary property as the function of individual authorial identity laid a fertile ground for equally personal metaphors of natural possession and influence such as those of paternity.

During the nineteenth century in Britain, then, metaphors of paternity were becoming increasingly relevant to discussions of intellectual property, to a large extent as a result of the new legal emphasis on the individual identity of the author. There also was undoubtedly an influence from continental law, which was much earlier in developing a doctrine of moral rights. In fact, the notion of moral rights as it exists under international law today has its origins primarily in French jurisprudence of the late eighteenth and early nineteenth centuries.[45] Legal historians have noted that the author's right of paternity as one of these moral rights "witnessed a rapid development" in the second part of the nineteenth century in European law. It was formalized in French copyright law by at least as early as 1826.[46] Although British law did not formalize the right of authorial paternity for another century, the language of paternity came to shape attitudes toward authorship during the Romantic period.

The reception of Byron shaped that discourse. In fact, the spurious and anonymous pamphlets dating the period of his separation resulted in one of the earliest legal instances of an author being granted an implicit right of paternity in his texts under British law. The case of *Lord Byron v. Johnston* came to trial in 1816 and at stake was Byron's right to prevent printers and publishers from publishing a series of "bad" poems under his name. Byron requested that an injunction be granted against the publisher James Johnston, who advertised for sale a spurious edition of "new" Byron poems, which he claimed to have purchased from the author for a copyright fee. In early December 1816, Byron wrote to Murray protesting this publication and requesting his agents in Britain to prevent any further circulation of the work, which included, according to the report Byron had received, "poems called a 'Pilgrimage to Jerusalem, a Tempest, and an Address to my Daughter.'"[47] Although the doctrine of paternity as a moral right of authorship did not yet have any legal standing in the British courts, in Byron's mind, the misappropriation had everything to do with his child and the complicated social, legal, literary, and emotional nexus that she represented in his life. "The answer to this is short," Byron wrote, "*I never wrote such poems.* . . . As to an address to little Ada, (who, by the way, is a year old to-morrow,) I never wrote a line about her, except in 'Farewell' and the 3d canto of *Childe H—d*."[48]

If Byron's concerns were essentially personal and parental, for the court at stake were questions of authorial character and its relationship to the statutory violation of copyright. As the court recognized, the author had certain rights that extended beyond mere issues of contract and profit and necessarily included certain natural rights pertaining to his or her own identity and to the identity of his or her text. It is for this reason that the case of *Lord Byron v. Johnston* still stands as an important legal precedent in British law. Unsurprisingly, connecting as it did the "public" and "private" rights of authors, plagiarism also became part of the legal case history.

The summary of the proceedings in the Court of Chancery on November 28, 1816, published in *The Morning Chronicle* two days later, records that Byron's friend and agent Scrope Davies testified on his behalf that "the works . . . are not the production of his Lordship, only so far as they may contain plagiarisms. . . . The Lord Chancellor observed, that the Noble Plaintiff did not ask the injunction . . . on pecuniary grounds, but on the grounds of character as an author."[49] The implication regarding plagiarism, of course, returns to the problem of style and authorial identity. It is precisely that same problem that Thomas Hope implicitly faced in the periodical review of *Anastasius*. If the spurious works at stake in the case of *Lord Byron v. Johnston* were in the style of Byron—in his character—then these poems were "his" in the sense that his identity had been plagiarized. He became, effectively, the author of something he had never written on the basis of authorial style and identity. The words, after all, were not his, and he had not composed them. But as a matter of aesthetic and cultural judgment, this fact did not prevent his imitators from being accused of plagiarism, even in an avowedly "new" text.

The legal remedy, however, was tangled. Because Byron acknowledged that he had not written the poems—in fact, because his precise contention was to prevent their publication on the grounds that he *had not* written them—it was impossible for the court to proceed on the basis that he had suffered any financial harm. After all, Byron could not hold copyright in a work that his labor and ingenuity had not created. But insofar as the "character" was Byronic, the spurious poems violated his private and natural rights to control his own identity. The idea, perhaps, is a plagiarism not of words, but of person—an idea certainly implicit in the etymological and earlier cultural understanding of the word as a form of kidnapping.

As Martin A. Roeder noted in the *Harvard Law Review* in 1940, *Lord Byron v. Johnston* was an early example of an author being protected under British law against "the false attribution of paternity" at a period when those terms still had only a cultural rather than a legal resonance.[50] Not coincidentally, I think, this *cultural* precedent of what would become an established *legal* convention protecting an author's "paternity" over the course of the next century is tied not only to Byron as an author, but to the same sort of spurious publications that were produced as part of the scandal surrounding his paternity and the moral questions tied to it. What I suspect is that the controversy surrounding Byron's poetry from 1816 until his death in 1824, bringing together as it did a number of urgent contemporary anxieties about anonymity, immorality, and illegitimacy, served as one important discursive moment in a representational shift, in which issues of private authority (either parental or literary) were overlaid with public and legal constructions of morality and natural rights. *Don Juan*, in particular, became a perfect storm of sorts. It was tied to a scandal about paternity. It was the subject of protracted legal and critical debates centered, despite the poem's provocative anonymous publication, on the personal immorality and identity of the author. It was the source of public allegations of plagiarism, and it was the most infamous and most widely read literary work of its era.

Don Juan, of course, confirmed Byron's status as a cultural anti-hero. But the simultaneously alluring and negative representation of the poet—that casting of him as "mad, bad, and dangerous to know" after 1816—was always a celebrity constructed in the language of fatherhood and moral seduction. Parental vigilance was the consistent message of nineteenth-century Byronism, from the didacticism of the Silver Fork society novels to the impulse that led Elizabeth Barrett Browning's father to use the lock and key in the library. It was a message that Byron's estranged wife and widow embraced with her characteristic zeal, going so far as to veil his portrait behind thick curtains to safeguard the wandering and innocent eyes even of his daughter Ada.[51] But, as I have argued here, it was a paternal vigilance that spilled over into the world of authorship as well. Perhaps one of modern history's first "brand-name" commercial authors, Byron's textual persona was so identifiably unique that his works confirmed, both legally and culturally, emerging perceptions about authorial identity as a guarantee of originality and, increasingly, as a guarantee of the natural—even paternal—rights of ownership over one's most intimate and private creations. Simply put, in the course of the Romantic period, the cultural metaphors used to describe plagiarism and an author's rights to his or her literary "progeny" changed, and they changed in ways that mirror the public controversy surrounding the poetry of Byron.

NOTES

1. Matthew Lewis, *The Monk*, ed. Louis F. Peck (New York: Grove Press, 1952). The advertisement highlights the extent to which questions of plagiarism in the period were separate from the formal matter of acknowledgment or citation. In addition to the layer of complexity posed by the anonymous publication of the novel, I also have argued elsewhere that the oral and popular, rather than self-consciously literary and "authored," origins of many of Lewis' source materials contributed to the plagiarism charges brought against him. In his prefatory note, Lewis reports that: "The first idea of this Romance was suggested by the story of the Santon Barsisa, related in The Guardian.—The Bleeding Nun is a tradition still credited in many parts of Germany. . . . The Water–King, from the third to the twelfth stanza, is the fragment of an original Danish Ballad—And Belerma and Durandarte is translated from some stanzas to be found in a collection of old Spanish poetry, which contains also the popular song of Gayferos and Melesindra, mentioned in Don Quixote.—I have now made a full avowal of all the plagiarisms of which I am aware myself; but I doubt not, many more may be found, of which I am at present totally unconscious" ("Advertisement"). See

Tilar J. Mazzeo, *Plagiarism and Literary Property in the Romantic Period* (Philadelphia: University of Pennsylvania Press, 2007), Chapter 3.

2. John Stacy, *Critique on the Genius and Writings of Lord Byron, With Remarks on Don Juan* (Norwich: John Stacy, 1820). Quoted in Samuel C. Chew, *Byron in England: His Fame and After-Fame* (New York: C. Scribners, 1924), 34.
3. On Byron's verse abuse, see Howard O. Brogan, "Byron So Full of Fun, Frolic, Wit, and Whim," *The Huntington Library Quarterly* 37, no. 2 (1974): 171–189, esp. 178; for a full account of the popular print culture surrounding Byron's marital difficulties, see Samuel C. Chew, "The Pamphlets of the Byron Separation," *Modern Language Notes* 34, no. 3 (1919), 155–162.
4. Malcolm Elwin, *Lord Byron's Wife* (London: Macdonald, 1962), 408.
5. Ibid., 467.
6. *Lord Byron: Selected Poems*, ed. Susan J. Wolfson and Peter J. Manning (New York: Penguin, 1996), 392–394.
7. William St Clair, *The Reading Nation in the Romantic Period* (Cambridge: Cambridge University Press, 2004).
8. Richard Godson, *A Practical Treatise on the Laws of Patents for Inventions and of Copyright* (London, 1823), 212.
9. John David Chambers, *A Practical Treatise on the Jurisdiction of the High Court of Chancery Over the Persons and Property of Infants* (London: Saunders and Benning, 1842), 90.
10. John Henry Adlington, *The Cyclopaedia of Law; or, The Correct British Lawyer: Forming a Complete and Concise Digest of the Various Laws and Statutes Comprehended in the Constitution of England, in Which Are Included an Epitome of the Acts of Parliament Passed in the Last Session, and a Glossary of the Technical Law Terms* (London: J. McGowan, 1820), n.p.
11. Byron to John Murray, October 8, 1820, in Thomas Moore, *Letters and Journals of Lord Byron, With Notices of His Life* (Paris: A. and W. Galignani, 1830), 347.
12. James Raven, "The Anonymous Novel in Britain and Ireland, 1750–1830," in *The Faces of Anonymity: Anonymous and Pseudonymous Publication from the Sixteenth to the Twentieth Century*, ed. Robert Griffin (New York: Palgrave, 2003), 143.
13. Godson, *Practical Treatise*, 221.
14. *Tonson v. Collins*, 96 *English Reports* 180; it was later clarified in *Beckford v. Hood* (1798) that the mere publication of a work anonymously could not constitute the abandonment of property unless there was intent, as well as action (101 *English Reports* 1164).
15. Matthew Bacon, *A New Abridgement of the Law* (Philadelphia: M'Carty and Davis, 1842), 149.
16. Godson, *Practical Treatise*, 221.
17. John Feather, *Publishing, Piracy, and Politics: An Historical Study of Copyright in Britain* (London: Mansell Publishers, 1994), 68.
18. Godson, *Practical Treatise*, 212.
19. Ibid., 226.
20. Lisa M. Wilson, "'Monk' Lewis as Literary Lion," *Romanticism On the Net* 8, (November 1997), available http: <http://www.erudit.org/revue/ron/1997/v/n8/005775ar.html>, (accessed February 1, 2008), para. 4.
21. *Southey v. Sherwood*, 35 *English Reports* 1006.
22. Byron to John Murray, August 24, 1819, in *Byron: A Self Portrait: Letters and Diaries, 1798–1824*, ed. Peter Quennell, 2 vols. (New York: Humanities Press, 1967), 2:485.
23. Byron to Richard Belgrave Hoppner, October 29, 1819, in ibid., 2:493.

24. Byron to John Murray, October 25, 1822, in ibid., 2:716.
25. Thomas Medwin, *Conversations of Lord Byron*, ed. Ernest J. Lovell, Jr. (Princeton: Princeton University Press, 1966), 168.
26. *Tonson v. Collins*, 96 *English Reports* 180 and 96 *English Reports* 169.
27. See particularly Martha Woodmansee and Peter Jaszi, *The Construction of Authorship: Textual Appropriation in Law and Literature* (Durham, NC: Duke University Press, 1994); Mark Rose, *Authors and Owners: The Invention of Copyright* (Cambridge, MA: Harvard University Press, 1993).
28. Mary Shelley, "Introduction," *Frankenstein* (London: Colburn and Bentley, 1831), xii.
29. Byron to John Murray, August 24, 1819, in Quennell, *Letters and Diaries*, 2:485.
30. Bryon to Douglas Kinnaird, October 30, 1822, in *Byron's Letters and Journals*, ed. Leslie A. Marchand, 12 vols. (Cambridge, MA: Harvard University Press, 1973–1980) 10:72.
31. *The Examiner*, August 10, 1822, 522.
32. Byron to John Murray, December 25, 1822, in Quennell, *Letters and Diaries*, 2:716; *The Letters of Elizabeth Barrett Browning to Mary Russell Mitford*, ed. Meredith B. Raymond and Mary Rose Sullivan, 3 vols. (Waco, TX: Armstrong Browning Library/Baylor University, 1983) 2:462. Quoted in St Clair, *Reading Nation*, 335.
33. Byron to Sir Walter Scott, May 4, 1822, in Quennell, *Letters and Diaries*, 2:693.
34. Byron to John Murray, December 21, 1822, in Marchand, *Byron's Letters and Journals*, 10:64; Byron to John Murray, December 25, 1822, in ibid., 2:716.
35. Byron to John Murray, August 23, 1821, in ibid., 2:661–662.
36. Byron to John Murray, October 12, 1817, in Marchand, *Byron's Letters and Journals*, 5:267; Benita Eisler, *Byron: Child of Passion, Fool of Fame* (New York: Vintage Books, 1999), 584.
37. "On *Anastasius*—by Lord Byron," *Blackwood's Edinburgh Review* 60, no. 10 (September 1821): 201–206.
38. Mazzeo, *Plagiarism and Literary Property*.
39. See Thomas Moore, *Tom Moore's Diary*, ed. J. B. Priestley (Cambridge: Cambridge University Press, 1925), 29; entry October 27, 1820.
40. On the question of improvement, see, for example, Wordsworth's further comment regarding Byron's alleged plagiarisms in *Childe Harold's Pilgrimage*: "Says Wordsworth, 'The celebrated passage about Solitude, in the first canto of *Childe Harold*, is taken from me, with this difference, that what was naturally expressed by me has been worked by Byron into a labored, antithetical sort of declamation.'" The point, I take it, is that Byron has borrowed from Wordsworth and simultaneously perverted it. Quoted in "Moore and the Byron Memoirs," *The New York Times*, May 26, 1854, 2.
41. *Tonson v. Collins*, 96 *English Reports* 169.
42. Godson, *Practical Treatise*, 215.
43. See Byron to John Murray, July 22, 1820, in Marchand, *Byron's Letters and Journals*, 7:138; Bryon to John Murray, September 28, 1820, in ibid., 7:182.
44. *Halsbury's Laws of England*, ed. Lord MacKay (London: Lexis Nexis/ Butterworths, 2006), vol. 9, pt. 2, 16; *Copyright, Designs, and Patents Act* (1988), pt. 1, chap. 4, ss. 77–89, as amended.
45. William Strauss, "The Moral Right of the Author," *The American Journal of Comparative Law* 4, no. 4 (1955): 506–538, esp. 506.
46. See particularly Strauss, "The Moral Right of the Author," 508–509, nn. 10–12, citing the decisions of the Cour de Paris (Court of Appeals, March

20, 1826) and the Civil Tribunal Seine (March 12, 1836; December 17, 1838; and December 18, 1838). See also Martin A. Roeder, "The Doctrine of Moral Right: A Study in the Law of Artists, Authors and Creators," *Harvard Law Review* 53, no. 4 (1940): 554–578, esp. 556.

47. Byron to John Murray, December 9, 1816, *The Works of Lord Byron*, ed. Ernest Hartley Coleridge and Roland E. Prothero, 13 vols. (New York: C. Scribner's, 1898–1905), 4, pt. 2:19–22.
48. Ibid.
49. "Court of Chancery, Westminster, Nov. 28, Lord Byron's Poems," *The Morning Chronicle*, November 30, 1816, quoted in *The Works of Lord Byron*, ed. Ernest Hartley Coleridge and Roland E. Prothero, 4, pt. 2:19–22.; see also *Lord Byron v. Johnston*, 35 *English Reports* 851.
50. Roeder, "Doctrine of Moral Rights," 563.
51. For more on this topic, see Frances Wilson, "Portrait of the Artist as an Icon," *Times Literary Supplement*, online edition, July 29, 2005, available http: <http://www.timesonline.co.uk> (accessed October 31, 2007), n.p.

7 Originality in the Enlightenment and Beyond

John Vignaux Smyth

An original is not someone who imitates no one, but someone whom no one can imitate.

—Chateaubriand

The most terrible fight is not when there is one opinion against another, but when two men say the same thing.

—Kierkegaard

Every time I want to say something someone else says it at the very same moment.

—Kierkegaard

Hardly any literature other than ours can exhibit so many monstrosities born of a mania for originality. Here too we are proved Hyperboreans. For among the Hyperboreans asses were sacrificed to Apollo, who would then take delight in their marvelous leaps.

—Friedrich Schlegel

INTRODUCTION

It is perhaps even more difficult to be original about originality than it is easy to be plagiaristic about plagiarism, twin topics today almost as fashionable as they were in the Enlightenment. Attacks are common, for example, on Romantic and post-Romantic ideas of originality, but it often feels as if these do not add up to much more than Voltaire's often plagiarized joke that an original is someone who imitates many people.

What "originality" is supposed to mean is, of course, a main problem. Does it pertain only or primarily to humans, selves, or agents (including perhaps animals or at least some animals)? Are subatomic particles (or at least some of them) "original"?[1] Are concepts of originality (or at least some of them) logical concepts? Historical concepts? Metaphysical ones? Economic ones (as in patent and copyright law)? The trouble is that a theory of originality seems sometimes to amount to a theory of almost everything and sometimes to almost nothing. Worse, we often seem to oscillate between two platitudes: that the only constant is change and there is nothing new under the sun.

Originality is ambiguous in that it can refer to both origins "at the beginning" and more proximate origins, such as human beings. For example, the Big Bang, supposing it occurred, was presumably original in one sense; "free" actions in the present, supposing they occur, are presumably original in another. Even the novel—to descend from physics and metaphysics to literary history—is marked by this double sense of originality as old and new. For although the "novel" in English seems tautologically on the side of novelty—and it is no coincidence that Romantics like Friedrich Schlegel regarded the novel as the Romantic or modern literary form *par excellence*—"roman" in French and German ("romanzo" in Italian) harks back to something past: romance, romance languages, Roman, and so on.

Schlegel singled out as especially proto-Romantic the works of Sterne and Diderot, my primary foci here.[2] For those accustomed to viewing, say, Wordsworth as prototypical of Romanticism, this may seem strange. For not only were they not lyric poets, but their overt and playful embrace of novelistic plagiarism seems at the opposite end of the spectrum from solemn Romantic stereotypes of the solitary genius emphasized, for example, by Martha Woodmansee and Peter Jaszi in *The Construction of Authorship: Textual Appropriation in Law and Literature* (1994). They may seem, perhaps, chameleons between what are called the "Ages of Reason" and "Romanticism."

For this reason, it may be helpful to begin with *The Construction of Authorship*, whose "blurb" announces: "This volume argues that contemporary copyright law, rooted as it is in a nineteenth-century Romantic understanding of the author as a solitary creative genius, may be inapposite to the realities of cultural production." The editors Woodmansee and Jaszi further specify that "the modern regime of authorship, far from being timeless and universal, is a relatively recent formation—the result of a radical reconceptualization of the creative process that culminated less than 200 years ago in the heroic self-presentation of the Romantic poets" as "secular prophet[s] with privileged access to experience of the numinous and a unique ability to translate that experience for the masses of less gifted consumers."[3]

This dating to post-1794 ("less than 200 years ago") narrowly lets off Sterne and Diderot, who had the grace to die slightly earlier, if not Schlegel, who, as I have said, regarded them as original Romantics and thus part of a "culminating reconception" *par excellence* (Hegel also singled out *Rameau's Nephew* as a model of modern consciousness). To take these shameless comic plagiarists as Romantic, even proto-so, would hardly suit Woodmansee's and Jaszi's polemic, and even Schlegel might not so easily fit the bill because he not only punningly took the *roman* (rather than, say, poetry of the "I wandered lonely as a cloud" variety) as paradigm of Romanticism, but defined it as the modern form of Socratic dialogue[4]—hardly, on the face of it, an activity of "solitary" genius. It is therefore not neutral that Woodmansee and Jaszi seize rather on the example of Wordsworth as a model of Romantic—and, by extension, apparently also Capitalist ("experience for the masses of less gifted consumers")[5]—delusions of originality.

The point here is not, however, to debate Romanticism as such—we may agree all too readily that the term is "plural." The point is that this stereotype of solitary genius, far from subjecting to critique Wordsworth's original ideas of originality *if any* (e.g., by analyzing his work), merely has recourse to the rather hackneyed notion of "self-aggrandizement"—hardly, one supposes, a uniquely Romantic sin—in "his misrepresentation of a collaborative creative process as a solitary, originary one." "In this self-presentation Dorothy [Wordsworth] and even Coleridge figure primarily as sources of 'inspiration,' or encouragement."[6] What a surprise!

If we felt sorry for Wordsworth here, not to mention his sister and Coleridge, we might mention that "inspiration" for him is not exactly a denigrating term. But such niceties aside, my point is that the Woodmansee/Jaszi critique of Wordsworth accomplishes little with regard to the concept of originality, Romantic or otherwise. For it would seem in these terms that the whole issue—both of copyright and originality—could be resolved by resorting to a Wordsworth/Coleridge or Wordsworth/Coleridge/Dorothy consortium along the lines of Lennon/McCartney or Jagger/Richards (although all fans know more or less who wrote which songs and which poems). But this just multiplies the problem, for now we ask whether the Coleridge/Wordsworth or Jagger/Richards consortia were original. The question of originality, if we pooh-pooh merely "solitary" claims to it, merely poses itself again in terms of groups and, worse, of potentially unlimited size and complexion. (Are some groups or some types of groups or even cultures more original than others? Was "sexuality," as Michel Foucault amusingly claimed, invented in the Enlightenment?) Posed in a more general form, the problem of originality thus becomes provocative in a way that is merely veiled by this attack on Wordsworth and Romanticism, even supposing it to be vaguely adequate to either of them.[7]

Turning now briefly from art to science, we may observe that Nobel prizes tend of course to be allocated in a manner reminiscent of patent law or athletics (first past the post), hence tussles of the "self-aggrandizing" kind as portrayed by Woodmansee and Jaszi are common between competing scientists. Whether Leibniz and Newton, much to the latter's horror (because he accused Leibniz of plagiarism),[8] would have jointly received the prize for independently inventing the calculus is moot, but we would nevertheless hardly be inclined to call Newton *more* original merely had Leibniz not existed, been killed by Newton, or turned his attention to other matters. Rather, it is part of their originality *that they both came to the same conclusion* (i.e., that they were *not original* in relation to each other).

(It is an irony of the Woodmansee/Jaszi approach that, had Wordsworth even more comprehensively acknowledged the influence of Coleridge and Dorothy than he did, he might have ended up ascribing his own supposedly deluded conception of originality to them!)

But if, say, we discovered that calculus was really invented hundreds of years earlier in India (a culture in many ways more mathematically advanced than old Europe, whose introduction of zero, for example, revolutionized European mathematics), would this change our view? Yes, doubtless.[9] But not necessarily because we would now downplay Newton's and Leibniz's individual originalities (or, as above, Wordsworth's). Rather, we would be inclined to modify our view of the history of culture in this respect, not to mention possibly revising our conception of mathematics.

Too close a priority reduces originality to a mere athletics or Nobel prize race. However, *too distant* a priority—suppose Cain and Abel invented the calculus to be rediscovered by Newton and Leibniz—is equally problematic because it may change our ideas about more or less everything. The idea of originality *qua* priority, as I have said, is ambiguous. To take an athletic example: when pundits discuss the greatest or most original tennis players of all time and pick, say, X and Y from 1927 and 2007, they may pick X as the most original, the "greatest," even though he or she would have been beaten by Y. Moreover, this is not on the basis merely of historical priority, although it may include that, because any number of other earlier players would fit that bill. Some more basic judgment of priority or originality, however questionable, is evidently at stake.

Diderot puts the problem in characteristically frivolous fashion when his character Bugger in *Jacques le fataliste* loses his virginity more than once. He is, of course, lying to his girlfriends, but nevertheless his "real" loss of virginity, or the effectively "original" copulation, may or may not be technically the first. Gottlob Frege, the logician, put the point as follows: When one iterates the natural numbers (1, 2, 3, etc.), is one always doing the same thing or something different? He compares this to saying every day that one is giving up smoking: is one always doing the same thing or something different? Frege refuses even to grant, unlike many logicians and mathematicians, 0 and 1 status as originary or somehow uniquely different from the rest of the numbers that can be derived from them by iteration.[10] So much for logic!

But this kind of problem—and joke—is omnipresent in Sterne and Diderot, and in Sterne's many contemporary plagiarists, one of whom was Diderot. The latter opens *Jacques le fataliste*, for example, with an overt plagiarism of *Tristram Shandy* and concludes the novel with another, while joking that Sterne might really have plagiarized him rather than vice versa. The joke seems harmless enough and indeed not terribly funny—it is predictably hackneyed in the considerable annals of Sterneana (pastiches, imitations, quasi-criminal impersonations, etc.) where claims that *everything* is pastiche or plagiarism, and that there are therefore *no* genuine originals, abound in a manner that makes avante-garde, Dadaist, Deconstructionist, and Postmodernist dicta of this sort seem almost recherché. Because Diderot openly acknowledges Sterne moreover, there seems to be no question of "real" plagiarism; until, that is, we note that, like Sterne, Diderot frequently acknowledges overt influence in a way that can actively conceal more covert appropriations and ones that are sometimes much more important than those openly acknowledged.[11]

But who cares? These are comic writers, it will be said, engaged in an ironic and (hopefully) amusing game. Quite so. But even if, for instance, Diderot's overt indication of Sterne's influence in *Jacques le fataliste* may be said to encourage us to search for other more covert echoes and appropriations, only a thorough reader of both authors may actually find them, and even a thorough reader may be seriously misled: "irony" may, of course, deceive as well as amuse us. Suppose Sterne's works were all destroyed just after Diderot read them. Would this matter? Because Diderot never plagiarizes word for word at considerable length, he is presumably exonerated from the kind of plagiarism charges normally leveled at students, newspaper hacks, academics, and the like. But would we not ask a student to cite the source of a novel *idea* he or she appropriated even if it were clothed in language different from its author's? To put the same point differently, if Newton's work had been destroyed before publication, what would we think of a Leibniz who (having read that work) acknowledged some, say, relatively minor influence of Newton on a different issue, but said nothing about his development of the calculus? Even if Leibniz developed the calculus independently, as he seems to have done, many would surely regard this suppression as heinous. But surely then the same would go for people like Sterne and Diderot,[12] unless they were exonerated by some rather obscure assumption about artistic license or, perhaps more frankly, the assumption that novels of this sort are essentially "not serious"—or at any rate not "original"—in the manner that the calculus is serious and original.

The interdisciplinary phantom raised here—the rivalry between art and science or between art and thought—is, of course, not foreign to either Diderot or Sterne, and modern commentators still cannot make up their collective minds about how far either is to be considered a "philosopher" as well as a "writer." *The Construction of Authorship* also contains several essays that call for an "aggressively" (as the "blurb" puts it) interdisciplinary approach to the problem of authorship, for example, in the domain of legal theory and practice (e.g., copyright law). But debates between literary and legal theorists, although now frequent and sometimes ferocious, rarely raise explicitly certain basic problems that arguably underlie both and indeed all disciplines—for example, "metaphysical" problems (metaphysics being decidedly démodé), whereas Sterne and Diderot raise such problems with relentless comic repetition. I have mentioned that Schlegel evidently had no difficulty in reconciling Sterne's and Diderot's plagiarist habits with his idea of Romantic originality presumably because he conceived such originality differently from Woodmansee and Jaszi. He may be said to have regarded Romanticism as historically original in a collective sense, not merely in terms of "solitary genius"—without, for all that, repudiating the notion of individuality or genius—and indeed as original precisely in developing the modern idea of history. According to Schlegel's own aphorism, however, the idea of history is tricky: "The historian is a prophet facing backwards."[13]

This aphorism puts into question the nature of law in general and its relation to both the origins (or history) and the future (or originality); in short, it plays with the ambiguity of originality as suggested earlier. We have said that originality is often understood as novelty—a fairly trivial equation that underlies, for example, patent law (provided that the novelty in question, however tenuous, is deemed economically useful). To be original is supposedly to be new—at some point—whether one is the Big Bang or Wordsworth. Of course, because the Big Bang is supposed to have occurred at a specific time "prior" to which all laws of physics break down, we face some catastrophic problems if we start originally there—far worse, one might say, than those posed by the Biblical *Genesis* or so-called primitive origin myths (which, however false, at least seem to maintain *some* kind of coherence)—before descending to the originality, or lack of such, of Wordsworth. Thus, preparatory to what follows and taking a cue partly from Diderot's references to Spinoza in *Jacques le fataliste*, I conclude this introduction with a brief glance at the interdisciplinary issue as such, if such a locution is permitted.

We have said that the Big Bang may have been original in one sense and human beings (not to mention animals or plants) in another—one that usually and indeed necessarily involves assumptions about freedom one way or the other. If humans are "free" or autonomous, even relatively so—compared, let's say to cats, rocks, or quarks—they must be "original" even when imitating others. (As Theodor Adorno put it: "Mimetic power is effectively the power of qualitative distinction.")[14] The connection between originality and freedom (i.e., "novelty" in a radical sense) is profound in both commonsensical and most philosophical views. Almost all conceptions of criminal law, for example—Spinoza's notably excepted—take it for granted that justice requires the assumption of relatively free choice (*more or less and whatever that means*) to establish guilt. This acknowledged, it must also be acknowledged that if a theory of originality depends on a theory of freedom, its intellectual knickers are likely in a bit of a twist. (That the same goes for criminal justice need hardly be belabored.)

Perhaps, then, we should begin with the basic interdisciplinary problem posed here: that human originality conceived as contingent on freedom excludes disciplines (e.g., the natural sciences) that have no concept of freedom (supposing a coherent concept or *axiom* of freedom to be possible).

But if this is the tacit assumption behind most humanist and even "posthumanist" treatments of the subject, is it valid?

Spinoza is an amusing card to play in this context, as exploited by Diderot in *Jacques le fataliste*, because he notoriously denied the coherence and thus existence of freedom as usually conceived (i.e., as an exception to necessity or law). For Spinoza, freedom does exist absolutely for God or Nature (which are virtually identical, hence the suspicion that he was an atheist) and, relatively speaking, for humans, but only insofar as freedom is conceived as freedom from *some* laws, not from law or necessity in general. (Hence, in this sense, even God or Nature is unfree except insofar as we can speak of what Spinoza calls "free necessity," and rational humans are freer than irrational ones precisely insofar as they act and think under the compulsion of more coherent or extensive laws.) Therefore, a corresponding conception of originality would have to break with the idea that originality breaks with the past, with law or necessity. Originality should not be defined in terms of mere novelty, but of the working out of the logic and necessity of the origins (the causes) as such.

Spinoza's denial of the coherence of exceptions to law finds an echo, from a rather different point of view, in Kafka. As René Girard has put it, Kafka was "one of the few to perceive that the absence of law is in fact identical with law run wild [*i.e. not an exception to law but its apotheosis*] and that this identity constitutes the chief burden of mankind."[15] Though Kafka's (and Girard's) position may seem to concern law in the merely human sense (moral, political, psychological, etc.), whereas Spinoza's in both human and universal senses (physical, metaphysical, logical, etc.), we see how "law run wild" can be conceived analytically and even mathematically. Meanwhile, Jacques' captain puts the point in quasi-Spinozan form: "The enjoyment of freedom which could be exercised without any motivation would be the real hallmark of a maniac."[16]

Thus, if the usual "existentialist" conception of freedom—and here I mean also the ordinary or commonsensical one—entails a momentary suspension of law, of causal determinism, in which the act of "free will" (originality in this sense) occurs, the Spinozan counterargument raises the question of what exceptions to law could possibly be, and this is where humanistic approaches usually fall short of even raising the general interdisciplinary problem. Because if human freedom means at least a provisional suspension of law, causality, determinism, and so on, it also presumably presupposes what such a suspension means when *not* applied to humans (or cats). That is, whether we accept that originality should be understood as an exception to law, or at least to law as hitherto understood, what *is* an exception to law?

We have cited the Big Bang—which has no cause unless we are prophets looking backward, and we could cite God if we were not Spinozans. But such grandiose originalities aside, we could appeal more obviously to chance or arbitrariness, the latter term etymologically bridging will or decision (arbitration) and randomness, but not obviously—or rather *obviously not*—resolving the opposition between the two. Here the problems multiply, but in interesting ways that will turn out to have their correlates in Sterne and Diderot. Because if we forget for a moment the problem of human beings (who will sufficiently entertain us later), the concept of arbitrariness is already quite difficult enough in science, mathematics, and logic. In *Fact, Fiction and Forecast*, for example, the philosopher Nelson Goodman claimed that the meaning of a "random sample" is not analytically clear; indeed, this falls under his list of other unclear but presumably fundamental terms that includes the concept of "likeness"—and hence originality, if that means "unlikeness."[17] In mathematics, the problem is even more or, should I say, even *less* clear because every irrational and transcendental number (e.g., the square root of 2 or pi) takes on the appearance of an infinite arbitrary sequence, although it is clearly *not* random. Meanwhile all "properly" random sequences may turn out to correspond to *some* law. (J.A. Benardete has suggested that a mathematical proof, supposing it were forthcoming, that at least some infinite sequences of numbers were governed by no law—unlike the real and transcendental numbers that look so similarly lawless—would at least give a clearer analytical meaning to the term "random." But it is possible that the contrary could be proved or that no proof either way emerges—even a proof that no proof is possible.[18]) The logician and philosopher Charles Sanders Pierce pithily summed up another related aspect of the matter when he remarked that "*if the world were governed entirely by chance it would be much more orderly than it is*; that is to say, chance is far from being the opposite of law: rather the intervention of law makes life *less* orderly!"[19] Chance, like originality, appears at one level as the opposite of law, but at another as its apotheosis. In this respect, it seems a bit like—but, as Goodman might add, what the hell does "like" mean here?—freedom as discussed previously.

Nevertheless, this becomes a little clearer if we consider the definition of a random sequence. Samuel Beckett put this wittily in connection with his character called "Py" (i.e., the transcendental number) in *Molloy*, where Py—who is a dentist or rather transcen-dental-ist! (the joke is implicit)—claims that he "*will do everything possible, necessarily*" for his patient.[20] The joke is that doing everything possible necessarily is the definition of an infinite arbitrary sequence. That is, if we throw a die indefinitely, we expect no possible finite sequence of numbers to be excluded in the long run. Everything possible must necessarily occur if the sequence is truly random. Thus, chance appears as the pandemic apotheosis of necessity, of "law run wild" (to use Girard's phrase)—one that cannot to date be distinguished from the "random" *form* of necessity or law, such as that of the real numbers.

Such considerations may appear excessively abstract, not to mention philosophically inconclusive, and therefore understandably often tacitly considered irrelevant by, for example, legal and literary theorists, although, of course, Spinozan-type debates still occur, for example, in the philosophy of science. Yet disciplines like biology, which would seem to be necessary bridges between physics or metaphysics and cultural theory or anthropology. maintain the centrality of the problem because conventional theory of evolution, for example, appeals to "random" genetic mutations (interacting with the environment) to explain biological originality: the generation of new species. The humanist temptation to found human originality (and law) on human freedom, conceived as a suspension of necessity, finds its quasi-counterpart in scientific appeals to chance. More important, the lack of conclusiveness of debates of this sort—as Kant understood in his assertion of an antinomy between necessity and freedom—hardly means that this inconclusiveness is irrelevant to morality, art, philosophy, science, criminal or civil law, and so on. Rather the contrary.

However, because the concepts of "positive" chance and "positive" freedom (i.e., of genuine autonomy in one sense or another) can be interpreted as resulting from our lack of knowledge, rather than their validity, perhaps we should begin by conceiving originality in a way that does not beg these questions. Thus, we may remain circumspectly agnostic, for example, vis-à-vis Einstein's famous declaration that God does not play dice with the world versus the indeterministic or antinomic interpretation of Quantum physics advocated by Neils Bohr, not to mention even more problematic arguments about *human* freedom. Indeed, it would seem that the problem of originality can, in certain respects, be posed more coherently without recourse to such arbitration. Frege, for example, famously argued that numbers—although in Kant's system analytic or tautological—should really be regarded as synthetic in Kant's sense because, although the natural numbers, for instance, are generated by mere iteration or repetition (1 + 1 + 1, etc.), they are nonetheless unique in their properties (such as the prime numbers), and therefore extend our knowledge, according to Frege, beyond tautology and into discovery or originality.[21]

In short, originality and repetition, law of the most banal sort, seem to be bed-fellows. They are certainly bed-fellows with a vengeance in Sterne and Diderot—*double entendre y inclus* (as we have glimpsed via Bugger's "virginity")—where the question of exceptionality as it concerns relations between human beings, the relation between the individual and the group, for instance, is intimately bound up with the question of exceptionality more generally. The real problem of originality is therefore by no means just a question of "solitary genius," as we may wholeheartedly agree with Woodmansee and Jaszi, but of understanding more generally. But are we not prepared to admit that the sheep or the ape is a "solitary genius," however hypermimetic (or for this reason), in comparison with, let's say, the ant?

An essay by Thomas Pfau, in *The Construction of Authorship*, cites Adorno to the effect that the more art works conceive themselves as individual, the more they are likely a result of social labor.[22] But Pfau does not mention the obvious dialectical corollary—and Adorno was nothing if not a dialectician—that the more such works conceive themselves as a result of social labor, the more they are likely to be individual (i.e., original, presumably like Adorno).

Spinoza—almost as perverse as *Jacques le fataliste*—makes the comparable claim that the more we think we are free, the less free we are. Hence, the less free we think we are, the more free we may be.[23] Oh dear! It all sounds, *mutatis mutandis*, a bit like the saint who is proved to be one by thinking he is not one.

MONSTROUS BIRTHS IN STERNE AND LOCKE

Sterne's most obvious technique, openly imitated by Diderot in *Jacques le fataliste*, stages the abstract difficulty of distinguishing between law and arbitrariness concretely for his readers because precisely where he and Diderot appear or claim to narrate most arbitrarily we would be well advised to suspect the opposite. The problem becomes particularly pointed, moreover, when it is a matter of deciding whether, say, what looks superficially like an arbitrary or "original" maneuver is, in fact, a conscious plagiarism or whether the resemblance we see belongs to a more fundamental law, where (like Leibniz and Newton) two authors arrive independently at similar results.

Diderot's obviously false joke that Sterne plagiarized him rather than vice versa finds more "serious" confirmation in other, often anonymous plagiarists of Sterne, some of whom actually seem to predict the future of Sterne's own work (*Tristram Shandy* was published in installments over nine years).[24] Because he apparently delighted in some of these plagiarisms—unlike, say, Daniel Defoe, who demanded that spurious sequels to *Robinson Crusoe* be punishable by laws like those governing household robbery (for which punishment was death)—he might well also have amiably plagiarized his plagiarists.

But if a plagiaristic prediction of the future of the author plagiarized recalls the ambivalence of originality *qua* historical priority mentioned earlier, that ambivalence is even better illustrated by an author who *predicts the past* of another author—recalling Schlegel's aphorism about the historian who is a prophet looking backward. This is the theme of Borges' famous story (*Pierre Menard*) of a nineteenth-century author who rewrites—or rather *writes*—*Don Quixote* word for word. To coincide with the past is arguably to be even more original than writing something genuinely new.[25]

I turn now to the theme of "monstrous births" as emblems of originality in Sterne and Locke, partly for its own interest and partly because Sterne may plausibly be regarded as having *either plagiarized or predicted* Locke in this respect. Locke's almost obsessively repeated example of monstrous births in *An Essay Concerning Human Understanding* illustrates the problem of what is meant by such ideas as "man." His concern is with the general uncertainty of concepts of "natural substances" (and "complex ideas" in general) and hence, for example, with how physically or mentally deformed or even cross-specied a baby has to be—he rather amusingly cites apocryphal examples of such monstrous babies as if they were real—before we cease to call it human. Locke, a philosopher who emphasizes the ambiguity or relative indeterminacy of natural species, may here be said to be concerned with originality in its pejorative sense of oddity, deformity, freakishness, and so on—a pejorative sense that became fashionable during this time.[26]

Now Sterne refers to or plagiarizes Locke innumerable times in *Tristram Shandy*, sometimes by name, sometimes not. He even surreptitiously attributes to Locke views espoused by Locke's arch opponents, such as Sir Robert Filmer (the defender of absolute monarchy and patriarchy), as if Locke were in perverse "plagiaristic" complicity with them. I cannot develop these matters here except to mention that, although Sterne refers to Locke throughout, he sometimes fails to mention arguably the most important references (just as Burton, who is also an important source for the novel, is never mentioned by name).[27] For example, Locke's highly rhetorical attack on rhetoric in the *Essay* famously descends to the chauvinist simile that rhetoric is "like the fair sex," an instrument of deception. This suits Sterne's feminist critique of Locke perfectly—and he singles out many other Lockean metaphors, examples, and so on for consideration—but he does not mention this one explicitly, whether by accident or design. Similarly, there is no explicit reference to my knowledge in *Tristram Shandy* to Locke's exemplum of monstrous births. However, the whole comic structure of the novel can be said to be that of a kind of gigantic "monstrous birth"—from the *coitus interruptus* of the first chapter, via Tristram's own birth (which famously takes several volumes), to the delayed twin births in the final chapter of a child and a calf, where the child is as hairy as the calf. (Because newborns are often hairy, Sterne's comic rhetoric is, in this respect, more realistic than some of Locke's supposedly actual examples of monstrous births, as is his lengthy comic citation of the actual religious debate over at what point a fetus can be baptized by holy water squirted up the vagina. This, after all, is our own decidedly unfunny debate over abortion *in nuce*.)

Whether we think Sterne's use of the monstrous birth motif is of a piece with his evident appropriation of other aspects of Locke—rather than, say, of a conventional idea "in the air" during the more than half a century spanning the *Essay* and *Tristram Shandy*, or perhaps of another author altogether (e.g., Rabelais)—depends on how original and precise we think Sterne's reading of Locke to have been; or, if you like, how extensively and cunningly plagiaristic of Locke he really was. I have argued elsewhere[28] that the point is not so much whether we can prove that Sterne had Locke's monstrous births specifically in mind (perhaps synthesized with other examples), but that the question is pregnant. Suppose we imagine that Sterne had access only to highly edited or expurgated versions of the *Essay*, such as modern students and professors usually read, or that he had got his Locke as much from encyclopedias, as some editors suggest, as from Locke himself (i.e., versions in which Locke's almost obsessive recurrence to this example is attenuated by being edited down from many instances to few or even none), we might almost regard him as predicting the past of Locke's text. In fact, although most modern commentary on Sterne's relation to Locke is notably silent on this particular connection, at least one of Sterne's anonymous contemporary plagiarists was not. For he (or she) not only grasped the general obstetrical metaphor whereby Sterne is said to paint using the placenta, but also connects this specifically to Locke and monstrous births. If a mother is too much influenced by Locke's notorious "association of ideas that have no connection in nature" (a phrase cited by Sterne), "'tis ten to one but that the child is born with the head of a dog," and "in some countries it would have been made a question, whether I should have been christened as a man, or thrown into the sea, as a monstrous birth, or *lusus naturae*."[29]

Though I have taken this example because it serves to illustrate something of what is at stake when we make detailed judgments of originality (is Locke, Sterne, or perhaps Sterne's plagiarist most "original" in his handling of monstrous births?), it is all the more exemplary, as I have said, because conception and birth are figures in Sterne (as elsewhere) for originality or novelty (or conceptuality) themselves. Nor can they be considered *mere* metaphors because, for example, Locke's appeal to monstrous births is quite literal: nature herself is capable of originality and novelty in a pejorative sense. Indeed, although Locke was obviously not privy to the modern theory of evolution, he would doubtless have also recognized the possibility of natural originality in a nonpejorative sense, the development of new species. Thus, the *natural* model of the monstrous birth already offers something of the ambivalence concerning originality that we find in the rather dramatic development or even reversal of its *cultural* meaning during the course of the eighteenth century.

Before coming to Sterne's explicit playing out of obstetrical *labor* as a (deformed) metaphor for his own originality, we should first note that he also alludes directly to Locke's doctrine of property rights as derived from *labor* in the ordinary sense, a doctrine frequently cited and/or criticized in modern treatments of originality and copyright law.[30] Without mentioning Locke by name in this context, what Sterne does with the doctrine—formulated by Locke in the context of material property—is precisely to apply it to *intellectual property rights*, just like modern commentators. Walter Shandy, Tristram's philosopher father, is said to pick up his ideas just as a man in a State of Nature picks up apples—and it is this example, which is Locke's own, that comically gives away the Lockean subtext.[31] For a clergyman like Sterne, the example of picking apples must have been particularly amusing as exemplum of the natural origin of property rights because picking apples is, of course, the Biblical example of original crime. Be that as it may, the standard modern leftist critique of Locke *qua* original Capitalist—that Locke's treatment of master–servant relations and property rights conveniently fails to mention that labor now operates in a context that is far removed from any hypothetical State of Nature and, moreover, manifestly unjust because *property has already been claimed* (and that the "natural marketplace" and individual autonomy appealed to by modern Capitalists is no less a fiction than Locke's State of Nature)[32]—finds a farcical parallel in the intellectual property claimed by Walter Shandy because he has, of course, "picked up" his own ideas from numerous sources and previous owners or claimants, including Locke. But the Shandyan critique obviously goes much further than the domain of economics or intellectual property rights because it calls into question the concept of labor as a fundamental source of value—a concept shared, *nota bene*, by both Locke and Marx, both capitalist and communist. For obviously one does not "own" an idea, let alone claim it as original, because one has labored on it because someone else who labored less could have come up with it first; hence, we have observed that intellectual property rights such as patents and Nobel prizes tend to degenerate into a matter of temporal priority, however slight. But we have also seen that even more substantial temporal priority is no more definitive than labor as a measure of either intellectual ownership or originality because Borges' nineteenth-century author of *Don Quixote* is arguably even more original than Cervantes and at least co-owner of the text.

In contrast to what Leo Strauss has identified as Locke's philosophy of labor[33]—both in the theoretical *Essay* and the political *Treatises on Government*—it is a critical platitude that Sterne seems to advocate "play." But it is not generally recognized, I believe, that his critique of labor as the natural basis of property rights turns punningly into an implicit critique of reproductive labor as the natural basis of sexual relations, where nature hopefully copies herself without too great a deviation, monstrosity, or originality. Once again, the anonymous plagiarist makes the appropriate feminist point in *Yorick's Meditations*: that to understand the *lusus naturae* or monstrous birth, we must understand that "dame nature has her frolicks as well as other females."[34]

But Sterne's or Tristram's own figure of originality departs altogether from natural reproduction, "playful" or otherwise, and hence from natural female labor as counterpart to the manly sort—although he maintains a kind of transvestite "feminine" and concealing/seductive role. Commenting on the most typical element of his rhetoric, aposiopesis (the Sternean dash in punctuation), Tristram compares this to someone who hides a "*BAMBINO*" up his sleeve to produce, pop, at the right moment.[35] *Yorick's Meditations* appears to predict the image of hiding something under one's (classical) cloak before it appeared in *Tristram Shandy*—a technique compared to that of a certain Athenian who, when asked what he is concealing under his cloak, replies, "with all the composure of a philosopher, I hide it that you may not know. In a like manner, I, Mr. Critic, write that I may not be understood."[36] Sterne's prophetic plagiarist does not, unlike Sterne, turn this act of concealment explicitly into a kind of artificial childbirth. However, we may recall in this connection another Athenian whose irony is traditionally associated with his intellectual midwifery, analogous to the midwifery of his mother. Kierkegaard wrote, for example, that Socratic irony created or gave birth by proxy "as it were by artificial demonstrations," and that its creativity or originality in a certain sense "borders upon a theft."[37] Such descriptions apply not just to Sterne's plagiarism, but to his figure of the bambino, where ironic concealment is in addition eroticized as a lure that artificially gives birth. But this erotic foreplay that results, so to speak, in a play-birth is far from merely playful in its consequences; we are told quite seriously, I think, that, when timed correctly, this kind of originality or monstrous birth can unhinge the principles and politics of "half a nation." We see in a moment, in connection with Diderot's use of Sterne, how this can be illustrated more concretely.

First, however, we should observe that, whereas Woodmansee and Jaszi accuse Wordsworth and the Romantics of turning originality into a mystification, *Sterne presents mystification as a special mode of originality.* Moreover, if we combine the maeutic figure of artificial birth with the *coitus interruptus* of Chapter 1 and other comparable figures in the novel, originality appears as a mode of *interrupted reproduction, conceptual labor, or replication.*

What does this mean? Intentional mystification is, of course, endemic not only to the art of ironists like Sterne and Diderot, but also to everyday life. If cultures and human relations are structured, in part, by concealment, as they evidently are, then the relations between old and new, originality in its double sense, also must be so structured. However, much mystification also is naturally unintentional and occurs willy-nilly ("To a person who hasn't got it," as Schlegel remarked, "[irony] will remain a riddle even after it is openly confessed. It is meant to deceive no one except those who consider it a deception"[38]), and the blatantly artificial Sternean gesture of concealment in a sense "imitates" the natural kind, as his artificial birth "imitates" the natural one. Hence, if Sterne defines his own originality as a kind of sham aposiopesis, we should recall that aposiopesis technically means not concealment as such, but the interruption of a grammatical sequence: it conceals or leaves something out *because it is incomplete*, and thus *not only imitates, but enacts* the incompletion, which is not only a part of all perception and interpretation, but of course constitutes the definition of history—because history is only history insofar as it is incomplete, uncertain, and/or deceptive in its upshot, law, or lack of such (i.e., regarding the future as well as the past). Originality, incompletion, and mystification go hand in hand.

Thus, we may distinguish between two modes of originality. The calculus—*insofar* as Newton's and Leibniz's slightly different notations can be reduced to the *relatively* clear and complete system that we employ today—was "original" in the Enlightenment. Thus, we do not generally refer to their original texts for precisely this reason, whereas Shandean or artistic originality seems to repeat itself, like a "nothing" that monstrously and erratically gives birth to itself (as *Yorick's Meditations* puns on *ex nihilo nihil fit*) from generation to generation. Of course, this distinction is only relative—one can well imagine a future in which Leibniz's and Newton's relatively distinctive treatments and conceptions of the calculus (including its relation to other things, including earlier anticipations of the calculus) become again a source of novelty, just as, conversely, artistic forms of originality are also obviously rooted in their periods. What used to be sentimentally called the "universality" or "timelessness" of great art (or indeed great science)—its originality *sensu eminentiori*—is, to some considerable extent, a trick or *trompe-l'oeil*, as we have just seen Sterne emphasize with his *bambino*. This *trompe-l'oeil* or illusion, one might say, derives partly from the deceptive nature of the universe and partly from the guile of human beings. It is therefore to the interesting relation between these in Diderot that I now turn.

MIMESIS IN *TRISTRAM SHANDY* AND *JACQUES LE FATALISTE*

The relatively abstract considerations concerning law with which I began pay off when it comes to reading Diderot. For example, though the details of Spinoza are arguably much less important to understanding *Jacques le fataliste* than the details of Locke to understanding *Tristram Shandy*, Spinoza's critique of freedom—his critique of conventional concepts of law in physical, metaphysical, moral, and legal senses—provides a stark index to the conceptual landscape. Diderot finds a model in Sterne, as we have noted, for the pretense of narrating "freely" and even at random—when, *in fact*, both writers are highly systematic—but this point is sharpened by Spinoza's denial of the possibility of acting freely or at random. It is not so much a question of whether Diderot agrees or disagrees with Spinoza[39]—although we note that Jacques, who has inherited his brand of Spinozism from his Captain, contradicts himself constantly—but rather that the relations of chance and law, as well as freedom and necessity, constitute what Kant calls an antinomy (i.e., a determined ambivalence in which contradictory and/or incommensurate interpretations of the same phenomena are incapable of being logically refuted). Spinoza, for better or worse, provides a rather spectacular illustration of the point.

This "Spinozan" problem occurs to the second power or at the metalevel in *Jacques*, not just regarding the kind of events and actions being described, but (as in Sterne) regarding the coherence of the text. The question is not merely how well the fiction copies or allegorizes the original called life—and Jacques, in contrast to his name ("a John" whose brother is naturally called "Jean"), is notoriously called an incomparable original—but whether it is even coherent in its own terms. I have argued elsewhere that the key to this coherence is to be found in *Jacques*—and this is also true of the two other Diderot texts I consider here, *The Paradox of the Actor* and *Rameau's Nephew*—in a conception of mimesis that moves beyond the so to speak abstract epistemology of the relations between originals and copies to mimesis conceived as a pattern of *mutual* imitation between humans. We have seen that many plagiarists or imitators of Sterne, like Diderot, insist that the question of originality cannot be solved simply by a decision about who is plagiarizing whom or who is copying what, but only by conceiving it as the upshot of a generalized system of reciprocal plagiarism or mimesis, leading to the "joke"—as in T. S. Eliot's conceit that every new poem changes the past history of poetry, or Borges' rewriting of *Don Quixote*, or Oscar Wilde's insistence that nature imitates art—that time or causality can run backward or stand still (a "joke" that appears monstrously serious in some interpretations of, say, Quantum physics). This joke occurs by inference in *Tristram Shandy*, whose opening chapter narrates a failure to wind up the clock (hence, one piece of Sterneana is entitled *The Clockmakers Outcry*).[40] It also occurs in Diderot when Jacques' watch is stolen just after the narrator's allegory of a chateau in which people are said to have been there before they arrived and still there after they have left and *which belongs to everybody and nobody*—although presently occupied by some bandits (38 ff.). Many readers do not perceive that the seemingly realistic theft is, in fact, a continuation of the allegory. (Flann O'Brien's *The Third Policeman* [1939], which plagiarizes Sterne in certain respects, makes a similar allegorical gesture when the narrator claims that his American gold watch has been stolen, although he has never actually had one, a fact that he subsequently forgets.[41]) The abolition of clock time and ownership go together in the allegoric chateau. Jacques elsewhere fails to notice that one of his master's stories entails an important temporal contradiction.[42]

Despite Jacques' explicit dislike of repetition, which he associates with the Bible, and despite the disparate and even seemingly random stories told in the novel—to the apparent effect that *everything is different*—one particular model nevertheless repeats itself systematically: that of duelers whose imitative reciprocity becomes more and more naked as the story is repeated. I do not repeat here what I have said about this elsewhere,[43] except to add that the coherence of the repeated story contrasts amusingly with at least one editor's judgment that it illustrates the "uniqueness" and "bizarreness" of human nature.[44] Precisely when the text points most emphatically to mimetic reciprocity—in short, to a relative lack of "uniqueness," the *opposite is inferred*—as if ironic deception contrives to occur even when the "secret" is made most visible.

I thus suggest, as I have said, that Diderot develops from the classical artistic and philosophical problem of *mimesis of* law to the anthropological problem of *mutual mimesis as* law. Moreover, just as we have discussed the antinomic ambivalence of the concept of law, and hence of origin, so a model of strictly reciprocal mimesis—which René Girard has metaphorized as "monstrous doubling" (recalling twins frequently killed as "monstrous" in ancient societies[45])—naturally also leaves the point of origin relatively undetermined or even arbitrary. In effect, originality is generated by mimesis, rather than, or as well as, vice versa. (We have already cited Adorno's claim that "*mimetic power is effectively the power of qualitative distinction.*") But this does not mean that originality—qualitative distinction—is merely subjective or even intersubjective. Ludwig Wittgenstein defended himself against just such a charge in his *Remarks on the Foundations of Mathematics* when considering an analogous issue: the relation between rule or law conceived as repetition (or mimesis in this sense) and agreement (or mimesis in the other). Only our agreement distinguishes what we consider genuine rules from nonrules, says Wittgenstein; but this emphatically does *not* mean that rules or laws are *founded* merely on agreement. (On the contrary, he says in a rather Shandyan vein—and he was incidentally an admirer of Sterne—that rules are founded on "nothing."[46])

I have said that Jacques' hatred of repetition is belied by the novel's repeated stories of mimetic dueling, as it is belied by his hiccoughs—and in this image of stammered repetition, I believe Diderot covertly recalls the servant Trim in *Tristram Shandy*, who tells a story that amounts to a single line interrupted and repeated over and over. Jacques hates repetition because he associates it with "portraits" and the Bible (i.e., moral judgment), as contrasted with his quasi-Spinozan belief in Fate and dismissal of good and evil. Hence, the stories he tells seem designed to avoid repetition and affirm difference, potentially running through every possible sequence of events and combination of characters and, in principle, fulfilling the definition of randomness as "doing everything possible necessarily." Jacques desires to demonstrate, among other things, that a so-called good action or person can always lead to bad and vice versa, or that there is no stability in moral judgments (here he is not really Spinozan, or only so in a perverse sense, because Spinoza provides an ethics modeled on the deductive logic of Euclidean geometry). The appearance of exhaustive or at least exhausting arbitrariness in the stories is thus a kind of law: the law, as Kierkegaard put it, that the only genuine repetition is the repeated demonstration of its impossibility.[47]

Yet the story of the duelers is not only repeated several times in the novel—with the supposed difference between them becoming ever more flimsy—but it is explicitly generalized to every kind of rivalry in life, and hence is arguably also the key to all of Jacques' other stories and indeed to the rivalry between master and servant. It might seem, in this connection, that Diderot's plagiarism or mimesis of the master-servant relation in *Tristram Shandy* (as Sterne in turn can be said to appropriate the master-servant couple in *Don Quixote*) effectively reveals a qualitative distinction between Diderot and Sterne because the edifying friendship between Toby and Trim is never allowed to degenerate into rivalry, whereas Jacques explicitly claims that he is the real master and is even allowed to be in erotic rivalry with his master. Indeed, it might appear that Sterne's portrayal of master and servant is the opposite of politically revolutionary in implication—in the English tradition, the clergyman Sterne is often regarded as politically (if not sexually) quietistic—whereas Diderot's emphasis on their rivalry is commonly seen as anticipating the French Revolution. But this ignores the fact that French imitations of Sterne were produced before, during, and after the revolution in a manner that often makes the reference to Sterne appear subversively "left-wing" (as indeed is also suggested by some English Sterneana of the period).[48] Moreover, a careful reading of *Tristram Shandy* reveals that there *is* a relatively concealed mimetic relation between master and servant, and one that runs the wrong way for the status quo, because it is the master who imitates the servant rather than vice versa. For example, although he is not permitted to fall for any of Trim's girlfriends, Toby significantly falls in love only after hearing the story of Trim's love, and it also takes Trim to suggest the obviously eroticized objects (model towns) of Toby's bowling-green wars. Trim, in short, is Toby's erotic model.

Although it is not pivotal for my argument, I suggest that Diderot was likely a careful and original enough reader of Sterne to recognize that the mimetic relation and hence potential rivalry between master and servant is already, although covertly, central to *Tristram Shandy.* In short, what looks like Diderot's original divergence from Sterne may illustrate rather the contrary—the depth of his "plagiarism" (or understanding) that makes him original in relation to other, more superficial interpretations. Be that as it may, Diderot's own treatment of the master–servant rivalry is not without its own equivocations and subtleties from a political point of view. For precisely in the episode in which Jacques openly rebels against his master and goes downstairs in a huff, their rivalry is solved not by an open battle, let alone by an unequivocal declaration of the equality of men, but only by the mediation of a third party, a woman, the hostess at the inn, who tells them that *they are equal and unequal at one and the same time*![49]

This is the double-bind or "paradox," one might say, that characterizes all forms of political equality because theoretical equality (whatever that may be) is always negated in practice. Gregory Bateson has made famous the double bind: "Be spontaneous!"—in short, "Be original!" But the correlative double bind is: "Be like me!" Of course, mimesis occurs not just between two people, a master and a servant, but between all masters and all servants. There are always mediating third parties, and indeed nth parties, and the mimetic double bind or "paradox" of origin can therefore perhaps be better expressed by the following: A imitates B imitates C. . . . imitates Z imitates A, and so on, although this obviously merely schematizes the notion of collective mimetic behavior whose dynamics are vastly more complex. For a further, rather extraordinary exegesis of these dynamics, I turn to two other texts by Diderot.

PATHOLOGIES OF ORIGINALITY IN *PARADOXE SUR LE COMEDIEN*

The ambiguity surrounding our conceptions of law and originality obviously does not mean that laws and originalities do not exist, but it does open them to pathological misinterpretations. One of the most obvious of these is the assertion of originality or difference by way of what Girard calls "negative mimesis"—claiming to be different from the crowd in a way that remains dependent on the crowd. Woodmansee and Jaszi seem to regard Wordsworth's idea of originality as an error of this kind (although, even if true, this does not mean that Wordsworth was not original), and the post-Romantic world (i.e., our own) admittedly treats originality rather fetishistically. The mimetic idolization of the so-called original, as "stars" are fond of pointing out, is fickle and can quickly turn to indifference or worse, and the *reductio ad absurdum* of originality or difference is perhaps Warhol's now hackneyed "15 minutes of fame." The pejorative meaning of originality (eccentric, odd, gratuitous, grotesque, etc.) is well illustrated by Dr. Johnson's mistaken view of *Tristram Shandy*: "nothing odd will last long."

The Paradox of the Actor develops precisely this kind of apparent "paradox" or double bind of mimesis in its relation to originality. The dialogue begins with the argument that the actor is most original who imitates best (i.e., who is least original and least 'natural'). Geoffrey Bremner's introduction claims that Diderot is "at pains to stress that the stage is a different world, different in kind from everyday life." But Bremner also states, without seeming to notice the incongruity, the immediate complication of the text that collapses this difference: "Action, persuasion, making things happen, is, like acting, best achieved in a state of moral and emotional detachment."[50] It gets worse: The just person is accordingly compared to an actor on stage (114); the genius will love justice without experiencing its sweetness (106); and good actors are "unbelieving priest(s)" (108). Worse still: People of natural sensibility, of which the "first speaker" (perhaps closer to Diderot than the second)[51] says he is one, are said to be mediocre geniuses, weak, and immoral; yet as the dialogue progresses, the evaluation seems turned on its head. In society, mimetic self-control (the actor's talent) becomes the court hypocrite, and good actors are said to make indifferent people, both morally and otherwise, because of their mimetic propensities. The first speaker accuses himself of having wanted to be an actor, a "non-natural" mimetist, out of a "natural" desire to frequent loose actresses (135) because the hot-blooded people are on stage and the geniuses in the audience (106)! The "paradoxical" development seems not so much dialectical as schizophrenic.

The dialectic between art and nature is faulty or pathological because, as it is slyly admitted, nature and art are *both* mimetic: "What the naturally sensitive person will show me will be weak; the other's [the actor's] imitation will be powerful; and if it did happen *that their imitations were equally powerful*, a point which I won't grant you, not in a million years . . ." (153; italics added). The difference between nature and art, the original and the imitation, is not a difference of kind, as Bremner claims, but of degree, of self-control and self-consciousness, of *power*.

The dialectic of original and copy now degenerates even further into a pathology that is sadomasochistic or sacrificial to an even more comic and programmatic degree. We are told not only that the actor is morally and otherwise indifferent, but that he is a slave to the public, which despises while needing him, and, worse, that the author is slave to the actor, a slave of a slave (139). The pattern of victimage is not only serial, but reciprocal because the actor is also later said to be a victim of the poet—his subjection to the latter's genius or originality being, in many cases, positively harmful to him. The public is said to lose its vices for an instant in the theater (138), but meanwhile the actors take on all the vices of the public, of slavery and domination in equal measure. Precisely because of his mimetic susceptibility and/or originality (talent)—depending on how one valorizes it—the actor becomes a kind of sacrificial surrogate for the public. (It is worth noting that Kafka's "Josephine the Singer" analyzes the star in precisely such terms. For when a child pipes up in the audience with a voice exactly like Josephine's, it is swiftly silenced or sacrificed. Meanwhile, the public and Josephine are said to be mutual victims as well as beneficiaries of each other.)

Far from being different in kind, the spectacles of art and life are therefore closely related, although this has to be hidden by the exaggerations of modern art and by a hygienic distance established in the modern age between actor and spectator. Thus, to explode this hygiene, we are told of an actress who is deceiving her actor husband with another actor, "this actor with the Chevalier, and the Chevalier with a third, whom the Chevalier catches in her arms." (Here we have the circular model A loves/imitates B, C, D . . . A mentioned earlier.) The Chevalier plans his revenge by taking up a position as *a spectator on the stage* to disconcert her, but she is able to respond to him *without for one moment departing from her role.* The second speaker responds to this undifferentiation between art and life, original and copy, disgustedly: "It's enough to turn me off the theater" (119–120)! In the so-called private theater, too, the spectator is at almost the same level as the spectacle (144).

Just as their thematization of mimesis is played out to the second power or at the metalevel by Sterne, Diderot and their plagiarists, in their plagiaristic relations, so *The Paradox of the Actor* concludes by increasingly and pointedly *acting out* the violence that it thematizes. First of all, the dialogue is now staged pointedly on the street or in the Tuileries "where [the first speaker, "the man of paradox"] would have bumped into everybody who came towards him if they had not avoided colliding with him," and where his interlocutor is now called his antagonist and several times physically approached and grasped. Indeed, the dialogue concludes with an anecdote concerning a Roman actor who killed a slave on stage, collapsing the sacrificial distance between art and life entirely. Moreover, the first speaker (perhaps close, as I suggested, to Diderot) defines his own role, his own originality, as marking him out as a potential scapegoat, claiming that he could be stoned in the streets for espousing these views of the theater (143)! One of these views is apparently that the ancients wrote lines that could be almost equally spoken on and off stage and that the modern hygienic distance between life and art is a sign of modernity's inferiority. Not to avoid comic paradox, one might say that the first speaker's—perhaps by proxy Diderot's or rather "Diderot's" (for, if so, he would of course be *acting* himself)[52]—claim to originality or genuine modernity here consists precisely in his rejection of modernity in favor of the originals, the "classics," in which the sacrificial basis of art and mimesis is more naked, if not more advanced. We see this hypothesis at least partially confirmed below.

PATHOLOGIES OF ORIGINALITY IN *LE NEVEU DE RAMEAU* (AND *LA RELIGIEUSE*)

Given the centrality of the concept of mimesis in Diderot, it is neither surprising nor particularly naive that his *Eloge de Richardson* takes seriously the powers of mimesis-as-verisimilitude, either genuine or illusory. However, in his "Richardsonian" novel *La Religieuse* (as *Jacques* is his "Sternean" novel)—a novel that, despite its putative verisimilitude, is filled with intentional inconsistencies (although more concealed than in *Jacques*), not to mention its origin in a real-life prank or mystification played on one of Diderot's friends—it is the latter, the illusory or deceptive element, that ultimately predominates. Diderot's theory of fiction, as Rosalina de la Carrera suggests, is to be found less in the *Eloge* of Richardson's so-called realism than in what she calls the indirect or "ternary" communication of the *Preface-Annexe* to *La Religieuse*, where truth and fiction enter into an ambivalent reciprocity produced by the ternary or tertiary mediators of communication (recalling the hostess in *Jacques* discussed earlier), transparent neither to one another nor to the reader—who is thus said by Carrera to be incorporated "as an integral term of the fiction," which produces "the illusion of reality."[53]

Carrera's identification of Diderot's theory of fiction with a theory of mediation or "ternary communication" dovetails well with the centrality of mimetic mediation I am proposing. Her adoption of Michel Serres' definition of dialogue—"*To hold a dialogue is to suppose a third man and seek to exclude him*; a successful communication is the exclusion of the third man"—provides a triangular model of communication that, as Serres well knew, is identical (or similar) to the models of triangular mimetic desire and sacrificial mimesis proposed more notoriously by René Girard.[54] Without mentioning Girard's theory of the sacred, Carrera provides a properly sacred model of ternary communication via Serres' interpretation of Leibniz, to the effect that all communication takes place "by the intermediate of God." Moreover, she acutely argues that in some of the most crucial dialogues in *La Religieuse*, the mediation of *music* "show[s] that Leibniz's model of communication is still effective even without the theological foundation. Music, instead, takes over for God as the universal encoder. . . ."[55] This claim recalls Kafka's sacrificial treatment of music mentioned earlier and prepares us for the entirely fundamental mediation of music in *Rameau's Nephew.*[56]

Music is partly a metaphor in *Rameau's Nephew*, as in Kafka, because, unlike his uncle, *he is not so much musician as mime.* The text is about "musical" mimesis that is often as much visual or intellectual as aural. But it is well worth noting that literal music in the modern world has gained an extraordinary semblance or actuality of power, not only in terms of defining "cutting-edge" originalities and fashions, but in being frequently hailed as (in the hackneyed phrase) "the universal language." Rameau maintains a mimetic analysis that recalls the tertiary mediations of *The Paradox*, claiming that instrumental music "imitates" the singing voice just as the singing voice "imitates" speech.[57] Now we only need the voice to imitate instrumental music for the mimetic circle to be complete. Indeed, this, with logical precision, is precisely what the text serves up. For Rameau is figured as a kind of pandemonic and universal mime—"*l'homme-orchestre*" or one-man band—who stretches his voice grotesquely to imitate the entire range of musical intruments whose deformations were supposed to imitate the voice. Rameau is "original" (the term is even more insistent here than for Jacques and even more paradoxical or antinomic)[58] in imitating or trying to imitate everything, *in doing everything possible quasi-necessarily.* He is a monstrous freak who might remind us of victims of Tourette's syndrome or "arctic hysteria."[59]

However, it is entirely plausible that Diderot has staged the dialogue at least as much on the side of Rameau as of "Moi" (the philosopher) (i.e., that Rameau really is a model of originality and not mere freakishness). The so-called freak is often a horrific victim, but so may be the original often confused with the freak, not to mention that these may coincide. Georg Lukács observed that "it cannot be by mere chance" that *Rameau's Nephew* is the sole modern work of literature cited by Hegel in *The Phenomenology of Spirit*, where Rameau is regarded as a model of the modern dialectic of "unhappy consciousness" (closely connected by Hegel to Romantic irony).[60] Stephen Werner further argues that Diderot's "2nd satyre" (subtitle of *Rameau*) anticipates not only Schlegel's concept of irony, as opposed to resembling the satire of Voltaire, but also "key documents of music and the coming of the new," such as Nietzsche's *Birth of Tragedy* and Kierkegaard's *Either/Or.* Werner observes that the subtitle "2nd satyre" has a double significance. First, it was *not* his second 'satyre,' but his first, and in this we recognize a pattern of comic confusion between original and copy, first and second, that is by now quite predictable. But Werner ventures further, arguing that this highlights "the hidden project of Diderot's text . . . the modernization of satire," and, moreover, that the archaic spelling of "satyre" signals that this modernization occurs by way of a "throwback to an earlier form."[61] Even if this interpretation of the detail as such stretches our credulity or seems "original" in a pejorative sense (although Werner may well be perfectly right), it nevertheless confirms the pattern of seemingly reversible temporality I have stressed throughout. Werner's contention about the "satyre" is moreover plausible not only in the light of relatively commonplace recognition of Diderot's consciousness of classical musical models in general—such as the flaying of the satyr-musician Marsyas by Apollo[62]—but in terms of his insistence on the mystificatory violence associated with the *philosophes*' or French Enlightenment satire in particular.[63] Above all, we are told that "*Mime is also violent*" (italics added), connected to "feelings of *ressentiment*," "the spirit of rebellion," and "schemes of revenge." "Diderot's *spectacle* endorses the primitive aesthetic called for in his early writings. It is theater as a Dionysian experience . . . whose center is music."[64]

Though we might perhaps beware Werner's and Carrera's differing tendencies to romanticize music (a topic I cannot pursue here),[65] their combined insistence on it—in one case as the center of Dionysiac and mimetic violence, in the other as a structure of tertiary mediation substituting for God—seem together remarkably suggestive as regards its role in both Diderot and beyond. What is at stake in the "Dionysian experience" is further specified by Werner in his definition of the term "énergumène" as applied to Rameau:

> Energumène is a satirical term. It conveys the excitability and frenzy of a tub-thumper or ranter. Yet the word also has a more exacting meaning. It signifies demonic possession or frenzy . . . possessed by the devil, requiring a kind of exorcism.[66]

Musical mimicry thus doubles here for both God and the devil and "requires a kind of exorcism"—one perhaps performed by the "original" or comic text. Rameau, like Shakespeare's fools (who are so often given the most correct lines), appears as a kind of carnival fool who epitomizes "dialogism" (or "double-talk")[67] in the sense that Werner borrows from Mikhail Bahktin. But beyond the attenuated scapegoat rituals of carnival lies not only what Werner rather sanguinely calls "the sublimity of an early state of imagination," but also what he cites directly from Diderot: "*La poésie veut quelque chose . . . de barbare.*"[68] Poetry—*mimesis and originality*—wants something barbarous, a victim, and it is no accident that Werner links Rameau to the martyrdom of (the dialogic) Socrates, while Otis Fellows (citing O'Gorman) links him to the flayed satyr Marsyas.[69] To be sure, Rameau is not flayed alive like Marsyas for his musical performance, but his moment of "sublimity" or originality as the *homme-orchestre* leaves him drained and shaken—and, more important, finally deserted by the crowd that has gathered around. Even his famous hackneyed parting shot to the philosopher—"Who laughs last laughs best"—is not so much a transcendence of his sacrificial role as a translation of the principle of sacrifice into that of comic irony, a translation of "satyre" into "satire" as Werner neatly puts it, or of literal (physical) into symbolic (mental) violence.[70] We may recall that the jester-priest Yorick, appropriated from Shakespeare in *Tristram Shandy*—and Sterne's pseudonym in both the *Sermons* and *A Sentimental Journey*—dies from the combination of others' malice and his own jokes in the first volume (from a broken heart it would seem) and is the tragicomic sacrificial victim *par excellence.*

CONCLUSION

The original as victim? Well, maybe. It is not too cheap, I trust, to recall the post-Romantic or modern stereotype of "genius" as linked to mental disorders, indifference from the contemporary public (like the proverbial prophet spurned in his or her own country), social alienation, even criminality, and the like: in short, *exceptionality* in various and often incompatible senses. Van Gogh's failure to sell his work, not to mention his cutting off his ear, provides a conventional illustration of both sacrificial and self-sacrificial behavior as regards the painter who now adorns chocolate boxes. Something similar goes for mathematicians like John Nash, whose work has been made famous to the public by the recent film that portrays his mental breakdown. The world of so-called pop music—Jimi Hendrix, Janis Joplin, John Lennon, Marvin Gaye, Kurt Kobain, etc.—is no less stereotypically associated with sacrificial or self-sacrificial behavior, some of which is thematized in the lyrics. A hardly more recondite example is Baudelaire, whose association of poetry or beauty with evil in *Les Fleurs du mal* is classic (like The Rolling Stones' "Sympathy for the Devil" or Bob Dylan's songs mentioning Baudelaire), but whose identification of the artist as "*sacred prostitute*" is even more pointed. For the sacred prostitute is doubtless a substitutive victim of sorts, to be sure, but a victim not without privileges and prerogatives, just like Kafka's Josephine the Singer.

Baudelaire's metaphor reminds us that, although we may be suspicious of Romantic and post-Romantic idealizations and pathologizations of originality in equal measure, the problem extends far into the past. The kind of secular mimetic-sacrificial reciprocities we have seen in *The Paradox of the Actor*—which we linked via Werner's and others' views of *Rameau's Nephew* to more archaic sacred and sacrificial phenomena—can be related, in turn, to the mimetic-sacrificial substitutions that define "sacred prostitution" in Baudelaire.[71] In this connection, it is worth recalling Girard. For in Girard's anthropology, it is not so much *the original who is victim* (although *that is true too* because, of course, sacrificial victims were and are chosen for their perceived exceptionality, whether "good" or "bad," "beautiful" or "deformed," first or last born) *as the victim who is original*—because according to him, the essentially arbitrary sacrificial scapegoat is the origin of all human religions and societies and the ambivalent source of all social and semiotic structures.[72] Original arbitrariness is here the source of original law—a fundamental sacrificial error according to Girard's exposition, but one that underlies the development of truth (*both the historical facts about us and our ability to analyze them*). Moreover, we have seen how a genuinely analytic perspective makes necessary and rigorous the confusion between law and arbitrariness, necessity and chance, not merely for so-called primitive or superstitious societies, but for the most reasonable and up-to-date logician or scientist.

I began this chapter by remarking that a true theory of originality would probably have to be a theory of everything, something that no one (perhaps fortunately) is capable of providing—although ambitions to do so have frequently degenerated into the most grotesque or "original" errors, both theoretical and practical. The point here is not, however, to make some so-called relativist or subjectivist point about originality (or law) as such. Rather, it is to recognize the simple fact that, however objective originality may be, or indeed precisely for this reason, it enters into the basic structure of human relations, which are *objectively* constituted by judgments about it. Human originality is, therefore, to a certain extent a self-fulfilling (or self-denying) prophecy.

Contemporary quasi-scientific and commonsensical interpretations of the post-Romantic cliché about genius and mental abnormality—that abnormal or exceptional mental states, perhaps biochemically induced and often regarded as deleterious or sick in ordinary people, may lead to originality in the lucky or unlucky few—should thus be tempered by the possibility of the reverse causality (i.e., the "Romantic" cliché that the original may be made [even "biochemically"] sick or exceptional by his or her relation to others). For probably no one, however genuinely original, including in fields that have nothing in theory to do with humans, is indifferent to whether his or her work (or self) is valued by others, if only in the future (hence, the appeal so often made by originals to a posthumous audience).

Kierkegaard distinguished the genius from the rest of us by saying that, whereas we imitate others, the genius tends to imitate him or herself—a point perfectly in order from a logical point of view. But such imitation, as Kierkegaard is at pains to stress, is no less subject to pathological originalities or sacrificial deviations than the other; according to him, the genius often brings to a kind of masochist fruition the "creativity" that belongs to us all (including, I must add, perhaps our cats), a creativity or originality that is both real and fraudulent in almost equal measure (unless we piously assume our cats incapable of fraud).[73] Diderot, in characteristically frivolous fashion, makes the equation between sacrifice and *communication* (as we saw Rosalina de la Carrera and Michel Serres do in their insistence on *dialogue as the exclusion of the third man*)—and surely the capacity to communicate is the origin of human originality, if any, one way or another—by pointing out that our liking for executions is a sign not of our inhumanity, but our humanity, because executions encourage us to talk![74] (Is this then the difference between our originality and our cats', a kind of tragicomic version of Girard's sacrificial distinction between humans and animals?)

I conclude by repeating that nowadays it is fashionable to pooh-pooh originality—to be quasi-eighteenth century in short, like some of Sterne's plagiarists—in a world that actually venerates it to the point of idolatry and where the pooh-poohers are usually would-be idols. Contemporary talent and so-called reality TV shows ("American Idol," "The X-Factor," "Big Brother," etc.) are a kind of allegory or comically empirical demonstration of what has been said here, where, for example, the public votes contestants *out* each week before the winner, the "original" by default, is voted *in*. The originality game is a kind of scapegoating technique, where, however, even those "victims" voted out often become mini-stars in their own right. It's not so bad!

There is much healing power—and doubtless much truth too—in the idea that *everyone is original*, and this perhaps is the edifying subtext of modern and postmodern attacks on so-called Romantic ideas of originality, to the similar or identical effect that *no one is original* (although the Romantics were perhaps significant originators of the former proposition). But there is no question that we make judgments, willy-nilly or otherwise, and that our judgments about originality in all its senses inform everything we do and think.

I personally think that Beethoven is more original than Mozart, just as a friend of mine thinks Neils Bohr is more original than Einstein. This does not mean, however, that we think Einstein and Mozart to have been lesser "geniuses" (perhaps the contrary depending on our definition of "genius"). It is a question of our views of the world. If I have succeeded in being *genuinely* incoherent or arbitrary here (something rare as Kierkegaard observed),[75] then perhaps I have succeeded in being as original as if I had been genuinely coherent on this formidable topic. But I fear not. My "own" idea of originality—to finish somewhat whimsically like my authors—is the apparently absurd equation $e^{i\pi}=-1$.[76]

NOTES

1. Either in the sense of being fundamental building blocks of the universe or of being apparently (relatively) spontaneous in behavior. In *Constructing Quarks: Sociological History of Particle Physics* (Edinburgh: Edinburgh University Press, 1984), Andrew Pickering warns against attributing "agency" to particles, as opposed to the supposedly objective scientists who study them.
2. See Friedrich von Schlegel, "Letter About the Novel," in *Dialogue on Poetry and Literary Aphorisms*, translated, annotated, and introduced by Ernest Behler and Roman Struc (University Park: Pennsylvania State University Press, 1968), 94–99.
3. Martha Woodmansee and Peter Jaszi, eds., *The Construction of Authorship: Textual Appropriation in Law and Literature* (Durham, NC: Duke University Press, 1994), 2–3.
4. Schlegel, "Selected Aphorisms From the Lyceum," no. 26, in *Dialogue on Poetry and Literary Aphorisms*, 123.
5. The connection or analogy between this conception of Romantic autonomy and capitalism can be made more precise if we recall the axiom of individual (rational) autonomy that underlies, for example, mathematical game theory as applied to marketplace economics. It is, of course, more than doubtful whether Wordsworth would have accepted the analogy.
6. Woodmansee and Jaszi, *The Construction of Authorship*, 3–4.
7. A more historically precise and detailed critique of Woodmansee and others can be found in Robert Macfarlane, *Original Copy: Plagiarism and Originality in Nineteenth-Century Literature* (Oxford: Oxford University Press, 2007). "[T]he myth of 'Romantic' originality to which Leader, Gregory, Woodmansee, McGann, and others so confidently allude did not originate with the Romantics. Rather, it crystallized afterwards, notably during the late 1820s and 1830s, when the Romantic doctrine on the subject of originality was simplified and mythified" (33). Aside from Macfarlane's claims as to the historical inaccuracy of Woodmansee's position, one might observe that several pieces in *The Construction of Authorship* seem to regard—rather peculiarly given the Romantics' tendencies (at least in their youths) toward revolutionary politics—Romantic delusions of individual originality as at least implicitly "rightist," in contrast to a properly "leftist" and collectivist view of creation. But this kind of critique of Romanticism was also espoused by T. S. Eliot, who famously favored the idea of collective tradition over individual talent (e.g., in poets of the sixteenth and seventeenth centuries), but who is hardly known as left wing. Meanwhile, essays such as Anne Ruggles Gere's "Common Properties of Pleasure: Texts in Women's Clubs," in *The Construction of Authorship*, 383–399, which celebrates women's communal reading and writing clubs of the nineteenth century, presents them as if they documented a real collective liberation from individualistic and male-chauvinistic delusions of originality or "seminality." To point out that eighteenth-century Salons were often run by brilliant women well aware of patriarchal stupidity would perhaps distract from the main issue, and with Gere we may find the nineteenth-century women's clubs appealing. But all this leaves more basic claims to originality and, indeed, superiority (i.e., politics) unaffected. (We may well imagine Margaret Thatcher, supposedly an espouser of nineteenth-century British values and the first female prime minister, belonging to a women's reading club.)
8. Although the authors are usually credited nowadays with independently inventing the calculus, Newton began work earlier—while Leibniz published

earlier—and accused Leibniz of having had access to his notes. This caused a long-lasting controversy.

9. This example is far from far-fetched because many anticipations of the calculus have been documented in both India and elsewhere.
10. Gottlob Frege, *The Foundations of Arithmetic*, trans. J. L. Austin, 2nd rev. ed. (Oxford: Blackwell, 1953). I discuss Frege more extensively in "A Glance at SunSet: Numerical Fundaments in Frege, Wittgenstein, Shakespeare, Beckett," in "Mathematics, Science and Postclassical Theory," ed. Barbara Herrnstein Smith and Arkady Plotnitsky, special issue, *South Atlantic Quarterly* 94, no. 2 (1995): 619–654.
11. Sometimes these are relatively obvious, for example, the pain in knee vs. pain in groin debate that Diderot plagiarizes without acknowledgment. Others are arguably much more covert, as, for instance, the twisted parallel between Trim's brother and Jacques' and many other matters. I discuss another candidate, concerning the mimetic relation between master and servant, below.
12. I am not, of course, arguing that Diderot's subtle and deceptive use of Sterne cannot be convincingly defended or that he did not hope for readers careful enough to deduce the more recondite allusions. But the pattern of deception is no mere game.
13. *Athenaeum Fragments* no. 80, in *Friedrich Schlegel's "Lucinde" and the Fragments*, trans. with intro. by Peter Firchow (Minneapolis: University of Minnesota Press, 1971), 170.
14. Theodor W. Adorno, *Aesthetic Theory*, ed. Gretel Adorno and Rolf Tiedemann, trans. Robert Hullot-Kentor (Minneapolis: University of Minnesota Press, 1997), 331.
15. René Girard, *Violence and the Sacred*, trans. Patrick Gregory (Baltimore: Johns Hopkins University Press, 1977), 189.
16. Denis Diderot, *Jacques the Fatalist and His Master*, trans. Michael Henry, intro. Martin Hall (Middlesex: Penguin, 1986), 236. Subsequent page references are placed in the text.
17. I discuss Goodman's claims in more detail in Chapter 2 of *The Habit of Lying: Sacrificial Studies in Literature, Philosophy, and Fashion Theory* (Durham, NC: Duke University Press, 2002).
18. J. A. Benardete, *Infinity: An Essay in Metaphysics* (Oxford: Clarendon Press, 1964).
19. Charles Sanders Peirce, "Uniformity," in *Philosophical Writings of Peirce*, ed. Justus Buchler (New York: Dover Publications, 1955), 225.
20. I discuss Beckett's treatment of pi in "A Glance at SunSet," 642 ff. and *The Habit of Lying*, 118 ff.
21. See note 10.
22. Thomas Pfau, "The Pragmatics of Genre," in *The Construction of Authorship*, 151.
23. Pierre Macherey confirms this in his contribution to *God and Nature: Spinoza's Metaphysics*, ed. Yirmiyahu Yovel (Leiden: E.J. Brill, 1991), 167.
24. There are a number of candidates for this, more or less subtle. For instance, John Carr's *The Life and Opinions of Tristram Shandy* (London, 1760), published anonymously and as if it were Volume III (which Sterne published in 1761), seems to predict that Volume IV will contain a full-blown treatise on noses (as it actually does in Sterne's "Slawkenbergius's Tale" in Volume IV)—hardly in itself perhaps a prediction of genius, but not without other interesting details. Later in the essay, I also mention the anonymous *Yorick's Meditations* (also published in 1760, after the first two volumes of Sterne's novel) which seems acute in both interpretation and prediction.

25. A similar point is made in Richard Griffith's anonymous and Shandyan *The Posthumous Works of a Late Celebrated Genius, Deceased*, 2 vols. (Dublin, 1770), 2: 147: "So that all we can possibly say, of the most original authors, now-a-days, is, not that they say anything *new*, but only that they are capable of saying such and such things themselves, *[as] if they had never been said before them.*"
26. See Reginald McGinnis, "The Critique of Originality in French Letters," *Studies in Eighteenth-Century Culture* 31 (2002): 127–143, for analysis of the usage of the term in French.
27. Several aspects of what I say here are detailed at more length in the first two chapters of my *A Question of Eros: Irony in Sterne, Kierkegaard, and Barthes* (Tallahassee: Florida State University Press, 1986), and especially in Appendix 3 concerning monstrous births.
28. See note 27.
29. Anonymous, "Upon the Association of Ideas," *Yorick's Meditations upon Various Interesting and Important Subjects* (London: R. Stevens, 1760), 76–80; *A supplement to The life and opinions of Tristram Shandy, gent. Serving to elucidate that work. By the author of Yorick's meditations* (London, 1760), 2–4, 13–14. Richard Griffith's anonymous *The Posthumous Works* (vol. 2, part 3, sec. 14, 222) also remarks that "the Athenians always cast their children into the sea, that happened to be born with any manner of defect or deformity." The author says that he prefers his own scheme, whereby the deformed make up the most terrible battle group in the army!
30. See, for example, a number of the articles in Woodmansee and Jaszi, *The Construction of Authorship*.
31. Laurence Sterne, *The Life and Opinions of Tristram Shandy*, in *The Florida Edition of the Works of Laurence Sterne*, ed. Melvyn New and Joan New, 6 vols. (Gainesville: University Presses of Florida, 1978), 1: 263–264 (vol. 3, Chapter 34). Subsequent references placed in the text. See also Smyth, *A Question of Eros*, 18 ff.
32. This kind of "leftish" critique of Locke, although in some ways plausible (and indeed Shandyan), generally fails to observe that Locke may have been well aware of some of the contradictions or ironies in his own work, as Leo Strauss effectively argues in *Natural Right and History* (Chicago: Chicago University Press, 1953). It is moreover at least plausible that Locke's irony derives not just from his "rightist" or "capitalist" leanings (as they may be seen in retrospect), but from a desire to conceal the radical nature of his "leftish" originality for reasons of political persuasion (a hypothesis that may go also, as is seen below, for Sterne). After all, Locke proposed a pretty radical or original view of women's rights, slavery, revolution, and so on by the standards of his day. Had he advocated the abolition not merely of slavery, but of master–servant relations, not merely of absolute patriarchy, but of every male prerogative, not merely of absolute monarchy but of kings and queens, he might not only have failed to have the enormous influence he had ("le sage Locke," as Voltaire called him), but risked his life. Sterne's feminist and literary critique of Locke arguably grasps this point and is deceptive on these topics.
33. Strauss' remarkably original reading of Locke in *Natural Right and History* points out that, although the concepts of "nature" in the *Essay* and the *Two Treatises* are in strong tension, the concept of labor appears to bridge the intellectual (or epistemological) and economic senses of ownership.
34. "Upon Virtu," *Yorick's Meditations*, 92. The natural philosophers who study the *lusus naturae* should be called, we are told, "unnatural philosophers."

35. *Tristram Shandy*, vol. 3, Chapter 14, in *Works of Laurence Sterne*, 1: 217–218. See also *A Question of Eros*, 88 ff.
36. "Meditation on Obscurity in Writing," *Yorick's Meditations*, 67.
37. Søren Kierkegaard, *The Concept of Irony: With Constant Reference to Socrates*, trans. Lee M. Capel (Bloomington: Indiana University Press, 1968), 172–173. My assimilation of the "certain Athenian" to Socrates exploits the parallel with midwifery alongside irony, although *Yorick's Meditations* also recalls the opening lines of Burton's "Democritus to the Reader" in *The Anatomy of Melancholy*, which refer to Plutarch's invocation (in Chapter 3 of *De Curiositate*) of a certain Egyptian reputed to have replied in a manner almost identical to Yorick's Athenian. Sterne is also called a second Democritus in Richard Griffith's *Posthumous Works* and elsewhere. Hence, precise interpretation here plunges one into a plagiaristic maze typical of Sterne and Sterneana. But Democritus, a native of Thrace, is hardly more suitable than the Egyptian as candidate for the specifically *Athenian* philosopher. See also *A Question of Eros*, 97.
38. Schlegel, citing himself from the *Lyceum Fragments*, in "On Incomprehensibility," *Friedrich Schlegel's* Lucinde *and the Fragments*, 265.
39. Jacqueline Lagrée (in a reply to Pierre Macherey in the same volume) contrasts Diderot's apparent view of suicide as an expression of freedom with Spinoza's of unfreedom, in Yovel, *God and Nature: Spinoza's Metaphysics*, 184–185. But this poses, rather than solves, the problem.
40. *The Clockmakers Outcry Against the Author of The Life and Opinions of Tristram Shandy* (London, 1760).
41. Flann O'Brien (pseudonym of Brian O'Nolan), *The Third Policeman* (Normal, IL: Dalkey Archive Press, 1999), 36 ff. O'Brien's "atomic theory" of bicycles, whereby the atoms of the latter mix with those of their riders via their groins and asses, is plausibly a direct plagiarism of Sterne's hobby-horse described in similar terms. (Although Sterne plagiarized the figure of the hobby-horse from several writers, only Sterne, to my knowledge, twists the figure in this precise way.) Moreover, it is made clear by O'Brien that bicycles are the modern form of horses. (I believe that the bicycle motif was possibly also, in part, plagiarized from O'Brien by Beckett in *Molloy*, unless indeed they arrived at it independently. This resembles the Newton/Leibniz controversy because, although *The Third Policeman* was written well before *Molloy*, it was published much later and posthumously. Yet Beckett might well have read it in draft before writing *Molloy*.)
42. This is the famous story of Desgland's "spot" in *Jacques the Fatalist*, 228–233.
43. See note 35.
44. Martin Hall, *Jacques the Fatalist*, 13.
45. The figure of monstrous doubling, like his literal reference to the fate of twins, occurs throughout Girard's work, as in his *To Double Business Bound* (a title plagiarized from Shakespeare).
46. See Smyth, "A Glance at SunSet," 630.
47. Søren Kierkegaard, *Repetition*. Nevertheless, Kierkegaard ultimately conceives *freedom as repetition* (i.e., as the fulfillment of law, rather than its suspension).
48. English language examples of the association of Sterne with "leftish" or revolutionary tendencies include the pseudonymous D. Whyte, MD (late surgeon to English prisoners in France), *The Fallacy of French Freedom and Dangerous Tendency of Sterne's Writings* (London: J. Hatchard, 1799), and (more ambiguously) the anonymous *Tristram Shandy's Descriptions of General Elections and Septennial Parliaments* (Dublin, 1762). French language

examples include *Tableau sentimental de la France depuis la Révolution, par Yorick sous le nom de Sterne, traduit de l'anglois par l'Auteur du Poëme de Souza et d'Eléonore* (Londres, 1792), which was really written in French and likely published in France, not London. While directly citing Sterne's *A Sentimental Journey* (written under the pseudonym Yorick) in connection with the liberation of the Bastille, this text also seems to recommend a "sentimental" (nonvengeful) attitude toward aristocrats.

49. "I hereby annul the equality which has been established between them by lapse of time and hereby recreate it simultaneously" (159).
50. Diderot, *Selected Writings on Art and Literature*, trans. with intro. and notes by Geoffrey Bremner (London: Penguin Books, 1994), 99. Subsequent page references to this edition of *The Paradox* appear in the text.
51. This hypothesis is not in any way crucial to my argument, but it may be suggestive for various reasons, especially when it comes to the sacrificial status of the first speaker's views I mention below. Indeed, later in the text, there is an "I" who claims at one point to witness *both* speakers, but even there we hear for a moment *only* the first speaker (now explicitly called the "man of paradox"—presumably *like the author* of *The Paradox of the Actor*), where, moreover, we also hear that "The ideas of the man of paradox are the only ones I can vouch for" (151).
52. See note 51. The fact that Diderot was jailed for his early work and that many of his most original works were published posthumously may perhaps provide an ad hominem argument for why Diderot might have sympathized with the first speaker's fears of being stoned in the streets for espousing such views as are stated here. This is not to deny that Diderot is perhaps or even necessarily impersonated in *both* speakers, producing a kind of dialectic as to "his" identity.
53. Rosalina de la Carrera, *Success in Circuit Lies: Diderot's Communicational Practice* (Stanford: Stanford University Press, 1991), 37.
54. Carrera cites from Michel Serres, "Platonic Dialogue," in *Hermes—Literature, Science, Philosophy*, ed. Josue V. Harari and David F. Bell (Baltimore: Johns Hopkins University Press, 1982), 66–67. Serres' acknowledgment of the Girardian connection has been cautious (perhaps for reasons of intellectual politics), but is explicitly made, for example, in *Les Origines de la géometrie* (Paris: Flammarion, 1993), 195–291.
55. Carrera, *Success in Circuit Lies*, 50–51.
56. It is perhaps worth mentioning that Gilles Deleuze's *Spinoza: Philosophie pratique* (Paris: Éditions de Minuit, 1981) also stresses a musical metaphor for the operation of Spinozan power and law (170).
57. When "the model is alive and thinking; noise, if the model is inanimate." Diderot, *Rameau's Nephew and D'Alembert's Dream*, trans. Leonard Tancock (New York: Penguin, 1966), 98–100.
58. The narrator opens: "Nothing is less like him than himself," while Rameau concludes: "Isn't it true that I am always the same" (*Rameau's Nephew*, 34, 125).
59. I trust I will not be misunderstood to scapegoat such victims. I allude to these "mimetic" diseases at slightly greater length in "Tenuous Borders in Kafka's *A Country Doctor*," *Western Humanities Review* 60, no. 2 (2006): 89–100.
60. Georg Lukács, *The Young Hegel* (London: Merlin, 1975), 495, as cited by Stephen Werner, *Socratic Satire: An Essay on Diderot and Le Neveu de Rameau* (Birmingham: Summa Publications, 1987), 59.
61. Werner, 70–73, 5.
62. Otis Fellows in *Diderot* (Boston: Twayne Publishers, 1977), 93–95, praises Donal O'Gorman's *Diderot the Satirist* (Toronto: Toronto University Press, 1971) for the "truly coherent pattern" he develops in this connection.

63. Reginald McGinnis has written an original book on this subject, still in manuscript, entitled *Les Origines de la mystification au temps des Lumières.*
64. Werner, 50–51, 35.
65. Werner cites George Steiner, who in turn cites Claude Lévi-Strauss and others, on music conceived as "a primal universal language," entailing the view—in my view highly unlikely in any ordinary senses of the terms, and moreover explicitly denied in *Rameau*—that "speech comes later than music" (68). Carrera, despite an interesting analysis of how *Jacques* undoes the model of musical communication she proposes for *La Religieuse* (77 ff.), nevertheless tends to idealize music as incarnating the kind of "materialist rhetoric" she attributes to Diderot more generally (171 ff.) Her comments on its "catching" or "contagious" effects, however, are suggestive in mimetic terms.
66. Werner, 27. The term *énergumène* occurs interestingly enough also in the anonymous *Tableau sentimental de la France depuis la Révolution* (27) mentioned in note 48.
67. I steal "double-talk" as a pointed quasi-synonym for dialogism from Paul de Man's discussion of Leo Strauss and Bahktin in "Dialogue and Dialogism," *The Resistance to Theory* (Minneapolis: Minnesota University Press, 1986), 106 ff.
68. Quoted in Werner, 27. What Werner calls primitive or classical "sublimity" (27) and "comic travesty" (43) are thus closely interlinked rather than opposed, as he seems to imply, in Rameau's mimicry. Despite Werner's seeming approval of the sublimity of "primitive imagination," then, we should note that the sacrificial or "barbarous" structure of comedy or satire outlined here finds a parallel in Diderot's own violent view of the sublime: "a wild ass [is more sublime] than a donkey; a tyrant than a king; a crime even than virtue; cruel gods than good gods; and all this was well known to the sacred lawmakers" (*Selected Writings*, 314).
69. Werner, 57–58; Fellows, 85.
70. Fellows cites O'Gorman in concluding that "*Lui* (Rameau), like Marsyas, is destined by the author to lose out" (85), i.e., be a victim.
71. Reginald McGinnis, *La Prostitution sacrée: essai sur Baudelaire* (Paris: Belin, 1994). I am indebted to him for insisting on the importance of Baudelaire's figure.
72. Almost all of Girard's work develops this sacrificial hypothesis.
73. I treat Kierkegaard's *The Concept of Dread* [*Anxiety*] on this subject in "Sacrificial and Erotic Materialism in Kierkegaard and Adorno," in *Idealism Without Absolutes: Philosophy and Romantic Culture*, ed. Tilottama Rajan and Arkadi Plotnitsky (Albany, NY: State University of New York Press, 2004), 181–201.
74. "The populace is hungry for something to look at and goes there because it enjoys seeing it and even more enjoys telling others about it afterwards. The populace is terrible in its fury but that does not last long. Its own poverty has made it compassionate and it turns its eyes away from the spectacle of horror which it has gone to see, is moved to pity and goes home crying" (*Jacques the Fatalist*, 165).
75. "[I]t requires much study to succeed in being arbitrary. . . ." Kierkegaard, *Either/Or*, trans. David and Lillian Swenson, 2 vols. (Princeton, NJ: Princeton University Press, 1944), 1:245–246.
76. The relatively easy proof of the equation, in my view, does not make it less provocative. First, as commonly observed, it combines two of the most important real and transcendental numbers (e and pi) with the imaginary

or complex (i). But whether this apparent wizardry is merely analytic (tautological) or synthetic—either entailing the beautiful quasi-universal coherence of "original," in the sense of fundamental, numbers, or entailing human "originality" of the more or less pejorative kind (e.g., an invention or even artifice masquerading as discovery) that Wittgenstein and some others have tended to ascribe to the real and transcendental numbers, let alone the imaginaries—is up for grabs. Thus, the equation begs the questions of originality earlier discussed in an especially sharp manner.

Bibliography

This list does not include references to specific legal cases or to eighteenth- and nineteenth-century newspaper and magazine articles. Complete documentation of works cited is provided in endnotes to the chapters in this volume.

Addison, Joseph, and Richard Steele. *The Spectator*. Edited with an introduction and notes by Donald F. Bond. 5 vols. Oxford: Clarendon Press, 1965.

Adlington, John Henry. *The Cyclopaedia of Law*; *or, The Correct British Lawyer Forming a Complete and Concise Digest of the Various Laws and Statutes Comprehended in the Constitution of England, in Which Are Included an Epitome of the Acts of Parliament Passed in the Last Session, and a Glossary of the Technical Law Terms*. London: J. M'Gowan, 1820.

Adorno, Theodor W., Gretel Adorno, and Rolf Tiedemann. *Aesthetic Theory*. Newly translated, edited, and with a translator's introduction by Robert Hullot-Kentor. Minneapolis: University of Minnesota Press, 1997.

Agg, John. *Pilgrimage to the Holy Land A Poem in Two Cantos*; *to Which Is Added*, *The Tempest*, *a Fragment*. Philadelphia: Moses Thomas, 1817.

Aikins, Janet. "Richardson's 'Speaking Pictures.'" Margaret Anne Doody and Peter Sabor, eds. *Samuel Richardson*: *Tercentenary Essays*. Cambridge, UK: Cambridge University Press, 1989.

Angelo, Henry, H. Lavers Smith, Thomas Evelyn Scott-Ellis Howard de Walden, and Joseph Grego. *The Reminiscences of Henry Angelo*. London: K. Paul, Trench, Trubner & Co., 1904.

Anonymous. *The Clockmakers Outcry Against the Author of the Life and Opinions of Tristram Shandy Dedicated to the Most Humble of Christian Prelates*. London, 1760.

———. *An Enquiry Into the Nature and Origin of Literary Property*. London: Flexney, 1762.

———. *Lord Byron's Farewell to England*; *With Three Other Poems*, *Viz. Ode to St. Helena*, *To My Daughter*, *on the Morning of Her Birth*, *and To the Lily of France*. London: Published by J. Johnston . . . and sold by all booksellers, 1816.

———. *Pamela in High Life*: *Or*, *Virtue Rewarded*. London, 1741.

———. *Reasons Humbly Offered to Be Considered Before the Act for Printing*, *be Renewed*. [n.p, 1692].

———. *The Student*: *Or*, *The Oxford and Cambridge Monthly Miscellany*. Oxford: Newbury, 1751.

———. *A Supplement to the Life and Opinions of Tristram Shandy*, *gent*. *Serving to Elucidate That Work*. *By the Author of Yorick's Meditations*. London, 1760.

———. *Tableau sentimental de la France depuis la Révolution, par Yorick sous le nom de Sterne, traduit de l'anglois par l'Auteur du Poëme de Souza et d'Eléonore*. Londres, 1792.

———. *Tristram Shandy's Description of General Elections, and Septennial Parliaments*. Dublin: Printed for R. Lewis, 1762.

———. *A Vindication of the Exclusive Rights of Authors to Their Own Works*. London: Griffiths, 1762.

———. *Yorick's Meditations Upon Various Interesting and Important Subjects*. London: R. Stevens, 1760.

Astington, John H. "Dramatic Extracts in the Interregnum." *Review of English Studies* 54, no. 217 (2003): 601–614.

Astbury, Raymond. "The Renewal of the Licensing Act in 1693 and Its Lapse in 1695." *Library* (5th series) 33 (1978): 296–322.

Axtell, James L. *The Educational Writings of John Locke*. Cambridge: Cambridge University Press, 1968.

Bacon, Matthew, Henry Gwyllin, Charles Edward Dodd, Bird Wilson, and John Bouvier. *A New Abridgement of the Law*. Philadelphia: M'Carty and Davis, 1842.

Barchas, Janine G., Dorothy Bradshaigh, and Gordon D. Fulton. *The Annotations in Lady Bradshaigh's Copy of Clarissa*. ELS monograph series, no. 76. Victoria, BC, Canada: English Literary Studies, University of Victoria, 1998.

Barnett, George L. Eighteenth-Century British Novelists on the Novel. New York: Appleton-Century-Crofts, 1968.

Bate, Jonathan. *Shakespeare and Ovid*. Oxford: Clarendon Press, 1993.

Beaumont, Francis, John Fletcher, and Fredson Bowers. *The Dramatic Works in the Beaumont and Fletcher Canon*. 10 vols. Cambridge: Cambridge University Press, 1966.

Benardete, José A. *Infinity; An Essay in Metaphysics*. Oxford: Clarendon Press, 1964.

Benedict, Barbara. *Making the Modern Reader: Cultural Mediation in Early Modern Literary Anthologies*. Princeton: Princeton University Press, 1996.

Benkler, Yochai. "Free as the Air to Common Use: First Amendment Constraints on Enclosure of the Public Domain." *New York University Law Review* 74, no. 2 (1999): 354–446.

Bettig, Ronald V. "Critical Perspectives on the History and Philosophy of Copyright." *Critical Studies in Mass Communication* 9, no. 2 (1992): 131–155.

Blackstone, William. *Commentaries on the Laws of England*. 4 vols. Oxford: Clarendon Press, 1765–1769.

———. *The Letters of Sir William Blackstone, 1744–1780*. Edited by W. R. Prest. London: Selden Society, 2006.

Bloom, Edward A. "Samuel Johnson on Copyright." *Journal of English and Germanic Philology* 47, no. 2 (1948): 165–172.

Bloom, Harold. *The Anxiety of Influence: A Theory of Poetry*. 2nd ed. New York: Oxford University Press, 1997.

Boime, Albert. *The Academy and French Painting in the Nineteenth Century*. London: Phaidon, 1971.

Bond, Richmond P. *English Burlesque Poetry, 1700–1750*. Cambridge, MA: Harvard University Press, 1932.

Bongie, Laurence L. "Diderot Creator and Compiler." *Transactions of the Samuel Johnson Society of the Northwest* 15 (1984): 35–44.

Boswell, James. *The Decision of the Court of Session, Upon the Question of Literary Property; in the Cause [of] John Hinton of London, Bookseller, Pursuer; Against Alexander Donaldson.* Edinburgh: Donaldson, 1774.

———. *Journal of a Tour of the Hebrides* [with Samuel Johnson, *A Journey to the Western Islands of Scotland*]. Edited by Allan Wendt. Boston: Houghton Mifflin, 1965.

———. *The Life of Johnson.* Edited by G. B. Hill. Oxford: Oxford University Press, 1934.

Boyle, James. "Fencing off Ideas: Enclosure and the Disappearance of the Public Domain." *Daedalus* 131, no. 2 (2002): 13–25.

Boyle, James, ed. "The Public Domain." Special Issue, *Law and Contemporary Problems* 66, nos. 1–2 (2003).

Bracha, Oren. "The Ideology of Authorship Revisited." University of Texas Law, Public Law Research Paper No. 82 (2006). Available at Social Science Research Network: <http://ssrn.com/abstract=869446>.

———. *Owning Ideas: A History of Anglo-American Intellectual Property.* S.J.D. thesis, Harvard Law School, 2005.

Brewer, David A. *The Afterlife of Character, 1726–1825.* Philadelphia: University of Pennsylvania Press, 2005.

Broder, Janice. "Lady Bradshaigh Reads and Writes *Clarissa*: The Marginal Notes in Her First Edition." In *Clarissa and Her Readers: New Essays for the* Clarissa *Project.*Edited by Carol Houlihan Flynn and Edward Copeland, 97–118. New York: AMS Press, 1999.

Brogan, Howard O. "Byron So Full of Fun, Frolic, Wit, and Whim." *The Huntington Library Quarterly* 37, no. 2 (1974): 171–189.

Browning, Elizabeth Barrett. *The Letters of Elizabeth Barrett Browning to Mary Russell Mitford, 1836-1854.* Edited and introduced by Meredith B. Raymond and Mary Rose Sullivan. 3 vols. Waco, TX: Armstrong Browning Library of Baylor University, 1983.

Buelow, George J. "Originality, Genius, Plagiarism in English Criticism of the Eighteenth Century." *International Review of the Aesthetics and Sociology of Music* 21, no. 2 (1990): 117–128.

Bunyan, John. *The Pilgrim's Progress.* Edited with an introduction by N. H. Keeble. Oxford: Oxford University Press, 1984.

Burlington Magazine for Connoisseurs. "Gainsborough's Collection of *Pictures.*" *Burlington Magazine* 84, no. 494 (1944): 107–110.

Byron, Lord [George Gordon]. *Byron's Letters and Journals: The Complete and Unexpurgated Text of All the Letters Available in Manuscript and the Full Printed Version of All Others.* Edited by Leslie Alexis Marchand. Cambridge, MA: Harvard University Press, 1973–1980.

———. *Selected Poems.* Edited with a preface by Susan J. Wolfson and Peter J. Manning. London: Penguin Books, 1996.

———. *The Works of Lord Byron.* Edited by Ernest Hartley Coleridge and Roland E. Prothero. 13 vols. New York: C. Scribner's, 1898–1905.

———, and Thomas Moore. *Letters and Journals of Lord Byron With Notices of His Life.* Paris: A. and W. Galignani, 1830.

———, and Peter Quennell. *Byron, a Self-Portrait Letters and Diaries, 1798 to 1824, with Hitherto Unpublished Letters.* New York: Humanities Press, 1967.

Campbell, Archibald. *The Sale of Authors: A Dialogue, in Imitation of Lucian's Sale of Philosophers.* London, 1767.

Capell, Edward. *Reflections on Originality in Authors, Being Remarks on A Letter to Mr. Mason on the Marks of Imitation: In Which the Absurd Defects of*

That Performance Are Pointed out, and the Absolute Uncertainty of Imitation in General Is Demonstrated in Various Instances. London: Horsfield, 1766.
Carr, John. *The Life and Opinions of Tristram Shandy*. London, 1760.
Carter, Elizabeth, Catherine Talbot, and Elizabeth Vesey Vesey. *A Series of Letters Between Mrs. Elizabeth Carter and Catherine Talbot, From the Year 1741 to 1770: To Which Are Added, Letters from Mrs. Elizabeth Carter to Mrs. Vesey, between the Years 1763 and 1787*. 2 vols. London: F.C. and J. Rivington, 1808.
Case, Arthur Ellicott. *A Bibliography of English Poetical Miscellanies, 1521–1750*. Oxford: Bibliographical Society, 1935.
Cervantes Saavedra, Miguel de. *The Ingenious Gentleman Don Quixote of La Mancha*. Translated by John Ormsby. Edited by Joseph Ramon Jones and Kenneth Douglas. New York: Norton, 1981.
Chambers, John David. *A Practical Treatise on the Jurisdiction of the High Court of Chancery Over the Persons and Property of Infants*. London: Saunders and Benning, 1842.
Chew, Samuel Claggett. *Byron in England: His Fame and After-Fame*. New York: Charles Scribner's Sons, 1924.
———. "The Pamphlets of the Byron Separation." *Modern Language Notes* 34, no. 3 (1919): 155–162.
Clayton, Timothy. *The English Print 1688–1802*. New Haven, CT: Yale University Press, 1997.
Clifford, Timothy, Antony Griffiths, and Martin Royalton-Kisch. *Gainsborough and Reynolds in the British Museum*. London: British Museum, 1978.
Cockle, Mary. *A Reply to Fare Thee Well: Lines Addressed to Lord Byron*. London: R. S. Kirby, 1816.
Connaughton, Michael E. "Richardson's Familiar Quotations: *Clarissa* and Bysshe's *Art of English Poetry*." *Philological Quarterly* 60 (1981): 183–195.
Connor, Rebecca Elisabeth. *Women, Accounting, and Narrative: Keeping Books in Eighteenth-Century England*. New York: Routledge, 2004.
Coombe, Rosemary J. "Challenging Paternity: Histories of Copyright." *Yale Journal of Law and the Humanities* 6, no. 2 (1994): 397–422.
———. *The Cultural Life of Intellectual Properties: Authorship, Appropriation, and the Law*. Durham, NC: Duke University Press, 1998.
Coppa, Francesca. "A Brief History of Media Fandom." In *Fan Fiction and Fan Communities in the Age of the Internet: New Essays*, edited by Karen Hellekson and Kristina Busse, 41–59. Jefferson, NC: McFarland, 2006.
Creech, James. "Diderot and the Pleasure of the Other: Friends, Readers, and Posterity." *Eighteenth-Century Studies* 11, no. 4 (1978): 439–456.
Cumberland, Richard. *Henry*. In *Eighteenth-Century British Novelists on the Novel*. Edited by George L. Barnett. New York: Appleton-Century-Crofts, 1968.
Cunningham, Allan. *The Lives of the Most Eminent British Painters, Sculptors, and Architects*. 6 vols. London: John Murray, 1830.
De la Carrera, Rosalina. *Success in Circuit Lies: Diderot's Communicational Practice*. Stanford: Stanford University Press, 1991.
de Zwart, Melissa. "A Historical Analysis of the Birth of Fair Dealing and Fair Use: Lessons for the Digital Age." *Intellectual Property Quarterly*, no. 1 (2007): 60–91.
Deane, Bradley. *The Making of the Victorian Novelist: Anxieties of Authorship in the Mass Market*. New York: Routledge, 2003.
Deazley, Ronan. *On the Origin of the Right to Copy: Charting the Movement of Copyright Law in Eighteenth-Century Britain (1695–1775)*. Oxford: Hart Publishing, 2004.
———. *Rethinking Copyright: History, Theory, Language*. Cheltenham: Edward Elgar, 2006.

Defoe, Daniel. *An Essay on the Regulation of the Press*. 1704. Reprint, Oxford: Published for the Luttrell Society by Blackwell, 1948.

———, and Arthur Wellesley Secord. *Defoe's Review*. 22 vols. 1704. Reprint, New York: Published for the Facsimile Text Society by Columbia University Press, 1938.

Deleuze, Gilles. *Spinoza, Philosophie pratique*. Paris: Éditions de Minuit, 1981.

Delon, Michel. "Confessions et Contre-Confessions." *Les Collections du Magazine Littéraire*. Hors-Série, no. 11 (mars-avril 2007): 37–41.

Diderot, Denis. *Jacques the Fatalist and His Master*. Translated by Michael Henry, with an introduction and notes by Martin Hall. Middlesex: Penguin Books, 1986.

———. *Jacques the Fatalist and His Master*. Translated with an introduction and notes by J. Robert Loy. New York: New York University Press, 1959.

———. *Jacques le fataliste et son maître*. Chronologie et préface par Paul Vernière. Paris: Garnier-Flammarion, 1970.

———. *Lettre sur le commerce de la librairie*. In *Œuvres*. Edited by Laurent Versini. 5 vols. 3:59–116. Paris: Robert Laffont, 1994–1997.

———. *Rameau's Nephew, and D'Alembert's Dream*. Translated with introductions by L. W. Tancock. Baltimore: Penguin Books, 1966.

———. *Selected Writings on Art and Literature*. Translated with an introduction and notes by Geoffrey Bremner. London: Penguin Books, 1994.

Dobson, Michael. *The Making of the National Poet: Shakespeare, Adaptation and Authorship, 1660–1769*. Oxford: Clarendon Press, 1992.

Draper, John W. "Aristotelian 'Mimesis' in Eighteenth Century England." *PMLA* 36, no. 3 (1921): 372–400.

Drassinower, Abraham. "Sweat of the Brow, Creativity, and Authorship: On Originality in Canadian Copyright Law." *University of Ottowa Law & Technology Journal* 1, no. 2 (2004): 105–123.

———. "Taking User Rights Seriously." In *In the Public Interest: The Future of Canadian Copyright Law*, edited by Michael Geist, 462–479. Toronto: Irwin Law, 2005.

Dryden, John. *The Works of John Dryden*. Edited by Edward Niles Hooker, H. T. Swedenberg, Vinton A. Dearing, et al. 20 vols. Berkeley: University of California Press, 1956–2000.

Duff, William. *Critical Observations on the Writings of the Most Celebrated Original Geniuses in Poetry*. London: Becket, 1770.

———. *An Essay on Original Genius; and Its Various Modes of Exertion in Philosophy and the Fine Arts, Particularly in Poetry*. London: Dilly, 1767.

Eagleton, Terry. *The Rape of Clarissa: Writing, Sexuality and Class Struggle in Samuel Richardson*. Oxford: Basil Blackwell, 1982.

Eaves, T. C. Duncan, and Ben D. Kimpel. *Samuel Richardson: A Biography*. Oxford: Clarendon Press, 1971.

Echlin, Elizabeth, Samuel Richardson, and Dimiter Daphinoff. *An Alternative Ending to Richardson's Clarissa*. Schweizer anglistische Arbeiten, Bd. 107. Bern: Francke Verlag, 1982.

Edwards, Edward. *Anecdotes of Painters Who Have Resided or Been Born in England, With Critical Remarks on Their Productions*. London: Leigh and Sotheby, 1808.

Edwards, R. *A Narrative of the Circumstances Which Attended the Separation of Lord and Lady Byron Remarks on His Domestic Conduct, and a Complete Refutation of the Calumnies Circulated by Public Writers*. London: R. Edwards, 1816.

Eilenberg, Susan. *Strange Power of Speech: Wordsworth, Coleridge, and Literary Possession*. New York: Oxford University Press, 1992.

Eisler, Benita. *Byron: Child of Passion, Fool of Fame.* New York: Vintage Books, 1999.

Elwin, Malcolm. *Lord Byron's Wife.* London: Macdonald, 1962.

England and Wales. *An Act for Preventing the Frequent Abuses in Printing Seditious, Treasonable, and Unlicensed Books and Pamphlets, and for Regulating of Printing and Printing-Presses.* 13 & 14 Car. 2, c. 33. London, 1662.

———. *A Decree of Starre-Chamber, Concerning Printing.* London, 1637.

Farington, Joseph. *Memoirs of the Life of Sir Joshua Reynolds; With Some Observations on His Talents and Character.* London: T. Cadell & W. Davies, 1819.

Feather, John. "The Book Trade in Politics: The Making of the Copyright Act of 1710." *Publishing History* 8 (1980): 19–44.

———. "From Rights in Copies to Copyright: The Recognition of Authors' Rights in English Law and Practice in the Sixteenth and Seventeenth Centuries." *Cardozo Arts & Entertainment Law Journal* 10, no. 2 (1992): 455–473. Reprinted in *The Construction of Authorship: Textual Appropriation in Law and Literature*, edited by Martha Woodmansee and Peter Jaszi, 191–209. Durham, NC: Duke University Press, 1994.

———. *Publishing, Piracy and Politics: An Historical Study of Copyright in Britain.* New York: Mansell, 1994.

Fellows, Otis. *Diderot.* Boston: Twayne Publishers, 1977.

Ferdinand, Christine Y. *Benjamin Collins and the Provincial Newspaper Trade in the Eighteenth Century.* Oxford: Oxford University Press, 1997.

Fiedler, Leslie A. *Love and Death in the American Novel.* New York: Anchor Books, 1992.

Fielding, Henry. *The History of Tom Jones.* Edited by John Bender and Simon Stern. Oxford: Oxford University Press, 1996.

Fisk, Catherine L. "Authors at Work: The Origins of the Work-for-Hire Doctrine." *Yale Journal of Law & the Humanities* 15, no. 1 (2003): 1–70.

Fiske, John. "The Cultural Economy of Fandom." In *The Adoring Audience: Fan Culture and Popular Media.* Edited by Lisa A. Lewis. London: Routledge, 1992.

Fitzgerald, Lauren. "The Gothic Villain and the Plagiarist: The Case of *The Castle Spectre.*" *Gothic Studies* 7 (2005): 5–17.

Forster, E. M. *Aspects of the Novel.* San Diego: Harcourt Brace Jovanovich, 1985.

Frank, Marcie. *Gender, Theatre, and the Origins of Criticism: From Dryden to Manley.* Cambridge: Cambridge University Press, 2003.

Frege, Gottlob. *The Foundations of Arithmetic.* Translated by J. L. Austin. 2nd rev. ed. Oxford: Blackwell, 1953.

Frye, Northrop, Sheridan Baker, and George Perkins. *The Harper Handbook to Literature.* New York: Harper and Row, 1985.

Fulcher, George Williams. *Life of Thomas Gainsborough.* London: Longman, Brown, Green, and Longmans, 1856.

Gaines, Jane M. *Contested Culture: The Image, the Voice, and the Law.* Chapel Hill: University of North Carolina Press, 1991.

Gainsborough, Thomas. *The Letters of Thomas Gainsborough.* Edited by John T. Hayes. New Haven, CT: Yale University Press, 2001.

———, Michael Rosenthal, Martin Myrone, and Rica Jones. *Thomas Gainsborough: 1727–1788.* New York: Abrams, 2002.

Gardiner, Ellen. *Regulating Readers: Gender and Literary Criticism in the Eighteenth-Century Novel.* Cranbury, NJ: University of Delaware Press, 1999.

Gerard, Alexander. *An Essay on Genius.* London: Becket, 1771.

Gervais, Daniel J. "*Feist* Goes Global: A Comparative Analysis of the Notion of Originality in Copyright Law." *Journal of the Copyright Society of the USA* 49 (2002): 949–981.

Girard, René. *Violence and the Sacred*. Translated by Patrick Gregory. Baltimore: Johns Hopkins University Press, 1977.

Godson, Richard. *A Practical Treatise on the Law of Patents for Inventions and of Copyright With an Introductory Book on Monopolies, Illustrated with Notes of the Principal Cases*. London, 1823.

Goldgar, Bertrand. "Imitation and Plagiarism: The Lauder Affair and Its Aftermath." *Studies in the Literary Imagination* 34 (2001): 1–16.

Goldstein, Carl. *Teaching Art: Academies and Schools From Vasari to Albers*. Cambridge: Cambridge University Press, 1996.

Golinelli, Gilberta. "The Concept of Genius and Its Metamorphoses in Eighteenth-Century English Criticism." *Textus* 18, no. 1 (2005): 189–204.

Gombrich, E. H. "Reynolds's Theory and Practice of Imitation." *Burlington Magazine* 80, no. 467 (1942): 40–45.

Gordon, Wendy J. "Render Copyright unto Caesar: On Taking Incentives Seriously." *University of Chicago Law Review* 71, no. 1 (2004): 75–92.

Gower, Ronald Sutherland. *Thomas Gainsborough*. London: George Bell and Sons, 1903.

Great Britain. *An Act for the Encouragement of Learning by vesting the Copies of Printed Books in the Authors or Purchasers of such Copies, during the Times therein mentioned* [*Statute of Anne*], 8 Anne, c. 19. London, 1710.

———. *Copyright, Designs and Patents Act, 1988*. Chapter 48. London: H.M.S.O., 1988.

———. *The English Reports*. Edited by Alexander Wood Renton, Max A. Robertson, and Geoffrey Ellis. 178 vols. Edinburgh: W. Green & Sons, 1900–1932.

———. *The Manuscripts of the House of Lords*. London: H. M. S.O.

———, and John Norman Keates Whitford. *Copyright and Designs Law: Report of the Committee to Consider the Law on Copyright and Designs*. London: H.M.S.O., 1977.

Greene, Jody. *The Trouble with Ownership: Literary Property and Authorial Liability in England, 1660–1730*. Philadelphia: University of Pennsylvania Press, 2005.

Griffith, Richard. *The Posthumous Works of a Late Celebrated Genius, Deceased*. 2 vols. Dublin, 1770.

Gwynn, Stephen. *Memorials of an Eighteenth Century Painter (James Northcote)*. London: T. Fisher Unwin, 1898.

Hammond, Brean S. *Professional Imaginative Writing in England, 1670–1740: "Hackney for Bread."* Oxford: Clarendon Press, 1997.

Hanson, Laurence. *Government and the Press, 1695–1763*. London: Oxford University Press, 1936.

Hargrave, Francis. *An Argument in Defence of Literary Property*. 2nd ed. London, 1774.

Harrison, John, and Peter Laslett. *The Library of John Locke*. 2nd ed. Oxford: Clarendon Press, 1971.

Hart, Kevin. *Samuel Johnson and the Culture of Property*. Cambridge: Cambridge University Press, 1999.

Haslett, Moyra. *Pope to Burney, 1714–1779: Scriblerians to Bluestockings*. New York: Palgrave Macmillan, 2003.

Hawkesworth, John, Samuel Johnson, Richard Bathurst, and Joseph Warton. *The Adventurer*. 2 vols. London: Payne, 1753.

Haydon, Benjamin Robert, and Frederick Wordsworth Haydon. *Benjamin Robert Haydon: Correspondence and Table-Talk*. 2 vols. New York: R. Worthington, 1878.

Hayes, John T. *The Drawings of Thomas Gainsborough*. 2 vols. New Haven, CT: Yale University Press, 1971.

———. Gainsborough, Thomas. *Gainsborough Drawings*. London: Arts Council, 1960.
———. *The Landscape Paintings of Thomas Gainsborough*. 2 vols. London: Sotheby Publications, 1982.
———, and Lindsay Stainton. *Gainsborough Drawings*. Washington, DC: International Exhibitions Foundation, 1983.
Heaney, Howell J., and William Blackstone. "The Letters of Sir William Blackstone (1723–1780) in the Hampton L. Carson Collection of the Free Library of Philadelphia." *American Journal of Legal History* 1, no. 4 (1957): 363–378.
Héricourt, Louis de. *Mémoire en forme de requête à M. le Garde des Sceaux*. In *La Propriété littéraire au XVIIIe siècle: recueil de pièces et de documents*, edited by Edouard Laboulaye and Georges Guiffrey, 13–40. Paris: Hachette, 1859.
Higgins, David. *Romantic Genius and the Literary Magazine*. London: Routledge, 2005.
Hills, Matt. *Fan Cultures*. London: Routledge, 2002.
Hogarth, William. *The Analysis of Beauty*. Edited with an Introduction by Joseph Burke. Oxford: Clarendon Press, 1955.
———, and Michael Kitson. "Hogarth's 'Apology for Painters.'" *Walpole Society* 41 (1966–68): 46–111.
Horwitz, Robert B., and Judith B. Finn. "Locke's Aesop's Fables." *Locke Newsletter* 6 (1975): 71–88.
Howard, William J. "Literature in the Law Courts, 1770–1800." In *Editing Eighteenth-Century Texts*, edited by D. I. B. Smith, 78–91. Toronto: University of Toronto Press, 1968.
Howell, Dorothy. *Intellectual Properties and the Protection of Fictional Characters: Copyright, Trademark, or Unfair Competition?* New York: Quorum Books, 1990.
Hughes, Justin. "Copyright and Incomplete Historiographies: Of Piracy, Propertization, and Thomas Jefferson." *Southern California Law Review* 79, no. 5 (2006): 993–1084.
Humphrey, Ozias. *Memoir*. London, Royal Academy, Humphrey Papers HU I/20–40 fol. 36.
Hurd, Richard. *The Early Letters of Bishop Richard Hurd, 1739–1762*. Edited by Sarah Brewer. Woodbridge, Suffolk: Boydell Press, 1995.
———. *A Letter to Mr. Mason; on the Marks of Imitation*. London: Dodsley, 1757.
———. *Q. Horatii Flacci Epistola ad Augustum. With an English Commentary and Notes. To Which Is Added, A Discourse Concerning Poetical Imitation*. London: Dodsley, 1751.
Italia, Iona. *The Rise of Literary Journalism in the Eighteenth Century: Anxious Employment*. New York: Routledge, 2005.
Jackson, H. J. *Marginalia: Readers Writing in Books*. New Haven, CT: Yale University Press, 2001.
Jackson, William. *The Four Ages Together With Essays on Various Subjects*. London, 1798.
Jacot-Grappa, Caroline. "Redites et identité: *Jacques le fataliste* et la pédagogie des Lumières." In *Le Travail des Lumières*, edited by Caroline Jacot-Grappa, Nicole Jacques-Lefèvre, Yannick Séité, and Carine Trévisan, 405–425. Paris: Champion, 2002.
James, Henry. *The Critical Muse: Selected Literary Criticism*. Edited, with an introduction, by Roger Gard. London: Penguin Books, 1987.
Jaszi, Peter. "On the Author Effect: Contemporary Copyright and Collective Creativity." In *The Construction of Authorship: Textual Appropriation in Law and Literature*, edited by Martha Woodmansee and Peter Jaszi, 29–56. Durham, NC: Duke University Press, 1994.

———. "Toward a Theory of Copyright: The Metamorphoses of 'Authorship.'" *Duke Law Journal* 1991, no. 2 (1991): 455–502.
Jenkins, Henry. *Convergence Culture: Where Old and New Media Collide.* New York: New York University Press, 2006.
———. *Textual Poachers: Television Fans & Participating Culture.* New York: Routledge, 1992.
———. "*Star Trek* Rerun, Read, Rewritten: Fan Writing as Textual Poaching." *Critical Studies in Mass Communication* 5, no. 2 (1988): 85–107. Reprinted with revisions in *Close Encounters: Film, Feminism and Science Fiction*, edited by Constance Penley, Elisabeth Lyon, Lynn Spiegel, and Janet Bergstrom, 171–204. Minneapolis: University of Minnesota Press, 1991.
Johns, Adrian. *The Nature of the Book: Print and Knowledge in the Making.* Chicago: University of Chicago Press, 1998.
Johnson, Samuel. *The Rambler.* Vols. 3–5 of *The Yale Edition of the Works of Samuel Johnson.* New Haven, CT: Yale University Press, 1958.
Kaufman, Paul. "Heralds of Original Genius." In *Essays in Memory of Barrett Wendell by His Assistants*, 192–217. Cambridge, MA: Harvard University Press, 1926.
Kayman, Martin A. "Lawful Writing: Common Law, Statute and the Properties of Literature." *New Literary History* 27, no. 4 (1996): 761–783.
Kenrick, William. *An Address to the Artists and Manufacturers of Great Britain.* London: Domville, 1774.
———. Review of *A Vindication of the Exclusive Rights of Authors. Monthly Review* 27 (1762): 183.
Kernan, Alvin. *Samuel Johnson and the Impact of Print.* Princeton, NJ: Princeton University Press, 1987.
Kewes, Paulina. *Authorship and Appropriation: Writing for the Stage in England, 1660–1710.* Oxford: Clarendon Press, 1998.
Keymer, Tom. *Richardson's "Clarissa" and the Eighteenth-Century Reader.* Cambridge: Cambridge University Press, 1992.
———, and Peter Sabor. *The Pamela Controversy: Criticisms and Adaptations of Samuel Richardson's "Pamela,"* 1740–1750. 6 vols. London: Pickering & Chatto, 2001.
———. *"Pamela" in the Marketplace: Literary Controversy and Print Culture in Eighteenth-Century Britain and Ireland.* Cambridge: Cambridge University Press, 2005.
Kierkegaard, Søren. *The Concept of Irony: With Constant Reference to Socrates.* Translated with an introduction and notes by Lee M. Capel. Bloomington: Indiana University Press, 1968.
———. *Either/Or.* Translated by David F. Swenson, Lillian Marvin Swenson, and Walter Lowrie. 2 vols. Princeton, NJ: Princeton University Press, 1944.
Kreissman, Bernard. *Pamela-Shamela: A Study of the Criticisms, Burlesques, Parodies, and Adaptations of Richardson's "Pamela."* Lincoln: University of Nebraska Press, 1960.
Kunzle, David. "Plagiaries-by-Memory of the *Rake's Progress* and the Genesis of Hogarth's Second Picture Story." *Journal of the Warburg and Courtauld Institutes*, 29 (1966): 311–348.
Kurtz, Leslie. "The Independent Legal Lives of Fictional Characters." *Wisconsin Law Review*, no. 3 (1986): 429–525.
Lamb, Caroline. *Glenarvon.* 1816. Reprint, Delmar, NY: Scholars' Facsimiles & Reprints, 1972.
Lamb, Patricia Frazer, and Dianna L. Veith. "Romantic Myth, Transcendence, and *Star Trek* Zines." In *Erotic Universe: Sexuality and Fantastic Literature*, edited by Donald Palumbo, 235–256. Westport, CT: Greenwood, 1986.

Langbaine, Gerard. *An Account of the English Dramatick Poets*. Oxford, 1691. Reprinted with a preface by Arthur Freeman. New York: Garland Publishing, 1973.

———. *Momus Triumphans; Or The Plagiaries of the English Stage, and The Lives and Characters of the English Dramatick Poets*. Reprint of the London, 1688 (or 1687) edition of *Momus Triumphans*. With a preface for the Garland edition by Arthur Freeman. New York: Garland Publishing, 1973.

Lange, David. "Recognizing the Public Domain." *Law and Contemporary Problems* 44, no. 4 (1981): 147–178.

Leach, Frederick D. *William Hogarth's Subscription-Tickets: A Vehicle for Eighteenth Century Satire on Contemporary Taste*. PhD thesis, State University of Iowa, 1955.

Lessig, Lawrence. *Free Culture: How Big Media Uses Technology and the Law to Lock Down Culture and Control Creativity*. New York: Penguin, 2004.

———. *The Future of Ideas: The Fate of the Commons in a Connected World*. New York: Random House, 2001.

Lewis, M. G. *The Monk*. Edited by Louis F. Peck. Introduction by John Berryman. New York: Grove Press, 1952.

Litman, Jessica. "The Public Domain." *Emory Law Journal* 39 (1990): 965–1023.

Lizé, Émile. "Une source de Diderot dans *Jacques le fataliste*: Qui était Monsieur Le Pelletier d'Orléans?" *Revue d'histoire littéraire de la France* 82, no. 3 (1982): 438–440.

Locke, John. *The Correspondence of John Locke*. Edited by E. S. De Beer. Oxford: Clarendon Press, 1979.

Loewenstein, Joseph. *The Author's Due: Printing and the Prehistory of Copyright*. Chicago: University of Chicago Press, 2002.

Lukács, György. *The Young Hegel: Studies in the Relations between Dialectics and Economics*. London: Merlin Press, 1975.

Lynch, Deidre. *The Economy of Character: Novels, Market Culture, and the Business of Inner Meaning*. Chicago: University of Chicago Press, 1998.

Macfarlane, Robert. *Original Copy: Plagiarism and Originality in Nineteenth-Century Literature*. Oxford: Oxford University Press, 2007.

Mack, Robert L. *The Genius of Parody: Imitation and Originality in Seventeenth- and Eighteenth-Century English Literature*. New York: Palgrave Macmillan, 2007.

Mackay of Clashfern, ed. *Halsbury's Laws of England*. Vol. 9. London: LexisNexis Butterworths, 2006.

Marks, Michael. "The Legal Rights of Fictional Characters." *Copyright Law Symposium (ASCAP)* 25 (1980): 35–92.

Marsden, Jean I. *The Re-Imagined Text: Shakespeare, Adaptation, & Eighteenth-Century Literary Theory*. Lexington: University Press of Kentucky, 1995.

Martinez, Cristina S. "The Painter's Eye and the Lawyer's Tongue: The Artist as Witness." In *Trials of Art*, edited by Daniel McClean, 105–133. London: Ridinghouse, 2007.

Mason, John Hope. "Thinking about Genius in the Eighteenth Century." In *Eighteenth-Century Aesthetics and the Reconstruction of Art*, edited by Paul Mattick, Jr., 210–239. Cambridge: Cambridge University Press, 1993.

———. *The Value of Creativity: The Origins and Emergence of a Modern Belief*. London: Ashgate, 2003.

Mazzeo, Tilar J. *Plagiarism and Literary Property in the Romantic Period*. Philadelphia: University of Pennsylvania Press, 2007.

———. "Plagiarism, Composition Pedagogy, and the History of the Book." *Pacific Coast Philology* 40, no. 2 (2005): 90–105.

McGinnis, Reginald. "The Critique of Originality in French Letters." In *Studies in Eighteenth-Century Culture* 31, edited by Ourida Mostefai and Catherine Ingrassia, 127–143. Baltimore: Johns Hopkins University Press for the American Society for Eighteenth-Century Studies, 2002.

———. *La Prostitution sacrée: essai sur Baudelaire.* Paris: Belin, 1994.

McKillop, Alan Dugald. *Samuel Richardson: Printer and Novelist.* Chapel Hill: University of North Carolina Press, 1936.

Medwin, Thomas. *Conversations of Lord Byron.* Edited by Ernest J. Lovell, Jr. Princeton, NJ: Princeton University Press, 1966.

Milhous, Judith, and Robert D. Hume. "Profits from Play Publication: The Evidence of *Murphy v. Vaillant.*" *Studies in Bibliography* 51 (1998): 213–229.

Moore, Thomas. *Tom Moore's Diary.* Edited by J. B. Priestley. Cambridge: Cambridge University Press, 1925.

Morris, William. *The American Heritage Dictionary of the English Language.* New York: American Heritage Publishing Co., 1969.

Mortier, Roland. "L'original selon Diderot." *Saggi e ricerche di letteratura francese* 4 (1963): 139–157.

———. *L'originalité: une nouvelle catégorie esthétique au siècle des lumières.* Paris: Droz, 1982.

Mounsey, Chris. *Christopher Smart: Clown of God.* Lewisburg, PA: Bucknell University Press, 2001.

Murphy, Arthur. *The Gray's-Inn Journal.* London: Vaillant, 1756.

Nelson, Robert S., and Richard Shiff. *Critical Terms for Art History.* Chicago: University of Chicago Press, 1996.

Nemetz, Steven L. "Copyright Protection of Fictional Characters." *Intellectual Property Journal* 14, no. 1 (1999): 69–70.

Nevins, Francis M., Jr. "Copyright + Character = Catastrophe." *Journal of the Copyright Society of the U.S.A.* 39 (1992): 303–344.

Nichol, Don. "Arthur Murphy's Law: The Man Who Won the First Decisive Battle in the Literary Property Wars." *Times Literary Supplement* 4855 (April 19, 1996): 15–16.

———. "Warburton (Not!) on Copyright: Clearing up the Misattribution of *An Enquiry into the Nature and Origin of Literary Property* (1762)." *British Journal for Eighteenth-Century Studies* 19, no. 2 (1996): 171–182.

Nimmer, Melville B., and David Nimmer. *Nimmer on Copyright.* 10 vols. New York: Matthew Bender, 1997.

Northcote, James. *Conversations of James Northcote, R. A. with James Ward, on Art and Artists.* Edited and arranged from the manuscripts and note-books of James Ward by Ernest Fletcher. London: Methuen & co, 1901.

O'Brien, Flann. *The Third Policeman: A Novel.* Normal, IL: Dalkey Archive Press, 1999.

O'Gorman, Donal. *Diderot the Satirist: Le Neveu De Rameau and Related Works; An Analysis.* Toronto: University of Toronto Press, 1971.

Orgel, Stephen. "The Renaissance Artist as Plagiarist." *ELH* 48, no. 3 (1981): 476–495.

Patry, William F. *The Fair Use Privilege in Copyright Law.* Washington, DC: Bureau of National Affairs, 1985.

Patterson, L. Ray. *Copyright in Historical Perspective.* Nashville, TN: Vanderbilt University Press, 1968.

———. "The Worst Intellectual Property Opinion Ever Written: *Folsom v. Marsh* and Its Legacy." *Journal of Intellectual Property Law* 5 (1998): 431–452.

Paulson, Ronald. *Hogarth: His Life, Art, and Times.* 2 vols. New Haven, CT: Yale University Press, 1971.

Peirce, Charles S. *Philosophical Writings of Peirce*. Selected and edited with an introduction by Justus Buchler. New York: Dover Publications, 1955.

Pepys, Samuel, and Helen Flora McAfee. *Pepys on the Restoration Stage*. New York: B. Blom, 1964.

Petrarca, Francesco. *Letters from Petrarch*. Selected and Translated by Morris Bishop. Bloomington: Indiana University Press, 1966.

Pettitt, Clare. *Patent Inventions: Intellectual Property and the Victorian Novel*. Oxford: Oxford University Press, 2004.

Pickering, Andrew. *Constructing Quarks: A Sociological History of Particle Physics*. Edinburgh: Edinburgh University Press, 1984.

Pigman, G.W., III. "Versions of Imitation in the Renaissance." *Renaissance Quarterly* 33, no. 1 (1980): 1–32.

Plumer, Francis. *Three Criticisms of Richardson's Fiction (1749–1754)*. New York: Garland Publishing, 1974.

Poirson, Martial. "Portrait de l'artiste en propriétaire: le dramaturge fortuné ou les avatars du statut de la propriété intellectuelle au XVIIIe siècle." *Littératures classiques* 40 (2000): 119–140.

Pope, Alexander. *The Correspondence of Alexander Pope*. Edited by George Sherburn. Oxford: Clarendon Press, 1956.

Posner, Donald. "Concerning the 'Mechanical' Parts of Painting and the Artistic Culture of Seventeenth-Century France." *Art Bulletin* 75, no. 4 (1993): 583–598.

Posner, Richard. *Law and Literature: A Misunderstood Relation*. Cambridge, MA: Harvard University Press, 1988.

Proust, Jacques. "Pour servir à une édition critique de la *Lettre sur le commerce de librairie*." *Diderot Studies* 3 (1961): 321–345.

Pugh, Sheenagh. *The Democratic Genre: Fan Fiction in a Literary Context*. Bridgend, Wales: Seren, 2005.

Pye, John. *Patronage of British Art*. 1845. Reprint, London: Cornmarket Press, 1970.

Ranon, Christina Z. "Honor Among Thieves: Copyright Infringement in Internet Fandom." *Vanderbilt Journal of Entertainment and Technology Law* 8, no. 2 (2006): 421–452.

Ransom, Harry. *The First Copyright Statute: An Essay on An Act for the Encouragement of Learning, 1710*. Austin: University of Texas, 1956.

Raven, James. "The Anonymous Novel in Britain and Ireland, 1750–1830." In *The Faces of Anonymity: Anonymous and Pseudonymous Publication from the Sixteenth to the Twentieth Century*, edited by Robert J. Griffin, 141–166. New York: Palgrave Macmillan, 2003.

Redgrave, Richard, and Samuel Redgrave. *A Century of British Painters*. London: Phaidon Press, 1947.

Reynolds, Joshua. *Discourses on Art*. Edited by Robert R. Wark. New Haven, CT: Paul Mellon Centre for Studies in British Art (London) Ltd. by Yale University Press, 1975.

Richardson, Jonathan. *The Works*. 1773. Reprint, Hildesheim: G. Olms, 1969.

Richardson, Samuel. *The Case of Samuel Richardson, of London, Printer With Regard to the Invasion of His Property in the History of Sir Charles Grandison*. London: [s.n.], 1753.

———. *The Correspondence of Samuel Richardson, Author of Pamela, Clarissa, and Sir Charles Grandison*. Edited by Anna Lætitia Barbauld. New York: AMS Press, 1966.

———. *Selected Letters of Samuel Richardson*. Edited by John Carroll. Oxford: Clarendon Press, 1964.

———, Johannes Stinstra, and William C. Slattery. *The Richardson-Stinstra Correspondence, and Stinstra's Prefaces to "Clarissa."* Carbondale: Southern Illinois University Press, 1969.

———, and R. F. Brissenden. *Clarissa: Preface, Hints of Prefaces, and Postscript.* Los Angeles: William Andrews Clark Memorial Library, University of California, 1964.
———, and Tom Keymer. *Samuel Richardson's Published Commentary on Clarissa, 1747–65.* 3 vols. London: Pickering & Chatto, 1998.
Roeder, Martin A. "The Doctrine of Moral Right: A Study in the Law of Artists, Authors and Creators." *Harvard Law Review* 53, no. 4 (1940): 554–578.
Roget, John Lewis. *A History of the "Old Water-Colour" Society.* 2 vols. London: Longmans, Green and Co., 1891.
Rose, Mark. *Authors and Owners: The Invention of Copyright.* Cambridge, MA: Harvard University Press, 1993.
———. "The Author as Proprietor: *Donaldson v. Becket* and the Genealogy of Modern Authorship." *Representations*, no. 23 (1988): 51–85.
———. "Copyright and Its Metaphors." *UCLA Law Review* 50, no. 1 (2002): 1–15.
Rosenthal, Laura J. *Playwrights and Plagiarists in Early Modern England: Gender, Authorship, Literary Property.* Ithaca, NY: Cornell University Press, 1996.
Rosenthal, Michael. *The Art of Thomas Gainsborough: "a little business for the eye."* New Haven, CT: Yale University Press, 1999.
Ross, Trevor. "Copyright and the Invention of Tradition." *Eighteenth-Century Studies* 26, no. 1 (1992): 1–27.
Rouquet, Jean André. *The Present State of the Arts in England.* London, 1755.
St. Clair, William. *The Reading Nation in the Romantic Period.* Cambridge: Cambridge University Press, 2004.
Sale, William Merritt. *Samuel Richardson: Master Printer.* Ithaca, NY: Cornell University Press, 1950.
Sambrook, James. "The Psychology of Literary Creation and Literary Response." In *The Cambridge History of Literary Criticism*, edited by Hugh Barr Nisbet, 614–632. Cambridge: Cambridge University Press, 1989.
Schellenberg, Betty A. " 'The Measured Lines of the Copyist': Sequels, Reviews, and the Discourse of Authorship in England, 1749–1800." In *On Second Thought: Updating the Eighteenth-Century Text*, edited by Debra Taylor Boreau, 25–42. Newark: University of Delaware Press, 2007.
Schlegel, Friedrich von. *Dialogue on Poetry and Literary Aphorisms.* Translated, introduced, and annotated by Ernst Behler and Roman Struc. University Park: Pennsylvania State University Press, 1968.
———. *Friedrich Schlegel's "Lucinde" and the "Fragments."* Translated with an introduction by Peter Firchow. Minneapolis: University of Minnesota Press, 1971.
Schoch, Richard W. "'A Supplement to the Public Laws': Arthur Murphy, David Garrick, and *Hamlet, with Alterations.*" *Theatre Journal* 57, no. 1 (2005): 21–32.
Serres, Michel. *Hermes—Literature, Science, Philosophy.* Edited by Josue V. Harari, and David F. Bell. Baltimore: Johns Hopkins University Press, 1982.
———. *Les origines de la géometrie: tiers livre des fondations.* Paris: Flammarion, 1993.
Shakespeare, William. *Antony and Cleopatra.* Edited by David M. Bevington. Cambridge: Cambridge University Press, 1990.
Shelley, Mary Wollstonecraft. *Frankenstein, or, the Modern Prometheus.* London: H. Colburn and R. Bentley, 1831.
Shelley, Percy Bysshe. *Queen Mab 1813.* Revolution and romanticism, 1789–1834. Oxford, England: Woodstock Books, 1990.
Sherman, Brad, and Lionel Bently. *The Making of Modern Intellectual Property Law: The British Experience, 1760–1911.* Cambridge: Cambridge University Press, 1999.

Siebert, Frederick Seaton. *Freedom of the Press in England, 1476–1776: The Rise and Decline of Government Controls.* Urbana: University of Illinois Press, 1952.

Smyth, Adam. *"Profit and Delight": Printed Miscellanies in England, 1640–1682.* Detroit: Wayne State University Press, 2004.

Smyth, John Vignaux. "A Glance at SunSet: Numerical Fundaments in Frege, Wittgenstein, Shakespeare, Beckett." In "Mathematics, Science and Postclassical Theory," edited by Barbara Herrnstein Smith and Arkady Plotnitsky. Special Issue, *South Atlantic Quarterly* 94, no. 2 (1995): 619–654. Reprinted in *Mathematics, Science, and Postclassical Theory*, edited by Barbara Herrnstein Smith and Arkady Plotnitsky, 212–242. Durham, NC: Duke University Press, 1997.

———. *The Habit of Lying: Sacrificial Studies in Literature, Philosophy, and Fashion Theory.* Durham, NC: Duke University Press, 2002.

———. *A Question of Eros: Irony in Sterne, Kierkegaard, and Barthes.* Tallahassee: Florida State University Press, 1986.

———. "Sacrificial and Erotic Materialism in Kierkegaard and Adorno." In *Idealism Without Absolutes: Philosophy and Romantic Culture*, edited by Tilottama Rajan and Arkadi Plotnitsky, 181–201. Albany, NY: State University of New York Press, 2004.

———. "Tenuous Borders in Kafka's *A Country Doctor.*" *Western Humanities Review* 60, no. 2 (2006): 89–100.

Spahn, Kenneth E. "The Legal Protection of Fictional Characters." *University of Miami Entertainment and Sports Law Review* 9 (1992): 331–348.

Stark, Louisa-Jayne, and Timothy J. Perfect. "Elaboration Inflation: How Your Ideas Become Mine." *Applied Cognitive Science* 20, no. 5 (2006): 641–648.

———, Timothy J. Perfect, and Stephen E. Newstead. "When Elaboration Leads to Appropriation: Unconscious Plagiarism in a Creative Task." *Memory* 13, no. 6 (2005): 561–573.

Starobinski, Jean. "Diderot et la parole des autres." *Critique* 28, no. 296 (1972): 3–22.

Stacy, John. *A Critique on the Genius and Writings of Lord Byron, with Remarks on Don Juan.* Norwich, 1820.

Steinke, Martin William. *Edward Young's "Conjectures on Original Composition" in England and Germany.* New York: Stechert, 1917.

Stern, Simon. "*Tom Jones* and the Economies of Copyright." *Eighteenth-Century Fiction* 9, no. 4 (1997): 429–444.

Sterne, Laurence. *The Florida Edition of the Works of Laurence Sterne.* Edited by Melvyn New and Joan New. 6 vols. Gainesville: University Presses of Florida, 1978.

Stone, Lawrence. *The Family, Sex and Marriage in England, 1500–1800.* Abridged Edition. New York: Harper & Row, 1979.

Strange, Robert. *An Inquiry into the Rise and Establishment of the Royal Academy of Arts.* London, 1775.

Strauss, Leo. *Natural Right and History.* Chicago: University of Chicago Press, 1953.

Strauss, William. "The Moral Right of the Author." *The American Journal of Comparative Law* 4, no. 4 (1955): 506–538.

Strowel, A. *Droit d'auteur et copyright: Divergences et convergences: Étude de droit comparé.* Bruxelles: E. Bruylant, 1993.

Suckling, John. *The Works of Sir John Suckling.* Edited by Thomas Clayton and L. A. Beaurline. 2 vols. Oxford: Clarendon Press, 1971.

Swift, Jonathan. *The Writings of Jonathan Swift.* Edited by Robert A. Greenberg and William Bowman Piper. New York: Norton, 1973.

Taylor, Gary. *Reinventing Shakespeare: A Cultural History, From the Restoration to the Present.* New York: Oxford University Press, 1989.

Temple, Kathryn. *Law and Authorship in Britain, 1750–1832*. Ithaca, NY: Cornell University Press, 2003.

Terry, Richard. "The Circumstances of Eighteenth-Century Parody." *Eighteenth-Century Life* 15, no. 3 (1991): 76–92.

———. "'In Pleasing Memory of All He Stole': Plagiarism and Literary Detraction, 1747–1785." In *Plagiarism in Early Modern England*, edited by Paulina Kewes, 181–200. New York: Palgrave Macmillan, 2003.

Thicknesse, Philip. *A Sketch of the Life and Paintings of Thomas Gainsborough, Esq*. London, 1788.

Tompkins, J. M. S. *The Popular Novel in England, 1770–1800*. London: Constable, 1932.

Travis, Hannibal. "Pirates of the Information Infrastructure: Blackstonian Copyright and the First Amendment." *Berkeley Technology Law Journal* 15, no. 2 (2000): 777–864.

Trusler, John. *An Essay on Literary Property*. London, 1798.

Turner, James Grantham. "Novel Panic: Picture and Performance in the Reception of Richardson's *Pamela*." *Representations*, no. 48 (1994): 70–96.

Tushnet, Rebecca. "Legal Fictions: Copyright, Fan Fiction, and a New Common Law." *Loyola of Los Angeles Entertainment Law Journal* 17, no. 3 (1997): 651–686.

United States. *Copyright Law Revsision Supplementary Report of the Register of Copyrights on the General Revision of the U.S. Copyright Law: 1965 Revision Bill. Part* 6. Washington, D. C.: U.S. G.P.O., 1965.

Vaughan, William. "Magic in the Studio." In *Sensation & Sensibility: Viewing Gainsborough's Cottage Door*, edited by Ann Bermingham, 165–179. New Haven, CT: Yale Center for British Art, 2005.

VerSteeg, Russ. "Rethinking Originality." *William & Mary Law Review* 42, no. 3 (1993): 801–883.

Vertue, George. "Vertue Note Books, Volume III." *Walpole Society* 22 (1933–1934).

Walpole, Horace. *Anecdotes of Painting in England With Some Account of the Principal Artists*. Edited by Ralph N. Wornum. 3 vols. London: Chatto and Windus, 1876.

Warburton, William. *A Letter From an Author to a Member of Parliament Concerning Literary Property*. London: Knapton, 1747.

Warner, William Beatty. *Licensing Entertainment: The Elevation of Novel Reading in Britain, 1684–1750*. Berkeley: University of California Press, 1998.

Watt, Ian. *The Rise of the Novel: Studies in Defoe, Richardson and Fielding*. Berkeley, University of California Press, 1957.

Werner, Stephen. *Socratic Satire: An Essay on Diderot and Le Neveu De Rameau*. Birmingham, AL: Summa Publications, 1987.

White, Harold Ogden. *Plagiarism and Imitation During the English Renaissance*. Cambridge, MA: Harvard University Press, 1935.

Whitley, William T. *Artists and their Friends in England 1700–1799*. 2 vols. London: The Medici Society, 1928.

———. *Thomas Gainsborough*. London: Smith, Elder & Co., 1915.

Whyte, D. [pseud]. *The Fallacy of French Freedom, and Dangerous Tendency of Sterne's Writings, or, An Essay Shewing That Irreligion and Immorality Pave the Way for Tyranny and Anarchy, and That Sterne's Writings Are Both Irreligious and Immoral Concluding with Some Observations on the Present State of France*. London: J. Hatchard, 1799.

Wilson, Arthur M. *Diderot*. New York: Oxford University Press, 1972.

Wilson, Frances. "Portrait of the Artist as an Icon." *Times Literary Supplement*, online edition, July 29, 2005. <http://www.timesonline.co.uk>.

Wilson, Lisa M. "'Monk' Lewis as Literary Lion." *Romanticism On the Net* 8, November 1997. <http://www.erudit.org/revue/ron/1997/v/n8/005775ar.html>.

Wind, Edgar. "'Borrowed Attitudes' in Reynolds and Hogarth." *Journal of the Warburg Institute* 2, no. 2 (1938): 182–185.

Woodall, Mary. *Gainsborough's Landscape Drawings*. London: Faber and Faber, 1939.

Woodmansee, Martha. *The Author, Art, and the Market: Rereading the History of Aesthetics*. New York: Columbia University Press, 1994.

———. "The Genius and the Copyright: Economic and Legal Conditions of the Emergence of the Author." *Eighteenth-Century Studies* 17, no. 4 (1984): 425–448.

———, and Peter Jaszi, eds. *The Construction of Authorship: Textual Appropriation in Law and Literature*. Durham, NC: Duke University Press, 1994.

World Intellectual Property Organization. *Berne Convention for the Protection of Literary and Artistic Works* (1886, as amended). <http://www.wipo.int/treaties/en/ip/berne/>.

Yen, Alfred C. "Restoring the Natural Law: Copyright as Labor and Possession." *Ohio State Law Journal* 51, no. 2 (1990): 517–559.

Yeo, Richard R. *Encyclopaedic Visions: Scientific Dictionaries and Enlightenment Culture*. Cambridge: Cambridge University Press, 2001.

Young, Edward. *Conjectures on Original Composition in a Letter to the Author of Sir Charles Grandison*. London: Millar, 1759.

Yovel, Yirmiahu. *God and Nature, Spinoza's Metaphysics: Papers Presented at the First Jerusalem Conference (Ethica I)*. Leiden: E. J. Brill, 1991.

Zimmerman, Diane Leenheer. "It's an Original! (?): In Pursuit of Copyright's Elusive Essence." *Columbia Journal of Law & the Arts* 28, no. 2 (2005): 187–212.

Zionkowski, Linda. "Aesthetics, Copyright, and 'The Goods of the Mind.'" *British Journal for Eighteenth-Century Studies* 15, no. 2 (1992): 163–174.

Contributors

Elizabeth F. Judge is an associate professor at the University of Ottawa, Faculty of Law, Common Law Section, where she is a member of the law and technology group, specializing in intellectual property, law and literature, privacy, and legal history. She is the coauthor of *Intellectual Property: The Law in Canada* and a founding editor and the editor-in-chief of the *University of Ottawa Law & Technology Journal*. Her current research focuses on the intersections between eighteenth-century legal and literary ideas of originality and authorship. She holds a BA from Brown University, a JD from Harvard Law School, an MA in English from the University of Toronto, and an LLM and a PhD in English from Dalhousie University. Prior to joining the University of Ottawa's Faculty of Law, she practiced law in Washington, DC, and served as a law clerk at the Supreme Court of Canada.

Reginald McGinnis is Associate Professor of French at the University of Arizona. His publications include a book on Baudelaire, La Prostitution sacrée (Paris: Belin, 1994), as well as articles in *Studies in Eighteenth-Century Culture, l'Atelier du roman, PO&SIE, Cahiers de l'Herne* and the *Romanic Review.*

Cristina S. Martinez completed her PhD degree in Art History and Law at Birkbeck College, University of London, where she was a Commonwealth Scholar and the recipient of a Social Sciences and Humanities Research Council of Canada Doctoral Fellowship. She also holds a BA with Honors in Theory and History of Art from the University of Ottawa and an MA in Art History from McGill University. Her publications include articles in *Les Cahiers du Musée national d'art moderne Georges Pompidou* and *History of Photography*, as well as a chapter in *The Trials of Art* (London: Ridinghouse, 2007).

Tilar J. Mazzeo is an assistant professor of English at Colby College and the author of *Plagiarism and Literary Property in the Romantic Period* (University of Pennsylvania Press, 2007).

Robert W. McHenry, Jr. holds BA and MA degrees from Boston University and a PhD from the University of Michigan–Ann Arbor and has taught at the University of Hawai'i since 1970. A specialist in Restoration and eighteenth-century literature, Professor McHenry is the author of *Absalom and Achitopel* (Hamden: Archon Books, 1986) and editor of *The Temper of John Dryden* (East Lansing: Colleagues Press, 1993) and *Critics on Dryden: Readings in Literary Criticism* (London: Allen and Unwin, 1973).

Anne Sechin graduated with a PhD in French Literature from the University of Manitoba in 2005, with a doctoral dissertation on "Sexuality and Textuality in the Novels of Diderot." She also holds MA degrees in French Canadian literature from the University of Manitoba and in English Literature from the Université des Sciences Humaines de Strasbourg. She is currently an assistant professor in the School of Translation at the Collège Universitaire de St Boniface in Winnipeg. Her publications include articles in *Dalhousie French Studies* and the *Western Humanities Review.*

John Vignaux Smyth holds BA and MA degrees from Cambridge University and a PhD from the University of Pennsylvania. A specialist in eighteenth-, nineteenth-, and twentieth-century British literature and critical theory, Professor Smyth is the author of *The Habit of Lying: Sacrificial Studies in Literature, Philosophy, and Fashion Theory* (Duke University Press, 2002) and *A Question of Eros: Irony in Sterne, Kierkegaard, and Barthes* (Florida State University Press, 1986).

Simon Stern is an assistant professor of Law and English at the University of Toronto. He has published articles in critical journals and law reviews on *Tom Jones* and copyright law, the early history of jury nullification, the history of authorship, and various aspects of the law of search and seizure. With John Bender, he is coeditor of the World's Classics edition of *Tom Jones*. His current research includes projects on cognitive heuristics and probable cause, as well as detective fiction and the history of legal education.

Index

For Product Safety Concerns and Information please contact our EU representative GPSR@taylorandfrancis.com Taylor & Francis Verlag GmbH, Kaufingerstraße 24, 80331 München, Germany

Batch number: 10725979

Printed by Printforce, the Netherlands